Cambridge Studies in Islam

Social history of Timbuktu:

the role of Muslim scholars and notables
1400–1900

Cambridge Studies in Islamic Civilization

Titles in the series

ANDREW M. WATSON. *Agricultural innovation in the early Islamic world: the diffusion of crops and farming techniques 700–1100*

ELIAS N. SAAD. *Social history of Timbuktu: the role of Muslim scholars and notables 1400–1900*

G.H.A. JUYNBOLL. *Muslim tradition: studies in chronology, provenance and authorship of early Ḥadīth*

BASIM MUSALLAM. *Sex and society in Islam: birth control before the nineteenth century*

SURAIYA FAROQHI. *Towns and townsmen of Ottoman Anatolia: trade, crafts and food production in an urban setting 1520–1650*

Social history of Timbuktu:

the role of Muslim scholars and notables 1400–1900

ELIAS N. SAAD
Wellesley College

Cambridge University Press
Cambridge
London New York New Rochelle
Melbourne Sydney

CAMBRIDGE UNIVERSITY PRESS
Cambridge, New York, Melbourne, Madrid, Cape Town, Singapore,
São Paulo, Delhi, Dubai, Tokyo

Cambridge University Press
The Edinburgh Building, Cambridge CB2 8RU, UK

Published in the United States of America by Cambridge University Press, New York

www.cambridge.org
Information on this title: www.cambridge.org/9780521136303

First published 1983
This digitally printed version 2010

A catalogue record for this publication is available from the British Library

Library of Congress Catalogue Card Number: 82-14687

ISBN 978-0-521-24603-3 Hardback
ISBN 978-0-521-13630-3 Paperback

Contents

Acknowledgements

This study is the product of two related efforts: a search for sources and historical data on Timbuktu, and secondly an attempt to synthesize the data within a meaningful framework of analysis. In both respects I have received the assistance of many scholars and librarians, as well as the cooperation of traditionists at Timbuktu. I mention below only those whose assistance was exceptionally valuable.

For data which have directly contributed to the making of this study, I wish to express my deep gratitude to John Hunwick. During my brief visit to Cairo he kindly opened to me his personal library, including the notes taken by him over the years from manuscript libraries dealing with West Africa. Since it was not always possible to acknowledge his contributions and suggestions in their proper place in the text, it is necessary to emphasize them here. Similarly, I would like to thank Professor Jean Devisse of the University of Paris for lending me personal copies of sources which otherwise may not have been accessible.

The search for the multitude of fragmentary and dispersed sources on Timbuktu is a difficult one. I am grateful for a Fullbright–Hays grant and a Social Science Research Council fellowship which made my overseas documentary and field research possible. Hans Panofsky and Dan Britz of the Africana Library at Northwestern University kindly exerted their efforts in procuring for me in advance some of the manuscript sources from abroad. In Paris, the staff of the Institut de France was most helpful, while in Rabat I found cooperation both at the National and Royal libraries. Additionally, I should mention the special assistance of Muṣṭafa N'jai of the Institut Fondamental d'Afrique Noire at Dakar.

In Mali my research was greatly facilitated by the assistance and companionship of Almamy Malik Yettara of the Patrimoine Historique et Scientifique. I am also most grateful to the staff of the Centre Aḥmad Bāba of Timbuktu, especially to the director, Maḥmūd Zoubeir, whose ideas contributed substantively to this study, and the assistant director, Nuri Muḥammad al-Amīn, who exerted a special effort to facilitate my research. The elders and alfas of Timbuktu were most forthcoming in their information and assistance. I am deeply grateful to Alfa Humal, *Imām* of Jingerebir, Mulay Aḥmad Babir, present-day chronicler of Timbuktu, Alfa Salum, *Imām* of Sankore, Alfa Aḥmad Banio, *Imām* of Sīdi Yaḥya, al-Shaikh 'Issa Wuld Muḥammad Mawlūd, Alfa of the Keltina al-Ḥājj, al-'Alim Zubeir, held by some to be the honorary *Qāḍi* of Timbuktu, and the Songhai elder Aḥmadu Badiji. Equal gratitude is extended also to the young Alfa Yaḥya Ibrāhīm, educator and sometime historian in Timbuktu.

I should reserve my deepest gratitude to Ivor Wilks. His suggestions have helped shape many of the directions taken by this study. His advice during the past few years has combined sensitive criticism with warm encouragement in a singular manner. From the planning of the research to its completion, his help has been most consequential. It is therefore important that I should especially associate his assistance with any contribution that the study may make.

Since completing the original draft of this study, I have had an opportunity to revise it in certain important ways, including the addition of a concluding section, besides a much longer introduction (Chapter 1). In this respect I would like to thank Dr Michael Cook and Dr Martin Hinds who read the manuscript on behalf of Cambridge University Press and who offered a significant and valuable set of suggestions. Additionally, I would like to express my appreciation to Wellesley College whose support greatly facilitated the revision of the study.

Finally, I should credit the special effort and exertions of my wife Julianna. At various stages of this study, and especially during the overseas research, her assistance and encouragement was most important. I owe to her many substantive suggestions as well as numerous editorial corrections and improvements.

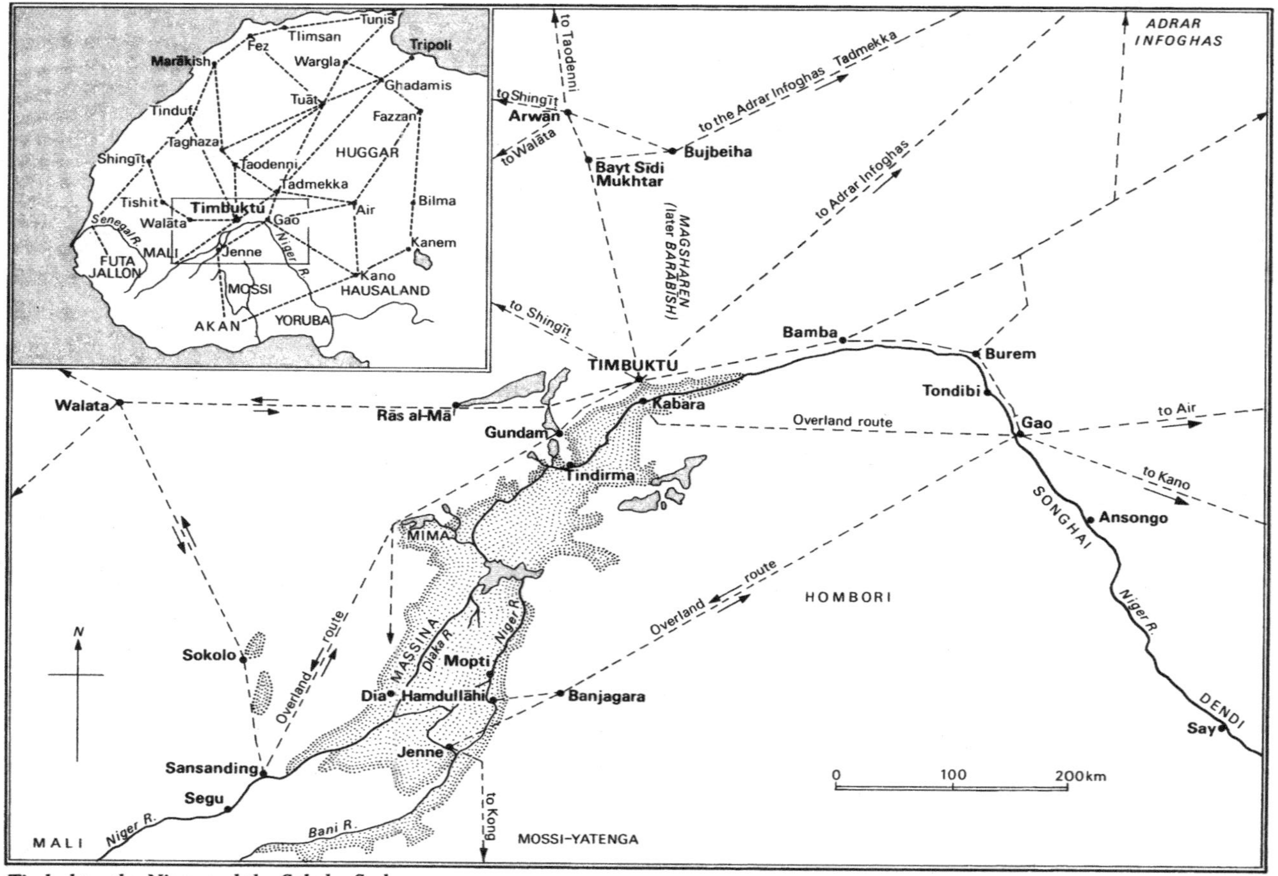

Timbuktu, the Niger and the Sahelo–Sudan

Dotted areas show the limits of the inundations of the Niger. Lines with arrows indicate the major trade-routes, especially during the sixteenth century. A major network of routes not indicated on this map were along the waterways of the Niger.

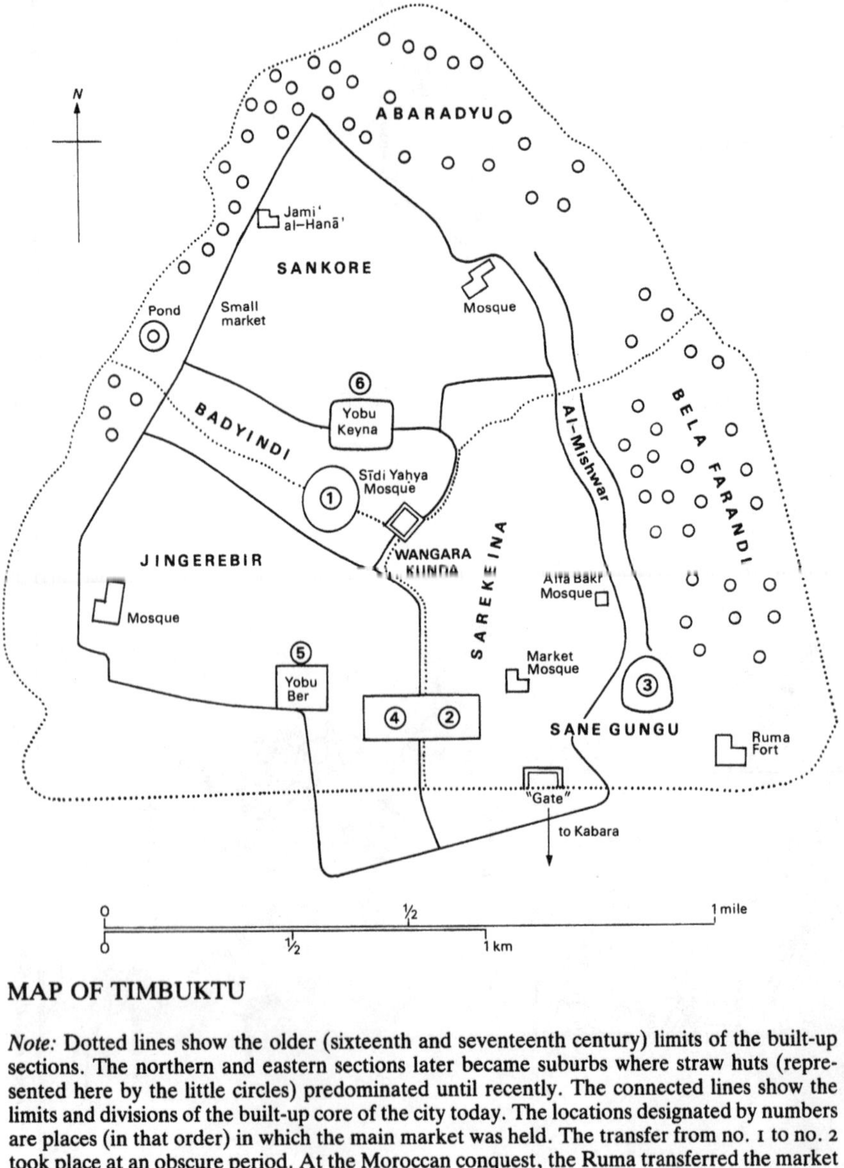

MAP OF TIMBUKTU

Note: Dotted lines show the older (sixteenth and seventeenth century) limits of the built-up sections. The northern and eastern sections later became suburbs where straw huts (represented here by the little circles) predominated until recently. The connected lines show the limits and divisions of the built-up core of the city today. The locations designated by numbers are places (in that order) in which the main market was held. The transfer from no. 1 to no. 2 took place at an obscure period. At the Moroccan conquest, the Ruma transferred the market closer to the Qaṣba, but it later reverted to the old place and gradually moved westwards during the eighteenth century. In the present century it was transferred to Yobu Keyna by the French.

CHAPTER 1

Introduction

The once-fabled city of Timbuktu holds a special place in the consciousness of people who are concerned with Africa, its past and its future. Particularly within the West African context, Timbuktu is one of several cities and states which affirm that the region had as much as any other, a long history of its own. For the historian, the special interest of Timbuktu lies in the fact that the city has left us a tolerably detailed record, not only of its own experience over several centuries, but also of the experience of its neighbours. This record derives principally from the well-known Arabic chronicles, or *tārīkhs* of Timbuktu, which have come down to us from various periods, beginning as early as the late sixteenth century. The history of Timbuktu is known to us almost exclusively from these chronicles. Indeed, it is also of considerable interest that the history of the area, namely the West African Sudan, is known to us in greater detail from the Timbuktu chronicles than from any other corpus of source materials pre-dating the nineteenth century.

The place of Timbuktu in West African history must be a point of emphasis in any study on the city. This is particularly true of the present study, for in approaching Timbuktu from the standpoint of its Arabic sources and its Islamic traditions, we risk conveying to the reader the sense that the city has historically belonged to a realm other than the sub-Saharan or Black African. The risk is not contingent upon our approach *per se*, for Timbuktu conceived itself as an Islamic city throughout its history. Rather, the risk is contingent upon the widespread misunderstanding which still persists even in academic circles concerning both Islam and Africa. For one thing, we have to contend with the conventions of East and West (now West and 'non-West') which for a long time left Africa out of the world historical picture. Other conventions have tended to project even stronger barriers against the historical processes of interaction between cultures. We frequently encounter notions of 'cultural' antithesis (as between the 'Islamic' and African, or between the 'Islamic' and Indonesian) when the evidence points more strongly to synthesis. In our case, the synthesis of Muslim and African pertains to the West African

Sudan generally rather than just Timbuktu. We must likewise remember that the division between northern Africa and sub-Saharan Africa (White and Black) is no more than a convention. Otherwise, we will fail to see how Timbuktu was at once Saharan and sub-Saharan, quite besides being at the same time African and Islamic.

Aside from the conventions mentioned above, or perhaps because of them, Timbuktu has long been the subject of an unusual lore of mystery and enigma. The name now often invokes the image of a remote, inaccessible place which never at all existed, anymore than the fabulous City of Brass of the *Arabian nights*. Horace Miner's ethnographic study of 1953, which characterized Timbuktu in the present century as an example of the so-called 'primitive city', certainly brought our subject closer to the realm of reality. Timbuktu was never the sumptuous or idyllic place which floated in the imagination of Europe up to the early nineteenth century. However, the place of Timbuktu in history is far from inconsequential. For here, just south of the great Sahara, was a substantial dynamic city by the sixteenth century when urbanization was still at a nascent stage in many parts of Europe. Moreover, the region of Timbuktu (or the Western Sudan) was remarkable for its large cities, including the metropolis of Gao, capital of the Songhai empire to the east, and the city of Jenne, the commercial centre of the Middle Niger Delta to the south. By the nineteenth century, these cities were no longer what they used to be, but to the historian at least they do not quite exemplify the theoretically formulated concept of the 'primitive city'.

The research of the past two decades has allocated to Timbuktu an important place in African history. The city is now famous as an ancient centre of commerce where a sophisticated tradition of learning flourished in the medium of classical Arabic, the language of Islam as a whole from Indonesia to Hausaland. Among the products of the Timbuktu tradition of scholarship, the best known are the chronicles because they have been widely utilized to reconstruct the outlines of early West African history. Although Timbuktu itself has not been the subject of concerted study, nonetheless the chronicles have contributed towards giving the city a new sort of fame more consistent with its real history than the earlier legends which circulated outside the area about Timbuktu.

The 'mystery' of Timbuktu

Our study approaches Timbuktu more from the standpoint of the chronicles and documentary records than of its legend or its present-day ethnography. Indeed, it might perhaps be said that the legend of Timbuktu and its mystery (including at the latest Miner's notion of the primitive city) pertain principally to the European approach to Timbuktu rather than to the actual history of the city. The history of European knowledge and exploration of Africa has been well written, and the 'discovery' of Timbuktu has received its share of attention. In the process, Timbuktu became famous for many things, ranging from its fabled slave-trade to its so-called Sankore University. However, any serious look at the city's legend will show that Timbuktu became famous merely for being 'famous'.

The mystery of Timbuktu is perhaps primarily the mystery of the full-fledged city which flourished south of the Sahara, in a continent which is not widely reputed for having historically had extensive urban centres. Secondly, the *real* mystery of Timbuktu pertains primarily to its relatively unknown origins and to the enigma of its early periods, when Timbuktu began acquiring the status of a metropolis which flourished almost in the desert, instead of at the centre of an agriculturally rich and well-populated region. Thirdly, and as far as the social scientist is concerned, the mystery of Timbuktu is that of the city which was not the modern European township, governed and thought to have been shaped by its municipal institutions, nor a mere conglomeration of villages, as some 'non-Western' cities have been described. Like many Asian and African cities yet to be studied seriously, Timbuktu was not necessarily shaped by the experience of a powerful kingdom, nor can its history be assimilated under that of the empires which successively controlled the area. Yet Timbuktu was a cosmopolitan city which attracted countless ethnic groups to become its sons and citizens.

Let us reaffirm at this point that Timbuktu is not historically the 'city' *par excellence* in sub-Saharan Africa. At most it can be said that no other town in sub-Saharan Africa has so far presented us with historical detail sufficient to make possible an internal view of the organization of the city over an extended period prior to the colonial era. The historian of urbanism in Africa may perhaps legitimately find more substantive basis for focusing on such major cases as Kano in Northern Nigeria, Jenne in the Middle Niger Delta, or Kumasi in modern Ghana. These settlements, too, are of great interest, for although they became the capitals of important kingdoms, we simply do not know whether city preceded state or *vice versa*. Other settlements of greater antiquity are attested by the remains of Zimbabwe in southern Africa, or by the art remains of Ife in Yorubaland. Remotely, the proliferation of ancient town–kingships affiliated to Ife by tradition may have a corollary in the phenomenon of city–states in the history of Hausaland. But in all these cases, and others, the research and documentation available so far has not yielded a body of evidence sufficient for a comparative approach in our study of Timbuktu. At most, we can readily arrive at comparisons with the nearby towns of Gao, Jenne and Walāta, all in the Western Sụdan, though in these cases we have to rely to an appreciable extent on the documentation available in the Timbuktu chronicles.

Similarly, we should affirm that Timbuktu was not the Islamic city *par excellence* in sub-Saharan Africa. Here, we need hardly emphasize the differences between the various African Muslim towns and cities, a theme which is often reiterated by Islamicists concerning the cities of North

Africa and the Middle East. Kano in Hausaland, Harar in Ethiopia and Kilwa on the East African coast have historically been different from Timbuktu and from each other. The role of scholar–notables was probably quite as strong in the case of Harar, an otherwise unique city which Richard Burton once described as the 'Timbuktu of East Africa'. What might be said of Harar need not be true of either Kano or Kilwa, though all three were Islamic cities and Islam played an important role in their history. Certainly, the Islamic factor was very strong in the organization of Timbuktu, and indeed one might even say that at times it loomed stronger than in the older cities of North Africa and the Middle East.

Given the importance of Islam in the history of Timbuktu, the risk is quite great that the city might somehow be seen as characteristically 'Arab' or more vaguely as 'Moorish'. We have already alluded to this problem, but we might perhaps further explain it when we recall that the Islamic cities of the East-African coast, for example, were thought until recently to have been the product of importation and settlement from southern Arabia and Persia. Indeed, writers on East Africa, till recent decades, tended to refer to African Muslims quite ambiguously as Arabs, just as the Portuguese, three or four centuries earlier, used to designate them 'Moors'. Fortunately, historians of West Africa have not had to contend with problems of nomenclatural ambiguity quite so commonly. For it was realized from an early date that Islam achieved an independent growth in West Africa, a fact which now increasingly appears to have been true of the mediaeval East-African coast as well. In both cases, one of the more significant findings of the historian is that we can identify no single event which accounts either for the introduction of Islam in mediaeval times nor for its subsequent growth locally. The 'mystery' in this case becomes in and of itself an important historical datum. It simply suggests that Islam was introduced gradually and informally as a result of processes of commercial intercourse whose origins would seem to pre-date the Islamic era in both cases. In East Africa, Islam remained for the most part restricted to the coastal regions, the area of Harar being an exception, while in West Africa Islam diffused widely, especially among mercantile communities of the Sahelo–Sudan. The process began long before Timbuktu came into being around 1100, and indeed even a full-fledged tradition of Islamic learning had witnessed considerable local development further to the south before the rise of Timbuktu to importance in the thirteenth and fourteenth centuries. Indeed, the very growth of Timbuktu to importance cannot properly be understood without appreciating the scope and nature of the southern influence.

Niger, Sahara and Sudan

Timbuktu belongs in the middle between two worlds which elsewhere in the Sahelo–Sudan are more distinct from each other. One is the world of the

Sudanic black peoples of the Savannah belt of West Africa, who have been characteristically agriculturalists, while the other is the world of the nomadic pastoralists of the southern Sahara, the 'whites' of the Sudan, who ultimately owe their origin either partly or fully to a pre-historic (and pre-Islamic) migration from North Africa. These two worlds come together along the Sahelian belt which separates the Sahara from the Savannah. However, the two worlds nowhere come so close as they do in the region of Timbuktu. The main factor is the unusual course followed by the great Niger river in its archlike journey across the West African sub-continent.

Much as Egypt was long ago described as the 'gift of the Nile', so Timbuktu and the cities and states of its region may perhaps be described as the gifts of the Niger. From its sources far to the south, the great Nile of the Sudan (as the Niger used to be called by the Arab geographers) bears resemblance to the Nile of Egypt in that it flows due north towards the Sahara. In the process, the Niger brings the more thickly populated regions of West Africa into the southern Sahara and, hence, closer to North Africa. Timbuktu's indebtedness to the Niger will become apparent when we consider that the great river changes its course eastwards precisely in the region of Timbuktu. From there, it takes a long journey through territories which would have been barren and uninhabitable until, in the regions of Bourem and Gao, it changes its course again, southeastwards, and from there flows along the longest part of its journey via Hausaland and Nupe to the Atlantic.

Perhaps it could be said that the Niger attempts the formidable feat, accomplished by the Nile, of actually crossing the Sahara. Even as it dissipates its strength in its course northwards, the Niger produces an inland delta on a scale which has no match elsewhere. The Middle Niger Delta, as the region south of Timbuktu is called, is a vast floodplain seasonally transformed into an immense shallow lake by the Niger inundations. The result is historically one of the richest regions in Africa, both agriculturally and in fishery. The area has aptly been described as the bread-basket of the Sudan, but the full impact of the floodplain upon the history of West Africa is far from satisfactorily understood.

Timbuktu owed its existence, as well as its long historical *floruit* as a commercial town, largely to the Niger and its inundations. Certainly, the same must also be said of the ancient city of Jenne which, along with the two important towns of Dia and Kābura, flourished in the midst of the Niger floodplain. Similarly, the city of Gao owed much of its history to its location along the eastern bend of the Niger. Timbuktu itself enjoyed the advantage of being located precisely at a point where the Niger inundations reach furthest north into the Sahara. Hence, for a portion of each year, some of the outskirts of the town are transformed into a cultivable region. More importantly, the rise of the Niger for a few months each year made it possible for boats of considerable capacity to navigate the river from Gao, *via* Timbuktu, to Jenne and beyond. Though not itself at the main course of the Niger, Timbuktu was nonetheless able, through its port at Kabara (to be distinguished from Kābura), to occupy an axial position in the commerce of the Niger bend area. The city linked various parts of the Niger with each other, besides standing at a particularly strategic location for linking the Sudan with the Sahara and, through the Sahara, with North Africa.

Seen from the vantage point of the Sahara, Timbuktu itself could perhaps be described, though in a special sense, as a 'port-town'. It is relatively well known that the mediaeval Arabs looked upon deserts as seas, and indeed the great Sahara separating northern Africa from the rest of the continent came to be known as *the* desert (*al-saḥrā'*). That is precisely why the two belts immediately to the north and south of the Sahara earned the name Sahel (*sāḥil*, literally coast). Timbuktu was as much a port-town along the West African Sahel, as Kilwa was a port-town along the coasts of East Africa. The main difference appears to be the fact that, while Kilwa interacted principally with other coastal regions, Timbuktu interacted most with, and probably owed much of its origin to, areas further 'inland' or further south.

The origins of Timbuktu are obscured in part by the scantness of the evidence, but they are perhaps more thoroughly overshadowed by certain conventions which have evolved around the earliest periods in West African history. Foremost among these conventions is a tendency to see history in the Sudan as proceeding from north to south, as it were, from North Africa, via the Sahara, to the Sudan. Among other things, it is quite widely stated that the early great empires of the Sudan, including ancient Ghana, Mali and the Songhai, owed their wealth and greatness predominantly to the stimulus of the trans-Saharan commerce in gold with North Africa. Indeed, we ourselves set out from the standpoint of a similar assumption about Timbuktu (especially in view of the predominantly commercial character of the city), but it soon became clear that the origin of the town, much like its continued existence today, rested upon a local commerce, mainly between the Middle Niger Delta, on the one hand, and between the pastoralists of the Sahara. We need not de-emphasize the role of the trans-Saharan trade in stimulating the further growth of Timbuktu, especially during the sixteenth century when the city became the emporium for West Africa *par excellence*. Nonetheless, there is a distinction between the influences which gave rise to Timbuktu (including the impact of the salt-mines in the middle of the Sahara) and between those which gave added prosperity and importance to the city during long periods of its history. This distinction has not been observed by writers on the Sudanic empires with the result that even the origins of state-formation are associated with the influence of trans-Saharan commerce and, indeed, with a 'civilizing mission' said to have been exerted on the Sudan by the southern Saharans.

Technically speaking, the central difficulty which has emanated from this sort of approach pertains to our inability to determine the location of the earliest kingdoms of the Sudan (as mentioned by the Arab geographies) and most especially the kingdom of Ghana. This ancient kingdom was the first in the area to assume an imperial stature, but neither its original core nor the extent of its expansion is known with precision. Most frequently, the core of the kingdom, known in local traditions as Wagadu, has been associated with a rather tenuous Sahelian location skirting the Sahara in the region of Walāta and Kumbi Saleh, some 400 miles to the west of Timbuktu. There, the kingdom may well have participated directly in the trans-Saharan commerce, as is frequently suggested, but there exists equally as much evidence that Ghana was located in or along the Niger floodplain. Indeed, it would appear quite possible that the commerce of Ghana was instrumental in giving rise to Timbuktu as an emporium (much as earlier in the case of Kumbi Saleh) from somewhere around 1100 onwards.

For the most part, we have avoided the complexities surrounding the history of ancient Ghana largely because they fall outside the scope of this study. Nonetheless, the reader should take note of a detail (in Chapter 2), for example, that the people of Wagadu (ancient Ghana) were among the earliest merchants to come trading at Timbuktu. The seventeenth-century chronicler, al-Sa'di, who records this information, also attributed Timbuktu's rise to prominence to its commerce with the city of Jenne, in the Niger floodplain. The interesting feature about both details lies in the fact that al-Sa'di confused the town–kingdom of Jenne, in an early phase of its history, and the kingdom of Ghana. Indeed, similar confusion is to be discerned in the sixteenth-century text of Leo Africanus, a source which exaggerated the extensiveness of the territories of Jenne while describing the town as Genni, Ghenoa and Ghinea.

One of the more fruitful lines of research pursued in this study concerns the chains of transmission of Islamic learning in the Sudan, a technical field of research (see Chapter 3) whereby the precise chains of transmission can be traced for many generations from teacher to student. We discovered that the chains of transmission at Timbuktu led us backwards, at the earliest, to a certain Muḥammad al-Kāburi, a black scholar who along with others bearing a Kāburi *nisba*, originated in the town of Kābura in the Niger floodplain. Beyond this scholar, the precise origins of Islamic learning in the Sudan are still not known. At most, the researches of Ivor Wilks (and partly those of Lamin Sanneh and Tom Hunter) have shown that many West-African Muslim clerics traced lines of transmission of learning which converge backwards upon a semi-legendary figure known as Sālim al-Suwari (Suware). It is of considerable interest that the origin of this scholar is associated with the town of Dia (Diakha, also Zāgha), a town near Kābura, where Ibn Baṭūṭa noted the existence of an Islamic learned tradition of long standing, already in the mid-fourteenth century. Remarkably, Suware is sometimes identified as son (almost certainly a putative son) of the Soninke founder–ancestor Dinga (Dinya) of ancient Ghana. Indeed, the traditions of ancient Ghana which are extant among the Soninke begin with relating the saga of travel for Dinga whereby the first places in which he resided in the Sudan are identified as Jenne and Dia (cf. Levtzion, *Ancient Ghana and Mali*, especially p. 15). This perhaps suggests that the ancient kingdom of Ghana flourished in the Niger floodplain or at least that it left an important legacy there at Jenne, Dia and Kābura. Timbuktu inherited the legacy to the extent that even its tradition of masonry is sometimes said to have been introduced from Jenne, a town which in turn is said to have been founded from Dia. There is no question that Dia was once a major metropolis, for it is indeed especially associated with masons and masonry, besides being an ancient centre of Islamic learning. Hence, although the evidence is neither complete nor fully reliable, it seems that the influences received by Timbuktu from the Niger floodplain had considerable impact upon the character of the city from its earliest periods.

The southern background of Timbuktu has been of interest to us in this introduction because it helps to amplify the African background of Timbuktu's traditions, including its tradition of Islamic learning. The world to which Timbuktu belonged did not see things in terms of a sharp distinction between Saharan and sub-Saharan, or between Black and White. Indeed, nor did it see civilization or history in terms of a movement from north to south. The traditionists of Timbuktu believed, for example, that the town of Tuat, across the Sahara in North Africa, was founded by Malinke from the empire of Mali. For all we know, the traditions may be correct, because the twelfth-century geographer, Abu'l-Ḥamīd al-Gharnāṭi, counted the town of Ghadāmis, also an emporium north of the Sahara like Tuat, as among the countries of the Sudan (*Sūdān*, Black people). Indeed, it is remarkable that people from Ghadāmis and Tuat have always been represented by settlers at Timbuktu. Other settlers from North Africa established themselves in the city at various times, but none contributed permanent settlers as much as the people of Tuat and Ghadāmis.

Perhaps the most interesting feature about Timbuktu historically is the great variety which characterized its settlers and its inhabitants. This factor is no longer apparent in the city today, because the majority speak the Songhai language. Indeed, Horace Miner saw Timbuktu as a *city* (albeit in his view a 'primitive city') because it was a multi-ethnic entity of Songhai, Arabic and Tamashagh speakers. In practice, the Songhai-speaking groups include Fulānis and Wangara besides Soninke and Sanhāja. Other groups who have gradually lost their ethnic identity include a variety of Tuareg and Hassāni settlers, besides Songhai and Ruma. We may note that southern Saharan 'whites' became more strongly associated with the northern Sankore quarter. However, it is interesting that other 'whites' from across the Sahara, including settlers from Tuat and Ghadāmis, historically settled in the southern parts of the city, at Jingerebir and Sarekeina.

The ethnic diversity of Timbuktu is historically the outcome of the fact that the city belongs to one of the most ethnically diversified regions in Africa. The Middle Niger Delta has historically been the home of Soninke and Malinke, Wa'kuri and Wangari, while Fulānis have figured prominently in the history of the region, alongside southern Saharan Sanḥāja Berbers. Arabs and North African Berbers might well have settled in the region, as individual merchants or merchant families, since the eleventh century when al-Bakri wrote the first detailed account of the countries of the Sudan. The area was likewise home for Songhai, not to mention other less-powerful groups, like the Bozo fishing communities and the semi-nomadic Zaghrānis. Owing to long processes of intermarriage, the colour lines in the region of Timbuktu are not clear-cut any more than elsewhere in the Niger bend area. By tradition, the Soninke, Fulāni and Songhai belong as much to a Sahelian as to a Sudanic background. What appears to be quite sharp, in any single period at least, is a distinction between settled townsmen and nomadic pastoralists. The latter in the expanse of the Sahara region adjoining Timbuktu are today divisible into Tamashagh-speaking Tuareg and into Hassāni Arabic speakers, often identified as Moors, Arabs or, earlier, as Barābīsh. Historically, both Tamashagh and Hassāni speakers owe their origin to the Berbers of the southern Sahara who are first known as Masūfa, Lamtūna and Judāla and who later make their appearance as Maghsharen, Kel Aghlāl, Kel Antasar, Kel al-Sūq, Barābīsh, Kel Tadmekkat *etc.* In the chronicles, these groups are identified by their clan and confederation names, rather than by any linguistic, ethnic or cultural criteria. Over the centuries Timbuktu has received (and indeed 'naturalized') settlers from all these groups, but more from among the settled peoples of the Niger than from among the pastoral southern Saharans.

The 'history' of Timbuktu

Conventionally, the history of cities, and especially of non-Western cities, is assimilated under the history of states, dynasties or empires which founded these cities, incorporated or dominated them. In regions which witnessed the rise and fall of several empires, like the Western Sudan, North Africa or the Middle East, this approach has the effect of projecting an idea of city (and especially of the 'Muslim city') as an entity whose character changes periodically. No one would seriously suggest that Mamluk Cairo was fundamentally different from Ottoman Cairo, but the studies available approach Cairo more from the standpoint of Mamluk and Ottoman than from the standpoint of factors which were constant and stable in the organization of the city. At most, the factors of stability are implicitly assimilated under the vague notion of changelessness which is said to characterize 'traditional societies'.

A good example of the emphasis on state, even in studies on the city, is Le Tourneau's *Fez in the age of the Marinids*. Fez has historically been an important North African city which could be an adequate subject for comparisons with Timbuktu, first because of the common factors of Islamic learning and Māliki jurisprudence, and secondly because of comparable economic features on both sides of the Sahara. Le Tourneau's study is one of a few important contributions in the field of Islamic (and indeed 'non-Western') urban history. The difficulty is that the work purports to study mediaeval Fez under the Marinids when, in fact, it is equally as frequently documented on the basis of much later data and, indeed, on the basis of contemporary observation of the organization of the city in the present century. Is it that Fez has remained the same over the centuries (in which case we should be interested in the factors of stability), or is it that Fez has remained Marinid?

In our own study we faced the difficulty that the entire corpus of historical data which is available on Timbuktu, though quite substantial by the standards of other sub-Saharan African cities, is nonetheless quite limited in comparison to the documentation available on North African, Middle Eastern or European cities during a comparable span of time. Particularly problematical is the fact that much of our information comes from the sixteenth and early seventeenth centuries, while the best details available on the commerce of Timbuktu, for example, pertained to the nineteenth century. It was quite tempting from the beginning to focus on one particular period while drawing upon data from other times. However, it proved quite important to focus precisely on the factors of stability over an extended period of time. Indeed, it was found more feasible to generate data around the theme of stability (and persistence of traditions) than around any other theme which could have constituted an adequate synthetical framework for a historical study of Timbuktu.

If we were to identify Timbuktu with one of the powers which controlled it over the centuries, the obvious choice would be the Songhai empire. The period of the Songhai empire was a relatively short one (*c.* 1468–1591), but it lies at the fulcrum of the city's own consciousness of its history, not only because the people of Timbuktu speak mainly the Songhai language today, but also because the sixteenth century was unquestionably the city's golden age. The difficulty is that the achievements of Timbuktu at that time cannot be credited to the Songhai empire, any more than the achievements of the Songhai empire can be credited to Timbuktu. Indeed, the key factor appears to have been a symbiosis between the two (following an initial period of extreme conflict) whereby both interacted to mutual advantage while observing a psychological distance from each other. This pattern had its precursors in the Sudan and it extended under the Songhai empire to the city of Jenne as well as Timbuktu.

Timbuktu does not lend itself to a conventional sort of historiography which relates the fortunes of the city to the rise and fall of dynasties and states in the region. For one thing, the town was clearly self governed during the first two centuries of its existence, though the settlers probably had to accommodate themselves to the nearby Tuareg confederations of the Masūfa. Subsequently, the city formed part of the empire of Mali for about a century, beginning around 1325, but the outstanding feature of the city's history during this period was its internal autonomy. During its period of decline, the empire of Mali finally relinquished its sovereignty over Timbuktu in 1433. There followed a period of continued autonomy for Timbuktu for a few decades, this time under the suzereinty of the chieftain of the nearby Maghsharen.

A great threat to the autonomy of Timbuktu in the early part of its history took place at the rise of the Songhai empire, and more specifically in 1468 when Sunni 'Ali conquered the city. The conquest was followed by a period of severe conflict and upheaval which came to an end only at the death of Sunni 'Ali in 1492. Subsequently, Askia Muḥammad established a new order of things which was as favourable to the interests of Timbuktu, as to those of other commercial centres in the empire. It was as part of this order that Timbuktu achieved its greatest prosperity, owing as much to the dynamism of its own leaders as to the accommodating attitude of the Songhai monarchs. During this period, Timbuktu was part of the Songhai empire, but it was not strictly ruled or dominated by the Songhai.

The most dramatic change in the history of Timbuktu took place in 1591, when the Moroccan Sulṭān al-Manṣūr sent an unprecedented expedition across the Sahara. The Moroccans put an end to the Songhai empire and established a new political order (patterned along Songhai lines) which controlled the Niger bend area. Henceforth, and for at least a century or so, Timbuktu enjoyed the dubious privilege of being the capital of an empire. The Ruma soldiery (as the Moroccans came to be known by their professional name locally) lost their connection with Morocco shortly after the conquest and, by around 1700, it was rare to find anyone among them who spoke Arabic, though the scholars of Timbuktu who were predominantly of non-Arab background continued to utilize that language in their scholarship, legal procedure and commercial correspondence. The assimilation of the Ruma by the Songhai whom they defeated is certainly an interesting phenomenon. Both remained for a long time distinct in Timbuktu as a military class, but the eighteenth century saw an erosion even of that distinction. The decline of the Ruma pashalik at Timbuktu was a long and gradual process, though it has often been said that the regime was destroyed in 1737, following a defeat of the main Ruma army at the battle of Tuwa by the Tuareg confederation of Kel Tadmekkat.

The 'political' history of Timbuktu during the rest of the eighteenth century continues to be quite fascinating. The early nineteenth century saw the rise of the famous *jihāds* (Islamic militant movements) in various parts of West Africa. One *jihād* gave rise to the caliphate of Massina, an empire based along the Niger floodplain at Ḥamdullāhi. This empire incorporated Timbuktu, at least from around 1825 until 1844, but again the key feature in this period is the autonomy of Timbuktu. The autonomy of the city was most threatened in 1862 when the jihādist al-Ḥājj 'Umar sought to bring Timbuktu more firmly under his authority. This gave rise to a counter *jihād* led by the Timbuktu scholar Aḥmad al-Bakkā'i, which put an end to Ḥājj 'Umar's caliphate at Ḥamdullāhi, though it did not give rise to an imperial theocracy based at Timbuktu. When the French conquered the city in 1894, they found it essentially autonomous, though reluctantly acknowledging the authority of the Kel Tingeregif, a Tuareg confederation which had succeeded the Kel Tadmekkat in supremacy over the Timbuktu portion of the southern Sahara.

Absorbing as the above outline may seem, by far the most interesting factor in the history of Timbuktu is its autonomy. Indeed, if we may except the first half-century or so following the Moroccan conquest, we can say that Timbuktu was always autonomous. Under the vast empire of Mali, the rulers were simply too distant, based to the southwest of the Niger floodplain, to influence the character of the city strongly or directly. Later, the Maghsharen ascendency during the mid-fifteenth century could not have shaped the character of Timbuktu in any fundamental way, because the city was in a greater position to influence the nomadic Maghsharen (as later the Wulmdān, Tadmekkat and Tingeregif) than *vice versa*. Indeed, the same holds true both for Songhai and Ruma, for while it is undeniable that Timbuktu exerted appreciable influence on the Songhai empire, it goes without saying that the city subsequently assimilated both Songhai and Ruma. Indeed, the reader will be surprised to find us suggesting (in Chapter 6) that Timbuktu even exerted an influence upon Morocco in the period immediately following the Moroccan conquest.

There is an unmistakable sense in which Timbuktu has its own character and its own history. In practice, this should be true of any city (or at least of most cities), whether Eastern or Western, African or European. We should not necessarily generalize from an example such as London, a city which has witnessed almost constant growth since the sixteenth century when, at that time, its size and possibly the scale of its commerce was not incomparable to that of Timbuktu. The point is not that such comparisons should not be made, for they are made implicitly in any case. The problem is that the present character and status of London (like Paris, *etc.*) is projected upon its past with the result that, when we turn to a case like Timbuktu, we gain the erroneous impression that we are dealing with a different sort of reality altogether in the phenomenology of human experience.

Naturally, a study of Timbuktu cannot be an adequate forum for discussing the varieties of urban experience in history. Indeed, it may be doubted that any systematic social scientific approach is yet possible on this profound dimension in history. Almost all generalization which has been made so far by the various writers and theorists remains subject to qualification. It has been said by Janet Roebuck, for example, that the Roman city (in the days of imperial Rome) depended on the empire for its existence. Similarly, and in a different context altogether, it has been said that the Chinese city had no personality of its own – that its personality was imparted to it by the Chinese empire and the imperial bureaucracy. These views (if valid in their own contexts) do not apply to Timbuktu, not only because of the city's 'internal' character but because the empires and states of the Western Sudan do not bear much comparison to the Roman or Chinese empires. Certainly, the Sudanic empires did not exert the centralizing stable influence of the Chinese imperial institution. As suggested earlier, there is greater scope for comparison with the Muslim cities of the Middle East and North Africa where the politico-dynastic feature of rise and fall stands to an extent in contrast to the relative stability of the city and of 'Muslim urbanism' generally.

Nonetheless, both in the case of Timbuktu and elsewhere, the personality of the city cannot be divorced from the impact of its region. In the most important respects, the character of Timbuktu was, indeed, imparted to it by the urban and mercantile traditions of its region. The city inherited its traditions from nearby commercial settlements and communities while, in turn, Timbuktu's own evolving traditions had appreciable influence upon those of its neighbours. In both respects, we must be aware of a certain sharing of traditions rather than overemphasizing a sharp distinction between the urban character of Timbuktu and the rest of the cities and societies of the Niger bend area.

Seen within the context of the history of the Western Sudan, Timbuktu over the centuries witnessed two main phases – gradual growth followed by gradual decline – rather than several phases corresponding to the dynastic or politico-military history of the area. The first phase, from 1100 to around 1600, was a period of constant growth, though the process clearly witnessed interruptions. In turn, this period may be divisible into Malinke, Maghsharen and Songhai, provided these are recognized merely as guidelines towards investigating the internal outlines of the city's history. Similarly, the second phase, from around 1600 to around 1900, may be subdivided into Ruma, Tadmekkat and Lobbo, but these subdivisions are even less coherent than the earlier ones.

At this point, we are able to pose coherently the central question raised in our study. Namely, what is the essential character or personality of Timbuktu? Naturally, it is not enough to say that Timbuktu was an African or Islamic city, or a diversified commercial centre or 'port-town'. The same could well be said of Kano, though the latter was not as much a 'port-town' nor was it quite as diversified as Timbuktu. Yet the fundamental character of Kano, unlike Timbuktu, was one of a capital city, the centre of a small kingdom or a city–state. Even after the nineteenth century *jihād*, which gave rise to a large territorial caliphate in Hausaland, the small kingdom or city–state tended to preserve much of its individual character in the area. The kingship tradition played a predominant role in the ordering of society at Kano and in securing for the city its relative stability. Similarly, we must seek the character or personality of Timbuktu in those factors which contributed most to the ordering of society and which provided a framework for stability.

City and scholars

Basically, the records and chronicles of Timbuktu do not leave us much scope to wonder about its personality or character. Most of what is known about the internal composition of the city historically, and even about its external relations, pertains to the scholars and to the structure of the learned hierarchy. To be sure, the chroniclers have left us a mass of detail about the Songhai empire, but this informs us about the structure of the Songhai state (and to a lesser degree about the capital city of Gao) rather than about the impact of the Songhai empire on Timbuktu. Similarly, the chronicles have left us much detail about the swift and long sequence of Pashas who 'reigned' at Timbuktu itself. Yet, even this body of detail does not tell us much about the ordering of society at Timbuktu. Instead, it highlights the existence of a distinct and separate military hierarchy – a hierarchy which coexisted with the religio-learned hierarchy of scholars and jurists. In the long run, the hierarchy of scholars and 'notables' (including civilian 'grandees' or *kubarā*') absorbed the topmost ranks of Songhai and Ruma families rather than the other way around. In this respect, the foremost consideration is a 'patrician' one, though the leadership of the patriciate (or 'upper bourgeoisie') in Timbuktu was primarily in the hands of scholars and jurists.

The status of scholars and jurists at Timbuktu was not divorced from the traditions of the city nor from those of its region. Indeed, in this sense the personality of Timbuktu (which was shared to an extent by other cities in the area) is to be found in its traditions generally, and more especially in the one tradition which revolved around the status and role of scholars and jurists. At an elementary level of analysis, this tradition was none other than the tradition of Islamic learning (and literacy) which flourished in the city. At another level of analysis, however, the impact of this tradition was felt most at the level of status and social stratification, besides parochial-type organization and administration. Hence, the varied factors which influenced and shaped the character of Timbuktu fell essentially within the framework of a special type of tradition – a social tradition.

Perhaps it would be accurate to say that every tradition has a history of its own, including a period of genesis and growth, followed either by decline or persistence. A key factor about the tradition which gave personality and character to Timbuktu is a dual feature in its formation. In part, the tradition came to the city with the immigrants who brought with them varying levels of subscription to Islam and Islamic learning from other Islamized mercantile settlements in the region. So long as Timbuktu was made up principally of immigrant settlers, the early periods in the history of the city are intertwined with those of the region. In another part, however, the tradition of leadership and autonomy under scholars was the product of local evolution at Timbuktu itself, especially in the fourteenth to the sixteenth centuries. The tradition achieved its period of maturity and its 'golden age' during the sixteenth century when Timbuktu interacted advantageously with the Songhai empire.

Another key element about the tradition which gave character to Timbuktu was that it persisted strongly, even when the city subsequently experienced a long and slow process of economic and demographic decline. The relative decline of Timbuktu relates in large part to shifts in the networks of commerce, both locally and internationally. Locally, it was principally the product of the periodic migration of Timbuktu merchants (and scholars) to various other locations which became more favourable for commercial enterprise. The 'dispersal' from Timbuktu (if we can apply the term dispersal to a very slow and gradual process) led to the partial diffusion of Timbuktu's social traditions both in the Sahara and the Sudan during the long period from the seventeenth to the nineteenth century.

Naturally, it may be asked to what extent Timbuktu derived its social tradition (and hence its personality and character), along with its tradition of Islamic learning, from the 'mainlands of Islam', that is from North Africa and the Middle East. In essence – and against the background of generalization about the 'Islamic city' – this is to ask whether Timbuktu should be seen typically as an example of the Islamic city. The social tradition which characterized Timbuktu amounted to a pattern of urban autonomy and autonomous leadership by scholars. There is little doubt that elements of this picture are found in the cities of Islam elsewhere. Indeed, the phenomenon of autonomous urban leadership by scholars and notables (*'ulamā'* and *a'yān*) may be a feature of Muslim urban history everywhere. Albert Hourani has written, for example, that 'the close connection of the *'ulamā'* with the bourgeoisie gave a distinctive shape to the urban society of the Islamic world'. To the extent that the leading merchant families of Timbuktu could be seen as a 'bourgeoisie' (or an upper bourgeoisie), their links to the upper ranks of scholars and jurists were most pronounced. Indeed, Hourani indicated that the leadership of the *'ulamā'* in Muslim cities generally tended to be drawn from the upper bourgeoisie and, for this and other reasons perhaps, they were the 'active leadership of the bourgeoisie'. In Timbuktu, and especially in the earlier periods, the scholars were unquestionably drawn from the wealthier merchant families and they were seen as *the* notables of the city *par excellence*.

Our study of Timbuktu was greatly facilitated by the questions which have been posed (and by the themes which have been discussed) in the existing literature on Muslim cities. Despite the absence of an adequate Islamicist study, it was quite clear that the stable curricula of learning at Timbuktu – and even the writings of Timbuktu scholars – bore strong comparison to the academic pursuits of Muslim scholars during the 'middle period' of Islam elsewhere, and especially in Māliki North Africa. Similarly, there were certain important grounds for comparison at the level of administration and administrative activities of scholars. In his study of Fez, for example, Le Tourneau noted that the 'administration of the city' tended to revolve around three main posts, namely those of 'governor', judge and *muhtasib*. At many periods of its history, Timbuktu did have a 'governor' (the Timbuktu-Koy or Timbuktu-Mundhu in Malinke and Songhai times, respectively) while the equivalent of the post of *muhtasib* was entrusted to special custodians of weights and measures. Even the primacy of the judgeship, which is a strong feature of the organization of Timbuktu, has been encountered by S. D. Goitein in a contribution on mediaeval Cairo ('Cairo: an Islamic city') and has also been suggested by Claude Cahen in an article on autonomist trends in early Muslim cities ('Mouvements populaires'). Additionally, the parochial character of urban organization at Timbuktu, both at the level of quarters and at the city-wide level, was suggested as a feature for early Muslim cities by Oleg Grabar ('The architecture').

Nonetheless, and despite the existence of a number of common themes, the scope for comparing Timbuktu to other Muslim cities across the Sahara remains quite limited. A key consideration is the absence of comparable studies which address themselves to the whole plethora of relevant questions concerning the stable features in the organization of any 'Islamic city'. Richard Bulliet (*The patricians*) alluded to this problem when he wrote about 'Islamic Nishapur' that 'an understanding of its character and composition will be little more advanced by a study of Islamic Fez than by an equivalent study of Christian Toulouse and Montpellier'. This may seem to be an exaggeration but it does amplify the difficulties and hazards of generalization about the 'Islamic city'. Many writers have emphasized the role of the *muhtasib* while Brunschvig ('Urbanisme medievale'), for example, noted the absence of any such post in mediaeval Tunis. At best, Louis Gardet contributed a remarkable work on the 'Muslim city' (*La cité Musulmane*) which, in fact, had little to do with either the 'physical' or 'sociological' city. His work suggests that generalization is possible only at the level of ideals (an ideal 'Muslim city') whereby the ideals themselves are adaptable in a multitude of different ways in each society. Indeed, the factor of adaptation is also suggested by the emphasis of Muslim scholarship – at the highest levels of learning, on jurisprudence and jurisprudential deduction. The very existence of a large body of accomplished scholars at Timbuktu, besides a broader stratum of lesser literati, is explainable in part by the need for jurisprudential adaptation of Muslim law – both at the level of daily practice and at the higher levels of formal 'interpretation' (or *futya*).

Given the factor of adaptation, it is perhaps legitimate to see the social (and even urban) tradition which evolved at Timbuktu and in its region as a variant upon the tradition of Muslim urbanism in the Middle East and North Africa. Nonetheless, the differences between the Middle Eastern and North African cities might themselves be quite appreciable. The entire question tends to be complicated by the extraordinary links which existed between scholars and scholar–notables across vast regions of urban Islam. In its 'classical period' (or its golden age), Timbuktu scholarship had strong links both with the Middle East and North Africa, though more especially with Egypt than the Maghrib. It is because of these links that the writings of Aḥmad Bāba achieved some currency in North Africa and the Middle East. Nonetheless, the links between scholars in the Sahelo–Sudan (or the West African Takrur) were much stronger than those which linked them to the mainstreams of Muslim scholarship across the Sahara. Just as Timbuktu had unmistakably a personality of its own, so the tradition of Muslim learning and leadership by scholars in the Western Sudan was a local tradition which evolved its own norms and conventions.

Let us be more precise and say that the phenomenon of a 'city of scholars' (which is so perceived as a matter of consciousness of historical experience) presents itself with greater immediacy in the Western Sudan. Elsewhere, as in the work of Lapidus on the 'Mamluk period', the important position of scholars is a matter of inference and analysis. Indeed, despite the superiority of the biographical sources, the integrative impact of the 'schools of law' in the Middle Eastern cities remains subject to varying interpretation. Lapidus, for example, described the *'ulamā'* (perhaps principally in Cairo) as 'auxiliaries' of the Mamluk regime. Yet, the same author found it necessary to say in the same work that 'all of the crucial political, economic, cultural, and religious roles of the society were entrusted to a broad and undivided class of professional, religious and commercial notables'. In other words, the relationship between scholars and other notables remains equally as problematical as the relationship between scholars and 'bourgeoisie' or scholars and 'city'. At Timbuktu on the other hand, the chronicles present us with an elusive sort of equation between city and scholars, as a point of departure for any analysis. Especially in the earlier periods, the scholars of Timbuktu were themselves *the* city's notables.

Insofar as Timbuktu inherited its social traditions from elsewhere, Timbuktu was not the sole city of scholars in the history of the Western Sudan. Rather, it shared its social traditions with other cities and towns and with mercantile communities in the area generally. The author of *Tārīkh al-Fattāsh* amplified this fact when he recalled the autonomy of Timbuktu prior to the Moroccan conquest. The key consideration was not so much the independence of the Timbuktu judges but a local tradition of jurisprudence which secured a position of primacy for the judge amidst a prominent class of jurists. Earlier, the pattern had been present in the city of Jaghaba (also Zāgha, now Dia) where judiciary authority was contingent upon the status of the city as a 'city of jurists'. Indeed, the author of the *Fattāsh* spoke directly of Dia as 'the town of jurists which had no authority other than that of its judge' in the age of the empire of Mali. The author also mentioned the now obscure city of Kunjuru as a 'town in the land of Kayaka which was the residence of the judge of that region and of its scholars'. By the sixteenth century, Timbuktu was the principal heir to this legacy whereby a whole town would be identified on basis of its autonomous leadership as a 'city of scholars' or a 'city of jurists'. In a sense, Timbuktu became the main point of convergence for scholars and literati in the region. Its reputation as a 'city of scholars' subsequently overshadowed that of other earlier towns and settlements. Nonetheless – and even in much later periods, the social tradition which characterized Timbuktu was well represented outside the 'urban' context of large settlements. The Western Sudan was remarkable for the fact that small settlements (among the Wangara and Dyula, for example) were viewed as 'clerical communities', while whole clans in the southern Sahara came to be seen as 'Maraboutic' clans of literate *tulba* or erudite *fuqahā'* or jurists.

Given the special nature of the evidence, it is tempting to say that scholars tended to play a far more prominent role in their communities than in the North African and Middle Eastern cities. This, at least, is true at the level of *perception* of the role of literati, scholars or jurists. Our task in this study is to look at the sociological context of this perception rather than to test its validity elsewhere. The sources at our disposal do not bear much comparison to the situation which enabled the Egyptian scholar al-Sakhāwi to compile the biographies of thousands of scholars and scholar–notables all belonging to the ninth century A.H. (the fifteenth century A.D.). Nor do we have the full continuity of evidence which is available on the Middle Eastern and North African cities from the mediaeval period down to the nineteenth century. Our entire corpus of available biographical evidence covers a body of scholars who number in the hundreds, not in thousands or tens of thousands. Nonetheless, the problem is not really one of scale nor a matter of documentation. At times, we learn much more from a single statement (such as we find in the *Fattāsh*) than from a long biographical entry. In that respect, we might even say that study of Timbuktu is facilitated by the modest size of the city and of its sources, while study of larger Muslim cities is often subject to the hazards of selectivity in the face of a far more extensive body of historical data.

Despite our attempt to synthesize the entire body of available evidence, it must be said, nonetheless, that those facets of Timbuktu scholasticism which pertain to Islam generally remain beyond the scope of comprehensive analysis. What is the significance, for example, of the fact that scholars in the Sudan, as in Mālikism generally, held study of *Kitāb al-Shifa'* as an important component in the education of a scholar? Numerous similar questions arise and, so long as they are not posed in the wider Islamicist context, they cannot be answered in the more restricted sphere of a study of Timbuktu and its region. Indeed, it is the limitations of generalization on Islam which led us to compare the scholars in the Sudan with the Chinese Mandarins. The common theme in this case has little to do with the 'content' of the learning process. Rather, it pertains to a more or less universal theme whereby leadership – along with administrative and quasi-administrative prerogative – was contingent upon learned status. The idea of a combined scholastic and social tradition is at least already quite familiar in the Chinese context. A central distinction lay in the fact that scholars in the Sudan were not strongly associated with 'state administration'. At Timbuktu especially, there appears to have evolved a distinction between the religio-legal hierarchy, including the judiciary post, and between the military–fiscal hierarchy of the state. This bears some resemblance to a delicate sort of balance (suggested by Hourani) between state and 'bourgeoisie' in Muslim urban civilization more generally. But the distinction in the Sudan appears to have been much sharper – and it is pertinent also outside the 'citied' context. Indeed, it helped give the scholars a position of intermediacy between states (even in the large territorial empires of Mali and Songhai) while giving rise in time to a distinction between warlike and clerical clans in the southern Sahara.

Approaching Timbuktu as a city of scholars is justified equally from the methodological standpoint as from the substantive standpoint. At the least, it may be said that the process of situating the scholars in Timbuktu society enables us to arrive at a more complete view of the society at large than an equivalent attempt to situate the rulers (or their representatives) in Timbuktu society. Thus, our treatment of scholars as 'academicians' (in Chapter 3) enables us to look at the wider diffusion of literacy and learning, a theme which cannot be discussed without reference in turn to the city's social composition and its historical demography. The interesting feature about Timbuktu is that we get our best information about the city's historical demography from data which are available on the literacy schools and rank-and-file literati during the sixteenth century. In this, as in other respects, the role and influence of scholars tells us more about the city than *vice versa*. Indeed, one might almost say that the history of Timbuktu cannot be investigated except from the standpoint of the traditions which evolved (and revolved) around the status and role of scholars.

Our discussion of the 'administrative' role of scholars (in Chapter 4) reveals an appreciable city-wide integrative role, first for the judgeship and secondly for the fluid '*Jamā'a*' of Timbuktu. Otherwise, the city was made up of quarters whereby, in some cases, the various ethnic groups were distinct. However, the ethnic–linguistic or colour distinctions were never strong, and we rarely have a case where ethnic group gives its name to an important city-ward or quarter. Instead, the two most important quarters were given their respective names by their mosques. This, too, is testimony to the influence of scholars who occupied the posts of *imāms* and were parochial leaders at the mosques.

Ultimately (and as seen especially in Chapter 5), the factors which determined the role and status of scholars were quite varied. They ranged from wealth to venerated descent and from erudition to piety. The factor of wealth is sometimes documented directly while in other cases it may be inferred from the city's commerce and commercial links. Nonetheless, it is quite clear that at least from around 1400 onwards, the city was controlled by a patriciate of wealth, learning and descent. As the reader will find, the ideological factors which conditioned the outlook of scholars, and especially their insistence on a distinctiveness and psychological distance from rulership and temporal authority, were likewise determinate of their status. Furthermore, whether in terms of commercial or pedagogical links, the role and status of scholars transcended the local urban 'patriciate' and (while bearing similarity to Marshall Hodgson's non-defined 'Islamicate') it characterized the city in the sense that it shaped the affiliations and status of Timbuktu in its region.

Our treatment of the 'Mandarinate' of Timbuktu and the Sudan in the central three chapters of the study is basically analytical rather than chronological. The data are not distributed evenly over the periods under consideration and hence it was important to feature an analytical framework. Nonetheless, in each of the three chapters, and indeed in each section of these chapters, we have tried as much as possible to present the data following a very rough chronological framework. This, of course, is much easier when one is considering the lines of transmission of learning, generation by generation, than when one is discussing the commercial links of Timbuktu. In the latter case, we get more information from Barth's account of his short residence in Timbuktu during the mid-nineteenth century (*Travels and discoveries*) than from any other single source. Nonetheless, even on this subject, the chronicles, along with a multitude of fragmentary documents which have survived, enable us to arrive at a reasonably clear picture.

The careful reader will no doubt note that much of our most detailed evidence derives either from the sixteenth and early seventeenth centuries or from the early and mid-nineteenth century. The well-known mid-eighteenth-century chronicle, the *Tadhkirat al-Nasyān* (*A reminder to the oblivious*) simply does not supply the wealth of detail which we find in al-Sa'di's *Tārīkh al-Sūdān* of around 1655. Indeed, Timbuktu never produced a monument to its own history equal in wealth of detail to al-Sa'di's chronicle. The author has left us a formidable source and his information is supplemented for the period up to the early seventeenth century both by *Tārīkh al-Fattāsh* (a chronicle which has a long history of its own) and by the numerous extant works of Aḥmad Bāba. Similarly, the nineteenth century is reasonably well documented by a number of short treatises and by a corpus of correspondence, including especially the correspondence of Aḥmad al-Bakkā'i. It is not fully clear why the works of the eighteenth-century scholars have not survived. Fortunately, however, some of the material from that time was incorporated into later sources, and especially the *Fath al-Shukūr*, a late-eighteenth-century compendium from Walāta.

The outline which we have adopted in the book is non-conventional in the sense that the chronological sections are to be found at the beginning and at the end. This, in part, is predicated upon the simple periodization which we adopted whereby the earlier periods (up to roughly around 1600) are characteristically seen as periods of growth, including a growth in the social traditions of Timbuktu to 'maturity', while the later periods (up to roughly around 1900) are viewed in terms of a persistence of traditions despite the Moroccan conquest and despite the long, slow process of economic and demographic decline. In writing the research, it proved necessary to analyse the social traditions which persisted, and to analyse the nature of the patriciate, before proceeding to document the sequence of events which made the persistence of the patriciate, and indeed its resurgence, possible. In this way, the organization of Timbuktu, as seen from the standpoint of the role of scholars (in Chapters 3–5), became part-and-parcel of the study, and indeed a central focus of attention from the analytical standpoint.

CHAPTER 2

Genesis of a social tradition

The role of Muslim scholars (*'ulamā'*) in Timbuktu is treated in this study as part of a social tradition which exerted a continuous influence upon the organization and character of the city throughout its history. The essence of this tradition was that status and influence, including recognition among the ranks of notables (*a'yān*), could most readily be derived through the acquisition of Islamic learning. Scholars in this tradition were the leaders of the urban community, its spokesmen *vis-à-vis* the rulers, and the regulators of its public affairs. In their combined roles as notables and a learned elite, the scholars could marshal considerable resources and mobilize wide sectors of the city's population. This gave them a dominant voice in the internal affairs of their community. In view of the religio-political organization of Islam, their impact was strongly felt at the administrative level as well as the political.

Some of the implications of the role of scholars in Timbuktu have already been observed by John Hunwick and Sekene Modi Cissoko in their contributions on the sixteenth-century history of the city. Cissoko underlined the prestigious position gained by Timbuktu, as an active and vibrant centre of learning, in the Songhai empire complex.[1] Hunwick, on the other hand, implicitly ascribed the phenomenon of autonomy to the unusual dynamism exhibited by the scholars, and especially by the Aqīt family among them, during the Songhai period.[2] The wealth and commercial importance of Timbuktu at that time, along with the legendary image which it evoked in post-mediaeval Europe, have made the pre-seventeenth-century history of the city a subject of commentary in many recent publications. However, there has emerged a tendency throughout to look at later periods as less significant in themselves or as constituting a dramatic departure from the patterns established up to Songhai times.[3]

The earliest surviving chronicles from Timbuktu are in large part responsible for this. Written in the middle of the seventeenth century by scholars who had experienced the transformative impact (and ravages) of the Moroccan conquest, these recall with marked nostalgia the essential independence of their city under Mali and the Songhai.[4] The intervening 60 or so years since the establishment of the Moroccan Ruma regime had witnessed a decline in the extent of literacy and this naturally had a reflection upon the tradition of higher Islamic learning. One almost senses a premonition on the part of the chroniclers of what was yet to come. The city which boasted of some 150 Qur'ānic schools in the sixteenth century had but some 20 to offer when the French gained control of it in the late nineteenth century. In the meantime, the population had declined to as little as one-quarter or one-fifth of what it had been and some of the central wards of the town remained uninhabited until recent years.[5]

Yet, for all that, the city retained much if not all of its essential characteristics (and its traditions) despite the decline. The seventeenth-century chroniclers attest equally to the sophistication of their own time as to that of the past they lament.[6] Many of the same families which had thrived under Mali and Songhai continued to wield their influence up to much later times. The tradition of learning remained so much alive that the French found it favourable to their interests to incorporate it partly into the new administration.[7] The assimilation of the Ruma which began as early as the mid-seventeenth century revived the power and influence of the scholars to such an extent that Paul Marty, one of the foremost researchers of West African Islam, described Timbuktu as 'a little democratic republic'. According to Marty, 'The city was at all times self-administered internally by its *Jamā'a*'.[8]

Approaching the history of Timbuktu from the standpoint of the tradition which conditioned the status and role of scholars offers the advantage of bringing out the element of continuity over the centuries. Indeed, and as a starting point, the approach enables us to enquire adequately (even if retrospectively) into the origins and growth of Timbuktu during a period of almost three centuries which are not sufficiently documented in the sources. Judging from later records, Timbuktu took on the character of an ethnically diversified settlement right from the beginning during the twelfth century when Timbuktu originated as a commercial town. The traditions which evolved in the settlement, and especially those which revolved around the role of scholars (parochial leaders and judges), enabled the town to develop its own personality and, in due course, to establish and preserve a power of collective action to a considerable extent. The scholars played a city-wide integrative role which transcended the organization of each quarter while at the same time drawing some of its strengths from it. Here, as in most non-Western cities, municipal institutions did not emerge independently, nor did Timbuktu ever become formally a city–state.[9] The ethnic diversity of the population, and especially that of the mercantile and learned elite, prevented the emergence of a strong kingship tradition such as we encounter further south at an early date in the city of Jenne.[10] Nonetheless, a strong sense of solidarity among the citizens did emerge and this was both symbolized and ritualized in the institution of the Friday congregation at the Main Mosque (Jingerebir).

The factor of Islam in the development of Timbuktu cannot strictly be treated along the same lines as in other Muslim cities north of the Sahara. For there existed an element of 'frontierism' in West African Islam which is perceptible only in the earliest periods in North Africa and the Middle East. In West Africa, on the other hand, in areas which are adjacent to each other we often encounter some of the same phenomena from the eleventh century, and earlier, up to the nineteenth century. The borders of Islamic diffusion remained quite fluid, and this led the Muslim or Islamized community, much more thoroughly than elsewhere, to define its own identity and its sense of solidarity in Islamic terms. The parochial aspects of Islam remained very strong here and exerted a city-wide impact, whereas in the mainlands of Islam they gave way to a process of fragmentation directly proportionate to the size (and sometimes ethnic divisions) of the city.[11] Likewise, predominantly politico-military considerations which gave rise to dynastic changes often came to be perceived in the Western Sudan in terms of Muslim conceptions of legitimacy.

When Timbuktu came into being in the twelfth century, Islam had penetrated many market-towns and state capitals to the west and east, as well as to the south. Already, in the eleventh century, we encounter the phenomenon of royal subscription to Islam (in varying ways) in kingdoms ranging from Gao in the east, to Takrur and Salli in the west, to the small kingdom of Malli (a precursor of Mali), to the southwest.[12] Presumably, a similar trend had been taking place among the small chieftaincies of the southern Sahara and the process was consolidated under the impact of the Almoravid militant Islamic movement of the late eleventh century.[13] The developments of the twelfth century are obscure, but it seems that the diffusion of Islam was aided by the formal Islamization of the kingdom of Ghana and by the growth of an important tradition of learning among the Soninke, or the 'people of Ghana'.[14] Future developments in the thirteenth and fourteenth centuries would incorporate Timbuktu along with practically the entire region of the Western Sudan into the empire of Mali, the greatest geopolitical formation in the history of West Africa. The legacy of this power came partly to be inherited during the fifteenth and sixteenth centuries by the more closely-knit Songhai empire which, like its predecessor, was strongly influenced by royal subscription to Islam and its propagation in varying degrees throughout its realms.[15]

Thriving under the auspices of first Mali and then the Songhai, Timbuktu's chroniclers and traditionists have impressed upon us two main features concerning the history of their city: first, that it originated as an exclusively Islamic settlement right from the date of its foundation at the hands of Tuareg tribesmen *c.* 1100 A.D; and secondly that the city's tradition of learning had begun to match those of much older cities in the heartlands of Islam when it was incorporated into the empire of Mali *c.* 1325.[16] These assertions reflect the collective memory of later generations and we have little by way of independent evidence to confirm them. Nonetheless, they help emphasize the extent to which the status and reputation of Timbuktu was enhanced by its Islamic image.

One of the implications of being an exclusively Islamic city in West Africa was to enjoy a high degree of autonomy with respect to the dominant state in the area. At the earliest, this amounted to a tendency towards quarantine on the part of the Muslim community, but the separation was never complete.[17] Owing to the predominantly commercial preoccupation of Muslims, the level of intercourse with non-Muslims was always high and it is this which facilitated the processes of conversion.[18] From as early as the tenth century we have the evidence of Ibn Ḥauqal to the effect that Muslim merchants who settled in the kingdom of Ghana, as also in the now obscure kingdom of Kūgha, enjoyed a distinct status and were administered autonomously by their judges.[19] By the eleventh century, Muslim settlements grew into virtual cities vying with the royal capitals at least at the twin cities in the kingdoms of Ghana, Salli and Gao.[20] Survivals of this tradition are exemplified by the town of Dia (also Zāgha, Jāgha) to the southwest of Timbuktu in Massina where, according to tradition, even the Malian kings did not enter the gates though they were the acknowledged supreme leaders of Islam in their time.[21]

The tradition of learning in Timbuktu, for which a precursor is found at Dia, assured the city a status and prestige which overshadowed the initial phenomenon of autonomism brought by waves of settlers from earlier Muslim settlements. Whether Soninke or Berber, from Ghana and its Sahelo–Saharan tributaries, or North Africans who had migrated extensively in the Western Sudan, the settlers all more or less subscribed to the importance of Muslim scholarship. Tuaregs who opted for a sedentary existence became major recruits to the ranks of scholars. They were to be joined by Wangara, or mercantile Malinke, during and after the supremacy of Mali, and by Songhai and Massina Fulāni throughout the earlier periods in the city's history.[22]

The Muslim sciences which the various settlers brought and fostered in the city went hand-in-hand with the widespread commercial contacts of these groups to secure for the growing town a measure of non-interference from outside. For one thing, the settlers themselves commanded considerable wealth along with widespread networks of trade and alliances in the area. Additionally, however, the security of the city was in its Islamic image; its mosques, schools and shrines began to be conceived early as its guardians. In the psychological mood which prevailed after the pilgrimage of Mansa Mūsa of Mali (and again on the return from the Ḥājj of Askia Muḥammad over a century and a half later), Timbuktu gradually gained an aura of 'sanctity' and assumed for itself a sort of inviolability. Its acknowledgement of Malian, and especially Songhai, rule at a later time, was perceived as a voluntary act which bound the city through the Muslim monarchs with the realm of Islam (the *umma*) as a whole. In both cases, the relationship was reciprocal. Recognition on the part of a thriving centre of learning reinforced the prestige of the ruler and he, in turn, bestowed some privileges on the scholars which greatly enhanced their influence. At the level of economics, similar considerations went into operation. Timbuktu, like other commercial centres, benefited immensely from the regularity and safety of trade brought about by the exigencies of empire-building. The rulers, for their part, had no interest in directly controlling these centres so long as a *laissez-faire* policy secured the flow of goods to and from their domains.[23]

There was no question, here as elsewhere outside Europe, of the city's evolving a corporate character with a legally defined body of citizenry. A rudimentary tendency in that direction (or at least a vague recollection of such a tendency) is evidenced in the case of Jenne, Timbuktu's major trade partner to the south, judging from the legends which recall the city–state's Islamization.[24] But the need for encouraging the arrival of merchants, whether for short or extended stay or permanent settlement, reinforced the *ad hoc* character of urban organization. It has often been pointed out that Muslim law and ideology recognized no permanent organizational unit other than the entire *umma* or community of believers.[25] This, though a highly theoretical premise difficult to reconcile with the historical fragmentation of the Muslim world, was not entirely irrelevant to the self-conceptions of Timbuktu. At all times the scholars betrayed a marked preference for associating their city, either directly or indirectly, with whatever power seemed to represent supreme leadership in Islam.[26]

Perhaps the most characteristic feature of Timbuktu was its openness to newcomers. For the people of its Sahelo–Saharan hinterland, its markets were a source of supply just as the tombs and shrines of its departed scholars were places of pilgrimage. The wealth of the city and its commercial *floruit* were perceived as an extension of the *baraka* (divine grace) with which it was endowed.[27] Most importantly, however, Timbuktu was a 'capital-city' for the pastoralists of the Sahara, just as it was an emporium for the people of the Sudan. The pastoralists of the region sought Timbuktu for their goods and some of their food supplies, as well as for learning and 'culture'. Similarly, students and scholars from various locations to its south came to the city to study and teach in the growing metropolis of the Sahelo–Sahara. The reputation for piety and learning of its leaders made Timbuktu a place of refuge and security. Moreover, in the emerging Islamic world of West Africa, the city was a main link along the caravan routes which led towards the pilgrimage in Mecca.[28]

Growth of a commercial settlement

Much as in the case of its social traditions, the demographic origins and growth of Timbuktu need to be investigated retrospectively on the basis of the information available for later, better-documented periods. The chroniclers have left us unmistakable evidence that they themselves did not know the precise outlines of the growth of the city. Much as in their case, we have to draw our own inferences on the basis of available knowledge concerning the groups who played an important role in the history of the city during the fourteenth and, more especially, the fifteenth and sixteenth centuries. Additionally, we are able to draw upon the evidence of the early Arab geographers concerning settlements which had preceded Timbuktu to importance in the area. Though limited in some basic respects, the available corpus of information enables us at least to offer an adequate outline of the areas from which Timbuktu inherited its settlers and its traditions.

The highly diversified ethnic composition of Timbuktu and the complexity of its demographic history are illustrated by the fact that Tuaregs, Berbers, Soninke, Songhai, Arabs, Malinke and Fulāni all played a prominent role in its leadership at various periods. The above groups do not exhaust the list and the high incidence of assimilation, through intermarriage and the integration of slaves, produced many mixed groups such as the Tamashagh-speaking Bella and the Songhai-speaking Ghabibi and Ruma. Among the latter, the Bella are sometimes alleged to be descendants of an autochthonous group which inhabited the location since time immemorial.[29] In practice, we cannot be sure about this any more than about the origin of the Maghsharen Tuareg who make an early appearance in the history of Timbuktu. The Tuareg as a whole were seen in the seventeenth century as a branch of the Masūfa who, in turn, were a branch of the Sanḥāja Berbers. The early ethnographic history of the region is quite obscure, and the most that can be said is that Timbuktu received a highly diversified and mixed body of settlers. Besides the permanent settlers, we should perhaps mention a 'floating population', especially of nomadic Tamashagh-speaking Tuareg and, later, of Arabic-speaking Barābīsh, who made their appearance in large numbers during the caravan seasons and at times of drought or instability.[30]

The data at our disposal indicate that the population of the city ranged between 30000 and 50000 inhabitants in the sixteenth century when Timbuktu experienced its 'golden age' of prosperity and Islamic learning.[31] By very indirect evidence we may also infer that the population amounted to some 10000 inhabitants when the empire of Mali incorporated Timbuktu around 1325, the growth being more or less gradual from then on.[32] However, it is not possible to arrive at an ethnographic breakdown of the community at any given period. Data from the present time, which indicate Songhai–Ruma predominance, reflect post-seventeenth-century transformations. Among other things, the past three centuries have witnessed a growth followed by a decline in the Fulāni element, as well as a general emigration of Berber (Sanḥāja) and Malinke groups who figured far more prominently in the early history of the city than is indicated by their numerical strength today.[33] Indeed, today, most groups except the Tamashagh-speaking Bella and the Arabic-speaking Hassānis (the latter being mainly relatively recent settlers) are indistinguishable. For, while most speak the Songhai language, it is only among a few families that actual lines of descent may be established with certainty.

The precise provenance of the various groups which settled the city in its period of growth is obscured by the high degree of geographical mobility which has historically characterized merchants in the Western Sudan.[34] What we know are the immediate locations from which some of the settlers came, and these were highly diversified settlements in themselves. Nonetheless, it would be useful to outline the general directions of these movements provided they are not equated strictly with questions of ethnic origin. These may perhaps be discussed in terms of northern, southern, eastern and western factors in the demographic growth of Timbuktu.

The northern factor, closely related to the Saharan and trans-Saharan trade, was important both in stimulating the rise of Timbuktu and in consolidating its economic and demographic growth. For, although Timbuktu owed much to the rich region of the Niger delta to its south, nonetheless the site may have remained marginal to the economics of the area if it had not been for the influence of Saharan commerce, as a first step, and for the influence of trans-Saharan commerce later. The key stimulus would seem to have come from the salt-mines of Taghāza located in the middle of the Sahara some 500 miles due north of the city. Al-Sa'di indicates that Tuaregs from the Maghsharen branch first used the location of Timbuktu sometime around 1100 A.D. as a permanent storehouse for their goods while they themselves persisted in their nomadic way of life which took them from the Niger to the town of Arwān to the north. Traditions of recent record have added to this detail the claim that the Bella were already in a servile relationship to the Tuareg and that they were entrusted with the upkeep of their stores.[35] It is possible indeed to visualize a rudimentary beginning for the trade which later predominated at the site in the exchange of cattle and hides for agricultural produce between the Tuareg (or their Berber ancestors) and between ancestors of the Bella drawn from among the agricultural societies of the Niger. But it seems that the salt-trade, possibly first carried by local Tuareg or Masūfa, was the main attraction for more dynamic merchant groups.

The salt-trade of Taghāza had previously been carried, and continued to be so for a very long time, to the much more extensive Tuareg settlement of Tadmekka. Also known as al-Sūq (Ar. 'the market'), in the Adrar of Ifoghas, Tadmekka had been the Saharan emporium of Gao, the old kingdom on the Niger some 250 miles to the east of Timbuktu.[36] The ancient importance of Tadmekka is attested by the fact that it gave its alternate names to the militant Kel Tadmekkat and the clerical and more peaceable Kel el-Suk (Kel al-Sūq). Both clans became prominent in the history of the area from the seventeenth century onwards. The ancient town was mentioned as a large well-built city during the eleventh century by al-Bakri, and it has since held a special position in Tuareg legend as a once-flourishing centre of learning which was allegedly destroyed by the defamed Songhai monarch, Sunni ʻAli.[37] It would seem, in fact, that its decline was a protracted one which, though possibly affected by the fortunes of Gao, began long before the rise of Sunni ʻAli in the late fifteenth century and continued thereafter. Essentially, the location of Timbuktu, with Kabara as its riparian port on the Niger, was far more advantageous for the exchange of salt in return for the products of the Middle Niger Delta. Indeed, during the eleventh century, al-Bakri had mentioned a town named Tireqqa whose location must have been in or near the location of Timbuktu and Kabara. Tireqqa had been a small town whose market was a meeting-place between the people of the kingdom of Ghana and the people of Tadmekka. Quite probably, Timbuktu replaced Tireqqa as a market town, beginning from around 1100, and in the process it drew settlers both from the Niger floodplain and from Tadmekka. The early prominence of Tuareg scholars in Timbuktu, not specifically related to the Maghsharen, would suggest that these moved to the settlement from Tadmekka and were probably (along with Soninke from Ghana) the first large-scale merchants at the location.[38]

The eastern factor in the demographic growth of Timbuktu is suggested by a general body of evidence which suggests that the city of Gao witnessed a gradual decline from the ninth century down to the fifteenth century prior to the rise of the Songhai empire at the site. As already mentioned, the kingdom of Gao had evolved into a twin settlement in the eleventh century and, although its earliest traditions have been overshadowed by those of the Songhai empire which made Gao its capital, the city would seem to have been the centre of an ancient state which attracted much of the produce of the Niger bend area and exchanged it for North African goods through the intermediacy of Tadmekka and, further to the east, Tagedda.[39] So far as we can tell, the decline of Gao had been gradual, though the funerary inscriptions nearby suggest a change of dynasty in the twelfth or thirteenth century.[40] Later, in the early decades of its incorporation by the empire of Mali, Gao probably witnessed some revival during the early to mid-fourteenth century. But it seems that a major upheaval resulted in the abandonment of the city beginning somewhere around 776 A.H. (1374/5 A.D.). At that time, the North African historian Ibn Khaldūn met a Sijilmāsi scholar named Muḥammad b. Wāsūl who had lived in Gao and had been employed in its judiciary. The latter told him of a devastating struggle over Gao between Mali and the Berber Tuaregs of the Tagedda region. The text of Ibn Khaldūn in the section on the Sudan is ambiguous but in the prolegomena the author says, 'Gao, . . . at this time is devastated'.[41] It seems quite possible that an exodus of the inhabitants took place at this juncture and the importance of the city was not revived until the rise of the Songhai empire. Ibn Baṭūṭa had visited Gao and associated with its scholars in its better days. He described it as 'a large city . . . one of the best and biggest in the Sudan'.[42] The decline of Gao during the late fourteenth century and the early fifteenth century almost certainly resulted in the diversion of much of its commerce westwards to Timbuktu. Similarly, it would seem almost certain that settlers from Gao (Songhai and others) contributed to the growth of Timbuktu, beginning even at a much earlier time.

The southern factor, or the extension of the trade of Timbuktu through Kabara along the Niger upstream, is emphasized in our sources to the point of seeming exaggeration. The ambiguity concerns the city of Jenne, some 250 miles to the southeast, in the eastern side of the Niger floodplain. The traditions of this city, like its demographic composition, seem to have incorporated those of earlier more important political and urban formations in that area. Jenne was allegedly founded in the second century of the Hijra (eighth and ninth centuries A.D.) and became officially Islamized towards the end of the sixth century (say somewhere around 1180 A.D.). At that time, we are told, when Timbuktu was still a minor settlement, Jenne boasted of no less than 4200 scholars already established in 'its lands'. At present, we have no confirmation of extensive Islamization at an early date in Jenne, except to say that the twelfth-century geographers did indeed emphasize the diffusion of Muslim learning among the people of the kingdom of Ghana. Interestingly, one of the geographers who emphasized this was al-Zuhri, an author who described the lands of Ghana by the name of 'Janāwa'.[43] Al-Sa'di heard that Jenne was the only power in the area which resisted incorporation into the empire of Mali. In this case too, we may suspect interpolation between the traditions of Jenne and those of ancient Ghana, especially since the geographer al-'Umari assigned a special sovereign status for Ghana within the domains of Mali.[44] Although the evidence is indirect, it would seem to us more than probable that al-Sa'di simply confused Ghana (or its legacy in the Niger floodplain) and Jenne. He heard that the lands of Jenne had once comprised over 7000 villages, close to each other, which would seem to designate the entire floodplain of the Niger. Jenne itself may have inherited a political legacy from Ghana, and that, besides the phonetic proximity of the names, may account for al-Sa'di's confusion.

The importance of Jenne (or Ghana, as the case may be) for this discussion lies in the assertion by al-Sa'di that, 'It was because of this blessed city that people flocked from all horizons to Timbuktu, from its east and west and from its north and south'.[45] Al-Sa'di also wrote that when Timbuktu first arose to commercial importance 'the people who came most to it for commerce were the people of Wagadu'.[46] It is now widely agreed that Wagadu was the native Soninke name for ancient Ghana, and hence the probable confusion between Jenne and Ghana is more strongly suggested. Indeed, perhaps al-Sa'di was unwittingly also referring to the commerce of Ghana (or at least that part of Ghana which flourished in the Niger floodplain) when he wrote that Jenne was the meeting place between salt-merchants from Taghāza and between gold-merchants from Bīṭu. The latter location can be identified with Bīghu, or some other earlier settlement, neighbouring the gold-producing area of the Akan forests. Although it is now believed that the exploitation of Akan gold did not begin as early as in the Bambuk and Bure regions, it seems to us quite possible that it began as early as the eleventh century, and possibly even earlier. The trade in gold, coupled with the agricultural wealth of the Middle Niger Delta, probably stimulated the earliest examples of state-formation and urbanization in the Western Sudan.[47]

Jenne itself probably remained a relatively unimportant settlement judging by the fact that it was not mentioned by any of the early Arab geographers and travellers. Though the city clearly had urban precursors in its region, its growth may well have been simultaneous with that of Timbuktu. A stimulus for the growth of Islam and for the regularization of trade, in both places, might have come from the city of Zāgha, located in the rich Massina area on the western side of the Niger floodplain. Zāgha has been identified with Dia and it holds a prominent place in the legends of dispersal of Soninke scholars and clerics who are associated with ancient Ghana.[48] In the fourteenth century, when what remained of Ghana was alone accorded sovereign status in the Malian imperial system, Dia, as already mentioned, enjoyed the privileges of an inviolable centre of learning and commerce. Its early importance and its tradition of Islamic learning are confirmed by external Arabic sources as well as by Soninke and Fulāni traditions. Though it remained a sizeable town for a long time to come, emigrations seem to have reduced its importance from the fourteenth century onwards.[49] Some of the migrants clearly moved south-west to Jenne, and probably also to Kābura and Bīṭu, while others, it seems, contributed to the commercial and demographic growth of Timbuktu.[50]

Traditions which attribute the introduction of architecture from Jenne to Timbuktu would seem to point either to the legacy of the kingdom of Ghana in the Niger floodplain or more specifically to Dia. For one thing, Jenne itself is sometimes said to have been founded from Dia.[51] Moreover, according to *Tārīkh al-Fattāsh*, Askia Muḥammad recruited fully 500 masons from Zāgha after the conquest of the town for the Songhai. Later, these masons were thought to have been responsible for building up Gao, the Songhai capital, as well as the provincial capital of Tindirma, not far to the southwest of Timbuktu.[52]

Al-Sa'di in the seventeenth century seems to have been aware of an extensive body of traditions which suggested that Timbuktu inherited its urban legacy, and with it its Islamic legacy, principally from further south. For reasons which are largely beyond us, however, he chose likewise to emphasize the Western influence on Timbuktu, from the regions of Walāta and Kumbi Saleh, it seems, in even stronger terms. He mentioned neither Tadmekka directly nor Dia but burdened us with the assertion that 'civilization' came to Timbuktu from further west. 'The techniques of town-building came from nowhere but *al-maghrib*', he said, 'and the same holds true for the tenets of religion and the procedures of commercial transaction'.[53]

By *al-maghrib*, al-Sa'di may have meant Morocco, or the Arab West, but the context of his statement suggests that he was referring to the Sahelo–Sudanic West. Particularly important was a town known by the name of Bīru, which has been identified with Walāta, some 400 miles due west of Timbuktu. This predominantly Berber Masūfa settlement had apparently served as the emporium of Wagadu, the core territory of the kingdom of ancient Ghana whose location is yet to be determined.[54] In its most flourishing days, Bīru was a most varied settlement, according to al-Sa'di:

> Companies of merchants travelled towards it from all over the horizons. The most elect of scholars and virtuous men, along with men of wealth of every tribe and country, settled within it. They came from Egypt, Wajal, Fazzān, Ghadāmis, Tuat, Teflālet, Fās, Sūs, Bīṭu and other places.[55]

All of these, along with Berbers from all branches of the Sanḥāja, eventually moved to Timbuktu. 'The growth of Timbuktu was the ruin of Bīru', the author says, but he does not indicate the chronological context of this migration. The itineraries of Mansa Mūsa's pilgrimage and Ibn Baṭūṭa's visit to Mali suggest that Walāta in the west, like Gao in the east, was still a major terminus for the trans-Saharan trade in the mid-fourteenth century.[56] Nonetheless, probable decline in the general region of Walāta is suggested by the fact that the important site of Kumbi Saleh, to the southwest of Walāta, appears to have been abandoned in the thirteenth century.[57] Hence, both in the East and West, we observe a pattern of gradual decline which resulted from or stimulated the growth of the central route via Timbuktu from the twelfth century onwards. Presumably, in the earliest phases, the commerce of the city centred upon the salt-for-gold trade, as on the exchange of cattle for grain between the pastoralists of the Sahara and the agriculturalists of the Middle Niger Delta. The extension of the Saharan trade past Taghāza all the way to North Africa probably accelerated with the transfer of the merchants of Bīru to Timbuktu.

The settlement of Timbuktu accordingly belongs to two main phases which probably overlapped with each other. The first phase brought settlers from north and south, and probably principally from Tadmekka and Dia. North African merchants long established at Tadmekka and in the Middle Niger Delta probably also contributed settlers to Timbuktu from an early date.[58] The initial growth of the city, principally at the hands of Soninke and Masūfa, encouraged the arrival of other settlers in much larger numbers during the second phase, including mercantile communities both from Walāta (or Bīru) and Gao. Presumably, the transplantation of the entire mercantile population from Bīru to Timbuktu was still apace when Ibn Baṭūṭa made his journey through the Sudan in the middle of the fourteenth century. During that same period, Timbuktu increasingly received Wangara settlers who had long been fabled for their participation in the gold commerce and who came to be closely associated with the commerce of the empire of Mali. The arrival of Songhai and Fulānis may have begun also in the fourteenth century, though, in all probability, both elements did not enjoy a strong position in the city prior to the fifteenth and sixteenth centuries.[59]

The ethnic diversity of the settlers naturally exerted a divisive influence, as Horace Miner has suggested in a general statement concerning the entire history of the city.[60] Certainly, in the earliest periods, the ethnic distinctions must have been quite strong, as many groups maintained their contacts with their original homes. Thus, it is no coincidence that a Malinke scholar, as we shall see, occupied the imamate of the Main Mosque (the parochial leadership of Timbuktu) during the last days of Malian sovereignty over the city. Later, after the revocation of Malian sovereignty, Tuareg scholars who were probably allied to the Maghsharen (at least by language) enjoyed an ascendent position in the city. Later, when the Songhai Sunni ʻAli rose against the Tuaregs, many scholars and merchants fled back to Walāta, while others possibly from Tadmekka fled further east to Tagedda. Finally, it may not be coincidental that Fulānis achieved prominence in the city when the Sultanate of Massina became an appreciable power in the sixteenth and seventeenth centuries.[61] The position of the various groups in the city was certainly influenced by their ethnic background and other alliances.

Nonetheless, there was a remarkable degree of sharing in the prerogatives of power and influence. The original kinship relations of the various groups became weaker from one generation to another, partly because of intermarriage, but especially owing to the exigencies of joint ventures in commerce. The tradition of Islamic learning confirmed this trend when individuals from various groups found it advantageous to study under scholars from outside their families. The standing of a scholar depended upon the recognition of his abilities in the entire community rather than his immediate kinship group. It was this primarily which determined the selection process to the major religio-administrative posts. Common subscription to the tradition of Islamic learning seems to have contributed to the integration of the city more than any other factor.

By the fifteenth century Timbuktu had become compactly built and the arrival of new settlers began to be balanced by the departure of groups which found more favourable commercial opportunities elsewhere.[62] The population became more or less stable and this consolidated the growing sense of common identity among the citizens. The Main Mosque, located in the southwestern section of the city, played a major integrative role. Presumably, the area around that mosque was the most thickly settled in the earlier periods. The influence of the Main Mosque (Jingerebir) was equalled only by that of Sankore, in the northern quarter, an ancient mosque which became the main forum for interaction among scholars and literati. Historically, and perhaps beginning in the sixteenth century, the Sankore quarter drew more settlers from among the 'whites' of the city, the Sanḥāja, the Tuaregs and the Barābīsh. Interestingly, however, one of the earliest references to scholars there suggests that these were 'blacks', presumably Soninke and Malinke Wangara. It seems more than doubtful that the earliest patterns of settlement followed strictly ethnic, linguistic or colour criteria. Perhaps they were patterned in part upon the directions from which the settlers came. Thus, Soninke and Sanḥāja who migrated from Walāta may have settled in one ward, while other Soninke from Dia may have settled close to Fulānis who migrated from the region of Dia. Certainly, we have evidence of intermarriage between Sanḥāja and Fulāni in the Massina region, while in the case of Soninke and Wangara it is often difficult to establish a distinction. The fact that the earlier settlements had already witnessed considerable intermixture probably facilitated the process of integration among the settlers in Timbuktu. Eventually, the strongest integrative factor was exerted by the institution of the judgeship (*al-qadā'*), especially as this institution assumed many of the prerogatives of rulership.

The emergence of patrician families

The political history of Timbuktu during its first two centuries of growth and development is summarized by al-Sa'di in a statement to the effect that the first introduction of 'government' (*al-mulk*, presumably a gubernatorial post) came about when the city was incorporated into the empire of Mali in the early fourteenth century. This, along with later indications on the area of Timbuktu more generally, suggests that the city and its region had no central authority in its formative periods. Indeed, even later under the authority of Mali, the role of 'government' *per se* appears to have been minimal. The same was true, as we shall see, of the period of Maghsharen ascendency during the mid-fifteenth century. At around 1400, or shortly thereafter, when the internal history of the city first comes to the limelight, we learn that Timbuktu was to all practical purposes governed by its 'patrician' families of scholar–notables. Hence, logically, we must consider that a similar pattern had been growing since the first beginnings of settlement at the site.

The silence of our sources on the first two centuries or so, from 1100 to 1300 A.D., lends itself to any number of explanations. The Masūfa Tuareg who roamed the adjacent Sahara, and who seasonally camped at the settlement for procuring their supplies of grain from the Niger, may have acted as the 'overlords' of Timbuktu in the special sense that they guaranteed its safety and the safety of its southern Saharan trade-routes in return for a tribute. This pattern was to be repeated on an informal basis at a much later time, during the late eighteenth and late nineteenth centuries, when the Kel Tadmekkat and the Kel Tingeregif respectively, became the dominant pastoralist powers in the area. In the earliest periods, however, there is no serious evidence of a centralized or appreciable power among the Masūfa Berbers of the region. Certainly, there exists no coherent support for the theory advanced by the early French writers to the effect that the militant Islamic Almoravid movement which arose in the Western Sahara during the late eleventh century gave rise to a vast but short-lived empire in the Sahelo–Sudan.[63] At most, we have a reference to a certain Yaḥya b. Abu Bakr as an *amīr* of Masūfa who exerted influence on Ghana around 1100 A.D. and succeeded in inducing its kings to adopt Islam. Conceivably, this *amīr* may well have been an important chieftain in the region of Timbuktu, and his obscure career may well have stimulated the first rise of Timbuktu around 1100, but we do not know the relationship between this *amīr* and the leaders of the western Almoravids who are specifically identified as Judāla and Lamtūna. Locally, the Masūfa seem to have been a junior partner (if anything) in an alliance which was headed by the kingdom of Ghana. Al-Zuhri indicates that the Islamization of Ghana was followed seven years later by the adoption of a 'true' Islam at Tadmekka, following a long struggle, it seems, which culminated in an ascendency for Ghana at Tadmekka.[64] Unless the information of al-Zuhri is in error, we may perhaps assume likewise an influence for Ghana in the region of Timbuktu along the route to Tadmekka. Nonetheless, it seems doubtful that this influence gave rise to any stable sort of government at Timbuktu, whether by Soninke or Masūfa, prior to the age of the empire of Mali. Pending further research on the earliest periods in the Western Sudan, the political legacy which the city inherited from its earliest periods seems to be one of autonomous self-administration by the settlers.

For the most part, we are inclined to suggest that the local Masūfa participated in the Saharan commerce, furnishing camels and escort, along with other settlers, but they enjoyed no privileges over them. Some of the settlers, and especially the Sanḥāja and Lamtūna Berbers, who shared an obscure kinship with the Masūfa, were slow to abandon their military inclinations when they settled to a sedentary or semi-sedentary mercantile existence. Similarly, the Soninke and, later, the Wangara and Fulāni settlers, who controlled the southern trade-routes, had probably adopted a measure of Islamic militancy in the wake of the Almoravid movement. Indeed, we have indirect evidence to suggest that the settlers at Timbuktu as a whole retained a militant, though obscure, sort of organization until the security of commerce by the early fourteenth century reduced their need for hardihood. The first permanent structures, aside from the mosques, were probably more in the nature of caravanserais for the storage of goods. The protection of these probably devolved on the whole community.[65]

This might explain why the judicial post of *qāḍi*, rather than strictly a politico-military post, ultimately became the main administrative function in the city. The *qāḍi* settled the occasional disputes which undoubtedly arose as of an early date and regulated the relationships of settlers with visiting merchants. Quite probably also he was the parochial leader of the community, recognized as *imām* at the existing structure which served as a mosque and which, judging by its later prominence, may have been an earlier and more modest version of the Sankore Mosque.[66] What appears certain is that the city drew increasing numbers of merchants and scholars to its confines. Traditions later recalled that the Hijazi settler 'Abd al-Raḥmān al-Tamīmi found the town virtually teeming with Sudani scholars (perhaps Soninke) when he first arrived there *c.* 1325.[67] The importance of the town is attested around the same time by the fact that it attracted the Andalusian architect Abu Isḥāq al-Tuwaiḥin and the wealthy Egyptian merchant and financier Sirāj al-Dīn al-Kuwaik.[68] A few decades later, Ibn Baṭūṭa made a point of visiting Timbuktu and his account indicates clearly that it was the most important town at the time along the main route between the Malian capital and Gao.

The incorporation of Timbuktu into the empire of Mali enabled the city to share in the extraordinary safety which Ibn Baṭūṭa observed (and marvelled at) throughout the domains of the empire of Mali. In other respects, the period of Malian sovereignty, and most especially during the mid-fourteenth-century heyday of Mali, did not transform the status of the city in any fundamental manner. At most, we gain a strong impression to the effect that the growth of Timbuktu accelerated most during the middle and last decades of the same century.

The long period of Malian sovereignty over Timbuktu witnessed one dramatic and probably devastating event when the city was conquered and sacked by the non-Muslim kingdom of the northern Mossi. The wording of al-Sa'di on this subject lends itself to the supposition that the conquest took place either in the 1320s or 1330s, shortly after the establishment of Malian sovereignty, or that it took place much later, somewhere around 1400 or shortly thereafter. An early-fifteenth-century date appears more plausible, first because Mali was fast declining at the time, and secondly, because Mossi power became a major factor in the Niger bend area during the fifteenth century. The failure of collective memory on this point may signify a break in Timbuktu traditions which was caused by the conquest. Similarly, it may reflect reluctance on the part of the chroniclers to admit an extended role or influence for a 'pagan' power in their Muslim city. They hasten to indicate that Timbuktu acknowledged the sovereignty of the empire of Mali for a full century of the Muslim calendar, corresponding to 1336–1433 A.D.[69] Mansa Mūsa was allegedly the one who established Malian sovereignty over the city during a visit on his return journey from the pilgrimage to Mecca. This event took place in 1324/5, as we know from external Arabic sources, and accordingly, it pre-dates the beginning of Malian sovereignty as remembered by later generations in Timbuktu.[70] All other indications in fact suggest that Malian rule, though a powerful constitutional legend in later times, had a limited effect upon the organization of Timbuktu.

The contemporary evidence of Ibn Khaldūn, by far the most reliable on Mali, enables us to arrive at a reasonably accurate interpretation of Timbuktu traditions. Mali's expansion northeastwards towards Gao, along the course of the Niger, dates apparently to 1300 A.D. or shortly thereafter. At that time, the reigning monarch, Sakūra or Sabkura, actually subjugated the kingdom of Gao, but he did not, it seems, venture north of the river.[71] Thus Timbuktu may have been left on its own until Mansa Mūsa's return journey from Mecca in 1324/5. Traditions first reported by Dubois in the nineteenth century claim that Mūsa was actually invited to the city by its inhabitants, presumably by the *qāḍi* and the scholars, when they heard of his presence at Gao.[72] This may seem somewhat fanciful in the telling but it probably holds a measure of truth. Mūsa remained long enough at Gao to have a mosque erected at the outskirts of the city.[73] His entry to Timbuktu may then have been negotiated and the scholars would have been more than willing to incorporate the city into the domains of a widely recognized Muslim monarch. He is alleged, though with some hesitation, to have been responsible for erecting the Main Mosque, Jingerebir.[74]

The association of Mali with the beginning of 'government' at Timbuktu seems to pertain principally to the erection of a governmental palace, the Ma'Dugu (perhaps Ma'a Dugu or Magha Dugu). This palace was located at the outskirts of the town near the canal which seasonally brought the Niger inundations towards Timbuktu. It is possible that Mansa Mūsa or his first two successors, Mansa Magha and Sulaimān, appointed Malinke governors in the city as we know they did in Walāta.[75] Alternatively, Mali may have stimulated the emergence of a recognized chieftaincy post (or a 'kingship') for the first time in the area's history at Timbuktu. When Ibn Baṭūṭa arrived in 1352, during the reign of Mansa Sulaimān, he found the government of the city in the hands of a Masūfa prince, named Farba Mūsa, who was drawn from among the Sanhāja–Tuareg settlers. Farba is clearly a Malian title, but it seems that Mūsa was largely independent of Mali. He was entitled to bequeath chieftaincy titles and honours without formally acting on behalf of the Malian monarch.[76] Though the evidence of Ibn Baṭūṭa is both brief and sketchy, a substantial Malian presence in the city did not come about until much later.[77]

A change in the fortunes of Timbuktu seems almost certainly to have taken place towards the end of the century, during the reign of Mansa Magha II.[78] Ibn Khaldūn's informant, already mentioned above, told him that in 1374 Mali was mounting campaigns to the area beyond Gao and planning an expedition much further east against the Tuareg of the Tagedda region.[79] This suggests probable breakdown of earlier accommodations with a variety of Tuareg and other Sanhāja clans, accompanied by a formidable Malian presence along the northern and eastern bend of the Niger.[80] Timbuktu probably received its share in the form of a Malinke garrison which was established now, perhaps for the first time, in the city. This garrison could not have been very strong, for we are expressly told that it was withdrawn from the city, sometime around 1400 or shortly thereafter, when the Mossi conquered Timbuktu.[81] However, the garrison did return and was to remain in Timbuktu until the revocation of Malian sovereignty in 1433 A.D.

The last years of the Malian regime are better documented than earlier times and they illustrate the extent that power was shared within the city. For one thing, it seems that a substantial Malinke community (and perhaps predominantly mercantile Wangara) had in the meantime settled at Timbuktu and came to be distinguished in its commercial and scholarly pursuits from the Malian garrison. The governor who held the title of Timbuktu-Koy ('King of Timbuktu') was a Sanhāja Berber named Muḥammad Naḍ whose Ajir clan had a presence both at Shingīṭ in the southwestern Sahara as well as in the Niger floodplain in the region of Massina.[82] He seemingly did not have full command of the garrison but managed nonetheless to dispose of an armed following of his own. Even the institution of the judgeship which might have helped centralize the administration was now fragmented in the transitional period, possibly as a result of the upheaval which had been caused by the Mossi conquest. The sources confront us with three scholars belonging to the early fifteenth century each of whom is given the title of *Qāḍi*. In practice, the information available on these three judges, in addition to the few details surrounding Muḥammad Naḍ and his family, provide us with our earliest internal view of Timbuktu society.

Mention should first be made of Muḥammad Muaddab (Modibo) al-Kāburi, a scholar of high stature, whose descent and age became somewhat confused in the memory of later traditionists.[83] He is described as a contemporary of 'Abd al-Raḥmān al-Tamīmi, who flourished from 1325 onwards, and at the same time he is assigned to the ninth century

A.H., which began in 1397 A.D. Judging from his relations with a few scholars whose chronology or genealogy is known, he acted as *Qāḍi* towards the very end of the Malian presence and lived for sometime thereafter teaching some of the most prominent scholars of the succeeding generation. His judicial functions may have centred on the Soninke element in the population of which he was apparently a member. He and thirty other scholars who shared his venerated graveyard originated in the town of Kābura, in the Niger floodplain south of Dia.[84] The legends which shroud them, along with other Sūdāni scholars, 'blacks' possibly from Dia, suggest that their families had been among the earliest settlers, probably pre-dating Malian times.[85]

The second judge, whose tenure of the *qaḍā'* is specifically assigned to the last days of the Malian regime was a Berber settler originally from Walāta or Bīru. Known variously as al-Qāḍi al-Ḥājj or al-Qāḍi al-Ḥayy, the man may have extended his jurisdiction over the Tuareg and Berber elements sometimes identified, along with North Africans, as 'whites' (*bīḍān*). He himself ultimately departed from the city, possibly under duress from the Malinke or Muḥammad Naḍ, and settled in Banku where his burial place became an object of veneration. But his sons remained in Timbuktu and their descendants figured prominently in its history for two centuries thereafter.[86]

The third judge, possibly the chief *qāḍi* at this time, was a Malinke scholar known to us by his personal name as Mūsa. In one instance he is described as Kātib Mūsa thereby suggesting that he had occupied a clerical-fiscal post earlier in his career.[87] He travelled to Morocco and studied in Fez before apparently assuming his judgeship. He combined that post with that of *imām* of the Main Mosque. As *qāḍi*, it seems, he was concerned with cases involving the Malinke community, as also probably the garrison, and he held court in front of his residence.[88] But as *imām* he was the acknowledged parochial leader of the whole city. It is rather interesting that a Malinke held this post, especially as he is described as the last of a series of Sudanic scholars to occupy it since the days of Mansa Mūsa.[89] Of his immediate relations we know very little except that a close associate of his, a Saharan Berber scholar named 'Abdallāh al-Balbāli ultimately succeeded him to the imamate. He himself probably lost the judgeship when Malian sovereignty was revoked but he maintained himself as *imām* under Maghsharen sovereignty until he died.[90] We may recognize a descendant of his in a prominent sixteenth-century scholar named Muḥammad b. Muḥammad b. 'Ali b. Mūsa, but the evidence is not clear-cut.[91] His family later gave way in the leadership of the Malinke settlers to scholars from the Baghayughu clan who migrated from Jenne.

The transfer of politico-military power, along with part of the city's revenues, from Malians to Maghsharen, is indicative of the *ad hoc* arrangements that conditioned the organization of the city. The Maghsharen continued to shy away from settlement in Timbuktu but they managed in the meantime to build a substantial military capability under a chief named Akil. Their presence is recorded at the village of Amdagha on the Niger and as far north as Arwān on the way to Taghāza.[92] They began, it seems, with a series of incursions on caravans and markets alike and possibly harassed the Niger port-town of Kabara, to the west of Amdagha. This naturally threatened the commercial existence of Timbuktu, but the Malian garrison did not respond. As al-Sa'di remarks,

The people grumbled on account of the damage and losses incurred and the fact that they (the Malians) did not stand up to them and fight them. They said: 'The country which is not defended by its sultan does not lawfully belong to him. The Malians then acknowledged [their loss of Timbuktu] and returned to their country.[93]

An arrangement was reached whereby Muḥammad Naḍ retained the post of Timbuktu-Koy while the Sulṭān of the Maghsharen was recognized as overlord. The revenues were distributed in three parts, one-third each for Akil and Naḍ apparently, the remaining third being allotted to a body of troops whose allegiance is not fully clear.[94] The arrangement outlived Muḥammad Naḍ and enabled his son 'Umar to succeed him. Ultimately, however, after 40 years, it broke down. This was partly because of internal strife and partly as a result of the rise of the Songhai empire under Sunni 'Ali.[95]

The career of Muḥammad Naḍ represents an attempt at establishing a Timbuktu-based dynasty. He had been 'one of the lords of the place' in Malian times, we are told, and this suggests that members of his family might have held the post of Timbuktu-Koy previously.[96] He established close and friendly relations with the scholars so that traditionists thereafter recalled him with respect. When a *sharīf* (a descendant of the Prophet) arrived in the city and settled there he erected a mosque in his name and appointed him its *imām*. This mosque of Sīdi Yaḥya al-Tādulsi was to remain the third most important in the city and, at times, it was identified as the mosque of Muḥammad Naḍ.[97] Muḥammad managed to keep Akil at a distance from the affairs of the city, but his son 'Umar was not as successful. After a falling out between them, 'Umar actually invited Sunni 'Ali to march on the city. This was to have dire consequences for some of the established families in Timbuktu, but 'Umar managed thereby to have his brother al-Mukhtār succeed him under Sunni 'Ali.[98]

The polarization of power between Akil and the Timbuktu-Koy greatly enhanced the influence of the major merchant families during the Maghsharen interlude. Though details are scanty, it seems that the family of al-Qāḍi al-Hājj, enjoying relations with Banku, became the most powerful. Its members allied themselves closely with a Tuareg family led by And-Agh-Muḥammad al-Kabīr. The latter's pedigree suggests an early establishment in Timbuktu with a possible origin in the city of Tadmekka.[99] Possibly on the initiative of Akil, And-Agh-Muḥammad was appointed *qāḍi* and he seems to have been the only one who held the title at the time. He apparently accumulated considerable prestige as a result and he passed it on to a multitude of descendants for several generations. It is probable, indeed, that the power which subsequently came to be lodged in the post of *qāḍi* was consolidated during his tenure. Whether by coincidence or as a direct result, the family which inherited the post for a long time to come was allied by marriage to him.

The family in question were recent settlers established in Timbuktu by Muḥammad Aqīt. H. T. Norris has found in the long pedigree of this man evidence of a possible descent from the leaders of the Almoravid movement in the eleventh century.[100] Even so, Muḥammad Aqīt's family had settled in Massina and this may suggest, once again, a southern influence from Dia. This does not deny the Mauretanian origin of the Aqīts for al-Sa'di describes the people of Massina, presumably the Sanhāja among them, as originally from Tishīṭ.[101] Muḥammad Aqīt must have been involved in the caravan trade at some point in his career for he is said to have had an engagement with Akil in which he wounded him. A Soninke family interceded on his behalf and he moved to the city early in Maghsharen times.[102] His son 'Umar married a daughter of And-Agh-Muḥammad al-Kabīr and this, along with his wealth, secured a position among the notables for his sons and their descendants.[103]

It is not possible to identify all the important families which acquired some of the characteristics of patricians in the city. Our sources being from a later time are subject to prejudices which resulted in the omission of many an important individual. Thus, for example, of the descendants of 'Abd al-Raḥmān al-Tamīmi, none is named except his grandsons Ḥabīb and al-Ma'mūn. This may result from the fact that Ḥabīb served as judge under Sunni 'Ali and al-Ma'mūn refused to join the posthumous propaganda campaigns against the ill-reputed Songhai monarch.[104] Other prominent scholars are mentioned only by their personal names and, in the absence of any references to their *nisba* or pedigree, it is impossible to determine their familial and kinship affiliations. Nonetheless, it comes out very clearly that the world of Timbuktu had long been dominated by its wealthy merchant families. Throughout Malian times they seem to have secured for Timbuktu its basic autonomy. Under the sovereignty of Akil the situation was ideal for them; the Timbuktu-Koy, Muḥammad Naḍ, represented a family which was only one among equals. Accordingly, during the 40 years which elapsed there appears to have grown a universal interest in maintaining the *status quo*.

The threat of Sunni 'Ali

The period of Songhai sovereignty over Timbuktu belongs to two phases which are sharply distinguished in our sources. The first, under Sunni 'Ali (*c*. 1468–1492) was marked by violence, while the second, under Askia Muḥammad and his successors (*c*. 1492–1590) gave Timbuktu the most peaceful and flourishing century in its history. Writing in retrospect, the chroniclers of the seventeenth century shower abuse against Sunni ʻAli, describing him as a tyrant, to the same extent that they sing the praises of Askia Muḥammad. The main reason for this is that Sunni ʻAli was an upstart who threatened the established order of things with no specific claims to legitimacy, while Askia Muḥammad gave a certain legality to the new order, firstly by accommodating the scholars and, more importantly, by undertaking the pilgrimage to Mecca. In the Timbuktu interpretations of history, he rather than Sunni ʻAli was held to be the founder of the new order.[105]

A number of opinions have been offered by recent authors to explain the more or less universal condemnation of Sunni ʻAli among scholars. Triaud went as far as to treat the early history of the Songhai empire in terms of a struggle between a 'Muslim party' which triumphed with the accession of Askia Muḥammad and a presumably anti-Muslim party led by Sunni ʻAli.[106] Trimingham put the same thesis in better perspective. He said:

> ʻAli had no use for Islam, the religion of urban communities. Its learned men constituted a state within a state and were critical of rulers for lukewarmness in Islam and indulgence in pagan rites. Confident in his own power, ʻAli did not need their support and refused to compromise with a religion which involved paying allegiance to a law higher than himself.[107]

This interpretation has much to confirm it in the chronicles, but it fails to take full account of their inconsistencies. For the sons and grandsons of Askia Muḥammad were also lax in the observance of Muslim rites, yet their sovereignty was recognized and supported even after the arrival of the Moroccan conquerors. The author of *Tārīkh al-Fattāsh* faithfully records the places where Sunni ʻAli performed the holiday prayers of Ramaḍān year-by-year during his campaigns, while al-Saʻdi says: 'Despite his ill-treatment of scholars, he acknowledged their worth and often said: "Without the *ʻulamā*' the world would no longer be sweet and good" '.[108]

The history of Timbuktu in this period can be readily understood in terms of a struggle on the part of patrician families to preserve their influence in the face of a rising power which threatened it.[109] The importance of their city, and its attractiveness to conquerors, lay strictly in the commerce which they attracted to its confines. Accordingly, their strength rested primarily in their ability to transfer their activities elsewhere and, thereby, deprive the conqueror of his prize. This is precisely what happened in three stages until the city was virtually evacuated.[110] It might have lain in ruins for a long time thereafter had not Askia Muḥammad subsequently reversed the policies of his predecessor.

Sunni ʻAli was a poor administrator, though a military genius, who was prone to react to events rather than shaping them himself. The expansion of his kingdom, begun under his immediate predecessor (and completed under Askia Muḥammad) promised to fill the political vacuum caused by the disintegration of the empire of Mali. Accordingly, he was liable to be supported by the scholars, provided he adopted the proper course of action, but he did not take advantage of the situation.[111] When he first appeared on the approaches to Timbuktu, he made no assurances to any of the inhabitants even though he had been in contact with the Timbuktu-Koy since the last days of Muḥammad Naḍ.[112] This precipitated a massive exodus of the wealthiest merchants and scholars, at least among Tuaregs and Berbers who inhabited the Sankore quarter.[113] Even 'Umar b. Muḥammad Naḍ who expressly incited him against Akil found it safer to join the exiles though he left his brother al-Mukhtār behind in charge of the family household. Akil himself, though unable to confront the Songhai ruler in open battle, took full advantage of the situation. He supplied a caravan of 1000 camels which enabled the evacuees to reach Walāta.[114]

Finding the city without its Timbuktu-Koy, Sunni 'Ali responded rather diplomatically by naming his brother al-Mukhtār as his successor. Concerning the more sensitive post of *qāḍi*, the evidence is suspiciously lacking. If the aged And-Agh-Muḥammad al-Kabīr was still alive at this time, it seems almost certain that he was abused and demoted. For we know that his sons, the scholars Maḥmūd and Aḥmad, were killed by Sunni 'Ali, while his daughter, the wife of 'Umar b. Muḥammad Aqīt, was imprisoned. Whether as a cause or as a result, the surviving head of this household, al-Mukhtār al-Naḥawī b. And-Agh-Muḥammad, fled the city to Walāta, along with 'Umar Aqīt and his sons.[115] These events, though the sequence is not fully known, closed the door upon any permanent accommodation between Sunni 'Ali and Timbuktu.

The Songhai commander tried to salvage the situation by showing great respect to some of the remaining scholars but mutual misunderstanding prevailed. He appointed a grandson of 'Abd al-Raḥmān al-Tamīmi, al-Qaḍi Ḥabīb, to the judgeship and showered favours on his cousin al-Ma'mūn. This act could not have been inconsequential considering that 'Abd al-Raḥmān had first come to the Sudan in the company of Mansa Mūsa. Sunni 'Ali also disposed himself favourably towards 'Abdallāh al-Balbāli who had succeeded Kātib Mūsa to the imamate. Indeed, when he later defeated the Fulāni Sanqara clan in Massina, he dispatched some of the captive women as slaves to the scholars in Timbuktu. This act, which probably enraged the Fulānis in the city, was far from universally acclaimed. As Muslims the women were not subject to enslavement, in the eyes of the scholars, and some of them, like 'Abdallāh al-Balbāli, found a way out of the difficulty by marrying the captives.[116]

It seems that some sort of uprising took place in Timbuktu similar to that which was to follow upon the Moroccan conquest in 1590. Sunni 'Ali might have been on the Niger at Kabara at that time for he is said to have ordered the enslavement of 30 women from the And-Agh-Muḥammad family and their dispatch thence. These never gave up their veils, according to our source, and were killed upon Sunni 'Ali's orders on the way. The same fate awaited two of And-Agh-Muḥammad's sons, as already mentioned, and his daughter was imprisoned. This precipitated a new exodus from the city which probably dates to 875 A.H. (*c.* 1470 A.D.), corresponding to a year or two after the conquest.[117]

The most victimized group among the inhabitants were from the family of al-Qāḍi al-Ḥājj and their kinsmen. Something of their influence is preserved in the tradition that Nāna Tinti, daughter of Abu Bakr b. al-Qāḍi al-Ḥājj, was a close associate of Askia Muḥammad's mother Kasa. The two met together on several occasions when Muḥammad, at that time a general in Sunni 'Ali's army, already suffered inconveniences at his hands. Later, Abu Bakr became a confidant of Askia Muḥammad while his son 'Abd al-Raḥmān was appointed to the judgeship of Timbuktu.[118] This may suggest, though the evidence is sketchy, that the notables of Timbuktu, now dispersed through a wide area, actively sought alliances against Sunni 'Ali.

We have it on record that Sunni 'Ali humiliated several members of the al-Ḥājj family and on one occasion caused al-Faqīh Ibrāhīm, son of Abu Bakr, to stand a whole day under the scorching sun as a humiliation and punishment. Subsequently, certain members of the apparently large clan fled to Tagedda to seek Tuareg support on a large scale. The Songhai commander retaliated by killing many of those remaining and imprisoning others, both men and women, and a party which fled towards Walāta was overtaken at Shīb and massacred to the man.[119] We do not know when precisely this happened, but stories of the martyrs became powerful legends among Tuaregs in the east where members of the al-Ḥājj clan settled permanently.[120]

The exodus of merchants and scholars to Walāta and Tagedda probably brought the commerce of the Niger bend to a standstill. Sunni 'Ali's forces, being accustomed only to river traffic, could not effectively control any portion of the southern Sahara. At one point he embarked on the almost impossible project of digging a canal from the Niger towards Walāta, but whether by coincidence or otherwise he had to give up the project to confront the more mobile forces of the Mossi kingdom threatening his rear.[121] While besieging Jenne around 1487 it seems, he realized that the exodus from Timbuktu had become irreversible. According to *Tārīkh al-Fattāsh*: 'He heard that the people of Timbuktu were all fleeing. Those originally from Bīru returned to Bīru. Others went to Fututi and Tishīt. Each group was returning to the place of its origin.'[122] At this point Sunni 'Ali ordered all the remaining inhabitants to transfer to Hawīki, a location across the Niger probably just south of Kabara. Having even imprisoned the Timbuktu-Koy al-Mukhtār, he apparently abandoned the notion of controlling the city and its neighbourhood. It is doubtful that Hawīki could have replaced the Timbuktu–Kabara axis as a terminus for the Saharan trade, but we know that many Timbuktuans lived in it virtually as captives for a full five years up to Sunni 'Ali's death. Among them, besides presumably the *qāḍi* and *imām* above mentioned, were Sīdi Abu'l-Qāsim al-Tuāti, of North African origin, and the two brothers Maḥmud and Aḥmad Aqīt.[123] It is extraordinary to find that the latter had returned to Timbuktu, for in the meantime he had travelled from Walāta on the pilgrimage to Mecca and resided for some time in Cairo. Later in his career, he travelled to Hausaland in northern Nigeria where he taught at Kano and Katsina.[124] After the death of Sunni 'Ali, his brother 'Abdullāh settled in Tazekht in southern Mauretania and refused to return to his birth-place when urged to do so. The lords of the Sankore quarter were divided amongst themselves, he explained, and he otherwise did not wish to reside where 'the seed of Sunni 'Ali' might have been living.[125]

Even in his own lifetime Sunni 'Ali approached an image comparable to that of an Antichrist in the minds of devout Muslims. The Egyptian scholar al-Suyūṭi, though he never visited the Sūdān, described his rise to power as a calamity comparable to the loss of Spanish lands by Islam.[126] In 892 A.H. (1486 A.D.) as Timbuktu later heard, invocations against Sunni 'Ali were made in Mecca in the presence of the jurist 'Abd al-Jabbār Kaku.[127] Al-Maghīli later contributed to the defamation of the Songhai ruler when, in his *risāla* to Askia Muḥammad, he questioned his qualification to a true Muslim identity.[128] Sunni 'Ali's hatred of the Fulānis and his persecution of the Sanqara clan among them became a point in their favour. In the nineteenth century it was claimed that Sunni 'Ali had persecuted the Sanqara because he knew that the twelfth true caliph was to arise among them.[129] Though there must have been quite a few, among them al-Qāḍi Ḥabīb, who refused to join the posthumous campaign against Sunni 'Ali, condemnation of his acts ultimately became a rallying force around which Timbuktuans could be unified.[130]

Askia Muḥammad became a beneficiary of the campaign when he deposed Sunni 'Ali's son, Abu Bakr Dā'u, and assumed the rulership of the newly carved empire. He reversed his predecessor's policies *vis-à-vis* Timbuktu, but the legacy could not be fully erased. Among other things, the And-Agh-Muḥammad family did not quite regain its former influence and the same could be said, though the picture is rather complex, of the descendants of al-Qāḍi al-Ḥājj. The And-Agh-Muḥammads, at least, gave way for a long time in the leadership of Timbuktu to their allies by marriage, the descendants of Muḥammad Aqīt. Specifically, Maḥmūd b. 'Umar Aqīt, who had studied under al-Qāḍi Ḥabīb and probably served as his deputy before the death of Sunni 'Ali, became virtually the lord of Timbuktu in the second part of Askia Muḥammad's regime. He was followed in that rôle by a succession of sons throughout the Askia dynasty.

Restoration of the patriciate

Our information becoming more and more detailed as we approach the fifteenth century, it becomes apparent that the major families in Timbuktu constituted a loosely-knit patriciate. Like other patricians known in history elsewhere, its members suffered considerable disunity but shared a great deal in common interests and attitudes. Sunni ʿAli had favoured some elements at the expense of others, but his policies proved catastrophic. By the end of his reign, Timbuktu was essentially abandoned, its inhabitants having relocated in a number of places, including Walāta, Tagedda and Hawīki. His successor, Askia Muḥammad, clearly dissociated himself from his policies and encouraged the process of resettlement. Those at Hawīki were apparently the first to return and, accordingly, they exerted considerable influence on the reorganization of the city. Others gradually followed suit and the city reassumed its former autonomous status.

If we may believe the sources, Askia Muḥammad was greeted as a saviour right from the beginning of his reign. This comes out most clearly from the opening pages of a contemporary chronicle which was incorporated later in the seventeenth century into a work by Ibn al-Mukhtār Qunbul, giving its name of *Tārīkh al-Fattāsh* to the whole compilation.[131] The original author, clearly a contemporary of Askia Muḥammad, says:

> God has favoured us by bringing forth in our own age this triumphant *imām*, the just caliph and victorious sultan, Askia al-Ḥājj Muḥammad b. Abu Bakr, the Tawradi of origin, the Kawkawi of residence . . . Lands opened before him to the east and the west while emissaries came to his court individually and in droves. Kings submitted to him [in large numbers] whether willingly or by force. By virtue of his *barakāt* we have attained a state of well-being and benefaction after we had been in difficulty and misery.[132]

The text of this chronicle, or at least its first part, has come down to us in a highly defective, nineteenth-century copy which was subjected to emendation under conditions which will be discussed in their own place. Enough remains, however, to indicate that it was written in or around 925 A.H. (1519 A.D.).[133] Traditions later assigned its composition to al-Qāḍi Maḥmūd b. al-Mutawakkil Kaʿt, a scholar of Soninke origin apparently, who died in 1002 A.H. (1593 A.D.).[134] In fact, it appears more likely that Maḥmūd b. ʿUmar Aqīt, or a close relative of his, was the original author.[135]

It seems that considerable disagreement arose among traditionists and chroniclers concerning the sequence of events in the transitional period between the later years of Sunni ʿAli and the early reign of Askia Muḥammad. Thus, the pilgrimage of Muḥammad *c.* 902 A.H. (1496/7 A.D.), by far the most significant of his actions so far as Timbuktu was concerned, is surrounded by controversy. According to the defective copy of *Tārīkh al-Fattāsh*, which claims that Maḥmūd Kaʿt, though belonging to a later generation, accompanied him on the journey, Askia Muḥammad was declared the eleventh of the twelve true caliphs by the Egyptian scholar, ʻAbd al-Raḥmān al-Suyūṭi, in Cairo.[136] This legend recalls an earlier visit by a monarch from the Western Sudan which, in fact, is recorded by Suyūṭi in his autobiography. He says:

Then in the year eighty nine (889 A.H. or 1484 A.D.), the pilgrim caravan of Takrur arrived, and in it were the sulṭān, the *qāḍi*, and a group of students. They all came to me, and acquired knowledge and traditions from me . . . A eunuch servant came in the company of the *qāḍi* as a present from his cousin. The sulṭān of Takrur asked me to speak to the Commander of the Faithful (the nominal Calīph ʻAbd al-ʻAzīz) about his delegating to him authority over the affairs of his country, so that his rule would be legitimate according to the Holy Law. I sent to the Commander of the Faithful about this, and he did it.[137]

It would be tempting to identify the *qāḍi* in question as Ḥabīb and his cousin as al-Ma'mūn wālid ʻAmarād of the Timbuktu sources.[138] But, in that case, we would have to assume either that al-Suyūṭi made an error concerning the date,[139] or that Askia Muḥammad undertook the pilgrimage long before his accession to Songhai rulership in 899 A.H. (1493 A.D.).[140]

The relations of al-Suyūṭi with West Africa are quite as complex as they are multifaceted. For one thing, they are closely bound with the Egyptian scholar's claim to recognition as the *mujaddid* (the renovator of the faith) of the ninth century.[141] Al-Suyūṭi was the author of an extended *fatwa* addressed to a certain Muḥammad b. Muḥammad b. ʻAli al-Lamtūni who, in the judgement of Hunwick, was from the region of Air.[142] The Egyptian National Library houses another letter addressed by al-Suyūṭi to the kings of Agades and Katsina in the Central Sudan.[143] Al-Suyūṭi's student and biographer, ʻAbd al-Qādir al-Shādhili mentions a correspondence with yet another unknown monarch of the Sudan. He says:

It happened that great strife broke out in the land of Takrur and a tyrant oppressed their sulṭān and they were unable to repel him. So they came and complained about this to the Shaikh, may God have mercy on him, and he ordered me to write a letter to the tyrant. When it reached him and was read to him, he turned back in retreat and withdrew. This was because of his (al-Suyūṭi's) prestige, his command of their respect, the greatness of their faith in him and their fear of opposing him.[144]

It is possible that the investiture obtained by al-Suyūṭi from the Caliph was in favour of a monarch other than Askia Muḥammad, though the latter's pilgrimage was the most celebrated of its time.[145] What is certain is that Askia Muḥammad met al-Suyūṭi during his passage through Cairo. This is confirmed in a commentary on one of al-Suyūṭi's works by the celebrated Timbuktu scholar, Muḥammad Bāba b. Muḥammad al-Amīn. This scholar died in 1014 A.H. (*c.* 1605/6 A.D.) at the age of 82 and was therefore a near-contemporary of Askia Muḥammad.[146] The author suggests an extended association between Askia Muḥammad and al-Suyūṭi in Cairo; he indicates that al-Suyūṭi dedicated to the Songhai monarch a composition on rulership entitled *al-Aḥādīth al-Mutqana fi Faḍl al-Salṭana*, which unfortunately is no longer extant.[147]

The difficulty surrounding Askia Muḥammad's relations with al-Suyūṭi is largely the product of a controversy among Timbuktu traditionists of the succeeding generations. One would expect that one scholar from Timbuktu, at least, and probably the *Qāḍi* Ḥabīb himself, accompanied Askia Muḥammad on the pilgrimage. Yet none of the scholars among the hundreds who made up the caravan, with the exception of the Soninke Mūr Ṣāliḥ Jūr, are identifiable.[148] We have two copies of *Tārīkh al-Fattāsh* which, though lacking their first parts, appear quite accurate. There the scholars named in the company of Askia Muḥammad are all obscure.[149] Al-Sa'di, on the other hand, betrays a marked reluctance to commit himself on this clearly controversial subject. He says: 'There made the pilgrimage with him those whom God destined to do so among that generation'.[150]

Our sources are in agreement on the fact that the Sharīf of Mecca, at least, formally invested Askia Muḥammad with the rulership of the Western Sudan.[151] This act may have been of great significance in legitimizing the Askia dynasty among the long-established inhabitants of Gao. As early as the eleventh century, al-Bakri observed that a sword allegedly sent by the Abbasid caliph had been used in the coronation ceremonies of the kings of Gao.[152] For his part Askia Muḥammad received one such sword from the Sharīf of Mecca and this remained an important symbol of sovereignty till the demise of the Songhai empire.[153] Returning as a pilgrim, the Askia secured recognition of his sovereignty throughout the southern Saharan areas from Walāta to Tadmekka without, it seems, campaigning in those parts. The Maghsharen submitted peacefully and supported the empire with thousands of mounted forces under the sons and nephews of Akil.[154] Elsewhere, Askia Muḥammad's campaigns, being even more extensive than those of his predecessor, reduced the northern Mossi of Yatenga as well as most of Mali while extending the influence of the empire as far as Hausaland.[155] In the new political unit the position of Timbuktu became so important that Leo Africanus, the author of an otherwise accurate description of the Sudan in the early sixteenth century, mistook the city for the capital of the empire and thought it to be the centre from which Muḥammad waged his campaigns.[156] The misinformation of the author may have resulted from the fact that Muḥammad's brother, 'Umar Kumzā'u, who acted as his deputy during his pilgrimage, established himself in the newly built city of Tindirma as governor of the eastern provinces adjoining Timbuktu. A son of the latter, Muḥammad Bankānu, who became Askia during 937–943 A.H. (1530–1536 A.D.), actually resided in Timbuktu during his youth and studied under its scholars in the Sankore quarter.[157]

The role of the Askias in the administration of Timbuktu became largely restricted to the confirmation of the *qāḍi* agreed upon by the scholars. Thus in 904 A.H. (1498 A.D.), when al-Qāḍi Ḥabīb died, there were three candidates, it seems, including Maḥmūd Aqīt, 'Abd al-Raḥmān b. Abu Bakr b. al-Qāḍi al-Ḥājj and, finally, al-Mukhtār al-Naḥawī b. And-Agh-Muḥammad. Disagreement between the families of the latter two caused Abu Bakr, apparently at a very advanced age, to forego the interest of his son and he pointed out Maḥmūd Aqīt to Askia Muḥammad as legitimate successor to Ḥabīb.[158] The man, thereby, combined the judgeship with the imamate of Sankore and came to wield unprecedented power. Traditions recall a disagreement between him and Askia Muḥammad caused by his refusal to allow the monarch's emissaries a say in the affairs of the city. Allegedly, the disagreement was settled in his favour when the monarch acknowledged his superior knowledge of Muslim law and precepts.[159] Whatever the case may be, it seems that Maḥmūd opted to leave the city in 915 A.H. (1509 A.D.) and embarked on the pilgrimage.

During his absence 'Abd al-Raḥmān b. Abu Bakr held the judgeship while al-Mukhtar al-Naḥawī held the imamate of Sankore. The latter held himself to be his deputy and, accordingly, he stepped aside in his favour upon his return. By this gracious act, it seems, he ensured that his own son, And-Agh-Muḥammad II, attained the post during Maḥmūd's old age. 'Abd al-Raḥmān, on the other hand, refused to accommodate the returning pilgrim, despite his prestige, and he acted as judge for 10 full years. Ultimately, around 1520, a difficult legal case came before him on which he passed a judgement which was contested by Maḥmūd. The body of scholars reached consensus on the superiority of Maḥmūd's judgement and word was sent to Askia Muḥammad which secured 'Abd al-Raḥmān's deposition.[160]

We have already indicated that the early chronicle partly incorporated in the defective section of *Tārīkh al-Fattāsh* was written *c.* 1519, around the time of this incident. This might explain why our sources gave so much attention to its details. In reality, however, the deposition of 'Abd al-Raḥmān became a *cause célèbre* which interfered with the politics of Timbuktu during the Moroccan conquest 70 years later. The judgeship at stake at this time amounted to full rulership of the city. This was so much the case that the chronicles in recording the death of the Timbuktu-Koy 'Umar b. Naḍ in 922 A.H. (1516 A.D.) do not even bother to name his successor.[161] Ultimately, towards the end of the Songhai regime, we find the post occupied by Naf' al-Musṭafa Kara, a grandson of a scholar named as al-Shaikh Aḥmad Bayukun who had been instrumental in informing Askia Muḥammad of 'Abd al-Raḥmān's inadequacy as Judge. The latter's grandsons opposed this Timbuktu-Koy while their kinsmen in Banku never quite reconciled themselves to the Aqīt family.[162] In Timbuktu, at least, they were the first family to cooperate with the conquering Ruma.

During his tenure of the judgeship, up to 955 A.H. (1548 A.D.) Maḥmūd Aqīt acted as some sort of moderator between the warring sons and nephews of Askia Muḥammad.[163] He managed to pass the post to his eldest son Muḥammad, who occupied it up to his death in 973 A.H. (1565 A.D.) during a good portion of the long and peaceful reign of Askia Daūd (*c.* 1549–1582 A.D.). Born of a Songhai mother wedded to Maḥmūd at the instance of Askia Muḥammad, the latter is remembered mainly for his wealth partly bestowed upon him by his godfather.[164] His brother al-'Āqib, however, whom he nominated to the imamate of Sankore at the death of al-Mukhtār al-Naḥawiy, acquired a widespread reputation as a brilliant judge and administrator during a long tenure of the *qaḍā'* from 1565 to 1583. He commanded sufficient funds, it seems, from sources other than the state revenues, to enlarge and embellish the Sankore Mosque and Jingerebir.[165] In one instance in 1569, when disagreement arose concerning the imamate of the latter mosque, he acted largely on his own in appointing Muḥammad Gidādu (Kidādu), the first Fulāni to hold the post.[166] Aḥmad Bāba, an Aqīt of the subsequent generation, mentions that many disagreements arose between him and the Askias, but he provides no detail except to say that al-'Āqib withdrew from the public view in such instances until his opinions prevailed.[167]

Though the Aqīts virtually constituted a ruling dynasty during most of the century, the prosperity of the city and its continuing population growth left ample scope for the influence of other scholars and families. We may mention, for example, Abu'l-'Abbas Aḥmad b. Muḥammad Sa'īd who, though he died at a relatively young age in 976 A.H. (1568/9 A.D.), left a lasting imprint by teaching some of the most prominent scholars of the time, including 'Umar b. Maḥmūd Aqīt, Muḥammad Baghayughu and Maḥmūd b. al-Mutawakkil Ka't.[168] Muḥammad Baghayughu himself migrated with his brother Aḥmad from Jenne, after undertaking the pilgrimage and studying in the East under prominent Egyptian scholars. Their father occupied the judgeship of Jenne for some time while they founded one of the most influential families in Timbuktu.[169] In 1566 A.D. both Muḥammad Baghayughu and his teacher Abu'l-'Abbās Aḥmad had a hand in the appointment of Muḥammad Kab b. Jabir Kab, a scholar from Jenne, to the post of Khatīb of Gao, an office in the Songhai empire which combined judicial with parochial functions and exerted some influence during the ensuing succession disputes.[170]

The Soninke Ka't family, strongly associated with the chronicling of events in Timbuktu, was partially based in the city of Tindirma where Maḥmūd Ka't became Judge. He was succeeded to the judgeship of that town by his son Isma'īl who apparently produced a first revision of *Tārīkh al-Fattāsh*.[171] The authorship of this chronicle is also associated with a son of Isma'īl's sister, believed to be Ibn al-Mukhtār Qunbulu.[172] The Qunbulu family, represented later by Muḥammad Qunbulu and his son al-Mukhtār, took over the judgeship of Tindirma in the late seventeenth and early eighteenth centuries.[173] In Timbuktu, the Ka't family was equalled in influence by that of 'Āmir al-Sa'di, whose descendant 'Abd al-Raḥmān, has left us our most important source.[174] Of comparable status also was the family of al-Amīn Kānu (Ganu) whose grandson Baba Gūru b. al-Ḥājj Muḥammad was the author of a chronicle entitled *al-Durar al-Ḥisān fi Akhbār Mulūk al-Sūdān* which has been lost to us.[175] Finally, so far as historiography is concerned, we may mention the prominent scholar al-Amīn b. Aḥmad whose authority is often quoted on the virtues of certain scholars from the family of al-Qāḍi al-Ḥājj. If he was a descendant of that family, traditions have suppressed the fact, for he is only described as the half-brother of 'Abd al-Raḥmān b. Aḥmad al-Mujtahid.[176] The latter's descendants assumed a measure of importance in the seventeenth and eighteenth centuries.

The Aqīt family maintained its ascendent position in Timbuktu by virtue of a complex network of interrelationships. Its members taught the Baghayughus while its sons studied under them. Tutor–pupil relationships had a strong ritual significance and were sometimes accompanied by the marriage of the student to his master's daughter. Maḥmūd Aqīt's mother, as already indicated, was daughter of And-Agh-Muḥammad. One of his daughters, in fact, came to be the mother of the influential and erudite Aḥmad b. Muḥammad Sa'id. Likewise, al-'Aqib married one of his daughters to Muḥammad Zankanu b. Abkar al-Maddāḥ whose descendants, allied by intermarriage to the prestigious Maghia family, remained important up to the nineteenth century.[177] The high incidence of intermarriage among the major families tended to reduce the instances of tension between them. At the same time, it secured a measure of cohesion which was sufficient to discourage undue intervention from the outside.

It is possible to see a tendency towards polarization of power between Gao and Timbuktu in the late Songhai period. Particularly instructive are a few details available on a crisis which ensued when al-Qāḍi al-'Āqib renovated and enlarged the Main Mosque of Timbuktu. Al-Sa'di's *Tārīkh al-Sūdān*, whose author had a distinct aversion to controversy, mentions the episode incidentally, offering what appears to be a reconciliation of various accounts current in the seventeenth century. According to him, Askia Daūd was returning from a campaign in Mali in 978 A.H. (1570/71 A.D.) when he heard that work on the Main Mosque was in progress:

He headed to Timbuktu and stopped at the backside of the mosque, in its courtyard, until al-Qāḍi al-'Āqib along with the jurists of the town and its notables came to greet him. He found that the building of the mosque had not yet been completed. He therefore said to the Qāḍi: 'The expenses of the remaining part are my share by way of cooperation on this pious project'. He gave him for that purpose what God willed to be given at his hands and, later when he reached his city, he sent him four hundred pieces of timber of the Kunku tree so that the work was completed in that year.[178]

However, *Tārīkh al-Fattāsh*, which is also quite reticent, suggests that a major disagreement arose between the *qāḍi* and the monarch in which they said of each other 'things which should not be said'.[179] When Daūd came to Timbuktu on his return from Mali, he went directly to the house of al-'Āqib, apparently in anger. Strange as that might seem, the Judge refused him admittance until the jurists and notables interceded on the monarch's behalf. According to this version, the crisis was resolved with the monarch declaring that 'he had no objection to all of that (i.e. the rebuilding of the main mosque) except that no share had been allotted to him and no part [of the mosque] had been left for him to build'. Daūd had to satisfy himself with patronizing the rebuilding of the tombs in the back courtyard, entrusting the Timbuktu-Mundhu, his representative at Timbuktu, with overseeing the remaining portion of the work, though the funds were given to al-'Āqib.[180] It is quite apparent that the Songhai monarchs (and certainly the long-reigning Daūd) were sensitive to the political advantages of patronizing the construction of pious foundations and, accordingly, mutual jealousy between them and the Aqits is not to be ruled out. The building of mosques had historically afforded Muslim monarchs in North Africa and the East, as indeed in the case of Mansa Mūsa of Mali, a means for enhancing their prestige. This was particularly true of the main mosques in each city where the sermon delivered at the Friday congregation ritually reaffirmed the sovereignty of the ruler. In classical Islam, authorizing the building of such mosques was the sole prerogative of the caliphs, great political significance being attached to this privilege.[181] It is tempting to conjecture that similar political considerations went into the crisis between Daūd and al-'Āqib, the former fearing a tendency towards full independence on the part of Timbuktu. But the bulk of the evidence, even in the more troubled times to follow, suggests that the Timbuktu scholars sought no more than securing the interests and internal autonomy of their city, besides enhancing as much as possible its prestige within the empire.

The death of al-'Āqib in 991 A.H. (1583 A.D.) shortly preceded by the death of Askia Daūd, gave rise to a more serious crisis which delayed the succession of Abu Ḥafs 'Umar, the eldest surviving brother of the deceased judge, for a full year and half. By this time, as we shall see below, Timbuktu began to be embroiled in the succession struggles of the Songhai ruling family. Al-Sa'di's *Tārīkh al-Sūdān*, the official history of Timbuktu as it were, maintains that 'Umar declined the judgeship when offered him by Askia al-Ḥājj, successor of Daūd. *Tārīkh al-Fattāsh*, on the other hand, claims that it was the Askia who refused to authorize the appointment of 'Umar. The two sources appear to disagree dramatically on this point, but the net impressions created by both are quite similar. Askia al-Ḥājj could not simply nominate his own candidate probably because no scholar of sufficient rank would accept the appointment at this juncture. This is perhaps what al-Sa'di tries to communicate to us in his account of how the crisis was eventually resolved: the Askia allegedly threatened to assign the judgeship to a non-learned person (a *jāhil*) unless 'Umar complied. This effective threat – really a conciliatory gesture – was made at the instance of Ṣāliḥ Takun, a scholar whose family's relations with the Aqīts pre-date Songhai times.[182] According to *Tārīkh al-Fattāsh*, Muḥammad Baghayughu, who discharged most of the judicial functions in the meantime, was the one who successfully interceded between 'Umar and Askia al-Ḥājj. When he finally dispatched the authorization in favour of 'Umar to Timbuktu, the Askia allegedly declared: 'If it was not for the intercession of Muḥammad Baghayughu we would not appoint al-Qāḍi 'Umar nor would we bring anyone from among them (the Aqīts) to the judgeship.' Since the crisis lasted over a year, it seems probable that the initial rejection of the post by 'Umar gave rise to an equally vehement anti-Aqīt attitude on the part of the Askia.[183]

The period of the vacancy of the judgeship is illustrative both of the extent of unity and disunity within the city. At first, following the death of the much feared and venerated al-'Āqib, the absence of a judge encouraged numerous cases of fraud in commercial transactions and some apparently involving the shares of inheritance legally owing to orphans. This caused Muḥammad Baghayughu, who occupied the Sīdi Yaḥya imamate in the centre of the city, to step forward into the breach and establish his own court. According to *Tārīkh al-Fattāsh*:

> After the morning prayers he would sit at the entrance of the Sīdi Yaḥya mosque, along with some of his students, then declare: 'Whoever has a claim against someone else unwilling to fulfil his obligations, let him bring his case forward.' The people would then bring their cases and he judged between them. He commanded and prohibited, passing prison sentences, while inflicting beatings on those deserving such punishments.[184]

As we know from his biography by Aḥmad Bāba, this instance was not the first in which Muḥammad Baghayughu settled legal disputes. But while at other times he acted mainly as a counsellor and mediator, in this case he assumed the full prerogatives of judge. This, in turn, caused anonymous complaints directed against him in which people blamed him in writing for assuming a function which he was not formally assigned. Since some of the letters were reportedly by the hands of scholars, Niamkey Georges Kodjo has suggested in a recent article that the agitation against Baghayughu was directed from behind the scenes by the Aqīts. This suggestion is not in keeping with the assertion of the *Fattāsh* that Muḥammad Baghayughu repeatedly wrote to Askia al-Ḥājj in the meantime pressing him to issue the appointment of 'Umar Aqīt.[185] Certainly, there are no grounds for the thesis by Kodjo of a long-term polarization in Timbuktu between Baghayughus and Aqīts. We may perhaps be misled by an accidental feature in the sources, but the relations between the Baghayughus and Aqīts are the strongest ever documented between two families in Timbuktu.[186] It appears to us probable that Muḥammad Baghayughu discharged the judicial functions in full consultation with the Aqīts in order to forestall the appointment of a judge who would not be acceptable to the body of scholars. It is possible that the opponents of Muḥammad Baghayughu were elements who were in close touch with the court in Gao, a factor which might explain their anonymity. Another stronger possibility is that the complainants against Baghayughu, led by mediocre literati as *al-Fattāsh* suggests, were residents of the Sankore quarter threatened by the fact that the court was not held at the Sankore Mosque where the Aqīts had previously presided. The account of al-Sa'di tends to suggest this, for he indicates that, at a later stage in the crisis it seems, Muḥammad Baghayughu sat in judgement over disputes between residents and visiting merchants while Aḥmad Maghia, the founder of a very important family, settled cases which arose in the Sankore quarter. In all probability Aḥmad Maghia did not pass any sentences and was concerned with cases (and perhaps appeals) on matters of legislative significance. He is assigned the title of Mufti (Supreme Jurisconsult) while, in later sources at least, Muḥammad Baghayughu earned the title of Judge.[187]

The cause of the disagreement between Askia al-Ḥājj and 'Umar Aqīt concerns us particularly at this point because it had ramifications at a shortly later time. The crisis had begun at the death of Askia Daūd when al-'Āqib was still living in extreme old age. At that time, Muḥammad Bankānu, the eldest and most favoured son of Askia Daūd, being away from the capital, lost his bid for the throne in favour of Askia al-Ḥājj. In order to allay the fears of his reigning brother, who dismissed him from the post of Kurmina Fāri, he fled to Timbuktu to reside there under the auspices of al-Qāḍi al-'Āqib. Yet, although he pleaded that he would devote himself to learning, he was nonetheless arrested and exiled to Kanatu. Al-Sa'di describes vividly the storming by veiled persons of the house in Timbuktu in which Bankānu resided. From another source, a fragment of an unidentified chronicle, we learn that the violent arrest actually took place in the house of al-'Āqib.[188] This outrage probably gave rise to one of those instances mentioned by Aḥmad Bāba when al-'Āqib withdrew from the judgeship. The Askia apparently did not reconcile the old Judge and, at his death, the Judge's brother, Abu Ḥafs 'Umar, if we may follow the evidence of al-Sa'di, declined to succeed him. The ensuing crisis, as described above, was eventually resolved to the satisfaction of both sides. However, the Askia subsequently opened the old wound by arresting another brother, Kurmina Fāri al-Hādi, in the house of the Khatīb at Gao. The royal contender in this case, after an aborted bid for the throne, had submitted to the intercession of the Khatīb, but he too was exiled to Kanatu.[189] Our sources do not provide the details that link these events together, but the sequence suggests that scholars now feared that their prestige was being undermined.

These events reached their climax when Askia al-Ḥājj was overthrown by his brother Muḥammad Bān. The new Askia opened his career by ordering the execution of the two exiles at Kanatu. This, no doubt, was the immediate cause for the dislike which he earned among the rank and file of literati both at Timbuktu and Gao. Writing in retrospect, al-Sa'di in a sense exonerates Askia al-Ḥājj by indicating that he did not, after all, kill any of his brothers and half-brothers.[190] Muḥammad Bān's actions, by contrast, created an intense fratricidal mood which embroiled Timbuktu in the bloodiest dynastic struggle in the history of the Songhai empire. The Moroccan conquest, taking place a few years after the upheaval, virtually found the empire undefended, especially in the Saharan fringes where the Moroccans would have been most vulnerable.

The immediate cause of the upheaval was a minor confrontation between an agent of the Askia who was in charge of the imposts at Kabara, the Kabara Farma 'Alwa, and the royal candidate Muḥammad al-Ṣādiq b. Askia Daūd, the Balma' in charge of the troops, just south of Timbuktu. During a scuffle between the two, 'Alwa was killed, and in the prevailing mood, Muḥammad al-Ṣādiq was left with no choice but to raise the standard of rebellion or risk execution. In a short time, the forces of virtually the entire Western provinces aligned themselves behind him in a march upon Gao. Since 'Alwa had committed extortions from the commercial boats which put in at Kabara, the merchants came readily to Muḥammad al-Ṣādiq's support. As for the scholars, we learn that even at Gao, they were the first to speak against the reigning Askia when they heard of events in the West.[191] When the rebels declared Muḥammad al-Ṣādiq lawful Askia, according to *Tārīkh al-Fattāsh*,

> The generality of the people of Timbuktu agreed with them on this, along with the merchants and some of the scholars. He was endorsed by officials of the Askia who were in Timbuktu, including the Timbuktu Mundhu and the Tusur Mundhu, while the chiefs of the merchants (*'umdat al-tujjār*) supported him with funds . . . The tailors of Timbuktu accompanied him, sewing blankets [for the soldiers] and mending shirts and caftans.[192]

The Maghsharen Tuareg also sided with Muḥammad al-Ṣādiq, but the reasons are unknown. The Moroccans had in the meantime, sent a small force which occupied the salt-mines of Taghāza and the Askia reciprocated by prohibiting caravans from going there. This, too, threatened the interests of merchants, though other salt-mines, possibly including Taoudenni, were exploited at this time.[193] Perhaps we are justified in speculating that the Maghsharen would have preferred a showdown with the Moroccans at Taghāza, had the Askia been so inclined. Indeed, it is remotely possible that Muḥammad al-Ṣādiq promised such a showdown if his march on Gao should result, as anticipated, in a successful *coup d'état*.

As it turned out, a huge force was assembled to intercept the rebels and, although the ailing Askia died before the confrontation, Askia Isḥāq II, who took over after a swift sequence of intrigues, could secure his position only in the imminent battle. This, according to *Tārīkh al-Fattāsh*, at least, proved to be the downfall of Songhai.[194] The rebels, including the choice forces of the Western provinces, were decimated, while the armies of the capital suffered comparable losses. Muḥammad al-Ṣādiq retreated with a few bodyguards to Timbuktu and, after spending a night at the house of Muḥammad Baghayughu, he was apparently advised to spare Timbuktu the risk of retaliation.[195] Another leader of the rebellion, the Baghana Fāri Bakar, approached the Qāḍi Abu Ḥafs 'Umar for refuge under his auspices but he was denied the privilege.[196] We simply do not know what was the official position of Timbuktu during the rebellion. The detail in *Tārīkh al-Fattāsh* that Muḥammad al-Ṣādiq was declared sovereign in the Friday *khutbas* seems to pertain to a brief period when rumours reached the city that he emerged victorious.[197] According to the lost chronicle *al-Durar al-Ḥisān*, quoted in *Tārīkh al-Fattāsh*, Timbuktu was spared full retaliation by the fact that Askia Muḥammad Bān had died before the battle. Askia Isḥāq proved less vengeful, but he nonetheless executed the chief of the Maghsharen Tuaregs, Tibirt. This, in the judgement of Kodjo, further alienated the Tuaregs at the crucial moment when their mounted Saharan troops would have been needed to intercept the Moroccan expedition.[198]

We owe it to Kodjo that he has dramatized in his brief article the interrelation between the weakness of Songhai resulting from the upheaval and the success of the Moroccan conquest shortly thereafter. However, he has burdened us with the thesis that the Aqīts, in collusion with the Tuaregs, were the 'architects' of the Moroccan conquest. This extravagant opinion, an extension of the Aqīt–Baghayughu polarization thesis, is consistently denied by the evidence at hand. It is quite plausible that the Maghsharen Tuaregs, or at least their allies in the Sahara, facilitated the passage of the Moroccan expedition. However, the Aqīts were not the permanent allies of the Tuaregs, any more than the Baghayughus were the natural allies of Gao. We have it on record that the Maghsharen-Koy Awsanbu, successor to Tibirt, turned against the Aqīts during the resistance to the Moroccans.[199] The Aqīts were the leaders of the resistance and, in consequence, they were the main victims of the establishment of the Ruma regime in Timbuktu.

As we will see in the last chapter, the Moroccan conquerors virtually had to destroy the power of the Aqīts, Baghayughus and Maghias before they could establish their regime in Timbuktu. The latter found influential allies in the descendants of Ahmad al-Ṣaqali, a Sharīf who had settled in Timbuktu in 925 A.H. (1519/20 A.D.), whose grandsons were among the main victims of the conquest. Ultimately, the tomb of Maḥmūd b. 'Umar Aqīt, like that of

Aḥmad Maghia, became a place of sanctity and pilgrimage. The Aqīts never recovered from the blow of the Moroccan conquest, but the descendants of Aḥmad Maghia regained their power to such an extent that for generations the judges were drawn from among them. Other families, both of older and more recent establishment, became increasingly influential as the conquering Ruma were gradually incorporated into the ranks of notables and commoners in the city. It will be argued throughout that the scholars took the initiative in extricating the Ruma from their relationship with the Moroccan state. However, as a military elite, the Ruma incorporated the previous Songhai institutions and intermarried with the Songhai to such an extent that the descendants of the two eventually became indistinguishable.

Basically, the factors which secured for Timbuktu its subsequent stability have been introduced only on a preliminary basis in this chapter. Our narrative has suggested so far that the 'patrician' factor was important. We have also suggested that the collective leadership of the patriciate tended to be centralized to an extent in the judgeship. In the following three chapters, we will look at these details more closely, beginning with an analysis of the structure of the learned hierarchy. In essence, the pedagogical links tended to reinforce the patrician dimension in the character of the city. Moreover – as will be seen in Chapter 4 – the institutional base of the learned hierarchy did not exclusively rest upon the power and function of the judgeship. Rather, it was strengthened also by parochial criteria of organization, besides factors of wealth, status and prerogative which will be explored more fully in Chapter 5. Eventually, it will be seen in Chapter 6 that these combined factors helped Timbuktu to preserve its essential character in the periods following the Moroccan conquest.

CHAPTER 3

The scholars as a learned elite

It has already been indicated in Chapter 2 that the origins of Muslim learning in Timbuktu have been lost to us. The reasons for this may possibly lie in the disruption caused by the Mossi conquest. Notwithstanding the ambiguity of our sources, we believe that this event took place around 1400 A.D. Our evidence on the transmission of learning begins with Muaddab Muḥammad al-Kāburi and al-Qāḍi al-Ḥājj. The latter is specifically associated with a crisis in Banku caused by the Mossi threat.[1] Quite probably, some demographic dislocation took place at the time comparable to that which was later occasioned by the rise of Sunni 'Ali. This may have led to the dispersal of some groups among the earliest scholars and resulted in a break in Timbuktu traditions. Indeed, excepting the associate of Mansa Mūsa, 'Abd al-Raḥmān al-Tamīmi, tradition did not preserve the name of any of the scholars who flourished in the thirteenth and fourteenth centuries.[2]

The memory of the earliest scholars may perhaps have been lost to fifteenth-century traditionists amidst conflicting claims concerning the first introduction of Māliki Islamic studies. Evidence from elsewhere in the Sūdān suggests the existence of an early Kharijite strain, especially of the Ibadi sect, which gradually gave way to Malikism.[3] As Islamic learning achieved more and more uniformity in the area, Māliki traditions came to be superimposed over others. In the Hausa city–state of Kano in Northern Nigeria, for example, disagreement arose concerning the first introduction of the basic *al-Mudawwana al-Kubra*. One set of traditions credited the first teaching of that work to the Wangara scholar, 'Abd al-Raḥmān Zaghaiti, while another credited it to a certain Shehu Tunus.[4] It is peculiar, indeed, that the first scholar in Timbuktu who is specifically associated with the teaching of *al-Mudawwana*, al-Ḥājj Aḥmad b. 'Umar Aqīt, travelled to Hausaland and actually taught in Kano.[5] Yet, while he is not mentioned there, it appears probable that the major Māliki juristic works formed part of Timbuktu scholarship since at least the fourteenth century. By and large, the sources confront us with a tradition of learning already in a mature state during the fifteenth century.

Attempts to link the Timbuktu tradition with its precursors in the Western Sudan are fraught with difficulty. The genealogical connection between the Aqīts and the Almoravids, suggested by Norris, might indicate survival of eleventh-century Sahelo–Sudanic scholarship among descendants of this family or its kinsmen, at least in Massina, but the evidence is not clear-cut.[6] In the case of Tuareg scholars, the traditions which link them with the early prominence of Tadmekka are surrounded by legends of eighth-century Islamization.[7] We encounter in seventeenth-century Timbuktu a scholar belonging to the Zaghaiti Wangara clan whose grandfather, al-Khaṭīb Muḥammad Zaghaiti, was associated with events leading to the evacuation of Gao at the time of the Moroccan conquest.[8] It has been suggested elsewhere that the name of this clan may reflect a *nisba* to a place of origin in Zāgha or Dia. But while the movements of the Wangara, like those of other Muslim mercantile groups, covered extensive territory, it is impossible to determine the strict flow of Islamic influences which gave rise to Māliki scholarship in Timbuktu.[9]

One set of traditions which probably has some relevance to our subject is reflected in the *isnāds* carried by Dyula scholars up to recent times. These trace the chains (*silsilas*) of successive teachers back to mediaeval times. In his study of a large number of *isnāds* (from the Ivory Coast, Ghana and Upper Volta), Ivor Wilks pointed to their convergence upon scholars of the Saghanughu clan dating to the eighteenth century.[10] Precursors in Muslim scholarship belonging to this clan were encountered by Ibn Baṭūṭa during the fourteenth century in the town of Zaghari, upstream from Zāgha along or near the Niger floodplain.[11] There, the group, which probably emerged out of Soninke descent, was identified as belonging to the Ibadi sect. Moreover, it was closely associated with black traders referred to as Wanjarata, presumably predecessors of the Malinke Wangara.[12] Their presence in Timbuktu is not specifically recorded, but al-Qāḍi Maḥmūd b. ʻUmar Aqīt is remembered to have secured the appointment of one of their descendants, Muḥammad Sānu (Saghanughu?) al-Wangari, as Judge of Jenne.[13]

The *isnāds* are also of interest in the sense that they are the only sources which drive back the Sahelo–Sudanic tradition of learning to an origin pre-dating the fifteenth century. A central figure in the chains is al-Ḥājj Sālim al-Suwāri, a scholar whose *floruit* is assigned by tradition to the twelfth century and whom Ivor Wilks, and more recently Thomas Hunter, on genealogical grounds, assign to the fifteenth century.[14] The chain goes backwards through him to the Malinke scholar al-ʻAbbās Mandawiyyu, then successively to the Soninke scholars Turi Kuri and Sissi Kuri. The latter two would seem to have been the last prominent representatives of a long-lived school which flourished in Dia during and before the fourteenth century.[15] Whether through its influence on Kāburans who ultimately migrated northwards, or directly through the dispersal of scholars from

Dia itself, Timbuktu would seem to have received its earliest influences in Islamic learning from this school.[16]

The section which follows will be devoted to tracing the transmission of learning in Timbuktu itself beginning with the figure of Muḥammad al-Kāburi. The tradition which describes him as contemporary of 'Abd al-Raḥmān al-Tamīmi, when in fact he lived to the days of his grandson Ḥabīb, may indicate that he studied under the erudite scholars whom 'Abd al-Raḥmān found established in the city when he settled there in the mid-fourteenth century.[17] After the Mossi conquest, he was probably the most prominent scholar remaining in the city and, accordingly, he overshadowed his predecessors. He may conceivably have exerted an organizational impact comparable to that of al-Suwāri further south in Dia and Diakha.[18] For although Kātib Mūsa and al-Qāḍi al-Ḥājj were probably his equals in learning, he alone is remembered for teaching the outstanding scholars of the succeeding generation. Indeed, al-Qāḍi al-Ḥājj is associated with an influential school referred to as Alfa Gungu (House of Learning), but Muḥammad al-Kāburi alone is credited with the title of Shaikh al-Shuyukh (Master of Masters).[19] In the absence of evidence on other chains of transmission, Muḥammad al-Kāburi stands out as the major link between the unknown scholars of the fourteenth century and the better-documented ones from the fifteenth century onwards.

Transmission of learning

Timbuktuan scholarship is distinguished from the tradition of the Dyula *isnāds* by a few factors which stem from the exigencies of a relatively extensive urban milieu. First, the Timbuktu tradition continually received input from the outside, both from local sources and through contact with North Africa and Egypt. This meant that the local *silsilas*, or chains of transmission, were always liable to be overshadowed by newer and more prestigious ones. Secondly, the curricula for acquiring the status of scholar were never strictly defined in terms of the completion of a specified set of works or commentaries which were studied by all aspiring scholars. Rather, they involved basic acquisition of Arabic grammar, along with such knowledge of Muslim doctrine and jurisprudence as could be acquired in any number of works.[20] Thirdly, the relative extensiveness of the body of scholars, at least in the fifteenth and sixteenth centuries, allowed for a degree of specialization and a corresponding tendency on the part of students to study under more than one master. Accordingly, the lines of transmission from one generation to another did not branch out in mutually exclusive directions, but rather crossed each other in complex patterns (see Appendices 12, 13, 14).

The acquisition of advanced learning (past the elementary stage of Qur'ānic literacy to be discussed further on in this chapter) was usually approached in a combination of two ways. First the student began by attaching himself to the school (*madrasa*) of an established scholar who held his classes usually at his home. Data on the number of such schools and their enrolment are essentially lacking except for the late nineteenth century. At the time of the French conquest, it is recorded that one school had an average of 75 pupils studying Qur'ānic interpretation (*tafsīr*), grammar, law and doctrinal theology. Two other schools of the same period, whose masters were descendants of Aḥmad Maghia and Muḥammad Zankanu, enrolled an average of 20–30 students each.[21] Closely related to the education offered in such schools were the more specialized lessons (*durūs*) occasionally instituted for advanced students. These either formed the last stage in the curriculum of a *madrasa* or, alternatively, they were offered by an established scholar at his home or at one of the mosques.[22] They were usually concerned with specific branches of Muslim learning and often focused upon a single theological or legal work. If the master was a very prestigious one, they could be attended by established scholars as well.[23] Similarly, but for a much wider audience, there were recitations and expositions (*iqrā'* and *tasrīd*) of individual commentaries, such as the exposition of *Kitāb al-Shifa*, a function which achieved permanency and high honour at the Sankore Mosque.[24]

Secondly, there coexisted with the above a system of tutorialships, essentially an extension of the *durūs*, whereby the relationship between the master and a few of his select students evolved on an individual basis. The student was admitted into such a relationship already in adulthood and often as late as the age of 30 or 40.[25] He was considered to be literally taking knowledge from his master and at the end he would be accredited to that effect in a certificate (*ijāza*, theoretically a teaching permit) which specified the works completed as well as the level at which they were studied.[26] The sources do not always distinguish between this type of transmission and that involved in the more open *madrasas* and *durūs*. Nonetheless, we may assume that in all recorded cases of transmission where the evidence is not otherwise specified tutorialships were involved. For, as one would expect, a student normally sought out as tutors scholars whose *madrasas* or *durūs* he attended. Sometimes, he did so while attending the more advanced courses or, more commonly, after having completed them and proved his long-term commitment to further education or his exceptional abilities as the case may be.

The tutorial system, on which the following discussion is primarily based, provided the context in which the student was gradually admitted under the patronage of his master into the ranks of scholars. Seeking out a prestigious tutor and, ultimately, a widely respected *ijāza*, was a complex process in which familial, kinship and economic ties played a role. Under this system, a student could most readily find a willing tutor in his own father, an older brother or some other close relative. But unless the relative in question was exceptionally reputed for erudition, the tutorialship was liable to go unnoticed both in the society at large as well as in the chronicles. This, in itself, encouraged many students to study under more than one master and, thereby, gain wide recognition of their learned abilities. In all cases, there was the concept of *mulāzama* whereby the student not only attended the lectures and lessons of his master but acted as his assistant and secretary and was present at his audiences at all times.[27] In this way, the abilities of the candidate became gradually known among the circles of scholars and this, over and beyond his *ijāzas*, secured his acceptance as scholar in the society at large.

The pedagogical system was ideal for the development of distinct schools differentiated from each other in their curricula depending on the preferences of their masters.[28] This tendency, however, was fully counterbalanced by the integrative role of the mosques, and especially Sankore, where the courses of study offered were essentially open to all students who could qualify. The combined result was the emergence of loose associations of scholars where kinship, intermarriage and neighbourhood ties were important factors. Each association was essentially made up of a few outstanding masters surrounded by their colleagues, their ex-students and their students. Though they never amounted to schools of learning as such, these associations may nonetheless be described as schools so far as the tutorial process of transmission is concerned.

Of the schools of transmission we may, partly for the lack of a better framework of reference, identify the most important ones during the fifteenth to seventeenth centuries as represented by the scholars of the three major families and their associates. The Aqīts and their circles, among whom the Baghayughus later became paramount, were by far the most influential. The main chain of transmission in this school passes from Muḥammad al-Kāburi to ʻUmar b. Muḥammad Aqīt and then to his son al-Ḥājj Aḥmad. Henceforth, the chain branches out from Ḥājj Aḥmad's younger brother, al-Qāḍi Maḥmūd, simultaneously to Aḥmad b. Muḥammad Saʻīd and Aḥmad b. al-Ḥājj Aḥmad.[29] Both taught a large number of scholars, including their common student Muḥammad Baghayughu, who inherited their prestige. Ultimately, he must be viewed as the founder of a new school centreing in the seventeenth to nineteenth centuries upon descendants of his brother Aḥmad. However, his most outstanding student was Aḥmad Bāba b. Aḥmad b. al-Ḥājj Aḥmad, who achieved widespread fame in exile after the Moroccan conquest and was the last of the outstanding Aqīts. Naturally, this brief outline omits a large number of scholars, some documented and others unknown, who attached themselves to the school. Besides the Baghayughus, the families of Maghia and Zankanu carried on the traditions of this school down to recent times.[30]

The other two main schools, identifiable with the And-Agh-Muḥammad and al-Qāḍi al-Ḥājj families, respectively, also contributed to the diffusion of learning, though perhaps on a smaller scale. The impact of the former was great during the lives of And-Agh-Muḥammad al-Kabīr and his son al-Mukhtār al-Naḥawī. And-Agh-Muḥammad might have been a student of Muḥammad al-Kāburi; his son is remembered only for having studied under al-Imām al-Zammūri while in refuge from Sunni 'Ali in Walāta.[31] Both contributed to the education of al-Ḥājj Aḥmad b. 'Umar Aqīt, but their descendants came to be relegated to a secondary position during the Songhai period. A member of the family identified as 'Abdullāh Boryo (also 'Abdullāh b. Aḥmad Boryo) taught Muḥammad Bāba b. Muḥammad al-Amīn and apparently revived the influence of the family shortly before the Moroccan conquest.[32] At this time the family produced an important book collector in the person of Aḥmad b. And-Agh-Muḥammad b. Maḥmūd b. And-Agh-Muḥammad who clearly owned a great library.[33] The author al-Sa'di may perhaps be a product of this school; for while he gives priority to the And-Agh-Muḥammads over the Aqīts, his main teacher seems to have been Muḥammad Sān b. al-Mukhtār b. Muḥammad b. al-Mukhtār al-Ṇahawī. Al-Sa'di suggests that the And-Agh-Muḥammads imparted their prestige to various in-laws besides the Aqīts.[34] They re-emerged in force during the seventeenth century, under the Ruma, in the person of Sayyid Aḥmad b. And-Agh-Muḥammad b. Aḥmad Boryo, who attained the judgeship, and Muḥammad b. Muḥammad Kara, a relative of the family through his mother, whose son Muḥammad also became Judge.[35] Al-Qāḍi Aḥmad b. And-Agh-Muḥammad taught some influential persons and his name appears in the *sanads* of much later scholars from outside Timbuktu.[36]

The school associated with the al-Ḥājj family had exercised a great though ill-documented influence before the rise of Sunni 'Ali. The Songhai monarch persecuted and killed some of the scholars from this family, including a number among them who lived, as we are told, at the Alfa Gungu.[37] However, the family seems to have maintained wide Sahelian connections, much like the Kunta of the eighteenth and nineteenth centuries. Al-Qāḍi al-Ḥājj, and his brother Ibrāhīm, are associated at once with Walāta and Banku, besides Timbuktu. Their sons and relatives fled Sunni 'Ali both to Walāta and Tagedda, while Ibrāhīm b. 'Umar, reputed to be a *walī*, became a judge at Jenje during the reign of Askia Muḥammad.[38] Today there exists an *ijāza* in the possession of al-Shaikh 'Īsa wuld Muḥammad Mawlūd, of the Keltina al-Ḥājj, which traces a long chain of transmission backwards to al-Amīn b. Abu Bakr b. al-Qāḍi al-Ḥājj.[39] The latter studied under al-Suyūṭi and, although he may have been the first to study under the illustrious Egyptian, he is not mentioned in the Timbuktu chronicles any more than his son Aḥmad and his nephew Muḥammad Ṣāliḥ. It may be that the activities of these scholars during the Songhai period were distributed over a wide area and left little impact on Timbuktu. Indeed, excepting the possibility that al-Amīn b. Aḥmad and 'Abd al-Raḥmān al-Mujtahid were products of their school, their impact on Timbuktu was not revived until after the Moroccan conquest when Muḥammad b. Aḥmad b. al-Qāḍi ʻAbd al-Raḥmān became Judge. He taught some influential scholars and thereby kept alive the *sanad* going back to his great-uncle, Muḥammad al-Amīn.[40] It is possible that his family later migrated from Timbuktu, much as happened to the And-Agh-Muḥammads. Alternatively, both families may have continued to contribute to the transmission of learning among the limited circles of their immediate relatives. This certainly appears to be the case among the Maghias and Gidados who monopolized the judgeship and imamate. During the eighteenth century, the diffusion of learning on a wider scale devolved primarily on the descendants of Muḥammad Gurdu.[41]

The coexistence of several schools of transmission is suggested by the occasional emergence of prominent scholars whose teachers are not known. Of these we know several who flourished just before and after the Moroccan conquest, including Muḥammad al-Amīn b. Ḥabīb, Aḥmad Maghia, ʻAbd al-Mawla al-Jalāli and ʻUthmān al-Filāli.[42] The presumption is that these scholars belonged to chains of transmission other than the main ones documented in the chronicles. These chains might conceivably lead us a few generations backwards to Sīdi Yaḥya al-Tādulsi, the most prominent student of Muḥammad al-Kāburi.[43] Alternatively, they may have branched out in Askia Muḥammad's time from the teaching activities of al-ʻĀqib al-Anṣamuni and Makhlūf al-Balbāli. In his biographical dictionary, Aḥmad Bāba devotes the same amount of attention to the latter two scholars as to his own kinsmen among the Aqīts, but he neglects to mention any of their students.[44] Similar omissions by al-Saʻdi, and more especially by later chroniclers, make it impossible to arrive at a full reconstruction of the complex patterns of transmission.

The selectivity of the evidence was largely forced upon the chroniclers by the records and traditions most accessible to them. These, being preserved among descendants of the scholars in question, were liable to overemphasize long tutorial relationships which were fortified by kinship and intermarriage ties. In the process, the teaching activities of outstanding masters who flourished outside the orbit of tutorial and familial ties were largely neglected. This would seem to apply to al-ʻĀqib al-Anṣamuni and Makhlūf al-Balbāli, as partly also to their precursor Muḥammad al-Kāburi. On the assertion of al-Saʻdi, we have it that the passage of every month was occasion for the completion of a course of study under Muḥammad al-Kāburi in *Tahdhīb al-Barādiʻi*. Yet only his tutorial relationships with Sīdi Yaḥya and ʻUmar Aqīt are specifically remembered.[45] Similarly, Muḥammad b. Muḥammad Kara, of several generations later, became *Imām* of Sankore and, presumably after instituting many courses of study there, came to be honoured as Master of Masters. But of those with whom he established a tutorial relationship only three are named, including Muḥammad Bāba b. Muḥammad al-Amīn, al-Muṣṭafa b. Aḥmad

Baghayughu and al-Imām Muḥammad Gurdu al-Fulāni. The fact that the three belonged to distinct ethnic groups suggests that his influence in the city was universal.[46]

From the obituaries recorded by al-Sa'di of scholars who died while he was compiling his chronicle in the mid-seventeenth century, it appears that the diffusion of learning was far more multidirectional than is indicated by the evidence of earlier and later times. The education of al-Imām Muḥammad Gurdu cut across all three main schools of transmission and included other teachers as well. Coming to Timbuktu as a youth from Massina, where his family had long subscribed to Māliki studies, Muḥammad Gurdu settled in the city under the auspices of 'Abdullāh al-Sa'di, father of our chronicler 'Abd al-Raḥmān.[47] He began his advanced education, it seems, under Aḥmad Bāba of the Aqīt family and later, after a long interruption until the master returned from exile, he payed him due respect by attending his lessons, though already learned and well advanced in age.[48] In the meantime, he had studied under Muḥammad b. Aḥmad b. al-Qāḍi 'Abd al-Raḥmān, of the al-Ḥājj family, and al-Qāḍi Sayyid Aḥmad, of the And-Agh-Muḥammad family. The latter two scholars both attained the judgeship and it was advantageous for Muḥammad Gurdu, like other aspiring scholars, to seek training in the practical application of Māliki law, besides its theory, under them. In fact, the accession of a scholar to the judgeship automatically expanded the sphere of his 'disciples' though an exception is found in the case of al-'Āqib b. Maḥmūd Aqīt who lacked either the time or the inclination to establish tutorial relationships.[49]

The one case where the teachers of a particular scholar appear fully documented is that of Muḥammad Bāba b. Muḥammad al-Amīn. In writing his obituary, al-Sa'di would seem almost certainly to have relied on the detail available in the lost chronicle, *al-Durar al-Ḥisān*, written by his son Bāba Gūru.[50] The scholar had studied under no less than seven masters, besides his own father, and each belonged to a different family.[51] His case is not entirely unique for this period, for al-Muṣṭafa b. Aḥmad Baghayughu enjoyed a succession of six masters while Muḥammad Gurdu studied under seven masters including Muḥammad Bāba himself.[52] What transpires is that the upheaval caused by the Moroccan conquest resulted in a disruption of the tutorial system and forced students to resume their education under new masters. Of the early teachers of Muḥammad Bāba, for example, Aḥmad Maghia was killed during an uprising against the conquerors while 'Abd al-Raḥmān Aqīt was exiled to Morocco and died there shortly after.[53] By and large, as is indeed suggested by the case of Aḥmad Bāba, it appears that scholars did not normally study under more than three or four masters and, even then, they usually acquired most of their education during an extended tutorialship under a single master.[54]

We have so far excluded from our discussion the input which Timbuktu scholarship received from the outside largely because this input did not substantially alter the patterns of transmission. We know of at least 15 scholars who travelled to North Africa and the East and associated with outstanding scholars there during the fifteenth and sixteenth centuries. But of these, only a few actually studied under known masters across the Sahara and their tutorial activities in Timbuktu were not extensive. Particularly interesting is the case of al-ʻĀqib b. Maḥmūd Aqīt whose pilgrimage and residence in the East is not dated though it clearly belongs to the period prior to his accession to the judgeship in 1565 A.D. According to Aḥmad Bāba, al-ʻĀqib studied in Cairo under the well-known grammarian, al-Nāṣir al-Laqqāni, and was accredited by him 'in everything that was creditable to him and through him'.[55] Yet, besides teaching and accrediting Aḥmad Bāba in his youth, al-ʻĀqib did not much engage in teaching in Timbuktu. Similarly, Makhlūf al-Balbāli studied under Ibn Ghāzi in Morocco while al-ʻĀqib al-Anṣamuni studied under the influential al-Maghīli in Tagedda. It is remarkable, in fact, that al-Anṣamuni acquired some learning under al-Suyūṭi as well, the subject of later Timbuktuan legend. Yet he and al-Balbāli, as already indicated, are not assigned any students whom they taught in Timbuktu.[56] One suspects a reticence on the part of local traditionists to admit the full contribution of external influences, especially since al-Maghīli's visit to the Sudan, which registered a lasting impact on Hausaland, is barely mentioned in the Timbuktu sources.[57] It may well be, however, that the local scholars of that particular generation recognized the erudition of the trans-Saharan masters, without holding them to be their superiors.

Al-Saʻdi especially shows no particular interest in the credentials acquired by the Timbuktu scholars during their pilgrimages. Aḥmad Bāba, on the other hand, pays great attention to scholars who were widely travelled and who had associated with famous masters in the East. His *Nayl al-Ibtihāj* was intended for a wide Muslim audience to cover the biographies of prominent Māliki scholars throughout Islam. The sections he devoted to Timbuktu covered mainly the scholars of his own family, the Aqīts, and their immediate associates. Had he set aside more space for his compatriots, erudite though they were, that would have been considered in ill-taste. As it is, the fame which *Nayl al-Ibtihāj* achieved in North Africa and the East placed Timbuktu permanently among the ranks of the major centres of learning in Islam.

Aḥmad Bāba sought consciously during his exile in Morocco to demonstrate that the tradition of learning which he left behind in Timbuktu had strong pedagogical links with the mainstream of Muslim Mālikism. He took pains to record the prestigious *sanads* which he, his masters and their masters, acquired through contact with Egypt. As already indicated, these *sanads* had only a minor influence upon the lines of transmission in Timbuktu. For example, Aḥmad Bāba records that he received an *ijāza* by correspondence from Yaḥya b. Muḥammad al-Khaṭṭāb of Mecca.[58] This *ijāza* hardly added anything to Aḥmad Bāba's credentials, especially since his father Aḥmad, as well as his kinsman al-Qāḍi al-ʿĀqib, had been accredited by Yaḥya's father, a famous commentator on *Khalīl*, during their pilgrimage. However, the variety of prestigious *sanads* which accrued to Aḥmad Bāba, over and beyond his erudition, made him widely sought after as a teacher in Morocco. Eventually he counted among his students some of the most influential men of the day, including the Tilimsani historian and jurist, Aḥmad al-Maqqari, and the Qāḍi of Fez, Abu'l-Qāsim al-Ghassāni.[59] Even after his return to Timbuktu, his *ijāza* was sought through correspondence by ʿAbd al-Raḥmān al-Jazūli. The latter treasured the brief *ijāza*, which reached him, though written at the master's dictation in old age by his son Muḥammad.[60]

For the most part, Aḥmad Bāba traced his *sanads* in the study of the major juristic works to Muḥammad (sometimes And-Agh-Muḥammad) b. Aḥmad b. Abu Muḥammad al-Tazikhti (Ayd Aḥmad). This scholar had been a student of Aḥmad Bāba's grandfather, al-Ḥājj Aḥmad, and he taught Aḥmad Bāba's main master, Muḥammad Baghayughu, besides others. Ayd Aḥmad had travelled from Timbuktu to Tagedda, where he studied under al-Maghīli, and in the east he was certified by al-Qalqashandi, al-Sunbāṭi and others of equal stature. We do not know how long he remained in Timbuktu on his return to the Sudan; he subsequently travelled to Hausaland and settled in Katsina where he became judge.[61] But his *sanads* left a lasting influence in the Sahel where they were eventually passed on to numerous scholars from Walāta, Shingīt and Tishīṭ.[62] Aḥmad Bāba himself did not contribute to the diffusion of these *sanads* except in Morocco. The biography of Sīdi al-Mukhtār al-Kabīr al-Kunti (of the late eighteenth century) features Aḥmad Bāba, besides Muḥammad Baghayughu, in the *silsilas* of the Kunta.[63] But these *silsilas* are almost certainly in error; they seem to confuse Muḥammad Baghayughu al-Wangari, Aḥmad Bāba's main teacher, with Muḥammad Baghayughu b. Muḥammad Gurdu al-Fulāni, of two generations later.[64]

Locally, the *sanads* of Ayd Aḥmad al-Tazikhti were transmitted by Aḥmad Bāba's father, Aḥmad, or alternatively, by Aḥmad b. And-Agh-Muḥammad. The former passed them on to Aḥmad al-Fazazi al-Yaʿqūbi, a teacher of Abu'l-Qāsim al-Ḥājji al-Waddāni who transmitted them to the scholars of Shingīt and Tishīt. Aḥmad b. And-Agh-Muḥammad, on the other hand, who received the *sanads* indirectly through Abu Ḥafs ʿUmar, passed them on to Muḥammad Gurdu. The latter combined them with the *sanads* of the al-Ḥājj family traced backwards to al-Suyūṭi. He transmitted them both to his son Muḥammad Baghayughu, a highly venerated master, who occupies a central position in later chains of transmission.[65]

One of the consequences of the early contact with North Africa, and especially with Egypt, was the fact that *silsilas* such as those of Ayd Aḥmad al-Tazikhti, fully overshadowed the previous local lines of transmission.

Table 1. *Scholars and the tutorialships given by them*

	Scholars	Tutorialships
Scholars whose masters and students are both known	28	60
Scholars whose masters alone are known (no students mentioned)	14	0
Subtotal (masters known)	42	60
Scholars whose students alone are known (masters unknown)	18	25
Total	60	85

Ivor Wilks suggests, for example, that Muḥammad and Aḥmad Baghayughu may ultimately belong to a Wangara chain of learning which goes back through their father Maḥmūd, a *qāḍi* of Jenne, to the tradition which had taken shape after the pilgrimages of al-Ḥājj Sālim al-Suwāri.[66] In adult life, just before settling in Timbuktu, the two scholars travelled on the pilgrimage and resided in Cairo where they met and 'benefited from' some of the most prestigious scholars of the time, including al Nāṣir al-Laqqani, al-Sharīf Yūsif al-Awmayūni and the mystic scholar al-Imān Muḥammad al-Bakri.[67] In Timbuktu, their teachers, Muḥammad b. Aḥmad Sa'īd and Aḥmad b. al-Ḥājj Aḥmad, were of such prestige as might have overshadowed the original chain of scholars to which they belonged. Their careers recall that of al-Siḍḍīq b. Muḥammad Ta'alla, a scholar originally from Kabūra who might conceivably also belong to the Zaghai tradition. While established at Jenje, he is alleged to have discovered that one of his ex-students who had travelled and studied in Timbuktu already surpassed him in juristic erudition. 'We have wasted our life in vain' he exclaimed, and set out to the city, as tradition recalls. However, we may in this case, once again, be faced with the reticence of traditionists to admit learned influence and contribution from further south. The man proved sufficiently erudite to be chosen for the imamate of the Main Mosque not long after his arrival.[68] Nonetheless, the reputation of his associates in Timbuktu, and especially of those whom he later encountered while on the pilgrimage in the East, surpassed that of his original master or masters.

The period *c.* 1450–1650, being relatively well documented by Aḥmad Bāba, al-Sa'di and the evidence of later *sanads*, affords some scope for systematization of the data. The known cases of transmission during the two centuries in question (up to the death of al-Sa'di) involve a total of 60 scholars to the exclusion of their trans-Saharan teachers and students. These scholars are hardly representative of the whole body of learned individuals since, by virtue of the attention accorded them in the sources,

Table 2. *Tutorialships*

	Relatives	Non-relatives	Totals
Under relatives only	12	0	12
Under relatives and others	15	27	42
Under non-relatives only	0	31	31
Total	27	58	85

they appear to have been among the most outstanding of their time. They include only those whose teachers and/or students are sufficiently known as to enable us to place them, without resort to inference, in the patterns of transmission. The relative uniformity of the group may be evidenced indirectly from its activities as represented in Table 1. There, we observe that scholars whose masters are not recorded (largely because no specific biographies are devoted to them) were equally as active in educating noteworthy scholars as those whose masters are duly mentioned. This suggests that the omissions of the sources, whatever else their significance, are largely haphazard as far as the lines of transmission of learning are concerned. Generally, we are dealing with a situation in which the masters of the earlier scholars tend to be unknown while the students of the later scholars (seventeenth century) are not recorded. The most striking example among the latter is Muḥammad Bāba b. Muḥammad al-Amīn. Having studied under a sequence of eight masters, one would expect that he taught others besides Muḥammad Gurdu. Indeed, the same applies to al-Muṣṭafa b. Aḥmad Baghayughu; no students are assigned him though he studied under six masters. He died at the age of 53, some 40 years before al-Sa'di (our main source of information), while Muḥammad Bāba died at the age of 83, ten years earlier still. By the time al-Sa'di embarked on his work, scholars taught by these two had probably left a great many students behind them.[69]

Of the 42 scholars whose masters are known, we find that 12 are associated with more than one teacher while, more significantly, all but one of these had three teachers or more. The total number of tutorialships under relatives, including in-laws, account for slightly over 30% (27 of 85) of the cases (see Table 2). The significance of this figure, which might in itself appear too low, is not necessarily diluted by the fact that many of the scholars involved studied under non-relatives as well. In a few important cases, for example, the role of family exhibited itself indirectly when the scholar studied under a non-relative who had been his father's student. Muḥammad Baghayughu studied under Aḥmad b. al-Ḥājj Aḥmad and, in return, taught the latter's son, Aḥmad Bāba. Baghayughu himself had no sons, but Aḥmad Bāba reciprocated by teaching his nephew, al-Muṣṭafa b. Aḥmad Baghayughu. The exchange of students between closely associated families minimized the need for remunerating the master in a society where the Islamic ethic looked upon teaching as an obligation besides an honour.[70] It cemented the ties between the families in question, sometimes resulting in (rather than from) intermarriage and often facilitated joint ventures in commerce. Moreover, it insured for the scholar that recognition of his learned status would rest on the testimony, and often the certification or *ijāza*, of masters other than his immediate relatives.

The above observations drawn from evidence on the fifteenth to seventeenth centuries would seem to apply also, with even greater emphasis, to the role of family during the eighteenth and nineteenth centuries. It appears certain, at least, that the basic features of tutorial relationships remained the same. While participating in the family business, its commerce or the management of its property, the student also acquired certain skills which he could place at the service of his master. We believe that the terms of the tutorialship, much like those of an apprenticeship in a particular craft, were implicitly known from the outset with the general understanding that a student would assist his master in whatever may have been his source of income. If the master was of modest means, as in the case of many known to us only by name, the student could be employed in manual labour at his master's farm or in conducting petty transactions at his retail business. In these and other cases, the master could take responsibility for his students' maintenance and, especially if several students were recruited, he could honourably seek funds for that purpose from rich merchants and rulers alike.[71] Some students could readily support themselves from their own private business or that of their family, and could supplement their income from notarial services as witnesses of legal deeds or from scribal activities as copyists of manuscript books.[72] The most distinctive feature of this system was a certain ambivalence which placed the student throughout a good portion of his early adulthood somewhere in the middle between his father's household, where he continued to dwell, and that of his master, where he formed enduring friendships and often sought a wife. In mediaeval and up to early Ruma times, the ambivalence could easily stimulate intellectual fermentation, on a modest scale at least, since a good proportion of the students sought the city from a number of directions and enlivened its quarters without being encumbered by close family ties.

Since the chronicles of the eighteenth century do not supply any information on the transmission of learning, our evidence for the period comes mainly from a few later *sanads* still extant at Timbuktu and others which were recorded in the late-eighteenth-century biographical dictionary from Walāta, the *Fath al-Shukūr*. Most of these *sanads* converge backwards on Muḥammad Gurdu through his sons Aḥmad and Muḥammad

Baghayughu.[73] The latter is honoured as 'the unique of his age', much like Aḥmad Bāba, but his teaching activities are not well documented. He accredited his son Muḥammad in an *ijāza* dated 1079 A.H. (1668/9 A.D.) which apparently achieved widespread fame.[74] The son (sometimes also identified as Muḥammad Baghayughu) passed on the *sanad* to some of the most influential scholars of the time. His student al-Wāfi b. Ṭālibna raised the town of Arwān, previously an unimportant village in the Sahara north of Timbuktu, to the rank of a centre of learning.[75] Another student, more influential yet, was Aḥmad Ag al-Shaikh al-Sūqi. The activities of this scholar fortified the reputation of his people, the Kel al-Sūq, as a clan of jurists (*fuquha'*).[76] He taught Sīdi 'Ali b. al-Najīb who, in turn, was the main teacher of Sīdi al-Mukhtār al-Kabīr al-Kunti, pontiff of the Sahara in the late eighteenth century.[77] The influential Sān Sirfi, who played an important role in the history of Timbuktu in the mid-nineteenth century, also traced his *sanads* to Aḥmad Ag al-Shaikh and, through him, to our illustrious Muḥammad b. Baghayughu b. Gurdu.[78] Finally, Muḥammad b. Baghayughu taught the celebrated Muḥammad b. Mūsa b. Ijil al-Zaidi. This scholar and his son Aḥmad b. Muḥammad b. Mūsa contributed to a school of learning which had great influence throughout the southern Sahara and counted among its students the author of *Fath al-Shukūr*, Muḥammad 'Abdullāh al-Bartīli.[79]

What is apparent is that Timbuktu scholarship in the eighteenth century became closely bound with a wide expanse of interrelationships spanning the areas from Arwān and Boujbeiha to Walāta, Tishīt and Shingīṭ. The area of Tuāt, across the Sahara, which like Ghadāmis, had always enjoyed strong commercial links with the Sūdān, was also part of the same complex of interrelationships. The migrations of scholars between these towns, coupled with the scarcity of the evidence, makes it difficult to distinguish scholars of Timbuktu from others. Sulaimān b. Daūd b. Muḥammad al-Husni al-Tunbukti, for example, is clearly a Timbuktu scholar. Yet nothing is known about him besides the fact that he was a logician and a *mufti* who had numerous disputations with the masters of al-Bartīli, presumably residents of Walāta.[80] The case of al-Mukhtār al-Kabīr al-Kunti is particularly problematical. He studied in Timbuktu as a youth and his later teachers were largely the product of the Timbuktuan tradition of learning. Moreover, in later life he exerted considerable influence on the affairs of the city. Yet, unlike his grandson Aḥmad al-Bakkā'i, who spent most of his active career in and around Timbuktu, he defies categorization as a Timbuktu scholar.[81] Muḥammad b. Mūsa b. Ijil al-Zaidi and his son Aḥmad, though not as influential in the Sahara, are equally as problematical. Their provenance is in doubt and we simply do not know when nor for how long they resided in Timbuktu. Muḥammad studied under Muḥammad b. Muḥammad Baghayughu and was, seemingly at a later time, accredited by him in an *ijāza* dated 1136 A.H. (1723/4 A.D.).[82]

The Baghayughu Wangara *imāms* of the Sīdi Yaḥya Mosque continue to this day to trace their *sanads* back to Muḥammad b. Mūsa.[83] His son Aḥmad taught Bāba Sa'īd b. al-Ḥājj 'Abd al-Raḥmān b. Isma'īl Yoro b. Muḥammad Gurdu. Descendants of Isma'īl Yoro eventually replaced the Gidādos as *imāms* of Jingerebir. In the meantime, Bāba Sa'īd's student and kinsman, al-Muṣṭafa b. Aḥmad, became teacher of 'Abd al-Qādir b. Muḥammad al-Sanūsi, Judge and Governor of Timbuktu under the Caliphate of Massina in the early nineteenth century.[84]

If inference on the basis of limited evidence is permissible, it seems that the scholars of Timbuktu who interacted with the growing world of Saharan scholarship gained the ascendency in the eighteenth century. The Maghias, in control of the judgeship, like the Gidādo *imāms* of Jingerebir, did not perhaps contribute to the cause of learning beyond their immediate familial circles and eventually they gave way to others in the leadership of Timbuktu. It is not clear whether the scholars of Jenne continued to sustain their traditionally close ties with Timbuktu. It seems almost certain, however, that the Fulāni scholars of Massina continued to interact with Timbuktu and Saharan scholarship. The expansion of Aḥmadu Lobbo's jihādist state northwards was facilitated by earlier links and did not, in any case, result in an upheaval. The name of Fulāni scholars, other than the Timbuktu Gurdus, appears occasionally among the masters of Saharan scholars.[85] More importantly, perhaps, Muḥammad al-Tāhir, one of the main ideologues of the Massina *jihād*, was a student of al-Mukhtār al-Kunti.[86] His famous manifesto, which made Aḥmadu Lobbo the spiritual successor of Askia Muḥammad, was sufficiently accepted in and around Timbuktu so that no complete copy of *Tārīkh al-Fattāsh* has survived which does not incorporate the manifesto.[87] The convergence subsequently of Saharan and Futa scholars on the region of Massina made it a radiating centre of learned influence. Even late in the nineteenth century we find that Aḥmad Bāba, *Qāḍi* of Timbuktu at the time of the French conquest, had resided for some time in Massina and presumably studied there.[88] Jenne likewise contributed its share of influence on Timbuktu in the person of Muḥammad b. Fadigh b. Aḥmad Zarrūq, one of the principal propagators of the Tijaniyya around the turn of the century.[89]

The traditional lines of transmission of juridical studies are overshadowed throughout the nineteenth century by the superior organizational impact of the Sufi *ṭarīqas* ('mystic' orders or confraternities). The Qādiriyya *ṭarīqa* must have made its first appearance in Timbuktu during the sixteenth century when a number of scholars established links with the rather eccentric Muḥammad al-Bakri in Cairo.[90] Indeed, Timbuktu itself apparently produced a devoted Sufi in the person of Abu Bakr b. al-Ḥājj Aḥmad b. 'Umar. However, while this scholar transferred his family to Mecca and settled there permanently, the influence of Sufism remained very limited.[91] We find it occasionally in certain poetical forms and especially in a seventeenth-century versification of al-Sanūsi's *Um al-Barāhin* by Muḥammad b. Aḥmad Baghayughu al-Wangari.[92] Judging from Aḥmad Bāba's views, it seems that the classical juridical orientation remained paramount. This prolific author has left us a composition purportedly on the virtues of scholars which, in fact, is more concerned with comparing (and implicitly contrasting) the conventional acquisition of learning (*'ilm al-zāhir*) with the gnostic approach (*'ilm al-bātin*). As in other compositions, Aḥmad Bāba surveys the whole spectrum of traditions and views on the subject but does not quite commit himself. The overall effect of his treatise, however, is to show a marked preference for the accomplished scholar. Learning leads to the benefit of the community as a whole, as Aḥmad Bāba saw it, while gnostic knowledge, even when it amounts to saintliness (*al-wilāya*), benefits only the seeker.[93] Though the evidence is not conclusive, it seems that this basic approach to Sufism remained prevalent until the propagation of the Qādiriyya in the late eighteenth and early nineteenth centuries by the Kunta. From then on, the *sanads* of the *tarīqa* took precedence over those of the juridicial sciences. Ultimately, most Qādiri scholars traced their *sanads* back to Sīdi al-Mukhtār (sometimes through his grandson Aḥmad al-Bakkā'i) while others traced them back to al-Mukhtār's teacher Sīdi 'Ali b. al-Najīb.[94]

At roughly the same time as the Qādiriyya became important in Timbuktu, the Tijāniyya made its first appearance in the area. It subsequently became a major force following the *jihād* of Ḥājj 'Umar which overthrew the Massina Caliphate of Hamdullāhi. The Bakkā'i-led struggle against Ḥājj 'Umar, which had repercussions until later in the nineteenth century, tended to minimize the influence of the Tijāniyya in Timbuktu. But by the time of the French conquest, or shortly thereafter, the new *tarīqa* became equally as important as the Qādiriyya.[95] Interestingly enough, few scholars from the area of Timbuktu traced their *sanads* in the Tijāni *wird* to the associates of Ḥājj 'Umar. Rather, the transmission and diffusion of the *wird* north of the Niger bend devolved primarily on Muḥammad b. Fadigh b. Aḥmad Zarrūq. This scholar from Jenne, sometimes known simply as Aḥmad Zarrūq, achieved considerable fame locally, and in the East he came to be associated with Sulṭān 'Abd al-Ḥamīd's pan-Islamicism.[96] His career however, little known as it is, falls beyond the scope of our study. The Tijāniyya, like the Qādiriyya, did not substantially alter the pedagogical process beyond the addition of their respective litanies to the curricula of study. They did provide added organizational power to the scholars at first, when they were more closely knit; but ultimately, their organization became almost as fluid as that of the schools of transmission of learning described above.

Academic pursuits of scholars

The Muslim sciences which lay at the core of the educational process in Timbuktu may be divided broadly into two categories. The first and most important was made up of four branches closely related in their subject matter, though varying in their source materials and methodology. They included Qur'ānic exegesis (*tafsīr*), traditions of the Prophet Muḥammad (*hadīth*), jurisprudence (*fiqh*) and the sources of the law (*usūl*). These branches all shared in common a preoccupation with the governance of society and the conduct of individuals along ideal Muslim lines. Their domains ranged from ethical standards and direct prescriptions to legal principles and precise laws. The first three of these sciences were required of all candidates of scholarship, while the fourth, which may be perhaps described as the methodology of Muslim jurisprudence, was reserved for the most learned and ambitious.

The second category of Muslim sciences included the fields of grammar (*nahw*), literary style and rhetoric (*balāgha*), logic (*mantiq*) and doctrinal theology (*tawhīd*). Of these, only the study of grammar formed an essential part of a scholar's education, the rest being designed to refine his learned capabilities or else earn him more versatility in juristic deductions and in Muslim doctrine. To these fields, we should perhaps also add the science of astronomy and history, along with an occasional interest in mathematics and medicine.[97] Finally, in cases where the scholar embraced the Qādiri or Tijāni order, study of the literature of that order and its body of doctrine often took the place of training in *tawhīd* or else complemented it.

Although it was not uncommon to engage in several fields of study at the same time, candidates to scholarship usually began their higher education in grammar, then in *tafsīr*. In Qur'ānic literacy schools (*maktabs*), these two fields at an elementary level were treated as one and the same; the instructor (*mu'allim*) introduced his students to Arabic grammar while teaching and dictating the text of the Qur'ān itself. At more advanced levels, the two fields were likewise studied simultaneously, though sometimes under different masters. The main distinction lay in the fact that the students were introduced to grammatical commentaries as such, while in *tafsīr*, the works of a wide range of authorities were used as textbooks.

The chronicles have not left us much information concerning the works studied in grammar, but copies which have survived since the sixteenth century suggest that a large number of commentaries, of foreign and local authorship, were utilized as textbooks.[98] It is quite apparent that versatility in the Arabic language was highly desirable in the circles of scholars. This much is suggested by the fact that the first Timbuktu scholar whose travels are recorded in detail, namely al-Ḥājj Aḥmad b. 'Umar Aqīt, made a point of associating with Khālid al-Waqqād al-Azhari, the master grammarian of his time (*Imām al-Naḥw*) in Cairo.[99] It is noteworthy, in fact, that al-Ḥājj Aḥmad's teacher in Timbuktu, al-Mukhtār b. And-Agh-Muḥammad, is known principally as al-Mukhtār al-Naḥawī (the Grammarian). Emphasis on grammar seems to have remained strong in the school of transmission centring around the And-Agh-Muḥammad family. For while Aḥmad b. And-Agh-Muḥammad b. Maḥmūd b. And-Agh-Muḥammad al-Kabīr is known to have excelled in grammar besides poetry, his distant cousin, 'Abdullāh b. Aḥmad Boryo, combined the 'vocation' of *mufti* (jurisconsult) with that of grammarian and philologist.[100] Moreover, 'Abdullāh's nephew, Sayyid Aḥmad b. And-Agh-Muḥammad, was author of a commentary upon the famous grammatical work, the *Ajerrūmiyya*, by Abu 'Abdullāh Muḥammad b. Daūd al-Sanḥāji (d. 1324). The conciseness of the latter work had since the early fourteenth century made it the subject for classroom elaboration and commentary throughout the Muslim world. Indeed, Sayyid Aḥmad's commentary on it, *al-Futūḥ al-Qayūmiyya fi Sharḥ al-Ajerrūmiyya*, may have come into wide use in North Africa and Egypt, judging by the fact that copies of it have been preserved in Cairo and in Morocco.[101] Locally, in the Sudan, the commentary continued to be widely used up to the late nineteenth century when several copies existed in the Umarian library at Segu.[102] For a reason which is not fully known, the Timbuktu chroniclers neglected to mention the compositions of Sayyid Aḥmad. This, however, is compensated for in a laudatory biography by the Moroccan scholar Muḥammad al-Qādiri. The latter composed a biographical addendum to Aḥmad Bāba's *Kifāyat al-Muḥtāj* on the prominent scholars of the Māliki school. He indicated that Sayyid Aḥmad's commentary came into great use as a textbook in Fez, on account of its clarity, and that the Timbuktu *Qāḍi* also authored certain *ta'āliq* (appendices) on *al-Murādi* before his death in 1045 A.H. (*c.* 1635 A.D.).[103]

Though more detailed commentaries often accompanied the teaching of the *Ajerrūmiyya*, the latter work, whose Sanḥāja author may conceivably have been of southern Saharan origin, has remained the basic text throughout the Sudan.[104] Other important works in the field included *al-Kāfiya al-Shāfiya*, by Ibn Mālik al-Dimashqi (d. 672 A.H., 1273 A.D.), a work whose abridgement, known as *al-Khulāṣa* (Alfiyyat Ibn Mālik) became the subject of advanced classroom exposition in which Sayyid Aḥmad is known to have excelled.[105] Similarly, Sayyid Aḥmad taught *Tashil al-Fawā'id al-Naḥawiyya*, also by Ibn Mālik which offered the advantage of surveying the views of the early linguists. This work was studied by Aḥmad Bāba under Muḥammad Baghayughu and no doubt contributed to his own compositions on the relation between verbs and nominal clauses.[106]

The science of *tafsīr* represented only a gradual departure from the

Qur'ānic studies offered in elementary schools. For although it introduced the student to the body of Muslim doctrine and to the primary source of legislation, it was among most scholars approached from the point of view of philological exegesis. Considerable variation existed in the degree of interpretation offered by various commentators in this field with the result that students had to study a number of works in succession. However, the *Tafsīr al-Jalālain*, begun by al-Maḥalli and completed by al-Suyūṭi, became the most widely studied from the sixteenth century onwards.[107] Occasionally we find reference to a more interpretative text (properly speaking in the field of *ta'wīl*), such as *Madārik al-Tanzīl* of al-Nasafi and *Lubāb Ta'wīl Ibn Khāzin*, but such studies were reserved for the most outstanding scholars.[108] By and large, scholars acquired versatility in the theological aspects of Islam in the last stages of their education. At that time, if they so chose, they could undertake some study in one or another of the works of al-Sanūsi (d. 1486), or some other commentary in the field of *tawḥīd*. This field acquired some vogue in the sixteenth and seventeenth centuries judging by the fact that Aḥmad b. al-Ḥājj Aḥmad and his son Aḥmad Bāba both wrote commentaries on *Sughra al-Sanūsi*.[109] By the nineteenth century, however, such studies were increasingly superseded by Sufi approaches to religious experience.

The field of *ḥadīth*, on the other hand, blended rather closely with the legalistic aspects of *tafsīr* and formed the basic source material for jurisprudence. Naturally, the abilities of a jurist came to be measured by his familiarity with the precedents set by the Prophet. The scholars took upon themselves to study as many *ḥadīths* as possible, to the extent that Sīdi al-Mukhtār al-Kunti is recorded to have studied all six authoritative collections (*saḥīḥs*).[110] Aḥmad Bāba, on the other hand, adopted the more representative approach of studying only *al-Bukhāri* and *Muslim*, and in his teaching activities he preferred to use abridgements by al-Qurṭubi of these two venerated collections alongside a redaction of the *Saḥiḥ* of al-Turmudhi.[111] *Ḥadīth* compendia being organized according to their legal subject matter, it was quite common for a student to study only selections from them, and especially those pertaining to marriage, inheritance and market laws, besides prescriptions for individual conduct. However, in most cases there was a tendency to study only a short collection, the most popular being *Jāmi' al-Saghīr*, of al-Suyūṭi. This, like the highly interpretative composition on the Prophet, the *Kitāb al-Shifa'* of al-Qāḍi 'Iyāḍ, became a basic textbook throughout the Sūdān.[112]

Kitāb al-Shifa' owed its popularity in North Africa and the Sūdān to the theoretical premises laid out by its theologically inclined author (d. 1149) concerning the mission of the Prophet and its implications for Muslim prescriptions and laws. It is surprising, nonetheless, that the exposition (*tasrīd*) of this work became a permanent function at the Sankore Mosque. Al-Mukhtār al-Naḥawī may have been the first to institute that tradition after having studied the *Kitāb* under al-Imām al-Zammūri in Walāta. In any case, we know that his son And-Agh-Muḥammad and his grandson Muḥammad both discharged the honorific function though the latter declined the imamate of Sankore when offered him at his father's death. Subsequently, it seems, the function remained distinct from the imamate and there exists some evidence that it persisted up to the late eighteenth century.[113]

In the field of jurisprudence as such (*fiqh*) there was considerable variety in the textbooks studied though these overlapped to a great extent in their subject matter. It seems that repeated study of the same legal principles in several works served as an alternative for studying the same book several times. The *Risāla of Ibn Abu Zaid*, studied by nearly all scholars, was concerned mainly with personal prescriptions ranging from proper observance of prayer to ethical aspects of individual conduct. Its deficiency, or brevity, in the field of civic law, was compensated for by study of *Tuhfat al-Hakkām*, by Ibn 'Āsim, a thoroughgoing summary in verse of court procedure, contracts, partnerships, market and land laws.[114]

By far the most important legal textbook, required of all scholars, was *Mukhtasar Khalīl*, by the Egyptian jurist Khalīl b. Ishāq al-Jundi (d. 1374). The popularity of this work is perplexing because, in view of its brevity, it lends itself to varying interpretations on numerous points in Māliki law. It seems almost certain that its use in Timbuktu dates back to the fifteenth century, but at that time it was overshadowed by the more detailed *al-Mudawwana al-Kubra*.[115] Subsequently, however, it became the single most important work in the entire educational system. Aḥmad Bāba is reported by a much later scholar to have declared: 'We are Khalīlis, if he erred we err'.[116] According to Ahmad Bāba in his biography of its author, no less than 60 commentaries were written upon the *Mukhtasar* in various parts of the Muslim world. Timbuktu, for its part, contributed an appreciable share. Of a total of 12 scholars whose compositions in the sixteenth and seventeenth centuries are specified in the chronicles, no less than seven contributed commentaries on parts or on the complete text of *Khalīl*.[117]

The earliest commentary, it seems, was in the form of notes (*taqāyīd*) in two volumes taken down by his students from the teachings of Maḥmūd b. 'Umar. This commentary came into some use in North Africa and came to be confused with a similar two-volume commentary on the difficult passages of *Khalīl*, which was edited by Aḥmad Bāba from the notes of his teacher, Muḥammad Baghayughu.[118] Maḥmūd b. 'Umar (d. 955 A.H.) is credited with having popularized the use of *Khalīl* as a textbook during a long teaching career which spanned the entire first half of the sixteenth century. He studied the work under a certain al-Shaik 'Uthmān al-Maghribi (also referred to as Aḥmad b. 'Uthmān) who may be related to al-Sayyid Aḥmad b. Muḥammad b. 'Uthmān b. 'Abdallāh b. Abi Ya'kūb, a mysterious scholar whose erudition is highly praised by al-Sa'di. The teacher of Maḥmūd b. 'Umar, namely al-Shaikh 'Uthmān, traced a *sanad* in the study of this work, through al-Nūr al-Sanhūri, to al-Shams al-Bisāṭi, a pupil of Khalīl in Cairo.[119]

Aḥmad Bāba, it seems, consciously sought to bring the works of the Timbuktu commentators to the attention of North African scholars during his exile in Morocco. For besides editing his master's work, he also abridged a commentary by al-'Āqib b. 'Abdallāh al-Anṣamuni on an important passage in *Khalīl*. The passage concerns the emphasis on intention, as distinct from action, a feature which distinguished Mālikism from the more formalistic attitude of other schools.[120] Other Timbuktuan commentators included Ṣālih b. Muḥammad And-'Umar (above-mentioned as Ṣālih Takun), a descendant of an ancient family in Timbuktu whose brother, Aḥmad Bīru b. Muḥammad al-Mukhtār b. Aḥmad, was killed during the uprising against the Moroccan conquerors in 1591. The connections between this family and the Aqīts suggest that the most dynamic legal commentators belonged to the schools of transmissions centreing upon the Aqīt–Baghayughu axis.[121]

Mukhtasar Khalīl combined with the far more detailed *Muwatta'* of Mālik b. Anas, reputedly the first legal compendium in Islam to occupy the attention of would-be scholars during several years of their educational training.[122] In most cases, the study of these works was followed by training in the field of *usūl*, the philosophy or theory of Muslim jurisprudence, which was the culmination of the educational process. Being concerned with the interrelationship between revelation and *hadīth* as sources of law, along with the function of *ijmā'* (consensus) and *qiyās* (analogy) in the classical legislative process, this field opened considerable scope for integration of the various sciences. Its methodology touched upon the science of *kalām* (philosophy) and the principles of philology, while dealing also with the classification and evaluation of the religious precepts (*ahkām*). Several textbooks were utilized in this field, including the *Jami' al-Jawāmi'* of al-Subki, a Shāfi'i jurist, but the main source was the *Jāmi' al-Ummahāt* (also *Mukhtasar al-Furū'*) of Ibn al-Ḥājib (d. 1249).[123] We are inclined to believe that the title of *faqīh* (jurist) was reserved only to those scholars (*'ulamā'*) who acquired ample training in the *usūl* (sources) as well as the *furū'* (branches) of the law. However, we should point out that most scholars mentioned in the sources, obviously the most outstanding ones, are identified as jurists. At a higher level of erudition yet, the title of *mufti*, jurisconsult, attached only to those whose learning qualified them to give formal legal opinions (*fatwa*) on difficult questions in the law.

In revolving around the concept of *fiqh* (jurisprudence in the wider Roman concept of the word), the curricula of study in Timbuktu were designed to give the scholars as wide a humanistic training as was in vogue in the Middle East at the time. Indeed, the prolific Egyptian scholar al-Suyūṭi, whose works in many branches were very popular, became something of a model to the literati of Timbuktu.[124] The writings of Aḥmad Bāba, which acquired widespread fame during his exile in Morocco and have been principally preserved north of the Sahara, are perhaps exemplary of this trend. Of a total of 56 compositions written by this scholar, 32 are still extant while the others are known only by their titles.[125] In most cases, the subject matter is known and it seems that fully a quarter are on theological themes, mainly divinity and devotion.[126] The bulk of Aḥmad Bāba's work, to a total of some 20–25 known compositions, falls more strictly in the legalistic aspects of jurisprudence. These include three general commentaries, among them a classification (*tartīb*) of the voluminous work known as *Jamī' al-Mi'yār* by al-Wansharīshi (d. 1507).[127] Most of the legal compositions, however, were concerned with specific sections of Sharī'a law, ranging from the marriage and divorce laws to market laws, in addition to three treatises hinging on the prerogatives of rulership.[128] Additionally, Aḥmad Bāba wrote some four compositions in grammar and a similar number in historical biography.[129] No doubt the learned interests of Aḥmad Bāba are representative of Timbuktu scholarship. For, although his fame overshadowed his predecessors and successors, he is reported to have testified that previous literati, from his own family at least, were equally as prolific.[130]

A key to the integration of Timbuktu into the wider mould of Islamic scholarship lies in the availability of manuscript books. Aḥmad b. And-Agh-Muḥammad's *al-Futūḥ al-Qayūmiyya*, for example, quotes directly from a bibliography of no less than 40 grammatical works listed at the end of one of the copies.[131] Likewise, Aḥmad Bāba's *Kifāyat al-Muḥtāj*, a major historical source on Māliki Islam, drew upon a bibliography of 23 biographical sources, besides numerous oral testimonies.[132] There exists no evidence so far that a public library was kept at Sankore or one of the other mosques.[133] However, extensive private libraries are known to have existed from an early date and these were often open to consultation and borrowing by interested scholars. One such library was left behind after a long teaching career by al-Ḥājj Ạhmad b. 'Umar. It boasted 700 volumes, including many which were copied and copiously annotated by the owner himself, at a time in the early fifteenth century when the importation and copying of books was fast gaining pace.[134] It was probably inherited by Aḥmad, son of al-Ḥājj Aḥmad, who is specifically remembered as a collector of books. According to his son Aḥmad Bāba, his library 'combined everything that was valuable and rare'.[135] At the time of the Moroccan conquest, the library must have been partly seized and sold, for Aḥmad Bāba is reported in Morocco to have lost as many as 1600 volumes.[136]

Leo Africanus suggests that books were the most valued among the various articles of trade which abounded during the sixteenth century in Timbuktu.[137] This, in turn, is fully borne out by the high praise accruing to Muḥammad

Baghayughu for his liberality in lending and giving away books to scholars who sought them.[138] The *Tārīkh al-Fattāsh* indicates that a copy of the *Qāmūs* (presumably of al-Firuzabādi) was once sold in Timbuktu for 80 *mithqāls*. This was an enormous sum which at the time in the sixteenth century exceeded the average price of a slave.[139] Unfortunately, we do not know how many volumes were involved; perhaps the copy was exceptionally well vowelled and ornamented. However, we do know that Aḥmad b. And-Agh-Muḥammad b. Maḥmūd b. And-Agh-Muḥammad owned a copy of Ibn Sīda's *Muḥkam fi'l-Lugha*, in 28 volumes, which almost certainly cost as much. The last several volumes of this copy, which at one point came into the possession of Aḥmad Bāba, are now preserved in Rabat. We learn from the colophons there that the copying of each volume was commissioned by Aḥmad b. And-Agh-Muḥammad for a sum of one *mithqāl* even though he supplied the paper to the scribe. An additional half a *mithqāl* had to be expended for remunerating a literatus, usually acquainted with the subject matter, who would proof-read the manuscript and correct its errors.[140] Since paper was imported from North Africa and Egypt, its cost must have been great, and we are inclined to believe that any large volume cost five *mithqāls* or more. Indeed, we learn that a volume of *Sharḥ al-Aḥkām* (a legal work thought to be by the Andalusian Muḥammad al-Ishbili) was purchased in 983 A.H. (1575/6 A.D.) by the same Aḥmad b. And-Agh-Muḥammad for slightly over four *mithqāls* even though the copy was seemingly worn.[141] The demand for Arabic books remained strong in Timbuktu up to the mid-nineteenth century. At that time Aḥmad al-Bakkā'i even approached the European traveller, Henry Barth, on the possibility of importing such books through trade with England.[142] What is remarkable is that the books in demand included the rarest and most voluminous besides the more basic texts used in the pedagogical process.[143]

The intensity of contact with North Africa and Egypt gave the scholars a wide span of subjects, both religious and secular, to choose from in their educational pursuits. It is interesting, for example, that the Egyptian al-Suyūṭi was opposed to the study of logic and is known to have had a correspondence with the North African al-Maghīli who championed it.[144] In this controversy, the scholars of Timbuktu clearly took the side of al-Maghīli to the extent that two among them from the Aqīt family wrote commentaries in the field of logic during the sixteenth century.[145]

Other secular sciences which were studied included mathematics and astronomy. The former was pursued only at the most basic levels of arithmetic; it formed such a secondary part of the educational process that the sources do not mention any commentary used as a textbook in this field. Astronomical treatises, on the other hand, are more frequently mentioned, and it appears that this field of learning, much like history, was a subject of popular interest as well as of training.[146] In some cases, as that of al-Ḥājj Muḥammad al-'Irāqi, whose descendants several generations later were paramount at the time of the French conquest, interest in astronomical phenomena was strongly tinged by astrological conventions.[147] What is apparent is that the scholars gained some training in meteorology: the chronicles often record unusually high floodings of the Niger, as well as heavy rains and winds, according to the solar as well as the lunar calendar.[148]

Finally, mention may be made of the sciences of rhetoric and prosody (*'arūd*) which formed a basic part of the education of all full-fledged scholars. In the former field, the famous *'Uqūd al-Jumān* was widely studied, but the *Alfiyya* of al-Suyūṭi became the basic text. It seems that Timbuktu produced an eminent scholar in this field in the person of Muḥammad Bāba b. Muḥammad al-Amīn, already mentioned as commentator on the *Alfiyya* and as having enjoyed the tutelage of eight prominent masters.[149] He seems to have enjoyed wide interests in *belles lettres*, judging by the fact that he wrote a treatise on *Maqāmāt al-Ḥarīrī*. It is perhaps testimony to the tendency of specialization in Timbuktu that one of his other compositions was a commentary on the *Khazrajiyya*, the most widely utilized textbook in prosody.[150] He, along with many other scholars, distinguished himself in his poetical output, through the conventional theme of *madīh*, praise of the Prophet.[151] Our earliest example of Timbuktu poetry is a work written in the mid-sixteenth century by Sīdi Yaḥya al-Tadulsi in commemoration of his master Muḥammad al-Kāburi.[152] This poetical form was also bound by conventions but it afforded ample scope for self-expression and imagery. The chroniclers have perhaps greatly overemphasized the pious themes in literature in their attempt to impart an aura of sanctity on the history of their city. The author of *Tārīkh al-Fattāsh*, for example, mentions the forty-eighth and fiftieth chapters of *Maqāmāt al-Harīrī* in such a casual way as to give the impression that all his local readers would be familiar with them.[153] Nonetheless, there is no doubt whatsoever that the learning process, whatever its practical implications for the social standing of the literati among the elite of the city, was built around religious rather than secular themes.

Hierarchy of learned status

A key to understanding the position of scholars in Timbuktu lies in the existence of a pyramidal socio-educational order in which the criteria of respectability and status ranged from mere command of literacy at the base to full erudition at the pinnacle. To begin with, there were great distinctions in prestige among the learned themselves including the possibility already mentioned that full-fledged jurists (*fuqahā'*) were more highly honoured than the main body of scholars (*'ulamā'*). Secondly, there was another socio-educational stratum comprising elementary school teachers (*mu'allims*), mosque functionaries (especially *mu'adhdhins*), scribes and governmental secretaries (*kātibs*) besides a horde of *Alfas* whose livelihood was partly enhanced by their education. These all enjoyed a level of learning approaching and sometimes equalling that of the scholars. Thirdly, it seems that the entire body of comfortable craftsmen and retail traders, forming a 'respectable stratum' in society, gave their sons one degree of literacy or another in the Qur'ānic schools (*maktabs*). By virtue of its aspirations to the advancement of its sons through education, this stratum naturally looked to the scholars for leadership and patronage.

Among the scholars themselves it is nearly impossible to reconstruct fully the hierarchy of prestige, even in the most richly documented periods, because of the selectivity of the sources. Aḥmad Bāba's biographical dictionary, for example, was intended for a wide Muslim audience to cover the most prominent scholars of the Māliki school in North Africa and Egypt, besides the Sūdān. Accordingly, the sections on Timbuktu are concerned strictly with the most erudite and, even then, the omission of Aḥmad Maghia, not to mention others, is remarkable. Similarly, al-Sa'di records the obituaries of some 50 scholars, along with some 20 notables who must have included a substantial proportion of scholars, for the period beginning with the Moroccan conquest in 1592 up to the completion of his chronicle in 1655. But a considerable proportion of these were relatives, friends and neighbours of al-Sa'di and his father. Accordingly, they contribute only in the most indirect way to assessing the number of those who fully qualify to the title of scholar. His genealogical evidence on the major families supplements the picture, but it remains a fact that many of the scholars whose testimony is cited on Songhai times in *Tārīkh al-Fattāsh* are not identifiable in any other source.

At the risk of a considerable margin of error we may perhaps estimate the leadership of the class of literati in Timbuktu, comprising fully qualified scholars, at some 200–300 in the sixteenth century. As much as half of the scholars, however, may have been drawn from a limited number of families, though the rest represented a wider spectrum of kinship groups. Thus, in the second half of the sixteenth century, the Aqīt and And-Agh-Muḥammad families contributed together some 15–20 prominent scholars, all belonging roughly to the same generation. A century later, or rather shortly after 1700 A.D., the Kidādu (Gidādo), Baghayughu and Maghia families contributed a yet larger number of prominent scholars. The latter detail is particularly interesting since by that time the body of scholars may have declined, along with the general fortunes of the city, to half of what it used to be. Despite the continued decline, the evidence of Caillié and Barth, coupled with that of a brief chronicle dating to around 1800 A.D., suggests that the influx of Kunta, Fulāni and other scholars from neighbouring clans, or at least their yearly residence in Timbuktu at the time of the caravan season in fall and winter, sustained the body of scholars at an appreciable numerical strength.[154]

The group usually gave recognition to a single individual as the most erudite of his time, but not necessarily to one of the holders of the major posts. For even during Maḥmūd b. 'Umar's long tenure in the judgeship (up to 1548 A.D.), when he was virtual ruler of the city, he may have been overshadowed in learning by the Tuareg Masūfa scholar al-'Āqib b. 'Abdullāh al-Anṣamuni. Aḥmad Bāba attributes to the latter the composition of a *risāla* entitled *al-Jawāb al-Majdūd 'ala As'ilat al-Qādi Muhammad b. Mahmūd.* This, as its title implies, was an answer to queries on the application of the law made to Anṣamuni by al-Qāḍi Muḥammad, Judge of Timbuktu from 955 to 972 A.H. Quite possibly, however, the treatise was addressed to Maḥmūd b. 'Umar himself, rather than to his son Muḥammad, for al-Anṣamuni appears to have died around 950 A.H. (1543/4 A.D.) while al-Qāḍi Maḥmūd was still alive.[155] Somewhere before that time, during Askia Muḥammad's reign, al-Anṣamuni's *fatwas* (formal legal opinions) were sought out by the Songhai ruler and led to the composition of a treatise entitled *Ajwibat al-Faqīr 'an As'ilat al-Amīr.*[156] It is not unreasonable to assume that this scholar influenced Askia Muḥammad in his organization of the Songhai empire. For, while al-Anṣamuni took some interest in parochial organization of towns and larger villages, as we shall see in the following chapter, Askia Muḥammad was remembered for having first introduced the institution of the judgeship in Jenne and 'other towns which deserved it'.[157] Al-Anṣamuni found equals in erudition in Makhlūf b. Ṣālih al-Balbāli and Ayd Aḥmad al-Tazikhti, both widely travelled scholars who taught in Hausaland besides studying in North Africa and the east. Aḥmad Bāba recalls live disputations in Timbuktu in which al-Anṣamuni, combining the influence of al-Suyūṭi and al-Maghīli, appears to have held the opinions most valued.[158] However, neither he nor any of the scholars of his generation left an imprint on Timbuktu equal to that of Maḥmūd b. 'Umar. The latter, living to the venerable age of 85 after a long teaching and juridicial career, acquired the image of a saint (*walī*) after his death and his tomb remained a place of pilgrimage venerated in Timbuktu and throughout the area.

The period towards the very end of the sixteenth century affords us the best picture of the hierarchy of prestige among scholars because the upheaval caused by the Moroccan conquest brought to the fore scholars of the second and third rank whose identity would otherwise not be fully known. At that time, leadership was in the hands of a 'triumverate' consisting of 'Abu Ḥafs 'Umar Aqīt, Muḥammad Baghayughu and Aḥmad Maghia. 'Umar, being the eldest living son of Maḥmūd b. 'Umar, stood to inherit the 'temporal' leadership of Timbuktu, while Muḥammad Baghayughu was certainly accorded higher recognition for the wide scope of his learning. Aḥmad Maghia, on the other hand, overshadowed them both in terms of the influence he commanded throughout the area, judging by the fact that he, like Maḥmūd b. 'Umar, was accorded the status of *walī* after his death. The court of his tomb (*rawda*) became a place of refuge and immunity from persecution throughout the seventeenth and eighteenth centuries.[159] His memory may have been accorded this honour because he fell a 'martyr' at the hands of the Moroccans following the uprising against them; however it is remarkable that he alone among the three so far mentioned is accorded the title of Mufti.[160] This may suggest that his legal opinions were widely sought, especially, it seems, in the areas stretching westwards towards his original home of Walāta.

Second in rank after the above three, we count several scholars, beginning with Abu Muḥammad 'Abdullāh b. Aḥmad Boryo who, besides being a grammarian and a linguist, is also accorded the title of Mufti.[161] The same generation boasted of two outstanding scholars in al-Amīn b. Aḥmad, eulogized for his knowledge of the *sahāba* (the Prophet's companions on whose testimonies the study of *hadīth* rested) and his half-brother 'Abd al-Raḥmān b. Aḥmad al-Mujtahid whose honorific nickname invokes the memory of the earliest jurists in Islam and may suggest that he favoured independent reasoning (*ijtihad*, as distinct from *taqlīd* or emulation) for elaboration and interpretation of revelation.[162] Naturally, Muḥammad b. Aḥmad b. 'Abd al-Raḥmān, of the al-Ḥājj family, who was raised to the judgeship by the Moroccan conquerors, ranked high in the hierarchy of prestige. The same was true of Ḥabīb b. Muḥammad Bāba who declined the judgeship when offered him by the Moroccans though that entailed the payment of a full 400 *mithqāls* simply to be relieved of the responsibility.[163] The latter, it seems, was the son of the erudite Muḥammad Bāba b. Muḥammad al-Amīn who was approaching the age of 70 at this juncture and no doubt also occupied a leading position in the hierarchy. His age-grade included Ṣāliḥ Takun, a Soninke scholar and author of a commentary on *Mukhtasar Khalīl*, whose intercession on behalf of citizens at the Songhai court is reported to have always been rewarded with success. Similar influence, even to the extent of being acknowledged *walī* in his lifetime, was commanded by Mūsa 'Aryān al-Ra's, especially it seems in the wake of the Moroccan conquest, when he dissipated a considerable fortune purchasing slaves to grant them their freedom.[164] Finally, Muḥammad Zankanu b. Abkar al-Maddāh, whose son al-Faqīh al-Mukhtār patronized the *Muddāh* and procured yearly shipments for the purpose from Jenne, probably enjoyed equal ranking to Maḥmūd Ka't, highly influential in Gao, to Muḥammad Gidādu al-Fulāni, *imām* of the Main Mosque at the time of the conquest, and to Siḍḍīq b. Muḥammad Ta'alla al-Kāburi, who shortly succeeded him.[165] To these we need only add Muḥammad b. Muḥammad Kara who attained the imamate of Sankore and paved the way for the emergence of his son, al-Qāḍi Muḥammad, as a major figure in the succeeding generation.

Leaving aside those scholars who were brothers, cousins and distant cousins of individuals already mentioned above, the third and the widest rank in the pyramidal hierarchy was comprised of fully qualified scholars covered only incidentally in the sources. Thus, the *imām* of the Market Mosque (*jamiʾ al-Suq*) is not even named, though his presence was probably required at all major meetings of the body of scholars. The *imām* of the mosque of the Tuātis, on the other hand, is referred to as Maḥmūd b. Muḥammad al-Zagharāni, his *nisba* suggesting Songhai descent.[166] Al-Saʿdi mentions among his own relatives and in-laws certain scholars who probably did not attain the rank which he himself enjoyed half a century later. They include his father, ʿAbdullāh b. ʿAmir, whose *sanad* was apparently traced backwards to al-Imām Ibrāhīm al-Zalafi, al-Shaikh Tamat al-Wankari, whose Wangara family of scholars seems distinct from the Baghayughu, and al-Sayyid ʿAbd al-Raḥmān b. al-Imām al-Qāḍi Sayyid ʿAli al-Anṣāri, whose father may have discharged the religious and legal affairs of the Tuareg Kel Antasar while resident in Timbuktu.[167] Al-Saʿdi's family also enjoyed intermarriage links with the grandsons of al-Sharīf Aḥmad al-Ṣaqali, among whom al-Shaikh Muḥammad b. ʿUthmān and Bāba b. ʿUmar played a leading role in the resistance to the Moroccans and fell 'martyrs' in the process.[168] Otherwise, we have reference in the pedigrees of their sons and grandsons to al-Mukhtār, Shaikh of the *muddah*, ʿAbdullāh Siri b. al-Imām Sayyid ʿAli al-Jazūli, al-Faqīh Abu Bakr al-Ghadāmsi and al-Faqīh Ṣālih Wankara. These, it should be emphasized, were not equal in stature to such educators as ʿAbd al-Mawla al-Jalāli, ʿUthmān al-Filāli and Muḥammad Kab b. Jābir Kab who were made famous by the erudition of their students. Nor were they equal to Muṣṭafa b. Misir And-ʿUmar, Muḥammad Bāba Misir al-Dalīmi, ʿUthmān b. Muḥammad b. Muḥammad Danbu Sili al-Fulāni and ʿAli Sili b. Abu Bakr b. Shihāb al-Walāti, who are mentioned in their own right. Nonetheless, they and all the above-mentioned are to be differentiated from such lesser literati as Alfa Muḥammad Wuld Adidar and Alfa Kunbaʿali who formed part of a delegation sent to the Moroccan Sulṭān.[169] Those referred to in the seventeenth-century chronicles as Alfa, it seems, belonged to an intermediate rank between fully qualified scholars and the whole range of literate persons in the city.

Focusing above on the hierarchy of prestige which pertained at the time of the Moroccan conquest in 1591, our discussion has rested so far on the assumption that this highly documented period is illustrative of later times. In the mid-seventeenth century, for example, Muḥammad b. Aḥmad b. Maḥmūd Baghayughu al-Wangari, occupied such a pre-eminent position that his death in 1066 A.H. (1655 A.D.) was construed as symbolizing the very extinction of that procession of erudition which gave Timbuktu its fame in its classical period.[170] Yet, while his brother's sons and grandsons achieved highly venerated positions in their own times, he himself was equalled in stature by Muḥammad Gurdu, ʿAbd al-Raḥmān b. Aḥmad Maghia and Muḥammad al-Wadīʿa b. Saʿīd b. Muḥammad Gidādu al-Fulāni. A century later, around 1750 A.D., Abu ʿAbdullāh Bābīr b. Aḥmad

b. Ibrāhīm b. 'Abdullāh b. Aḥmad Maghia earned the praise in *Tadhkirat al-Nasyān* of being 'the unique of his age', an honorific previously accorded only to Aḥmad Bāba and Muḥammad Baghayughu b. Muḥammad Gurdu.[171] Yet, a series of obituaries recorded around 1800 under the title of *Dhikr al-Wafayāt*, shows him only to have been one among equals, his main distinction being his assumption of the judgeship.[172] Even in the early twentieth century, Paul Marty recorded biographical notes on several prominent scholars in Timbuktu which showed that gradations of prestige and influence continued to be subtle and multi-faceted.[173] In the meantime, the pyramidal stratification of the literati remained strong, though the distinction between full-fledged scholars and other Alfas became less clear-cut.[174]

The rank and file of the literati comprised an extensive and heterogeneous group widely varying in its educational attainments. On the one hand they included well-to-do merchants who earned prestige, despite their limited education, by their attendance in the circles of scholars and their patronage of needy students and Alfas. On the other hand, the main body of the group was made up of retailers and craftsmen, especially members of the tailoring craft, whose means did not allow them to devote their full energies towards a complete education. From the sixteenth century on, a substantial portion of the latter came to be identified, by virtue of their specialization in laudatory poetry on the Prophet Muḥammad, as 'Praise Singers' or *Muddāh*. In that capacity they were entitled to some support made through alms at the mosques by wealthy scholars and notables as well as to gifts made on the occasion of Ramaḍān by state officials. The title 'Shaikh al-Maddāhīn' seems to refer to an acknowledged notable among the group, a literatus often drawn from one of the leading families.[175]

The corporation of tailors, if it was at all organized along corporative lines, occupied a unique position in the status stratification of society. For, whether by design or custom, or a combination of both, it was historically open only to alfas and would-be alfas. In a sense, this trade acted as a safety valve for those students with modest means who devoted themselves to study over several years without having a secure source of livelihood. In some cases, they were apprenticed to a master-tailor, himself a literatus, who provided them with a Muslim education besides a skill in the craft. In adulthood, tailoring, along with some commerce in textiles, could become the main means of income for an Alfa or, failing that, it could supplement his income from alms besides scribal and notarial activities.[176]

In view of their special position, it is not surprising that *Tārīkh al-Fattāsh* has left us some quantitative evidence concerning the tailors. It states that in the late sixteenth century Timbuktu boasted of 26 tailoring houses (*tindi*), each having an average of 50 apprentices serving under its master, while some of them had as many as 70 or 100. This piece of information, cited on the authority of a certain Muḥammad b. Mawlūd, was intended to emphasize the high value placed on learning in pre-Ruma times. It seems rather doubtful that the tailoring houses supported a full 1300 apprentices. The master in these houses is described at once as a Shaikh, Ra'īs (chief) and Mu'allim.[177] This suggests that his 'apprentices' included adults among the literati who, well beyond the stage of training, attached themselves to his establishment in order to secure their supply of textiles.[178] No doubt also, the tailoring establishments provided shelter and sustenance for students who came to the city from elsewhere until such time as they completed their studies or secured an independent source of income. Otherwise, the extensiveness of the tailoring craft is not surprising, though by the first two decades of the present century the city could boast of no more than five or six tailoring houses.[179] Textiles of various sorts accounted for a substantial percentage of the value of all commodities imported to West Africa through the trans-Saharan trade. Local manufactures were not unknown, judging by the importation of cotton and the general availability of wool in the area. But while most manufactures originated in Morocco and the east in the early periods, European and Hausa products from Kano increasingly found their way to Timbuktu in the eighteenth and nineteenth centuries.[180]

The tailor–alfas undoubtedly enjoyed a higher level of education than the members of other trades. They belonged to the same status stratum, in terms of socio-educational criteria, as elementary school teachers (*mu'allims*), mosque functionaries (*mu'adhdhins*) and scribes and lesser secretaries (*kātibs*). Of the status of *mu'allims*, hardly anything is known besides the reference to the exceptionally prestigious Mu'allim 'Ali Takariyya. Additionally, the anonymous author of *Tadhkirat al-Nasyān* in the eighteenth century refers to his grandfather, Alfa al-Amīn b. Muḥammad Mūdu, who died in 1657, as an 'instructor of youths' (*mu'allim al-sibyān*).[181] It is rather interesting that none of the earlier chroniclers devotes a biography or an obituary to his elementary school teacher; indeed, in the case of none of the prominent scholars is the name of a *mu'allim* listed among his teachers. This could either mean that the prominent scholars received their earliest training in their homes or else that the status of *mu'allims* was not sufficiently high to earn them attention in the chronicles. Towards the nineteenth century, however, and especially at its end, common adherence to the same Sufi confraternity (Tijāniyya or Qādiriyya) may have reduced the distinction between *mu'allims* and full-fledged scholars.

It would be hazardous to estimate the numerical strength of the rank-and-file literati beyond what is known about the tailoring houses. The group was broadly defined in terms of its acquisition of some learning in *tafsīr* and *hadīth* beyond the level of elementary schools. Some who received such training went on, often past their middle years, to become scholars. Others fully devoted their energies to tailoring or became mosque functionaries or scribes. Based on his participation in the life of Timbuktu around the turn of the century, Dupuis-Yakouba observed that, by virtue of the frequency of commercial correspondence, scribes could readily find employment.[182] Sometimes they served as assistants to the judge or one of the *imāms*, though most often the latter 'employed' the most promising among their students. Another avenue of deriving an income was to seek employment as secretary (*kātib*) to one of the state officials. Secretaries to the Songhai monarchs, and later to the Pashas of Timbuktu, were sometimes drawn from among the ranks of accomplished scholars. But provincial governors and the chiefs of the quarters and of neighbouring clans (if the latter were not themselves scholars enjoying the services of their students) had to satisfy themselves with the less qualified literati to assist them in their correspondence.

The sustenance of an exceptionally large number of literati in Timbuktu was made possible in part by occasional and yearly contributions from the rulers and state officials. The precedent for this may have been set as early as the visit of Mansa Mūsa in the fourteenth century, but it was Askia Muḥammad who was long remembered for his patronage of Muslim scholarship. Of his time in the early sixteenth century, Leo Africanus wrote:

> Here in Timbuktu there are great stores of doctors, judges, priests and other learned men, bountifully maintained at the king's cost and charges. And hither are brought divers manuscripts or written books out of Barbary, which are sold for more money than any other merchandise.[183]

Traditions dating to the nineteenth century which have been incorporated into the defective copy of *Tārīkh al-Fattāsh* have exaggerated the generosity of Askia Muḥammad to the extent of shedding some doubt on his administrative acumen. They claim, for example, that he bestowed the plantations of a whole region (*nāhiya*), including several villages, on the Sharīf Aḥmad al-Ṣaqali.[184] Such extravagant claims, however, are unique to the nineteenth century and are not reconcilable with earlier evidence.[185]

Nonetheless, it appears probable that the Askias made donations to the most prominent scholars who, in turn, contributed to the sustenance of a large number of needy students and Alfas. At the height of Songhai wealth and power, Askia Daūd set up farms manned by 30 slaves (presumably in each farm) devoted to the maintenance of the poor of Timbuktu.[186] Whether from these farms or additionally, he is recorded to have dispatched 4000 measures of grain (*sūniyyas*), on a yearly basis, to be distributed by al-Qāḍi al-'Āqib.[187] At that time, in the fifteenth century, the wealth of Timbuktu was such that two scholars were able to make donations of an equal value for the upkeep of the poor.[188] In the eighteenth century, however, the sum involved often exceeded the total taxation extracted from the city's merchants.[189] But despite the decline, a tradition survived whereby the Pashas made yearly gifts in the form of textiles at the end of Ramaḍān to the body of scholars and especially to the *Muddāh*.[190] Even in the nineteenth century, Aḥmad b. Aḥmad Lobbo, ruler of Massina and nominal sovereign over Timbuktu, dispatched to the city considerable gifts of grain. Aḥmad al-Bakkā'i alone received 800 *sūniyyas* despite the great tension between him and the monarch.[191] The contributions of rulers do not seem to have been made in the form of stable endowments, such as *hubūs*, which allotted revenues of a specific estate for the maintenance of the literati. Nonetheless, their rendition on a yearly basis during the month of Ramaḍān enjoyed the full force of custom and secured for the city 'repatriation' of a substantial portion of the taxes collected from its merchants.

Outside the small body of scholars and the much wider stratum of lesser literati, the chronicles have left us a unique piece of evidence concerning the extent of literacy in sixteenth-century Timbuktu. This occurs in *Tārīkh al-Fattāsh*, which reports that Timbuktu housed as many as 150–180 Qur'ānic schools (*maktabs*) in the last years of the Songhai regime.[192] The statement, in the context where it occurs, has certain important implications. First, the extensive number of schools, coupled with the data on the craft of tailors, served the seventeenth-century author as one of the major criteria for measuring the high fortunes attained by Timbuktu in the sixteenth century. This, at once, emphasizes the value placed in society upon literacy as a first step towards learning and erudition. Secondly, since the *Fattāsh* was completed sometime after 1665, its author implicitly indicates that the decline in literacy and learning which was to accompany the slow demographic decline of the city was already apace in the mid-seventeenth century. This fully confirms the evidence known from elsewhere that the Moroccan conquerors (Ar. *al-Rumāt*, locally Ruma or Arma), though contributing large numbers to the declining population, took little interest in learning.[193] Thirdly, the statement concerning the schools is made upon the authority of a certain al-Shaikh Muḥammad b. Aḥmad (possibly Muḥammad b. Aḥmad Baghayughu) who is said to have 'seen' them.[194] This, and the fact that the Songhai period was still live in the memory of traditionalists who had lived then, lends considerable credibility to the testimony.

The fact, otherwise, that some 150 *mu'allims*, each having his own Qur'ānic school, practised their trade in Timbuktu during the late sixteenth century need not be doubted. The chronicles mention in passing numerous scholars and literati who were not prominent enough to have specific biographies or obituaries devoted to them. The problem, however, lies in the fact that the author of *Tārīkh al-Fattāsh* gives us an inflated impression of the enrolment of these schools, for he suggests that one of these schools, belonging to Mu'allim Takariyya, enrolled as many as 200 students at one time. Al-Shaikh Muḥammad is recorded to have visited that school on a Wednesday, the day of the week when students brought to the headmaster donations from their parents in lieu of tuition. He later recalled: 'I looked around at the writing boards used by the boys in the court of his house and counted of them one hundred and thirty boards. I guessed that the whole of the Qur'ān might have been transcribed on these boards.'[195] While the text of *al-Fattāsh* suggests that Mu'allim Takariyya's school was exceptionally large, the author does not give us any direct idea concerning the average enrolment of other schools. Accordingly, we may be free to assume that of a total of some 150 schools, each had an average of some 50 students. This would give us a total elementary student population of some 7500. Possibly basing himself on the above data, Cissoko estimated the population of Timbuktu during the late sixteenth century at 75 000.[196]

The possibility that the elementary students comprised one-tenth of the population seems acceptable but does not directly help us assess the population of the city as a whole. For we have no information on the age distribution of the inhabitants at any one time nor do we know how long students remained enrolled in primary schools. Many probably enrolled for several years, and thereby secured full command of literacy, but others were able to attend for two or three years only. Their numbers, and especially in the 10–20 age bracket, were considerably augmented by outsiders to the city. These came from neighbouring towns and villages, as well as from the nomadic Barābīsh, Tuareg, Sanhāja and Fulānis who sent their sons for learning to Timbuktu. In practice, though not in theory, the literacy schools were beyond the reach of certain sectors of the population, including the sons of slaves, porters and street vendors, besides the servile agricultural groups living at the outskirts. In the *maktab* of Mu'allim Takariyya, the voluntary tuition ranged from five to ten cowry shells a week, a modest sum which over several years, however, could impose a financial burden on some of the more modest traders and craftsmen.[197] There is no doubt that some of the lesser schools were subsidized by the wealthy merchants and scholars, but in some cases these need not have served more than 15 students at a time.[198] By and large, we are inclined to believe that the *maktabs* enrolled an average of 25 students each, the total elementary student population never exceeding 4000–5000.

Our own rough estimate of up to 50 000 inhabitants for the population of Timbuktu during the late sixteenth century is based on a wide range of indirect evidence. This includes various indications concerning the size of merchant caravans and armies in the area, along with economic data which lend themselves only with great difficulty to systematization. Particularly significant is the comparative evidence on the size of cities throughout the Sudan which suggests, among other things, that Timbuktu was of equal demographic strength to Jenne, and that both fell short of the size of the Songhai capital, Gao, in the late sixteenth century. The author of *Tārīkh al-Fattāsh* mentions, for example, on the authority of a certain al-Shaikh Muḥammad b. 'Ali Drāmi, an argument which once took place in Gao at the time of Askia al-Ḥājj II with youths from Hausaland. The latter claimed that their metropolis of Kano was greater than any of the cities of the Songhai empire. This it seems led their opponents in Gao, including some resident youths from Timbuktu, to count the houses of the Songhai capital to a total of 7626 permanent structures, excluding straw huts on the outskirts of the city. Considering the patriarchal organization of commercial urban centres and the extensiveness of many households, this figure has often been used as evidence that Gao boasted some 75 000 inhabitants.[199] And indeed, when the evacuation of Gao was contemplated as a defensive measure at the time of the Moroccan conquest, it was asserted that 2000 boats, at the least, would be available for the purpose.[200] Other particulars from the sources unmistakably lead us to believe that the demographic growth of Timbuktu under the Songhai regime was not comparable to that of Gao, just as its decline after the Moroccan conquest was not as dramatic. Naturally, no definitive statements can be made on this subject, but it seems safe nonetheless to assume that the population of Timbuktu never exceeded 50 000 inhabitants.

Secondly, we have the evidence of the early European explorers and travellers. These visited Timbuktu at a time in the nineteenth century when the city had long been experiencing a process of decline. The most reliable among the early estimates, though conservative in range, was that made by Henry Barth in 1854 of 13 000–23 000 inhabitants. This was essentially confirmed by Lenz in 1877 when he placed the population at 18 000–20 000. Barth learned that the city had been twice as large in the past, presumably during Songhai and early Ruma times.[201] The topographical evidence which he and others observed shows indeed that a large part of the city had been gradually abandoned over the centuries. According to mid-nineteenth-century informants, the Sankore Mosque which stands at the northwest corner of the city had once been well within the limits of the built-up section. Likewise, the tomb of Maḥmūd b. 'Umar Aqīt, which stands half a mile north of the city's limits, had once been within it.[202] Remains of previous buildings stretching far to the north of the city are still quite evident though interspersed on account of the accumulating sand. These areas, as we believe, were probably abandoned during the late seventeenth and early eighteenth centuries.[203] Even in the nineteenth century, some portions of the city, principally to the south, were abandoned at a time when the trans-Saharan trade, and especially the Arwān–Timbuktu axis, was gradually succumbing to other trade routes.[204] Estimates which place the population at some 5000–10 000 at the time of the French conquest may be somewhat haphazard; but they reflect a further downward trend which was slightly reversed in the twentieth century.[205]

The main implication of the evidence surveyed above is that a minimal command of literacy was universal among all but the poorest sections of the free population. Indeed, Caillié observed after visiting the city in the early nineteenth century that 'all the negroes of Timbuktu are able to read the Koran and even know it by heart'.[206] The literate population probably included most of the male retail traders who, along with women active in the market, supported half to two-thirds of the inhabitants at any single time. Unfortunately, we have no detailed breakdown of the craftsmen and small-merchant community in precolonial times beyond indications that masons, leather-workers and tanners, tailors, butchers and muleteers, as well as inn-keepers, enjoyed guild-type organizations. These groups, and to a lesser extent silver- and wood-workers (manufacturers of jewellery, tools and utensils), were strongly integrated into the social order dominated by scholars. To them may be added commercial brokers (*teifa*), expert measurers of grain and precious metal, as well as the specialized scribes whose function was to mark the slabs of salt arriving in the seasonal caravans before their export further south.[207] In all these cases, command of literacy may have enhanced the individual's capacity in his trade, especially as virtually all craftsmen were merchants in those commodities which became the raw material for their manufactures. However, the main value of a childhood education in the *maktabs*, lacking as it does formal training in arithmetic or book-keeping, was perceived in terms of the pious purpose of securing some knowledge of Muslim precepts as well as a certain level of respectability among the established families of the city.

Given the extent to which the quest for literacy and learning permeated the whole city, the scholars naturally stood in a highly venerated position. Currents of intergenerational mobility, which were persistent though slow over the centuries, acted as a barrier against their differentiation into an upper caste of some sort defined by ethnic criteria. The influence of neighbouring nomadic societies, where differentiation between 'clerical' and other clans took place, tends to complicate the picture, especially in the eighteenth and nineteenth centuries. These factors, the influence of wealth, and the distinction between military and learned elites will be discussed more fully in Chapter 5. Before turning to that subject, however, we will address ourselves to the 'administrative' and related role of scholars in Chapter 4.

At this point, it is possible at least to say that the Songhai sector in the city's population did not contribute to the highest ranks of learning as much as the Soninke, Sanḥāja, Tuareg (Masūfa) or Malinke (Wangara) sectors. Indeed, even the Fulāni – a small minority in the population of the city up to around 1600 – were more prominent among the highest ranks of scholarship in Timbuktu than the Songhai. Perhaps the Songhai themselves were a small minority in the population of Timbuktu up to and including the Songhai period in the sixteenth century. Another possible explanation is that the Ka't scholars, who are conventionally identified as Soninke, were in fact Songhai. Regrettably, we cannot be certain on this point – nor are we sure about the ethnic identity of many scholars featured early in the sources. What is evident is that the Songhai, in the seventeenth and eighteenth centuries at least, came to be seen as a 'military elite', much like the Ruma. In all probability, the scholars among them tended to lose their ethnic Songhai identity, but not their language, much as among the Maghsharen Tuareg who settled at Timbuktu.

CHAPTER 4

The scholars as administrators

Investigation of the administrative functions of scholars in Timbuktu confronts us with by far the most problematical aspects of their activities. The difficulty arises mainly from the fact that they controlled a rather limited number of public posts and yet they were custodians over every aspect of society and state which was governed by the Islamic Sharī'a. This factor complicates the relationship between military–fiscal elites and the religio-legal administration throughout Islam, but it is particularly important in the context of the Sūdān. For the purpose of this study, it means that the politico-administrative impact of the scholars transcends the few posts they occupied and encompasses functions which they appear to discharge *de facto* when in reality these too are sanctioned by the Sharī'a.

Though the administrative tenets of the Sharī'a cannot be discussed at length here, it should perhaps be pointed out that Muslim political theory, originating in idealistic conceptions of a divinely guided community, did not evolve a complete and consistent system regulating social integration and delegation of authority.[1] The Ḥanafi and, to a lesser extent, the Shāfi'i schools did tend towards an organic view of Islam as governed by the organizing authority of the early rulers, as successors to the Prophet, *khalīfas* or caliphs. Even there, however, the stipulations specifically spelled out concerned only a few major posts, including viziers, provincial governors, *Qāḍis*, *Ḥukkām al-Maẓālim*, *Imāms* and *Muḥtasibs*.[2] In many areas, some of these posts, excepting provincial governors, *Qāḍis* and *Imāms*, did not make an appearance or else tended to take local titles and forms. This was particularly true in areas where Mālikism was predominant because the classical jurists of this school did not evolve an elaborate jurisprudential system. Ibn Khaldūn attributes this phenomenon to the relative underdevelopment of urbanism in North Africa, where the school had its main exponents and the greatest numbers of adherents.[3] Additionally, it seems that the ideological orientation of the founders, beginning with Mālik b. Anas, influenced the future development of the school as well as its potential spread in various regions.[4] In essence, the later jurists of this school had greater options to choose from, whether from practices of other schools, or by reference to the original sources of Muslim legislation, especially the voluminous compendia of the prophet's *hadīths*. This factor was of considerable importance for the spread of Islam and the growth of Muslim learning in the Sūdān. The prevalence of Mālikism there was originally a function of early commercial contact with the North African Maghrib and, to a lesser extent, the impact of the Almoravid movement in the Western Sudan.[5] However, even in the central Sudan, where interaction with Egypt was historically much stronger, Mālikism also established its prevalence at an early date.[6] Whatever the case may be, it seems quite evident that scholars operating within the Māliki tradition in the Sūdān sought to evolve such systems as were reconcilable with local customs and needs on basis of the broad frameworks of Islam.

The central feature of the system which arose in Timbuktu was the fact that the judge enjoyed an acknowledged ascendency over the entire civilian population of the city. We do not know to what extent this had parallels elsewhere, whether in the Sūdān or across the Sahara.[7] However, while the situation in Walāta and Jenne seems comparable, it is probable that the authority of judges in the Middle East and, to a lesser extent, North Africa, had witnessed some erosion, on the symbolic scale at least.[8] We learn from Ibn Khaldūn, and others, that the custom whereby *imāms* had been invested in their posts by judges had been a feature of early Islam which was outmoded by the late fourteenth century.[9] In Timbuktu the custom survived at least up to the mid-eighteenth century and probably well into the nineteenth century.[10] This practice in effect meant that the parochial leadership of Timbuktu, which was vested in the *imāms* and especially in the *Imām* of the Main Mosque, was essentially independent of the rulers. For although the Judge was himself formally appointed by the ruler, this was largely a theoretical premise because selection of the Judge ultimately devolved upon the body of scholars. It will be suggested in the sections shortly to follow that the judgeship occupied a central position in the integration of Timbuktu society.

Before proceeding, we should perhaps explain that the administration of Timbuktu, insofar as the scholars were concerned, was characterized by implicit emphasis on reciprocity in the delegation of authority. This no doubt had some bearing on the concept of consensus (*ijmā'*) which had been central to the classical legislative process in Islam.[11] Thus, the *imāms* were formally invested by the Judge but they cannot in any way be conceived as his deputies or inferiors. Similarly, the factors of erudition and piety would have made it impossible for a judge to adopt a posture of superiority *vis-à-vis* other accomplished scholars. This, perhaps more than anything else, helped sharpen the distinction between the fluid hierarchy led by the scholars and the stricter system governing the military elites. Furthermore, it seems that the same factor imparted a strong element of stability upon the various *liens* which linked the scholars to the society at large. Implicitly recognized criteria of prerogative and precedence governed the entire social and economic life of Timbuktu. The market organization and the chieftaincies of the various wards are factors on which little information is available. Nonetheless, these and the professional and age-set associations form important though subtle links in a complex of relationships which made it possible for Timbuktu to achieve a certain sense of order and unity without the need for an elaborate hierarchy.

The institution of the judgeship: al-qaḍā'

The institution of the judgeship which evolved in Timbuktu drew its strengths largely from its dual character as a representative of state authority in the city on the one hand and as spokesman for the whole city *vis-à-vis* the rulers on the other hand. This duality is best exemplified during the Fulāni regime when Timbuktu acknowledged the sovereignty of Ḥamdullāhi. When Barth visited Timbuktu at that time he found that the city had two judges. One represented the interest of the capital, and was appointed by the ruler, while the other stood for the interests of the city and was drawn from the ranks of the Timbuktu scholars.[12] Significantly, the governmental appointee is barely mentioned in the contemporary sources; he does not figure in later lists of the judges either. By contrast, the locally elected judge, Muḥammad b. Muḥammad b. 'Uthmān al-Kāburi, better known as Sān Sirfi (or Shirfi), became one of the most influential figures in the nineteenth century.[13] At most other times, Timbuktu had only one judge who combined governmental authority with city-wide leadership: the seal of governmental approval strengthened the position of the Judge and gave added weight to his decisions and court judgements. However, the impact of the judgeship as an instrument of urban autonomy or administration by scholars far outweighed its role as an extension of state authority.

The scholars availed themselves of certain principles among the various non-binding stipulations of the Māliki school which together tended to fortify the position of the Judge. Among these stipulations perhaps the most important was the principle that the *Qāḍi* should enjoy intimate knowledge of the constituency he judges.[14] This translated itself in the fact that all scholars who attained the post were native to the city and, moreover, tended to be drawn from the ranks of the long-established families. Thus, although we hear that al-Qāḍi al-Ḥājj came to Timbuktu from Walāta, the association of his sons with a *madrasa* of some sort, the Alfa Gungu, suggests a much earlier presence of members of this family in Timbuktu and elsewhere along the Niger bend.[15] As already indicated, similar considerations surround the figure of Muḥammad al-Kāburi and the same would seem to be true of Kātib Mūsa.[16] On the basis of genealogical and other evidence we have chosen to place al-Qāḍi al-Ḥājj, Muḥammad al-Kāburi and Kātib Mūsa, in that sequence, as the first three in our list of the judges in Appendix I.

The evidence on the early periods cannot serve as a basis for generalization concerning the selection of judges. The first judge ever to occupy the post in Jenne, for example, was a Saghanughu settler rather than a native-born Wangara; after migrating to the city northwards from Bīṭu, he simply proved to be the most qualified for holding the post.[17] The subsequent list of known judges in Jenne shows only one attempted case of imposing a *Qāḍi* from outside the circles of established families. This pertains to the period shortly after the Moroccan conquest when Songhai and Ruma sovereignty was still being contested. The evidence is complex but nonetheless requires some attention because it is quite instructive. It seems that the presiding judge at the time of the conquest, Banba Kanāti, had been either reluctant or else cautioned against endorsing the *bī'a* (a formal act of allegiance) to the Moroccan sulṭān. Some of the notables, probably out of fear of retaliation by the Ruma, formally sought the deposition of Kanāti. The Ruma in this case overstepped themselves: they imprisoned the *Qāḍi* in a humiliating way and named in his place a person who must have been a recent settler because al-Sa'di describes him as 'one from among the people of the Maghrib known by the name of Aḥmad al-Filāli'.[18] This turn of events, it seems, enraged the body of scholars, 'people of intelligence who knew the true state of affairs', as al-Sa'di described them, and they no doubt had a hand in what happened shortly thereafter. A body of Songhai troops and supporters made their way to the city and released the imprisoned *Qāḍi* who then apparently preferred to leave Jenne and ultimately settled in the sultanate of Ta'ba. The scholar-notables maintained their reservation concerning the endorsement of either Songhai or Ruma sovereignty, pending the outcome of the military contest.[19] Nonetheless, they proceeded to raise to the judgeship Mūr Mūsa Dābu, a member it seems of a long-established Soninke family in Jenne.[20] Subsequently, the Ruma proved irreversibly to have gained the upper hand, but they refrained from deposing the new judge appointed under the auspices of their opponents. Subsequently, the Dābu family contributed two more members to the judgeship of Jenne though one of them, as we shall shortly see, may not have been fully qualified by his learning.

The only instances in which state authority effectively intervened in the selection of judges at Timbuktu came precisely in the wake of political upheavals. As already suggested, the intervention of the Massina caliphate, which named its own counterpart to the Judge of Timbuktu, was indirect and largely ineffective. Even Sunni 'Ali had been aware of the disadvantages of alienating the body of scholars, but his choice of the prestigious al-Qāḍi Ḥabīb did not in the end reconcile the Timbuktu notables to his policies. The Ruma for their part proved to be no exception to the rule since, being largely drawn from a foreign and in any case distinct military elite in the organization of Moroccan society, they were predisposed to accept a limited and even marginal role in the ordering of urban society in the Sūdān. Indeed, it is interesting to learn that al-Qāḍi 'Umar Aqīt was informed of the swift sequence of events in Jenne mentioned above: he warned the notables of that town against compromising the position of al-Qāḍi Banba Kanāti.[21] As it turned out, this formed part of a series of developments which culminated in the arrest of al-Qāḍi 'Umar himself and his deportation virtually with the entire Aqīt family to Morocco. The Ruma in this case did not press their hand in their choice of a new judge but rather, after considerable deliberation, they induced Muḥammad b. Aḥmad b. al-Qāḍi 'Abd al-Raḥmān, scion of the al-Ḥājj family of judges, to accept the post. The chroniclers of a few decades later are more or less favourable to the memory of al-Qāḍi Muḥammad b. Aḥmad himself. Nonetheless, his acceptance of the post under the circumstances may have created a stigma against his family which helps explain the scarcity of obituary notices on his ancestors and kinsmen.[22]

We might mention other principles in Mālikism which helped raise the Judge in the public eye to a position of veneration and respect. Dignity in comportment, along with reservation in speech and judgement, were part of a whole assembly of ethical standards inculcated into jurists throughout the whole training process. Insight into the inner meaning of things was more desirable than cunning, just as reliance on direct testimony and evidence in court was more important than introspection. It is not clear to what extent individual judges conformed to these norms but the stylized praises which we encounter in the obituaries suggest widespread subscription to an ethical ideal among scholars at large.[23]

Of more practical importance than the above were the two stipulations in Mālikism that the Judge must be widely recognized as knowledgeable in the law, and must enjoy sufficient means and influence to place him above suspicion of accepting bribery and insure implementation of his rulings and decisions.[24] We have by way of exception to the first stipulation the heavy judgement of al-Sa'di that 'Abd al-Raḥmān b. Mūsa Dābu, who succeeded his brother Aḥmad in 1062 A.H. (1651/2 A.D.) to the judgeship of Jenne, was 'a *jāhil* who knew nothing of jurisprudential *ahkām*'.[25] We are not sure what to make of this, especially since al-Sa'di, an otherwise impartial observer of his own times, may have had personal reasons for overstating the case.[26] In any case, the selection of 'Abd al-Raḥmān at a very advanced age, after some 30 years in which the post had been held by his older brother, may have been intended to honour the family of the departed judge. During the remaining few months of his life, 'Abd al-Raḥmān's standing as a highly respected elder may have compensated for his inadequacy as an accomplished jurist. Muḥammad b. Marzūq Mawla al-Huwāri, who succeeded him, probably assisted in the post. The fact that al-Sa'di commented on the ineligibility of 'Abd al-Raḥmān, nonetheless, attests to the insistence of scholars on erudition as the prime qualification to the post. This factor remained crucial throughout the history of Timbuktu partly because Mālikism looked with disfavour upon the delegation of judicial functions to assistants or deputies of the Judge. Indeed, it was stipulated that the creation of any permanent functions in conjunction with the judgeship, presumably because it gave rise to vested interests, invariably leads to corruption.[27]

The stipulation that the *Qāḍi* be a man of some wealth had three important implications. First, it meant that he would not be dependent on the salary (*rātib*) which he was entitled to receive from state revenues. Aḥmad Bāba mentions in one of his treatises that the Judge in Muslim legal practice, or at least in the views of such early jurists as the philosopher–theologian Ibn Rushd (Averroes), was qualified by the nature of his responsibilities to receive remuneration, presumably for himself and for the *imāms* invested by him, from the state treasury. Such remuneration could be received either directly from the ruler or through the agency of an official who is empowered to dispense revenue at his discretion.[28] We do not know what this meant for the organization of Timbuktu since the few references to fiscal arrangement in Songhai times involve the Judge more than the Timbuktu Mundhu. We know of the existence of a Tusur Mundhu in Timbuktu, apparently an official in charge of taxation and imposts, much like the Kabara Farma on the Niger.[29] It is possible that this official surrendered a fixed portion of the revenues to the *Qāḍi* though there is no reference to such practice under the Ruma regime either. Fines and fees which were imposed upon litigants in commercial and inheritance disputes may have augmented the resources of the fluid administration presided over by the Judge. Whatever the case may be, the sources more often mention gifts than salaries and al-Qāḍi Maḥmūd b. ʿUmar is alleged to have distributed to the poor everything which he thus received.[30]

As a second implication, the independent means of the Judge helped place him above suspicions of corruption and favouritism. Throughout the area, the exchange of gifts and their dispatch over long distances from one region to another virtually constituted an important facet of commerce. Accordingly, it is difficult to distinguish the wealth which a judge brought independently with him to his position from that which he later accumulated in the course of his judicial career. Peculiar as this might seem, traditionists in Timbuktu today claim that the eighteenth-century Judge of Arw̃an, al-Wāfi b. Tālibna, actually sanctioned the acceptance of bribes in cases involving disputes over commercial transactions and the taxation of caravans by various clans in the southern Sahara.[31] As often happens in these cases, however, the specific composition in which al-Wāfi's putative *fatwa* was recorded is neither known nor extant. In all probability, the illustrious Judge indulged in some speculation on the theoretical kinship between bribes and disinterested gifts, and this factor made his views a subject of popular misunderstanding.

The third and main implication of the choice of judges from among the wealthy was a tendency for the post to be monopolized by a small circle of families. The 'inheritance' of the post, as it were, by brothers, sons, other kinsmen or in-laws of the deceased judge, or else by his favoured student, became a strong criterion in the succession system.[32] We have been able to assemble a more or less complete list of the Qāḍis from the early fifteenth century to the present.[33] Of a total of 35 known cases of succession we observe that only four judges were directly succeeded by sons as against five cases of succession by a brother. An overriding principle seems to be the fact that a judge who held the post for an exceptionally long time was often succeeded by a son. More commonly, however, the sons of the deceased did not command sufficient seniority in terms of age and veneration and, accordingly, the succession went either to a surviving brother or to a more distant relative or a non-relative especially esteemed for his learning. The result was a certain amount of alternation over the post and its occasional reversion to a family which had previously held it. Thus, a total of six families contributed some two-thirds of the judges of Timbuktu during the past 400–500 years.[34]

It is important to emphasize that the Ruma Pashas, though they formally invested the judges during the seventeenth and eighteenth centuries, had barely any influence on their selection. The overwhelming majority of Ruma hardly enjoyed their tenure of the Pashalik for over a year. Indeed, during the eighteeenth century, and especially towards its end, the Pashalik was often vacant, sometimes for extended periods of time. This all the more strengthened the hand of the judges, and indeed of the *imāms*, as a stabilizing force. It is no wonder then that the judgeship re-established its precedence though, as we shall see, the scholars evolved a vested interest in maintaining a gubernatorial post.

The powers of the judges were enhanced by the fact that they had some influence in all three spheres – the judicial, legislative and executive – which in modern theory are associated with the state. In the legislative sphere, the *qāḍi*'s judgements, though theoretically resting on interpretation of a divine and immutable law, became precedents which future judges would follow. Thus, for example, in his treatise on slavery, the *Mi'rāj al-Su'ūd*, Aḥmad Bāba quotes the Qur'ān, the Ḥadīth and the views of the classical jurists, but he also places a great weight on a judicial precedent set by Maḥmūd b. 'Umar. The jurists were all locally agreed that skin colour had nothing to do with legitimizing slavery; a captive could be reduced to slavery only if he was a non-Muslim or belonged to a group considered 'pagan' and hence beyond the pale of Islam.[35] To this general principle, Maḥmūd b. 'Umar added the stipulation that the captive, rather than his owner, enjoys the benefit of the doubt if he should claim to have been already a Muslim at his capture.[36] This stipulation, of course, had important implications since the distinction between Muslim and non-Muslim groups in the Sūdān often remained a vague and fluid one. Even Askia Muḥammad apparently contemplated sequestering the properties of Sunni 'Ali's heirs and followers on the grounds that his conduct placed him, and by implication them, beyond the pale of Islam.[37] According to al-Sa'di, none of the Songhai wars, excepting Askia Muḥammad's campaign against the Mossi in 904 A.H. (1498/9 A.D.), formally conformed to the prescriptions of *jihād* (or holy war).[38] Yet numerous other struggles were followed by reduction of the defeated parties to slavery. This caused Makhlūf b. Ṣāliḥ al-Balbāli to rule that the wars waged by the Songhai and the various states of Hausaland, like the raids of the nomadic chieftaincies on the fringes of the Sahara, led to indiscriminate enslavement of Muslims and non-Muslims alike. According to this scholar, 'It is not permissible to exercise a right of ownership of any sort on such individuals; liberty should be restored, by judiciary action, to those who originate from, or declare themselves to be natives of, these countries'.[39] It is not clear to what extent a legal opinion rendered formally as a *fatwa* had an effect on actual practice. However, the quasi-legislative power of the judges was shared by the body of scholars as a whole. Certainly, Aḥmad Bāba's views, on matters ranging from the question of customary law to the lawfulness of smoking tobacco, remained a framework of referral among scholars long thereafter.[40] His treatise on slavery, for example, became a basis for a comprehensive condemnation of the trans-Saharan slave-trade by the recent North African scholar, al-Nāṣiri.[41]

The judicial functions *per se* of the Judge were also shared in varying degrees by the general body of scholars. On a *de facto* basis, the scholars settled the frequent disputes which arose among members of their ethnic group or among inhabitants of their own neighbourhood, especially in matters of inheritance. Māliki law stipulated specific shares for wives, sons, parents and sometimes even for other kinsmen of the deceased, depending upon their number.[42] The process was often complicated by the need for selling immovable property to insure its proper distribution and for settling the claims of creditors and commercial partners whenever the estate of a merchant was involved.[43] The scholars acted as expert mediators in such disputes and, since the decision of the Judge alone was binding, they had to remain in close consultation with him. Thus, we are told that Muḥammad Baghayughu allotted a part of every morning for mediating between would-be litigants and often went to the Judge for that purpose. This scholar, who devoted a whole lifetime to the cause of teaching, was 'insistent on serving the affairs of the public and the judges whenever they could find to his intercession no alternative'.[44] On the whole, it seems that the scholars carried out on a *de facto* basis most of the judiciary functions and, as a result, litigation in Timbuktu was reduced to a minimum. This further explains why the judgeship never evolved an elaborate bureaucratic or hierarchical apparatus. The important place reserved for intention in Māliki adjudication meant considerable emphasis on weighing the value of testimonies. It seems that Maḥmūd b. 'Umar surrounded his court with a body of *shuhūd*, or character witnesses.[45] These formed part of *ad hoc* arrangements whereby scholars vouched for the moral rectitude of litigants and witnesses alike.[46]

Unfortunately, we have no details on individual cases of public prosecution (if the terminology applies) or private litigation. We know of one instance in the eighteenth century when four Shurfa notables were convicted in a murder case. But the details seem to point to a verdict by scholar–notables rather than a formal court action presided over by the judge.[47] In another case, the *Qāḍi* sat in judgement in a dispute between two Ruma families who had long struggled over short-term tenures of the Pashalik. The proceedings of this trial illustrate the fact that prominent scholars acted as attorneys for litigants on both sides in important cases.[48] Both this and the case of the Shurfa hinged on matters of high state politics or else they would not have been mentioned in the sources. They will again be discussed in their proper chronological context in Chapter 6.

The crucial factor which enhanced the power of the Judge was the fact that in most cases he saw to the implementation of his own decisions and judgements himself. Mālikism did not specify the means that could be employed to that end, but the *Qāḍi's* influence opened to him several alternative courses of action. First and perhaps most importantly, the Judge could call upon his constituency as a whole, especially at times of crisis, or upon personal followers or students as circumstances required.[49] Secondly, we are told that the Songhai state since at least the time of Askia Muḥammad empowered the judges to call upon the services of certain officials in any matter connected with the execution of justice. Thus, listing the exclusive prerogatives of the various officials of Askia Muḥammad, *Tārīkh al-Fattāsh* says of the monarch:

> No one in his lands was entitled to call upon his servant and send him to execute some command, whereby he could not refuse, and whereby he would treat his command exactly as he would treat that of the Askia, except the Qāḍi.[50]

Reference to this as an established feature in the 'Songhai system' (*tarīqat Sagha*) suggests that the Qāḍi-Khatībs in Gao could independently call upon the help of the highest officials in any judicial matter not involving the military hierarchy. At Timbuktu, it seems almost certain that the Judge enjoyed a similar power of recourse over the Timbuktu Mundhu. We may assume that the help of this official, as probably also that of the Maghsharen-Koy, was necessary for intercepting fleeing culprits, though the only case on record is surrounded by ambiguity.[51] However, the story that Maḥmūd b. 'Umar at one time expelled the Askia's emissaries, after actually having ordered them beaten, suggests that the Aqīt judges rejected infringement by state officials on their broadly-interpreted prerogatives.[52] By and large, it seems that their recourse to the help of such officials in matters affecting the civilian public was minimal.

Thirdly, the Judge in Timbuktu disposed of a formally constituted police force which, though probably quite small, combined with his local standing to make his decisions certain of implementation. The police force was in the hands of an official identified variously as Khādim al-Shar‘ (Ar. 'Servant of the Law') and as Ashra‘ Mundhu.[53] This official makes an appearance at the time of the rebellion against the Moroccan conquerors when he acted as emissary between Judge and notables. Being otherwise rarely mentioned, the Ashra‘ Mundhu enjoyed little prestige, but it seems probable that the position was staffed from among the rank-and-file literati. There are no grounds for comparing his role to the wide powers of the Muḥtasib over the market organization in the older cities of Islam. However, it seems that he was qualified to act against routine infractions and bring the offenders to court.[54] The post was probably even more reduced in importance after the Moroccan conquest when prison sentences made by judicial decisions were enforced, it seems, by Ruma officialdom.[55] The Ruma Pashas instituted the post of Ḥākim (Governor) who had a greater say in the daily affairs of the city, at first, than had been the case with the Timbuktu Mundhu. We know for certain that the governors despatched by the Pashas to Jenne had greater power than the Jenne Mundhu under the Songhai. Indeed, in recapitulating his history, al-Sa‘di lists the Ḥākims of Jenne (though not those of Timbuktu) before the *qāḍis* of that town.[56] However, a century later, reflecting a return to earlier criteria of precedence, the anonymous author of *Tadhkirat al-Nasyān* placed the Ḥākims of Timbuktu at the end of a rather long list.[57] The post of Ḥākim had, in fact, disappeared altogether in Timbuktu and, by and large, the entire Ruma hierarchical system had been slowly collapsing. The only post which ultimately survived was that of Pasha and even the title changed to that of Amīr when the scholar ‘Abd al-Qādir al-Sanūsi combined governmental power with the judgeship in the early nineteenth century.

As already suggested, the fiscal prerogatives of the judges are most ambiguous. On the whole, we are inclined to believe that no uniform system of taxation was ever imposed on the city (until some time after the French conquest) beyond imposts on the entry and export of goods.[58] However, the exactions of fiscal officials could sometimes be quite enormous, and the judges sought as much as possible to protect the interests of merchants. Thus, on one occasion when Askia Isḥāq I visited Jenne he found the notables in a resentful mood. He apparently made the mistake of declaring that he would punish anyone against whom a just complaint was made. The bold al-Qāḍi Maḥmūd Baghayughu then retorted:

No one here usurps the rights of another except on your behalf, by your order or by virtue of your power . . . This wealth which is taken to you from here, making you rich, does it really belong to you? Do you have slaves ploughing for you here or funds being invested on your behalf in commerce?[59]

The *Tārīkh al-Fattāsh* indicates that Maḥmūd was not yet *Qāḍi* at the time of this outburst. However, the evidence of al-Sa'di suggests that the presiding Judge, al-'Abbās Kab, was already nearing his end and that Maḥmūd, one of his principal *shuhūd*, was recognized as his successor *de facto*.[60] It seems that taxation and extortions reached an all time high during the reign of Isḥāq. At his death, according to al-Sa'di, it was found that two of his agents had collected a total of 70 000 *mithqāls* (of the order of 9000 ounces of gold) from the merchants of Timbuktu alone.[61]

Surprising as this might seem, the scholars looked upon most taxation as a superfluous source of wealth for rulers. According to their view, it was honourable for rulers, like other officials and non-officials, to augment their resources by employing clients and slaves either in agricultural plantations or in commercial enterprises. This attitude had its roots in widespread local custom which we find represented at an early date in faraway Hausaland.[62] Nonetheless, its endorsement by scholars is of some interest because they seem to have had some influence in the end, even among the Ruma. By the late seventeenth century, the Pashas derived much of the state income through revenue received on a mutually agreeable basis from the wealthy notables and plantation owners (*al-musabbibīn*). At a yet later stage, we find that the main Ruma families sustained themselves through ownership of plantations along the Niger.

Besides the factors discussed above, the Judge's administration rested on a number of *liens* with the chiefs of the professional corporations. Unlike the Ashra' Mundhu, these 'officials' did not fall directly under the judgeship. Their relationship with the *qāḍi* was based on reciprocity, much as in the case of *imāms*, though they occupied a far more modest position. To all intents and purposes, their authority was an autonomous one drawn from their recognition as chiefs or foremen by members of their respective trades and by society at large. It is possible that the Judge presided over the formal investment of these chiefs at times. In any case, they seem to have represented their constituency *vis-à-vis* the Judge (and at times perhaps the Pasha) and *vice versa*. Mutual recognition of the distinct criteria of precedence and status was a central principle in this type of fluid, yet ordered system.

Our information on the crafts is almost entirely drawn from recent French sources and contemporary observations. Nonetheless, the antiquity of the professional organizations and their links with the scholars and judges are not in doubt. In no case were the links as strong as in the case of the tailor–alfas; these were the representatives *par excellence* of scholars among the craftsmen. The corporation of masons, a yet more formal organization, attributes its foundation to a certain 'Ali who came to Timbuktu from Walāta at the same time, presumably in the mid-fifteenth century, as 'Umar Aqīt.[63] The chief of the muleteers, the Arukoy, is encountered in one instance in the eighteenth century when, during a period of insecurity, he sought refuge from persecution at the tomb of Aḥmad Maghia.[64] Most striking of all the current traditions is the story that the age-set associations of Timbuktu, which cut across the entire population, quarter by quarter, crystallized into their present shape in the sixteenth century when al-Qāḍi al-'Āqib rebuilt the Main Mosque, Jinger-ebir. According to this tradition, the illustrious judge called upon all the inhabitants of the city to help in the project and their participation was organized on an age-set basis.[65]

We are free to question the accuracy of these traditions but they do help us understand how the corporations and age-set associations supplemented the Judge's administration of Timbuktu. By analogy with mediaeval Tunis, for example, we may see the chief of the masons as a recognized expert in the customary application of the so-called Muslim Māliki *droit de voisinage*.[66] He probably saw to it on a routine basis that builders calling on the services of his corporation did not infringe on the property of neighbours or on public passageways and market spaces. Contact and consultation between him and the Judge would have been a continuous affair and especially at times of disagreement over urban property and litigation. The chief's post has always been attributed magical powers which, in repairing the mosques and the elevated two-storey buildings, protected the masons from falling or being hurt. Succession to the chieftaincy of the masons has been to a large extent hereditary, but authority also rested in a consultative body made up of the veterans of the craft.[67]

Similarly, the Arukoy, or chief of the muleteers, represented the members of his craft in all matters pertaining to the transport of merchandise between Timbuktu and Kabara on the Niger. The ten-mile tract, being unsuitable for camels, linked the Saharan and trans-Saharan caravans, which unloaded at the northern outskirts of Timbuktu, to the riparian trade with Jenne and elsewhere along the Niger. The Arukoy, a modest but respected official, presided at every large procession setting out to Kabara. In all probability, his subordinates were responsible to him for any merchandise lost or damaged and he, in turn, acted as an expert and character witness in cases when Tuareg warriors (Imoshāgh) or their clients (Imghād) plundered individual companies of muleteers.[68] A clue to the importance of the chieftaincy lies in the fact that merchants did not always accompany their merchandise, whether towards Jenne, or to the salt-mines in the Sahara and beyond. We find no reference to a chief of the camelteers, but the Maghsharen, the Barābīsh and other clans which monopolized the transport of goods and the escort of caravans in the Sahara contributed their own criteria of order (and sometimes disorder) to the mercantile organization of Timbuktu.[69]

The insecurity at times of transport and commerce tended to strengthen rather than weaken the city's subscription to legal formalism. For example, the contract drawn on behalf of Aḥmad b. And-Agh-Muḥammad b. Maḥmūd in 983 A.H. (1575/6 A.D.) concerning his purchase of a book is far more detailed than one would expect in a relatively minor commercial transaction. There were professionals in such *mu'āmalāt* who saw to drawing up the proper instrument for every transaction. The scribe and witness in this case is a certain Abu Bakr b. 'Ali b. Danbu Sili who appears distantly related to a later judge of Walāta.[70] His son, Aḥmad, is encountered in another context as a scribe who presented a copy of *Risālat Ibn Abu Zaid* in 1586 A.D. to Askia Muḥammad Bān.[71] The buyer in our contract, being a member of the respected And-Agh-Muḥammad family, did not need detailed introduction. However, the seller is described in the document in full as a stranger to the city, a tall youth from Bulāla named Mālik b. Muḥammad al-Fulāni. It is further specified that he came to Timbuktu in the company of known grandees (*akābir*) who would, presumably, testify to his character. We are assured that seller and buyer reached the agreement 'voluntarily and in full command of their faculties'. Finally, the document specified that the agreed price was in *mithqāls*, following the Timbuktu standard gold-weight. The last stipulation was important since the *mithqāl* of Timbuktu and the Niger bend area differed up to the nineteenth century from that of Bornu, Hausaland and elsewhere in the Sudan.[72]

The proliferation of *shuhūd*, scribes, modest chieftaincies and age-set leadership, insured for the entire population intervention at times of need at the highest levels of judicial and governmental authority. Among the Tamashagh-speaking Bella, who live at the eastern outskirts of Farandi, the problem is complicated by traditions of permanent subservience to the Tuareg. Modern sources, reflecting local views and idiom, often describe the Bella as having always been 'slaves' of the Tuareg.[73] We are not sure what this means, since dominance over the local Kel Inkundar has historically changed hands from the Maghsharen to Barābīsh, Tadmekkat and Wulmdān (Ouilimiden) and, in the late nineteenth century, to the Tingeregif.[74] The most that can be said is that they have been since perhaps the eighteenth century subject to whoever achieved dominance among the Tuareg. Augmented over the centuries by slaves of the Tuareg who have settled among them, they were nonetheless governed by internal and autonomous traditions of order.

Similar considerations affect the inhabitants of the northern Abaradyu (Abaraju) quarter, though these tend to be more recent in settlement and less uniform in traditions and language. Some would seem to be remnants of Barābīsh fugitives who, after a series of internal struggles in the Sahara during the eighteenth century, fled to Timbuktu in defeat and settled there.[75] They were at various times joined by impoverished settlers from Arwān, a substantial town in the seventeenth and eighteenth centuries which was particularly vulnerable to the ravages of periodic drought. The patronage of these settlers devolved on the chief lineages of their clans and to an extent on kinsmen among the established notables of the Sankore quarter.[76] We might mention that household slaves tended over the years to be assimilated along with the more modest craftsmen and petty traders into a fluid social-status grouping identified as the Ghabibi. These, though generally low in prestige, ranked higher than the suburbanites among the 'sons of the city' for two reasons: they inhabited the built-up quarters in permanent dwellings rather than straw huts; and their economic position, based on substantial contribution to retail trade and the crafts, seems always to have been of consequence. Historically, they have been viewed as clients of the wealthy families, including the families of scholar–notables and of Songhai and Ruma high officials.[77]

Finally, we might mention that the judgeship indirectly controlled the commercial organization of Timbuktu without there being any formal machinery entrusted with overseeing the market. The central market was never as great as one would associate with a predominantly commercial city. This resulted from the dominance of long-distance over retail trade and from the huge fluctuations in prices which were contingent upon the city's locality. The nomadic clans came for their supplies of grain, in return for hides and cattle, on a seasonal basis and the villages in the area were few and far between. A tradition took root whereby even the modest families purchased their vital supplies in bulk. The physical market dealt in a range of perishables, and it seems that the corporation of butchers achieved some considerable importance.[78] Other important merchandise were utensils, leatherwork, household goods and ornaments. Some of these, like textiles, cloth and books, and also shoes (in which the Ruma specialized), became objects of local export. Nonetheless, owning stores and market stalls remained unimportant, and the bulk of even the local trade was carried out through the agency of the *teifa* or the commercial brokers who acted as intermediaries between sellers and buyers. The system was given some regularity through the role of expert measurers, sometimes drawn from among the tailor–alfas, who were also the custodians of standardized weights and measures.[79] These experts, like the specialists who marked the salt-slabs following known categories of weight and quality, were usually remunerated by people who sought their services. They enjoyed an official capacity of some sort and may even have been the subjects of donations from judges and rulers. If so, then they may have helped oversee the market and secure some standardization in the levels of exchange. Whatever the case may be, they were potential expert witnesses in cases of litigation and, as a result of this, they helped complete the market organization of the city under the auspices of the judgeship.[80]

In the section to follow, we will consider the spatial aspects in the organization of Timbuktu. We have chosen to consider these factors alongside the role of the *imāms* because the mosques in which the latter presided were the most stable factors in spatial organization. Chieftaincies of the various wards were also important but the existence of these is documented only in the later periods.

Parochial leadership: imāms *and mosques*

Beginning as far back as the sources can take us, the topography of Timbuktu has always been dominated by its mosques. These pious foundations, devoted both for prayer and study, served also as the main centres in which the poor and needy sought relief at times of famine and crisis. Their architecture rose above everything else in the city and they became the main points of referal and congregation in their respective quarters. Elements of this picture have already been discussed in Chapter 1, but it is here that we are able to give full attention to the phenomenon. A starting point is to emphasize that the main mosques became the foci of social integration long before the formal delineation of specific wards and quarters. Indeed, it was the influence of the mosques which ultimately determined the directions in delineation of quarters.

We have already paid considerable attention to the Jingerebir, Sankore and Sīdi Yaḥya Mosques. To these we might now add the influential Market Mosque (*Jāmiʿ al-Sūq*). This was a modest structure up to the late sixteenth century when al-Qāḍi al-ʿĀqib renovated and expanded it, along with Sankore and Jingerebir.[81] This act, as it were, completed the parochial organization of the city during its height of prosperity and wealth. From then on, and up to the mid-nineteenth century, the topography of Timbuktu took a triangular shape. The Sankore Mosque defined and gave its name to the Sankore quarter at the northern portions of the triangle. Similarly, Jingerebir defined the southwestern portions of the triangle, while the Market Mosque, standing actually to the east of the Main Market (Yobu Ber) helped give structure to the Sarekeina quarter. Finally, the Sīdi Yaḥya Mosque stood at the very centre of the city and, although it never strictly belonged to any quarter, its first *imām*, who is buried there, has come to be seen as the spiritual patron of Timbuktu *par excellence.*[82]

The positions of the Sankore and Jingerebir Mosques, the two oldest, offer considerable scope for speculation. Sankore stands today, and has stood for a long time, at the very northwestern edge of the built-up section.[83] Jingerebir, on the other hand, has stood almost at the southeastern edge of the city. This phenomenon, whereby a mosque is not at the centre of a population concentration, testifies to a certain characteristic in the origin of Timbuktu which it was not possible to treat fully in Chapter 2: there exists a strong possibility that the city in its obscure and ill-documented periods prior to the Maghsharen ascendency was a twin settlement. We need not contradict the chroniclers, and especially al-Sa'di, in postulating that the northern sections were inhabited by Muslims while the southern sections were inhabited by 'pagans'.[84] However, there are certain important similarities to the twin cities described by al-Bakri and al-Idrisi which flourished in the eleventh to the thirteenth centuries on both sides of the Senegal and Niger rivers. There, and especially in ancient Ghana, one section of the city was dominated by king and court while the other section was autonomously administered by Muslim settlers.[85] In Timbuktu, the seat of government was in the southern sections at all but Maghsharen times. In contrast, the judges were most often drawn from the Sankore quarter. We should not overexaggerate the importance of these observations, but it remains a fact that Sankore has throughout the centuries drawn Sanhāja, Tuareg and Arabic-speaking settlers, while Jingerebir and Sarekeina have tended to draw Malinke, Fulāni and Songhai–Ruma settlers. According to some views at least, the former were the *Bidan* (whites) among the inhabitants, while the latter were the *Sūdān* (blacks) who tended to migrate to the city more often from further south.

Germane to the above considerations is some evidence that the Niger inundations used to reach Timbuktu in fuller force and in greater masses of water than they have in more recent centuries. Thus, Kabara appears in the early sources as the main port of Timbuktu, and perhaps even the sole one, during Songhai times. But judging from more recent sources, the seasonal inundations of the Niger have not been reaching it for a long enough time, and since the nineteenth century at the least it has had to compete with Day and Kuryummi further southwest on the Niger. In more ancient times we may perhaps assume that navigation in smaller boats all the way up to Timbuktu was possible in some seasons for quite a few months around January and February.[86] What now has become the commercial Badyindi quarter, located on low-lying ground, used to be reached and perhaps fully inundated in some seasons by the Niger.[87] It stood between and separated Sankore from Jingerebir, and its eastern portions were probably the original market place which linked the twin settlements together.

Among the various quarters and wards which at different times made an appearance in the topographic divisions of Timbuktu only Sankore and Jingerebir have sustained their distinct characters. The integration of the two and hence the unification, so to speak, of the city, belongs to Maghsharen times and the credit goes to the Timbuktu-Koy Muḥammad Naḍ. We have no details on other particulars of his policy, but his erection of the Sīdi Yaḥya Mosque, halfway in the middle along the Sankore–

Jingerebir axis, was a crucial step in integrating the two main centres of populations. Al-Sa'di indicates that Kātib Mūsa was the last among the Sudanic *imāms* who held the parochial leadership of Jingerebir. Recent scholars have sometimes understood this to mean that whites became dominant from the Maghsharen ascendency onwards.[88] This, however, overlooks the fact already mentioned in Chapter 2 that Kātib Mūsa's white successor, 'Abdallāh al-Balbāli, had settled in Timbuktu under Mūsa's auspices. Sīdi Yaḥya, for his part, graciously acknowledged the precedence of Sudanis, mainly from Kābura, in consolidating the cause of learning in Timbuktu.[89] We do not know who immediately succeeded him to the imamate of the Central Mosque but, beginning with Muḥammad Baghayughu, the post has been virtually monopolized by the Malinke Wangara up to the present time. Indeed, we know that Muḥammad was offered the prestigious imamate of Sankore but he declined it on the grounds that his responsibility to the Sīdi Yaḥya Mosque had 'prior claims'.[90]

It seems that the Maghsharen interlude in the mid-fifteenth century was also the period in which the unity of whites and blacks in the city was fortified by moral sanctions and constitutional legend. Thus, the 'whites' led by the And-Agh-Muḥammads and later by the Aqīts, gained a strong position through tenure of the judgeship, but most of the recognized *walīs*, scholars whose tombs became venerated at this time, were Sudanic scholars, or at least scholars who originated further south, including Soninke and Malinke.[91] Al-Sa'di, for example, relates that Muḥammad al-Kāburi was at one point insulted as a 'Kāfuri' by a *ṭālib* from Marākish. Tradition maintains that by virtue of insulting such a pious and venerated individual, the *ṭālib* was immediately stricken with elephantiasis and, despite all treatments and potions which were administered to save him, he perished shortly thereafter.[92] The moral and psychological sanctions against racial prejudices remained so strong that they barely made an appearance in the sources and they certainly never contributed to internal strife in the long history of Timbuktu.

The only case where colour distinctions are specifically recorded concerns al-Faqīh 'Ali Sili b. Abu Bakr b. Shihāb al-Walāti al-Tunbukti. This venerated scholar who died in 1013 A.H. (1604/5 A.D.) appears to be the father of the Abu Bakr who has been encountered above as a witness to a legal deed. It seems that when al-Qāḍi al-'Āqib rebuilt the tombs adjoining the Jingerebir Mosque, there arose a discussion concerning the identity of 'Ali Sili's grandfather, namely Shihāb al-Walāti. At that time there was in Timbuktu a visitor from Walāta, a *walī* who claimed that he had seen Shihāb in an apparition and wished to visit his burial place. On enquiry by the scholars, according to al-Sa'di:

> He turned to Muḥammad Baghayughu and said: 'You are darker in colour than him'. He told Aḥmad Maghia: 'You are lighter than him'. Finally, he pointed out al-Faqīh Aḥmad b. al-Ḥājj Aḥmad [Aqīt] and said: 'His colour was like the colour of this man'.[93]

We need not concern ourselves with questions of colour and race any more than it concerned the scholars themselves. Nonetheless, it seems that the ancient family in question, hailing from Walāta, like many others whose ethnic identity is not clear, belonged to a variety of Soninke groups originating in ancient Ghana.[94]

We observe in the sources a certain condescension, partly by the later Aqīts, towards the Zagharānis. The main body of this group, which intermarried with the Songhai, often makes its appearance alongside Fulānis in the area of Massina, and they may be Soninke who are linked to ancient Zāgha.[95] We encounter one of their scholars, Masara (Misir) Bubu al-Zagharāni, as a close friend of al-Qāḍi Maḥmūd b. 'Umar who taught his son 'Abd al-Raḥmān.[96] Later, however, the group apparently declined in prestige because their clan, to the west and southwest of Timbuktu, took no interest in learning and 'was not known for virtue'.[97] Still, we find that Maḥmūd b. Muḥammad al-Zagharāni, who died in 1011 A.H. (1602/3 A.D.), was respected as an accomplished grammarian and he became *imām* at the mosque of the Tuātis.[98] It is rather obvious that this mosque was not for the exclusive use of settlers from Tuāt, though they apparently built it. The location of this small mosque, probably in the Sarekeina quarter somewhere to the north of the Market Mosque, has long been forgotten. However, its last known *imām*, the eighteenth-century Bamoy b. Muḥammad Wangarab, judging by the usage of the nickname or title of Muri in his ancient family, appears to be of Soninke descent.[99]

One element of prejudice which remained strong throughout the centuries was directed against the Fulānis and especially the Dikko clan from whom the Ardo or rulers of Massina were drawn. We even learn that Muḥammad Aqīt had transferred his family from Massina to Timbuktu because he feared that his sons would intermarry with the Fulānis.[100] Resentment of the whole group in this case bears strong similarity to the attitude of scholars towards the warrior Tuareg. But while among the latter the permanent settlers in Timbuktu and elsewhere tended to lose their Tuareg identity, the scholars drawn from among the former continued up till recent times to be principally identified as Fulāni. Even as late as the nineteenth century, we find an element of almost racial bias in Aḥmad al-Bakkā'i's missives against the Lobbo dynasty, although they had overthrown the Ardo in a *jihād*.[101] This, however, had little influence upon the position of long-established Fulāni families of Timbuktu. Beginning with the late sixteenth century, these families have more or less monopolized the imamate of Jingerebir.[102]

We have given considerable attention to ethnic besides spatial factors in this discussion because the mosques were the main forums of interaction between the various groups. More importantly yet, the appointment of *imāms* each with his own deputy who might conceivably succeed him, served as a basis for the distribution of prestige and influence and, in

Songhai times at least, for the circulation of elites between the various quarters. The servile Bella were left out of the process and the same is probably true of the impoverished nomadic settlers of the northern outskirts. Artisans and small traders, however, often descendants of freed slaves who are identified as Ghabibi, were strongly integrated into the parochial organization. Modest *alfas* were often drawn from among the Ghabibi to become the *mu'adhdhins* (callers to prayer) who were also in charge of maintaining the mosques. However, we find, for example, reference to Sayyid Yaḥya Bāba b. Muḥammad b. Sayyid Kulum (or Gulun) as 'the Great Mu'adhdhin' of the Sīdi Yaḥya Mosque who died in 1154 A.H. (1741/2 A.D.).[103] The *mu'adhdhins* were probably at times formally remunerated by the *imāms* but in more recent times they derived their livelihood from alms directly contributed to them.

Besides the mosques already mentioned above there were numerous others which made their appearance in Timbuktu at various times. Caillié, for example, mentioned seven mosques in the early nineteenth century when the Market Mosque was probably no longer standing.[104] A few decades later, Barth mentioned three small mosques, besides Sankore, Sīdi Yaḥya and Jingerebir. These were the mosques of Sīdi Ḥājj Muḥammad, the Msid (Masjid) of Bilāl and the mosque of Sīdi al-Bāmi.[105] None of the latter three are identifiable in the local sources; they, like many others before them, were probably modest structures built by wealthy merchants and notables for members of their own neighbourhoods. Historically, we have reference to the mosque of Alfa Babakr, the mosque of al-Jazūlis (al-Jazūl) and the mosque of the Qaṣba, the latter being built by the Ruma early in their history for the use of the soldiery.[106] Another mosque which is listed in the chronicles is that of al-Qā'id 'Āmir, a late-seventeenth-century structure built by an unknown Ruma official. But the only important one among these smaller mosques is *Jāmi' al-Hanā'* (the Mosque of Felicity). It is peculiar that Timbuktuans chose this particular name, for al-Sa'di claims that al-Sulṭān al-Manṣūr, who dispatched the expedition to the Sudan, had hoped to give it to the principal mosque built by him in Marakesh. He died before the completion of the mosque however, and because of this, al-Sa'di claims, the mosque came to be known as *Jāmi' al-Fanā'* (the Mosque of Extinction!).[107] The *Jāmi' al-Hanā'* of Timbuktu fell into ruin in the year 1185 A.H. (1771/2 A.D.) but its remains have never been removed and the empty square in which it is located has come to be looked upon as an especially blessed place for burial. The proliferation of tombs in the courtyard has given rise to the popular legend that it had collapsed upon a congregation of 40 virtuous scholars who were then buried there.[108] A more credible version of the same legend is that it was built in the early seventeenth century by 40 scholars who wished to have their own mosque as an exclusive place of congregation for the virtuous.[109]

The importance of *imāms* rested on symbolic criteria of social and religious integration more so than on actual administrative prerogatives. To all intents and purposes they were simply leaders of the prayer with no official capacity other than being prominent in the public eye. They delivered the sermon during the Friday congregation and could, therefore, influence public opinion, but the sermons generally dealt with pious and ethical themes. Nonetheless, the original sources of Muslim legislation, studied by generations and generations of scholars, placed the *imāms* in an unsurpassed position of spiritual leadership. For even as Ibn Khaldūn observed:

> The religio-legal prerogatives (*khiṭāṭ*) of prayer, *futya*, *qaḍā'*, *jihād* and *ḥisba* all fall under the Great Imamate, which is the Caliphate. The leadership of the prayer (*imāmat al-ṣalāt*) is the highest among all these prerogatives and is higher than kingship (*al-mulk*) itself in its particular sense as a function under the Caliphate . . . If this is established, know then that mosques in a city are of two kinds: the great and spacious mosques devoted for the public prayers, and the smaller ones which belong to a particular group or quarter.[110]

In Timbuktu, it seems that Jingerebir, Sīdi Yaḥya and Sankore, as also at times the Market Mosque, were considered public mosques whose *imāms* were invested by the *Qāḍi.*[111] This status may have extended to the mosque of the Tuātis, *Jāmi' al-Hanā'* and other mosques, especially under circumstances during the eighteenth century when the influence of Jingerebir was restricted to its own quarter.

Throughout most of the history of Timbuktu, Jingerebir (al-Jāmi' al-Kabīr = The Great Mosque) was considered the mosque of the congregational prayers *par excellence.* The evidence is not clear-cut, but we are inclined to believe that the Friday congregation during Malian, Songhai and early Ruma times drew to this mosque the main body of scholars and notables from all quarters of the city. The *Imām* of Jingerebir was the acknowledged parochial leader of Timbuktu and the *khuṭba* which he delivered to the public on Fridays included a ritual proclamation of allegiance to the reigning monarch on behalf of the entire city. We do not know to what extent this formality, or its omission, had an effect on popular sentiment. But certainly in Songhai times this was an important consideration. The post of *khaṭīb* in Gao, as well as in Jenne, remained distinct from that of *imām*, and was often held by the judges. It is quite obvious that reciting the Friday sermon only symbolized the relation between *khaṭībs* and state, for they also acted as caretakers over the properties of the deceased monarchs between reigns.[112] In Timbuktu, the *imāms* also acted as witnesses over the transfer of state properties, especially during Ruma times when the Pashas overthrew one another in swift succession.[113] The evidence of *Tārīkh al-Fattāsh*, if credible, suggests that at the time of the rebellion against Askia al-Ḥājj several *imāms* acted independently in proclaiming the sovereignty of Muḥammad al-Ṣādiq in the *khuṭbas.*[114] However, judging by the details of the revocation of Moroccan sovereignty in 1070 A.H. (1659/60 A.D.), the *khuṭba* at Jingerebir alone seems to have had substantial significance.[115] This factor persisted up to the nineteenth century when Barth learned that the Lobbo dynasty sought to impose a fine upon anyone who absented himself from the Friday prayers at Jingerebir.[116]

The precedence of Jingerebir is further emphasized by the fact that its *imāms* alone are fully covered in the sources. This at least is true of the period from the early fifteenth to the late eighteenth century, but even in the nineteenth century the survival of a few documents helps to complement the information of living traditionists on the sequence of *imāms.* By contrast, the *imāms* of Sankore are virtually unknown except during Songhai times, when the northern quarter of the city, at that time sprawling all around the mosque, was the abode of the most prominent scholars. Sankore at that time was the main forum of interaction between scholars and, in the recitation of *Kitāb al-Shifa*, it boasted of at least one permanent professorial post. There is no doubt that various scholars held their advanced *durūs* at other mosques and that, thereby, each mosque had its own *madrasas.* But the position of Sankore under the patronage of the Aqīt judges was unsurpassed so far as erudition is concerned in the sixteenth century.[117]

Al-Sa'di makes a point of listing the *imāms* of Sankore during the Songhai period but he does not include their successors in recapitulating his account of the Ruma regime.[118] This is symptomatic of the swift decline which befell the Sankore quarter after the deportation of the Aqīts by the Moroccans. The *Jāmi' al-Hanā'*, built to the west of Sankore, within the same quarter, at times overshadowed the ancient mosque. Indeed, since the later chroniclers do not always identify the mosques in which the *imāms* presided, we are often unable to distinguish between the sequence over the two. It seems, however, that the judges continued to be largely drawn from the Sankore quarter and they often combined the *qaḍā'* with parochial leadership either at Sankore or at al-Hanā'.[119]

Of eight *imāms* at Sankore whose sequence in the sixteenth and seventeenth centuries is known with certainty, half held the post in conjunction with the judgeship. Indeed, it seems almost certain that attaining the imamate of Sankore served as a stepping-stone to the judgeship. Besides the four cases already mentioned, And-Agh-Muḥammad b. al-Mukhtār al-Naḥawī kept alive his family's claim to the judgeship by attaining the imamate of Sankore. Muḥammad b. Muḥammad Kara, on the other hand, paved the way for his son's accession to the judgeship. In the other cases, what appears surprising is that the judges, first the Aqīts and later the And-Agh-Muḥammads of the early seventeenth century, retained the parochial leadership of Sankore while serving as judges. This perhaps emphasizes the psychological precedence which accrued alone to the *imāms*.[120]

The monopoly of parochial leadership at Sankore by a limited circle of families tended further to emphasize the precedence of Jingerebir in the fifteenth and sixteenth centuries. At that time the alternation of numerous families in holding the post gave its *imāms* the posture of duly-elected officials. From Kātib Mūsa down to Wadī'at Allah al-Fulāni, his thirteenth successor who took charge in 1052 A.H. (1642/3 A.D.), we find little repetition of names. 'Abdullāh was followed by three settlers from north of the Sahara, the Biḍān (or Whites) of al-Sa'di, but they gave way to al-Faqīh Aḥmad, known only as father of Nāna Surku (Surgu), perhaps a Songhai name.[121] The only family which established a claim upon the post at this early time was that of Siddīq b. Muḥammad Ta'alla, the Sudani scholar from ancient Kābura. After a tenure of the post by Muḥammad Gidādu al-Fulāni, he was succeeded under the Ruma by two sons. By the early eighteenth century, however, after a brief interruption in the evidence, the grandsons and great-grandsons of Muḥammad Gidādu established a virtual monopoly on the post. From then on, this monopoly, coupled with other factors, tended to reduce the importance of Jingerebir until the early nineteenth century.

Before turning to these factors, a word should perhaps be said concerning the process of selection to the post. We find little basis for generalization, but it seems that the whole body of notables took an interest in the choice of the *imāms*. Sīdi Abu'l-Qāsim al-Tuāti, who attained the post shortly after the conquest by Sunni 'Ali, was a notable of the quarter itself who lived across from the mosque, patronized the *Muddāh* and established a school for children in the vicinity. Furthermore, it seems that Tuātis tended to settle around Jingerebir at that time, for the graveyard in the back of the mosque, which was in fact built by Abu'l-Qāsim, is described by al-Sa'di as the abode of 50 Tuātis equal in piety.[122] Al-Sa'di quotes his own father concerning another *imām* as saying: 'Our master Ibrāhīm al-Zalafi had great prestige among the people of Timbuktu because they believed in him; otherwise they would not have submitted to him in that post'.[123] It seems that the *imāms* were chosen from among the ranks of venerated elders who could secure for the mosque sufficient patronage for helping needy students and the poor. One such *imām* was Sayyid 'Ali al-Jazūli who, however, delegated the leadership of the prayer to an uninfluential deputy 'Uthmān b. al-Ḥasan b. al-Ḥājj al-Tishīti, shortly before his death. The congregation failed to contribute the customary 500 *mithqāls* a year under the auspices of this deputy, and al-Qāḍi Maḥmūd b. 'Umar had to intervene with the notables on this subject. This, among other things, may account for the fact that 'Uthmān al-Tishīti did not immediately become a full-fledged *imām*. As the story goes, he declined the imamate at the death of al-Jazūli and pointed out Siddīq b. Muḥammad

Ta'alla as a more qualified candidate. He continued to serve as deputy under Siddīq and a close friendship developed between the two which apparently became a subject of commentary by traditionists. At the death of Siddīq, he finally became *imām* in his own right but he only accepted the honour after al-Qāḍi al-'Āqib threatened that he would otherwise actually imprison him.[124]

The *qāḍis* were empowered formally to invest the *imāms* on the theoretical premise that they were the deputies of the Askias who in turn were seen, somewhat half-heartedly, as delegates of the central caliphate in Islam.[125] In practice, the intervention of the *qāḍis* in the selection of the *imāms* was restricted to two exceptional cases. At the death of Manṣūr al-Fazzāni, student and successor of Sīdi Abu'l-Qāsim al-Tuāti, the 'people of the great mosque' agreed upon al-Faqīh Aḥmad, the father of Nāna Surku, and he was accordingly confirmed by al-Qādi Maḥmūd b. 'Umar. Shortly thereafter, however, the eldest son of Sīdi Abu'l-Qāsim came to Timbuktu from Tuāt and some of the notables apparently changed their mind in his favour. At that point al-Qāḍi Maḥmūd said to them: 'After the investment of al-Imām Aḥmad you come to say this! If you do not go away from me I will imprison you all.'[126] Again, when 'Uthmān al-Tishīti died, the notables disagreed between themselves over Aḥmad b. Siddīq b. Muḥammad Ta'alla and Muḥammad Gidādu al-Fulāni. Al-Qāḍi al-'Āqib in this case was given the final word, and his choice fell upon Muḥammad Gidādu.[127] It seems that Fulānis by this time had a substantial numerical presence in Timbuktu and among the circles of scholars, especially in the Jingerebir quarter. They subsequently produced one *imām*, drawn from the warrior Dikko clan, not known for its interest in learning, before the imamate was ultimately monopolized by the Gidādus.[128]

The declining influence of Jingerebir as a forum for city-wide leadership partly resulted from the emergence and growth of other mosques in the southern quarters of the city, principally in Sarekeina. The name of this quarter stands for 'the little city', but over the years it actually became an aggregate of small wards. The richest of these wards, at the southeast corner of the city, was that of the Ghadāmsis (*Ḥawmat al-Ghadāmsiyyīn*) which was largely sequestered by the Moroccans at the time of the conquest, but re-emerged by the nineteenth century under the name of Sane Gungu, once again as the abode of wealthy merchants from Ghadāmis and Tuāt, across the Sahara.[129] Other wards within the same quarter included the Wangara Kunda, principally east of the Sīdi Yaḥya Mosque, the Sirfi Kunda, inhabited by descendants of Sīdi Yaḥya himself and of Aḥmad al-Saqali and, at a later stage, the Alfasin Kunda, which got its name from one of the main divisions of the original Ruma army.[130] The persistence of the name Tjefr Kunda (believed to mean 'Ward of the Infidels') further emphasizes the fact that Sarekeina was less integrated than either Jingerebir or Sankore. Indeed, it seems almost certain that most of the small mosques which made brief appearances in the history of Timbuktu arose in various wards of the Sarekeina quarter.[131] The transfer southwards of the Main Market (Yobu Ber: the Great Market), at a period unknown, to somewhere roughly at the meeting point between the Sarekeina and Jingerebir quarters however, helped to give character to the former quarter from the sixteenth century onwards. The Market Mosque, whose location is no longer precisely known, rose to the east or northeast of the market, somewhere in the proximity of the main 'Gate' which led the muleteers to and from Kabara. The Ruma contributed their share to the proliferation of mosques when they erected the Qaṣba Mosque, within the complex of barracks which they raised as a citadel over the Ghadāmsi ward. The imamate of this mosque, first held by Sa'īd b. Muḥammad Gidādu, robbed Jingerebir of some of its precedence as the mosque most closely associated with the elusive questions of sovereignty in Malian and Songhai times.[132] At this juncture, it seems, a certain distance arose between the northern quarters, surrounding Sankore and *Jāmi' al-Hanā'*, and between the southern quarters of Jingerebir and Sarekeina where the Ruma gradually settled and intermarried. In the north, parochial leadership alternated between two Waddāni families, originating north of the Sahara but long established in Timbuktu, and between the Maghia and Zankanu families of judges.[133] The Sīdi Yaḥya Mosque, presided over by the Baghayughus, became once again the main forum of interaction between north and south and was perhaps the most important in the city throughout the Ruma period. In the south, on the other hand, the Market Mosque achieved precedence for some time and its *imāms* were largely drawn from the Gurdu Fulāni family acknowledged as the most illustrious in learning throughout the eighteenth century.[134]

The main reason for this development is that the Ruma, once settled, produced their own families of notables which came to be divided between two contending factions. The distinction and the struggles between the Fāsiyyīn and the Marākishiyyīn is prominent in the sources; it originates in the alternation of the commanders of these two main military divisions over the Pashalik (Tibshāsha). The notables of these two also alternated over the command of a third division, however, that of the Drāwis; while a fourth division, identified as the 'People of the East' ('Ahla Shrāqa, mainly from Tlemcen), held its own until it was virtually destroyed in a struggle which largely took place outside Timbuktu. As will be indicated in Chapter 6, it is most difficult to establish the patterns of allegiance among the Ruma, but at many points they came to be defined in terms of city ward or quarter. The result was polarization between Jingerebir and Sarekeina, or at least certain adjacent parts of these quarters. Under the circumstances, Jingerebir lost its pre-eminence and was at certain times of strife inaccessible to worshippers from the eastern quarters. The Market Mosque may at times have overshadowed it as a more advantageously located parochial centre. The Main Market itself was, however, in one instance in 1125 A.H. (1713/14 A.D.) totally abandoned and replaced by three different smaller markets.[135] The Sīdi Yaḥya Mosque alone, by virtue of its central position, remained the subject of city-wide parochial allegiance.

Perhaps one of the outcomes of the struggles which took place in the eighteenth century between the Ruma was the delineation of quarters, and the emergence of quarter chieftaincies. We simply have no reference to any such chieftaincies prior to the nineteenth century and even there the evidence is not clear-cut. We know that Jingerebir and Sankore each had its own body of *Muddāh* presided over by a Shaikh al-Maddāḥīn, but these were closely linked to the parochial leadership of the *imāms.*[136] In the central parts of the city, other wards besides the Wangara Kunda looked to the *imām* of Sīdi Yaḥya for leadership. The Sharīfs, principally based in the Sirfi Kunda, had their own acknowledged leader at any one time, but while exerting great influence this leadership was not defined in terms of an official post.[137] In other words, though the craftsmen and traders had their own chiefs, there was for a long time no significant alternative to the spatial organization provided by the mosques.

The Ruma seemed to have introduced the new factor as a result of the dominance of the Marākishiyyīn in the Sarekeina quarter, led by the Mbārak al-Dara'i family, and the dominance of the Fāsiyyīn, led by the Tazarkīnis, in the Jingerebir quarter. The Masūdu family, though considered originally Fāsi, stood between the two and ultimately one of its descendants became the last city-wide *amīr* before the French conquest. The developments of that period are not fully known, but it seems that Jingerebir, Sankore and Sarekeina became distinct quarters and a fourth was added in Badjinde, to the northeast of the Sīdi Yaḥya Mosque, which came to have its own chief. For the most part, the Kunta and the closely-related Ahl Sīdi 'Ali, like the Tuareg Kel Inkundar and the settlers from Sasanding who specialized in dyeing, had their own chiefs.[138] The chieftaincies of the quarters, having in the course of the present century largely disappeared, are no longer a subject of interest to traditionists. Among other things, it is widely believed that succession to these posts was inherited, but the evidence of the early French colonial documents proves otherwise. What is certain is that the chieftaincies of the quarters tended to be held by descendants of the old military elites, both Ruma and Songhai. Among the Songhai, actual lines of descent, from the Askias, seem to have lost relevance after the mid-eighteenth century and, among the Ruma, this happened shortly thereafter.[139] Today we find that both the Masūdu and the Idji (Idye) maintain an unspecified descent from the old Pashas, but the French sources tended to identify the former as Ruma while designating the latter as Ghābibi.[140] Whatever the case may be, we notice that around the time of the French conquest the chieftaincy of Jingerebir was in the hands of a certain Ben 'Ali Masūdu (also referred to as Ibrāhīm b. Sīdi

Masūdu) while that of Sarekeina was in the hands of Hammey Hammam Idji, a notable who had previously held the lesser chieftaincy of Badyindi.[141] His predecessor at Sarekeina was the illustrious Alfa Sa'īd, a scholar who was elected by the notables as chief (*Amīr*) of Timbuktu at the French conquest.[142] His successor at Badyindi, a fluid quarter to which the Main Market reverted under the French, was a scholar named Muḥammad 'Umar b. 'Umar b. Sa'īd b. Bāba, a propertied individual and a large-scale merchant. This man was apparently also recognized as an honorary *imām* of Jingerebir, though the formal imamate was not in his hands.[143] Finally, the chieftaincy of the Sankore quarter had been held by Mahaman Tafa Idji at some point and he was succeeded by Sān wuld al-Qā'id Babakr.[144] The circulation of posts suggests that the chiefs were not elected solely by the notables of each quarter. Rather, under the leadership of the *Amīr* (or Kāhia, if Ruma) and Judge, succession to these posts was determined by the notables of the city as a whole.[145]

The complex administrative and extra-administrative configurations which emerged during the nineteenth century will be further discussed towards the end of this study. It will be suggested that the period witnessed an erosion of the sharp distinction which once existed between military and learned elites. The proliferation of posts outside the orbit of religio-legal prerogatives tended to reduce the importance of *imāms*. They continued to be a medium of intercession on behalf of the respective quarters with judges and *amīrs*. But their role as mediators in familial and neighbourhood disputes was increasingly shared by others; namely the chiefs of the quarters.

In the classical period the mosques presided over by the *imāms* were the main agencies for patronage and relief for the poor and for needy students. This was an important consideration owing to the cycles of drought which frequently hit the area and threatened to depopulate the city. It seems that only the Main Mosque had a tradition whereby a specific sum was collected on a yearly basis for relief and patronage. As already indicated, this amounted to 500 *mithqāls* and had to be delivered by wealthy notables to the *imām* by the end of each Ramaḍān.[146] In the nineteenth century such a sum could purchase some 75 tons of grain, whether rice or millet, and even the dates imported across the Sahara from Tuāt sold at less than half a *mithqāl* for each *nafaq*.[147] It seems probable that these donations were for the benefit of the Jingerebir quarter alone and that similar customs arose at Sankore, Sīdi Yaḥya and the Market Mosque. So far as Sankore is concerned, we have a unique piece of information from al-Sa'di suggesting, among other things, that the 'Master of Masters', Muḥammad al-Kāburi, may have held the imamate besides the judgeship.[148] The author relates that at one time, during a famine, Muḥammad induced a notable, possibly also a Kāburi, to donate 1000 *mithqāls* by declaring that he would guarantee a place in paradise to anyone who would give such a sum.[149] It seems that the story became celebrated from then on and a similar plea was made during 'Abd al-Raḥmān Aqīt's tenure of the imamate. Our text reads rather ambiguously on this point, but it is open to the possibility that ʿAbd al-Raḥmān himself made an equal donation.[150] At Sīdi Yaḥya, the Wangara *imāms* may themselves have been the foremost patrons of the mosque for at all times their family's participation in commerce appears substantial.[151]

Finally, so far as the role of *imāms* is concerned, we should point out that their posts helped them stand out markedly among the ranks of scholars. They were generally better placed for mediating in the familial and other disputes which arose in their neighbourhoods and throughout their respective quarters. By the same token they interceded more frequently on behalf of plaintiffs with the judges and, when necessary, with the Askias and, later, the Pashas. Muslim jurisprudence generally gave preference to full-fledged jurists (*fuqahā'*) over the other scholars (such as the *huffāz*) as the most qualified to become *imāms*.[152] In Timbuktu, this stipulation seems to have been observed during the fifteenth to the eighteenth centuries in the selection of the main *imāms*, including those of Jingerebir, Sīdi Yaḥya, Sankore and the Market Mosque. The result was that these *imāms* could join the judge to form a supreme court, on a temporary basis, for passing a particularly difficult sentence.[153] One or another of the *imāms* was also usually selected to head the arbitration commissions (*Mashyakhas*) often established to mediate between warring Ruma or else between Ruma and Tuareg.[154] We could perhaps suggest as well that the *imāms* acted informally as deputy judges in their respective quarters. In this, however, their decisions were only symbolically more binding than the decisions of other jurists whose intercession was also often sought.

The scholars as a semi-corporate **Jamāʿa**

As already indicated above, the semi-legislative powers of the Judge extended to all other scholars who were qualified to interpret the *Sharīʿa* or else advance formal *fatwas* concerning its applications. This, however, did not transform the scholars into a legislative body *per se* because their own frameworks of reference precluded such a development. Firstly, the scholars' sense of identity and their 'jurisdiction', so to speak, transcended the organization of their own city and, indeed, of the states which incorporated Timbuktu. Secondly, although the ultimate framework of reference was 'Islam' as a whole, Muslim jurisprudence had not allocated a formal status to scholars beyond the implicit stipulation that the *futya*, or rendition of formal legal opinions, should be based on learning. This left considerable scope for the influence of wealthy or powerful individuals other than scholars who ranked with them among the notables or *aʿyān*. In Timbuktu, the term *aʿyān* was a fluid one which in classical times designated principally the scholars, and especially those belonging to the major families. Even at that time however, notability status was extended to the Sharīfian family of Aḥmad al-Ṣaqali, though its members did not particularly contribute to the cause of learning.[155] Another factor was a tendency from that time onwards to admit to the ranks of notables recent settlers who had been prominent or influential, and especially if learned, in their original home towns. As will be further explained in the next chapter, a combination of factors all contributed to the definition of status, though learning was paramount. Putting it as briefly as possible, the concept of notables pertains to questions of power and influence, but had no direct bearing on administration as such.

One concept which did have some bearing on the organization of Timbuktu, and especially in its relations with the outside world, was that of the *jamā'a*. We have mentioned at the outset of this study that Marty saw Timbuktu as essentially an internally administered city whose public affairs were regulated by its *jamā'a*. This observation certainly applies to the nineteenth century when state authority was either minimal or altogether absent. The concept of the *jamā'a* however, rooted in parochial conceptions of social organization, was present in Timbuktu at a much earlier time. Each mosque had in a sense its own *jamā'a*, theoretically including everyone who attended the congregational prayers at that particular mosque. In practice however, the *jamā'a* included the scholars of each quarter and those notables who, by virtue of wealth, could patronize either the *tulba* or the mosque. Thus, it was up to the scholars and their patrons to elect the *imām*, or accept him in cases of familial succession, in each quarter. The *jamā'a* of Timbuktu therefore was a higher body drawn from the most influential among these lesser *jamā'as*.

We know that Timbuktu concerned itself at an early date with this concept from the fact that al-'Āqib al-Anṣamuni devoted a treatise to the matter calling it *On the obligatoriness of instituting the Friday congregation at the village of Ansamun* (*Fi Wujūb al-Jum'a bi-Qaryat Ansamun*). This treatise is no longer extant and, although the views of al-Anṣamuni prevailed, they seem to have been contested at the time by Makhlūf al-Balbāli.[156] We do not know the details of the controversy, but we know that the subject of the *jum'a* had been an important theme in the classical legislative process in Islam. Abu Ḥanifa, founder of the Ḥanifi school, had stipulated that the *jum'a* could be held only in cities, while Mālik postulated that is was permissible in any settlement which could become the seat of a full-fledged city. The most specific view was offered by the founder of the Shāfi'i school who maintained that the *jum'a* be held in a town which had 40 legally qualified male citizens (*min ahl al-Jum'a*) permanently established in that town.[157] We are inclined to believe that al-Anṣamuni adopted a variant on the latter view, for his home town of Anṣamun, though smaller than nearby Tagedda, appears to have been a small centre of learning in the east-central Sūdān.[158] In any case, this recourse to a theme forgotten in the Middle East denotes a tendency among the scholars of each settlement in the Sūdān to look upon themselves as a semi-corporate entity defined by parochial criteria.

The concept of *jamā'a* emerges again in one of the treatises of Aḥmad Bāba concerning the organization of an autonomous settlement in the Sahara. In response to a formal enquiry, he wrote:

If the *jamā'a* of Muslims agree among themselves, in a place which has no sulṭān or is not reached by the authority of a sulṭān, upon establishment of the stipulations of the law in the proper manner, then their authority becomes as that of the Qāḍi or that of the Sulṭān . . . If they establish special sanctions and rulings in accordance with the public interest that would be permissible provided that these are in consonance with the general outlook of the law (*jāriya 'ala wajh al-shar'*).[159]

Unfortunately, we have no detailed information concerning the special rulings established by the successive *jamā'as* in Timbuktu. The views of Maḥmūd b. 'Umar, al-Balbāli and Aḥmad Bāba on slavery are an exceptional case; they came in response to special circumstances in the Sūdān which required more than the usual elaboration of Muslim law. As we shall see, the views of scholars on this subject, for all their detail, remained open to varying interpretations. In other spheres, the adoption of special legal practices incorporating elements from customary law, did not receive their due share of attention from the chroniclers and jurists. The main reason for this is that reference to the original sources of Muslim law, and especially to the *Ḥadīth*, overshadowed the reliance of jurists on local or recent precedent or custom.

One exigency which required a definitive ruling on the part of scholars was the appearance of tobacco in the late sixteenth century. The novelty elicited contradictory opinions throughout the Sūdān, as indeed in North Africa, but Timbuktu seems to have subscribed throughout to a single view. This view, once again, is known at the earliest from a treatise by Aḥmad Bāba, whose writings tended to supersede earlier ones, until they themselves were superseded by the writings of al-Mukhtār al-Kunti and Aḥmad al-Bakkā'i in the nineteenth century. Aḥmad Bāba in this case had little or no recourse to the original legislative sources except in recalling the prohibition of alcohol and hallucinatory drugs. On comparison, he concluded that tobacco was neither an intoxicant nor a narcotic and was therefore perfectly permissible. This view was adopted by all later scholars in Timbuktu and tobacco indeed became one of the major items of commerce, grown locally and imported from Tuāt.[160] However, the leader of the Massina *jihād* ruled against the permissibility of tobacco and this, along with disagreements on questions of slavery, became the main bone of contention between Timbuktu and the Lobbo dynasty of Ḥamdullāhi.[161]

The political attitudes of scholars, or at least those affecting their attitude to military officials and the state, constitute a subject on their own and will be dealt with in the following chapter. Here, however, we may indicate that the concept of *jamā'a* was largely a dormant one which had practical significance only at times of crisis. During the Songhai period, it seems to have been embodied in the recognition of some 30–40 scholars, headed by the Judge, as the notables of the city or rather as the notables of the scholars (*a'yān al-'ulamā'*), and the representatives of the public interest. It seems rather doubtful that other wealthy notables were fully admitted to this body of erudites before the seventeenth or even the eighteenth centuries. The scholars appear to have been as wealthy as anyone else in this period, being drawn from the great merchant families. We learn that the Ghadāmsis were among the richest in the city but only one of them deserved mention by name in the chronicles, a certain Fayyāḍ, and this because al-Qāḍi Maḥmūd b. 'Umar presided in old age at his funeral.[162] At the time of the Moroccan conquest no one could intercede in matters of public policy or lead the resistance except the most notable scholars.

From the late seventeenth century onwards we get the impression that the distinction between scholars and other civilian notables ceased to be as clear-cut as it had been in the sixteenth century. Several factors contributed to this long-term development, but our evidence is in most cases indirect. First of all, the decline of literacy, more so than higher learning, meant that the older gradations of learned status were slowly eroded. An ultimate outcome of this was breakdown of the distinction between full-fledged *'ālims* and lesser *alfas*. During the course of the eighteenth century and thereafter, the two titles became gradually interchangeable.[163] Under the circumstances, merchants who enjoyed a sufficient literacy in Arabic could more easily attach themselves to the circles of scholars.

Closely related to the above is the fact that long establishment in the city, and especially descent from a venerated scholar, helped sustain the prestige of many non-learned families. Thus, the descendants of those Aqīts who survived the Moroccan conquest fell considerably in influence because they did not contribute to the cause of learning. Nonetheless, the name of Awlād Sīdi Maḥmūd, or Ḥafā'id Aḥmad Bāba, secured for these tolerably wealthy families a position of special respect.[164] The Shirfi descendants of Aḥmad al-Ṣaqali, on the other hand, enjoyed a powerful position in the eighteenth century, though the presence of scholars among them was probably limited to very few prior to the nineteenth century.[165] Additionally, the nearby Tuareg and Ḥassāni clans each tended to be represented by a settler in Timbuktu who, almost as ambassador, secured a voice for his kinsmen among the ranks of the *jamā'a*.

A crucial development took place in the fiscal sphere when the Ruma established a direct system of taxation whereby much of the income of the state came to be received by the Pashas from the merchant–notables. This meant formal recognition of a body of patricians, so to speak, defined by other criteria than the *jamā'a* of scholars. The two bodies overlapped to a great extent and it seems, indeed, that the *sharīfs* were especially equipped to stand in the middle. Their recognition as descendants from the prophet tended to place their leaders among the highest circles of scholars while the bare literacy of these leaders associated them more closely with non-learned merchants.[166] Since wealthy merchants tended to acquire one level of learning or another, the tradition of learning ultimately regained the initiative by a lowering of standards. Exceptionally gifted scholars, such as among the Gurdu, continued to thrive, but the broader body of scholars was no longer defined by the rigorous jurisprudential training of earlier times.

The late eighteenth and early nineteenth centuries witnessed a significant shift in the integration of Ruma elements into the body of notables. This was the product of a long development which began immediately after the conquest and received a thrust forward in 1150 A.H. (1737 A.D.) when the Ruma army was virtually destroyed in open battle by the Kel Tadmekkat.[167] Subsequently, the remnants of the army were reconstituted again and again, although the post of Pasha was often vacant, for a whole century. This was possible because of the tacit cooperation of scholars at a time when the leaders of the Ruma drew their strength from their position as notables of their own 'ethnic' group. Henceforth, a few of these leaders joined the ranks of the *jamā'a* which controlled Timbuktu up to the French conquest.

The size of the *jamā'a* is indicated to us, though at a rather late date, from a document which was drawn up in 1915 in response to a formal enquiry by the French concerning the attitudes of the notables towards Turkey and towards Germany and her allies in the war. This was signed by 26 notables, beginning with the *Amīr*, Alfa Sa'īd b. Guidādu, and the then very influential al-Qāḍi Aḥmad Bāba b. Abu'l-'Abbās. We note that the names of the main *imāms* are high on the list, while those of the chiefs of the quarters are lower on the scale. The signatories include two representatives of the Barābīsh, including a previous *qāḍi* of Arwān, along with one Kunta scholar. Otherwise, the list is interspersed by the names of eight notables from Timbuktu itself, mainly scholars, followed at the end by five Moroccan and southern Saharan settlers.[168]

We need not suggest that this list is fully representative of the configurations of influence. Still, it seems that a similar body of notables, led by al-Qāḍi Sān Sirfi, formally invited Aḥmad al-Bakkā'i into the leadership of a struggle against the authority of al-Ḥājj 'Umar in 1862. The document in which this invitation was made is actually a *bī'a*, or a formal act of allegiance, written in the name of 'the *Jamā'a* of the people of Timbuktu, its whites and its blacks'.[169] Similarly, it seems that a broad body of notables made the decision to send an embassy to Morocco at the time of the French conquest. In that instance a letter accompanied the embassy which was written in the name of 'All the people of Timbuktu, and its notables, and the adjoining people, both *'Arab* and *'Ajam'*.[170] Finally, in 1885 a letter was addressed to the French authorities requesting reduction of the taxation and imposts and pleading, among other things, on behalf of the whites (*bidan*) 'because they bring the salt and other merchandise and because the people of the Niger would otherwise not come trading in the city'.[171] The document was drawn up in the name of 'the chiefs of the people of Timbuktu', but it is obvious that in all cases the same body of notables, more or less, led principally by the scholars, acted as spokesmen on behalf of the whole city. Naturally, there were great differences in precedence and prestige within the body of notables and, including vicissitudes in careers, even within the same generation. Nonetheless, the continued presence of descendants of the ancient families of scholars – Maghia, Gidādu, Baghayughu, Zankanu, Gurdu, 'Irāqi and Ṣaqāli Sirfis – tended to impart a sense of stability to the internal notions of what constituted the core of the *jamā'a*.

In essence, the institutional base of the religio-legal hierarchy at Timbuktu should be described as 'semi-administrative' rather than strictly as administrative. It was mainly at the level of the judgeship that the scholastic establishment played a directly administrative role. This, in itself, was quite important, owing to the links between the judgeship and other urban organizations, like the corporations of masons and muleteers. Additionally, however, we should not underestimate the routine influence of most jurists over the daily commercial and legal affairs of the city. Nor should we overlook the organizational impact of parochial leadership by *imāms* at the mosques. The Muslim parochial conceptions of 'community' which underlie this impact are quite problematical and elusive. Nonetheless, this may be a function of the adaptability of these conceptions. At Timbuktu, they did afford some scope for conception of the city as a whole as a parochial entity led by its own *jamā'a.* So long as there was no formal 'council of elders' (or a council of scholars or patricians), the *jamā'a* of Timbuktu cannot be described as a formal institution. Nonetheless, the phenomenon of a collective leadership which is signified by the term *jamā'a* was always a factor of prime import in the organization of the city.

CHAPTER 5

The scholars as regional notables

The existence of a status group known as the notables (*a'yān*), among whom scholars occupy a prominent position, is an urban phenomenon which is quite widespread in Islam. The significance of the phenomenon has tended to vary vastly from one region to another depending upon local traditions of social structure and administration in each case. Among the towns and commercial centres which arose south of the Sahara, Timbuktu perhaps exhibits the closest parallels to the Muslim cities of North Africa and the Middle East. Certain aspects of its organization were in a sense an extension of North African urban culture into the northern reaches of West Africa. Nonetheless, the role of its scholars was conditioned by ideological, economic and social considerations which cannot simply be attributed to the influence of Islam from across the Sahara. Some factors were deeply rooted in local custom and civilization while others, especially pertaining to the influence of learning as a criterion of social advancement and status, are simply to be recognized as universal. In mediaeval and early modern Europe, for example, there was at one point an awareness of semi-official status defined to a large extent by jurisprudential learning: thirteenth-century Erfurt measured its prestige by the number and standing of its scholars.[1] Similarly, in connection with mediaeval Bologna, *Habita* was granted to 'all scholars who travel for the sake of study and especially to the professors of divine laws'.[2] Other examples could be found elsewhere, but these are overshadowed by a major transformation which took place in Europe: namely, the distinction between clergy and learned laity which did not materialize in Islam.

Perhaps under the influence of the European model, the study of scholars everywhere continues to be concerned primarily with intellectual history, or the evolution of ideas and ideologies. In the wider Islamic context there already exists some work which looks upon the scholars both as a status-grouping and as a social–structural body. The affiliations of scholars with the larger configurations of notables remain problematical however. S. M. Stern, for example, implicitly saw the notables as patrician elements who, irrespective of the presence of scholars among them, amounted as a group to a pre-modern bourgeoisie.[3] An extension of the same thesis, somewhat modified, was offered by Richard Bulliet in his study of Nishapur. According to Bulliet, the learning of an individual affirmed his patrician status but did not define it.[4] This model is relevant to the case of Timbuktu because it is quite clear that the acquisition of full-fledged learning, through years of almost exclusive devotion to study, was open primarily to the wealthy. In our case however, we have to contend with the fact that learning could be passed on from one generation to another within the family, through tutorialships under relatives, even though that family may have declined over the passage of time on the scale of wealth. The content of the learning process, and especially insofar as law and administration were concerned, was likewise an important factor. Additionally, as Carl Petry has pointed out in a study on the fifteenth-century scholars of Cairo, the elements of piety and veneration which attached to learning, were crucial in sustaining the leadership position of scholars over the affairs of the public.[5]

One additional model which may be relevant to our case, certainly on the methodological scale, is that of the Mandarins of Imperial China. There we have a highly formalized socio-educational order in which learned status was confirmed through standardized examinations and degrees often corresponding to specific grades in the Imperial and provincial bureaucracies. We need not claim that this example is fully pertinent to the case of Timbuktu. As we shall see in the concluding section of this chapter however, it helps provide a framework of reference for understanding the wider roles of scholars and their circulation as religio-learned elites throughout the Sahelo–Sūdān.

We should perhaps explain at this point that the outlook of scholars was characterized by a certain duality concerning their own sense of identity. On the one hand they belonged to a larger body of urban notables whose terms of reference rested upon allegiance to, and custodianship of, the interests of Timbuktu. Naturally, we may assume that a similar orientation existed among scholars in Jenne, Walāta and even Gao. In the latter case, at the time of the Moroccan conquest, the Songhai military and administrative hierarchy fully evacuated the city. But the scholars and the merchants stayed behind and, under the leadership of the *Khatīb*, they tendered their submission to the conquerors.[6] Similarly, in Jenne and Timbuktu, after considerable reluctance, the sovereignty of the Ruma was duly acknowledged and accepted. The allegiance of scholars and notables was principally reserved for their city itself and only theoretically to the state which incorporated it.

At another level of association, the scholars of each city and settlement felt a sense of solidarity with scholars elsewhere in the Sūdān. If there existed any sense of 'patriotism' as such, it pertained to all the Muslim regions of West Africa, an area designated by the ill-defined name of Takrūr.[7] There was a distinction between the northern and southern reaches of this area, the inhabitants of the former being generally looked upon as Whites (Bīḍān) while those of the latter were considered Blacks (Sūdān).[8] Besides the common subscription to Islam and Muslim learning however, this distinction was subordinate to other factors. Among the non-Saharans, the Songhai and Fulānis, at least, held traditions of Middle Eastern origins.[9] Moreover, even Tuāt and Ghadāmis, across the Sahara, were integrated by traditionists into the 'Takruri' culture complex. According to al-Sa'di, the town of Tuāt, always a main link in the commercial intercourse with North Africa, was founded by Mālinke who had accompanied Mansa Mūsa on his pilgrimage.[10] Equally important on the ideological scale, and somewhat more credible, is the current tradition in Ghadāmis that the Kel al-Sūq there migrated across the Sahara from Timbuktu around 1600. The tradition might strictly implicate the Ghadāmsis of Timbuktu who were displaced when their quarter was taken over by the conquering Ruma. In other words, their designation as Kel al-Sūq (a reference to ancient Tadmekka) does not reveal their ethnic identity any more than in the case of their distant kinsmen, both Kel al-Sūq and Kel Tadmekkat, who remained south of the Sahara. The Kel Infoghas, whom they joined in the region of Tuāt, became the major transporters of goods across the Sahara during the nineteenth century.[11] Further evidence of ethnic intermixture comes from a statement by al-Sa'di to the effect that the Sanhāja Ajir, of the Timbuktu area, were originally from Shingīṭ while 'the origin of the people of Massina is Tishīt'.[12] It is most difficult to arrive at any conclusion concerning the relationship between Sanhāja and Fulānis in the Niger bend area. We have, however, for example, a reference to a *qāḍi* of Tishīt who died in 1180 A.H. (1766/7 A.D.) as Muḥammad b. Yadghur b. Aḥmad b. al-Shaikh b. al-Amīn b. Muḥammad b. Gāb (Kāb) al-Masini al-Gābi.[13] This suggests a relationship to the Kāb family of Jenne whose member, Muḥammad Kāb b. Jābir Kāb, became Khatīb of Gao in 973 A.H. (1566/7 A.D.).[14] Jenne, for the most part, was looked upon as a Sudani settlement while Walāta was principally the abode of Saharan scholars. Yet despite the psychological precedence of Whites in Islam, Jenne was always venerated as a virtuous Muslim city. By contrast, Walāta fell victim in the late nineteenth century to a charge of 'enemies of the faith' directed against its notables from the recently Islamized Umarian capital of Segu. The Jamā'a of Walāta felt obliged to declare that their relationship with non-Muslims was restricted to trading with them 'as all Muslims do, in the east and the west, the 'Arab and the 'Ajam'.[15] Naturally, the *jihāds* in the nineteenth century tended to heighten the awareness among scholars in each area of the activities and attitudes of their colleagues elsewhere in the Sahelo–Sūdān. But long before that, the pedagogical links resulting from the travels and migrations of scholars, and especially merchant–scholars, strengthened the sense of belongingness to an extensive 'Takrūri' homeland.[16]

Before proceeding we should perhaps explain that comparison between the various towns and commercial settlements in the Sūdān is hampered by the scantity of the evidence. Timbuktu is the only city whose internal organization is documented over several centuries more or less without interruption. In some of the Hausa city–states we learn of an appreciable presence of scholars just before and after 1500 A.D., but from then on the evidence concerns only the most accomplished authors whose writings are quoted by the nineteenth-century Jihādists.[17] A similar pattern is observed in Massina where the literature of the *jihāds* more fully superseded earlier chronicles and jurisprudential writings. Even Jenne, which for centuries had the strongest familial, commercial and pedagogical links with Timbuktu, has left us no substantial chronicle of its own. Accordingly, in this and in other cases, we often have to rely on the limited information supplied by Timbuktu chroniclers.

So far as we can tell, the organization of Jenne differed from that of Timbuktu in one major respect. Namely, the criteria of order surrounding the kingship tradition of the Jennekoy almost always served as an alternative for leadership by scholars. This was because the kingship originated long before Islamic learning made an impact upon the city. By the Songhai period there was considerable integration between the two traditions. We note some evidence of a patrician tendency among the Baghayughu, Turfu, Kāb and Dābu scholars of Jenne. The parochial organization appears to have been very influential, especially since the topography of the city, concentrated in a relatively small space on a riparian island, was dominated by its Main Mosque.[18] The office of the Jennekoy survived long after the Moroccan conquest but, in a development which may also have affected the post of *qāḍi*, it seems to have lost considerably in prestige from the mid-seventeenth century onwards.[19] There have survived a series of obituaries from the eighteenth century which feature for the most part a number of notable Ruma families. These need not reflect the actual patterns of precedence any more than in the case of the *Tadhkira* and the *Dīwān* of Timbuktu.[20] It seems that the Ruma, at the time of their final absorption into the ranks of notables and commoners patronized some *alfas* to record the obituaries of their grandees. Subsequent developments were much the same in Jenne as at Timbuktu; the Fulāni Dikko clan established themselves as a regional power comparable to the Kel Tadmekkat. The *jihād* of Aḥmadu Lobbo overthrew the Ardo, and this, among other factors, reasserted the ascendency of scholars.[21]

The closest-documented parallels to the case of Timbuktu are, in fact, those pertaining to the scholars of Walāta. This city was virtually abandoned at some point during the Songhai period, as already mentioned in

Chapter 2, but it recovered its importance very swiftly in the wake of the Moroccan conquest. It is interesting to learn, for example, that Muḥammad b. Muḥammad b. 'Ali Sili, whose ancestors had migrated to Timbuktu in the fifteenth century, returned to Walāta in the early seventeenth century and became Judge there. Since the previous history of the settlement has essentially been lost to traditionists, he is in fact the first known Judge of Walāta.[22] He had a partner in the leadership of the town in a certain 'Umar al-Walī al-Maḥjūbi who is described as 'the pillar of learning' in his time. This scholar too may have migrated from Timbuktu, or else grew up there, for he is recorded to have studied under al-Qāḍi 'Abd al-Raḥmān b. Aḥmad Maghia.[23] The town of Walāta lay beyond the reach of the Ruma regime and offered to the scholars and the merchant–scholars a continuation of the virtual autonomy previously enjoyed in Timbuktu. A similar pattern is observed in the case of Arwān, well inside the Sahara to the north of Timbuktu, which was transformed into a virtual town in the seventeenth century. The weakness of Ruma authority there, and its complete absence in Walāta, indirectly compensated Timbuktu for its loss of independence. That is because the same merchant families often had branches in all three places, besides Jenne. In Walāta, as at Timbuktu, leadership devolved on *qāḍis* and *imāms*, and these posts seem to have been held in alternation by a small circle of families. The biographies assembled by al-Bartīli suggest that these families, including al-Bartīli's own, amounted to a stable patriciate over several generations. The main distinction is that the family tended to be a more extended one, almost a clan, in the case of Walāta.[24] In both cases, however, the scholars associated with their own ranks as notables the chiefs of the nearby clerical clans. Max Weber advanced the concept of the 'precommunal patrician city' to characterize the similar situation of Mecca in pre-Islamic Arabia.[25] In our case too, the economic and kinship factors were pronounced, but the presence of scholars among the notables contributed an important legitimizing and integrative role.

Wealth, status and influence

As partly suggested above, the status of town-based scholars in the Sahelo–Sūdān lends itself to two distinct analytical approaches. The first takes the notables (*a'yān*) as a starting point and views their learning as a factor which confirmed their status. This approach is justified by the fact that the term *a'yān* is a vague one which is often interchangeable with *'ulamā'*. The second approach, which we have adopted in this study, takes the scholars as a starting point and proceeds to show that their status and influence was strengthened both by economic and ideological factors. The present discussion is concerned with the economic factors, a subject which, however, is not as well documented in our sources as we would have hoped.

The evidence at hand suggests rather strongly, though indirectly, that the scholars at all times had people of great wealth among their ranks. The learning process itself, in its combined religio-legal aspects, placed the scholars in a position of advantage for participating in commerce. First of all, even aside from full-fledged scholarship, the factor of literacy had important psychological and practical implications. The clerics of the Sūdān (*malams* in Hausaland, *alfas* elsewhere, and *marabouts* in the Senegal regions) were represented virtually everywhere in the towns which lay along the main trade-routes in West Africa. Knowledge of Arabic, even though it was sometimes imperfect, facilitated and sustained the relations between towns over long distances through the agency of the clerics. Recent studies have sometimes emphasized the supernatural or magical powers attributed to clerics because of their command of literacy and their ability to write charms.[26] Above and beyond that, the clerics projected an image of neutrality between states, especially since the Suwarian tradition among the Jahanke and the Dyula had rested upon peaceful diffusion of Islam.[27] The result, as the English merchant Jobson observed in the early seventeenth century, was that the clerics

> . . . have free intercourse through all places, so that howsoever the kings and countries are at warres, and up in arms the one against the other, yet still the Mary-bucke (*marabout*) is a privileged person, and may follow his trade or course of travelling, without any let or interruption of either side.[28]

And, indeed, we learn from al-Sa'di that he himself had lived briefly and taught in a village called Shibla, southwest of Jenne, which was subsequently razed to the ground in a local war. He mentions, somewhat incidentally, that the house in which he had lived, belonging to a certain al-Faqīh Abu Bakr San'atar, was the only structure besides the village mosque which was spared.[29]

A second factor was that Muslim Māliki law, inasmuch as it pertained to commercial transactions and contracts, imparted a measure of uniformity and predictability to the procedures of long-distance trade. In the mid-nineteenth century, Barth commented on the Tuareg scholars of Air by saying: 'Under the authority of these learned and devout men, commerce is carried on with a security which is surprising'.[30] Indeed, in Walāta the seasonal caravan which was mounted across the Sahara to Tuāt was led by a full-fledged scholar (Shaikh al-Rakab) who 'was dreaded by robbers and feared by tyrants'.[31] Likewise, the internal market of Walāta was at one time regulated by an overseer (an *amin*) who received an obituary among the *a'yān al-'ulamā'* (the most notable scholars) because he acquitted himself admirably in his post. He did not himself rank among the scholars, but acquired ample knowledge of commercial law through constant recourse to their views and advice.[32] In Timbuktu, the expert measurers acted in lieu of an *amīn*, a title equivalent to the *muhtasib* of Muslim Spain and the earlier Middle East. The function in this case pertains strictly to the commercial urban context and is not to be confused with the *amīn* established under the early Ruma to represent the fiscal interests of the Sulṭān of Morocco.[33]

The present-day situation in Timbuktu suggests a strong divorce between the leading merchants, who are exceptionally wealthy, and the scholars or *alfas*, whose leading men enjoy moderate prosperity. This, however, might pertain to developments in the twentieth century; the sons of scholar–merchant families have tended to favour a secular Western education with the result that the body of *alfas* has become rather restricted. Traditions mention, for example, that Abu'l-'Abbās, the father of the late-nineteenth-century al-Qāḍi Aḥmad Bāba, was noted for his extreme wealth. Other indications may suggest that wealth had for a long time been competing with learning (and with descent from the learned) as a criterion for high status. Yet, it seems that a close relationship with the Kunta, who were at once venerated, learned and wealthy, was responsible for raising Abu'l-'Abbās' son to the judgeship.[34] Around the turn of the century, one of the earliest French military commanders over the region, Marc-Shrader (a 'Mayor of Timbuktu', as he called himself), observed that the lucrative salt-trade was in the hands of 'Moroccans' and a few indigenous merchants. He added, however, that there was a diffusion of profits from this trade because the Arabs (meaning in this case principally the Barābīsh) gave up the salt on arrival at Timbuktu to the local families which housed the caravaneers and supplied them with goods imported from the south. Otherwise, Marc-Shrader indicated that the 'erudites' themselves each controlled a portion of the commerce which was quite 'agreeable'.[35]

A problematical theme in the European sources of the nineteenth century results from the fact that they often give the impression that the commerce of Timbuktu was dominated by North African settlers (or more vaguely by the 'Moors') who are said to have periodically repatriated their profits. We have no reason to doubt that merchants from the main urban centres of North Africa (and even the Middle East) frequently found their way to Timbuktu and often ventured further south where the prices for their goods were appreciably higher. Such merchants, however, had little knowledge either of the patterns of supply or of the fluctuations in prices. The recorded travels of the Astrakhani Muslim merchant, Wargee, are a case in point; after traversing virtually the whole West-Central Sudan, this enterprising merchant arrived in the Kingdom of Asante quite destitute.[36] A development which began in the fifteenth century at least had resulted in a complex system of relays whereby the bulk of the trans-Saharan commerce was carried by proxy between the Saharan settlements on both sides. The French seem to have been unaware of this complexity and, additionally, the sources often confront us with a general misunderstanding of the actual ethnic and geo-economic configurations.[37] Leaving aside the very earliest accounts, based on hearsay, we find that René Caillié, after his visit, somehow came to the conclusion that the Songhai-speaking majority in the city belonged to one ethnic Sudanic group which he described as the 'Kisoor nation'.[38] Otherwise, he represented the Whites, under the general title of 'Moors', as though they were all temporary settlers who dominated the city's commerce. He wrote: 'They are engaged in trade and, like Europeans, who repair to the colonies in the hope of making their fortunes, they usually return to their own country to enjoy the fruits of their industry. They have considerable influence over the inhabitants . . .'[39] Even at a much later time, Oscar Lenz, who also actually visited the city, reported that the Moroccan Jewish Mordekhai family traded directly with Timbuktu and enjoyed specific rights there. Yet, a description of the city by a member of this family, being inaccurate and based on outdated information, shows no evidence of direct contact.[40] Immediately after their conquest of Timbuktu, the French established, or rather recognized, a certain Mīlād b. Bu Jmā'a as spokesman of a group vaguely identified as the 'white' or 'foreign' merchants.[41] The group included mostly Saharans from the Barābīsh, Tajkant and other Hassāni clans, besides Kunta and Tuareg, who had always contributed permanent settlers to Timbuktu.[42]

So far as we can tell, the long-established and influential North-African merchant families in Timbuktu were few in number and were principally drawn from the northern Saharan settlements of Tuāt and Ghadāmis. We likewise find individual reference to Filālis and Balbālis (originally from Tafilelt and Tabalbalat) but the *nisbas* do not always designate the actual provenance of such settlers. The Ghadāmsis may have been partly looked upon as foreigners since they do not seem to have contributed *imāms* to any of the mosques. After the Moroccan conquest, there arose a reverse migration to Ghadāmis which tends to complicate the picture. It seems that northern-Saharan merchants from several settlements came to relocate in Tuāt and were represented in Timbuktu. In the nineteenth century, we have some evidence that the Ghadāmsis especially identified with their original hometown and repatriated their profits.[43] Under the auspices of the Kunta, they were very visible in the city at the time of Barth's visit. The traveller formed the impression that, by European standards at least, their wealth was not considerable, 'the greater part of them being merely agents for other merchants residing in Ghadāmis, Swera (Mogador), Marākesh (Morocco) and Fās'.[44] This, however might simply mean that the Ghadāmsis linked the trade of the main North-African cities with the Sahara, much as the merchants of Timbuktu linked the Sahara to the trade of the Sūdān. At a shortly later time, we find al-Bakkā'i referring to the Ghadāmsis and other northern Saharans altogether as Tuātis.[45]

Representation of the same family both north and south of the Sahara appears to have always been a strong factor in the case of the Tuatis. Beginning with the time of Sīdi Abu'l-Qāsim, *imām* of Jingerebir in the fifteenth century, we seem to be dealing with a restricted number of families who were certainly not looked upon as foreigners or outsiders.[46] The most prominent and influential were two families who ranked among the scholars and are identified by a Waddāni *nisba*, in addition to a third whose members were also sometimes learned and are identified as Kūri (or Gūri). These would appear to have been the most permanently involved in the trans-Saharan trade and it is almost certain that they ranked among the most wealthy. Unfortunately, the evidence as it stands concerns the scholars among them with barely any information being available on their commercial activities or those of their kinsmen.[47]

The wealth of Timbuktu rested upon its position as a depot for the storage of goods and their subsequent distribution north and south depending upon the conditions of supply and demand. Huge fluctuations in prices were a yearly, and sometimes a monthly or a daily feature, which required constant knowledge of the markets elsewhere. Thus, we know that in one instance two boatloads of salt fetched virtually a fortune in Jenne at a time when the commodity had been absent from the market for only a short period.[48] The English Consul in Morocco, James Jackson, who also traded in gum arabic imported from Timbuktu, has left us a most remarkable document in the form of an invoice sent to North Africa by the Timbuktu merchant, 'L'Hage Hamed Elwangaree'. Among other things to be mentioned below, the Timbuktu merchant told his North African correspondent 'I will inform you by the spring caravan what merchandise to send here next autumn'.[49] Unfortunately, we are not able to identify this Ḥamed al-Wangari, especially since Jackson's information on Timbuktu, controversial in its own right, is surrounded by riddles.[50] In all probability, Hamed was a member of the Wangara Baghayughu family whose kinsmen, besides being *imāms* of the Sīdi Yaḥya Mosque, were to be found virtually in all the settlements along the way to the Akān goldfields. Besides gum arabic, an important product of the Timbuktu area by this time in the late eighteenth century, he exported gold-dust, gold-bars and locally-manufactured bed-covers, all in one consignment across the Sahara. The name Aḥmad, with the variants Ḥamad and Ḥammey, was too common in his family to allow a full identification without knowing his parentage.[51]

In his study on the Dyula–Suwarian tradition of learning, Ivor Wilks has pointed to the important fact that each family tended to devote only one son to a career of full-fledged scholarship.[52] This model is quite applicable to Timbuktu although among the major families we frequently find two or more brothers who were fully learned. The case of Maḥmūd b. 'Umar Aqīt's sons is an exceptional one whereby we find a sequence of several brothers all ranking among the scholars. This perhaps is what caused one traditionist to say: 'We favoured Maḥamūd b. 'Umar only on account of his virtuous sons'.[53] Far more commonly, each nuclear family produced only one or two scholars so that, for example, when we speak of several And-Agh-Muḥammad scholars all in one generation, we are really dealing with several families all descended from And-Agh-Muḥammad al-Kabīr. In their own time, the Baghayughus, Maghias and Gidādus each amounted to a whole clan, but the scholars among them were a minority. Indeed, Aḥmad Bāba's branch of the Aqīt family, which remained important for almost three centuries, produced no more than six or seven known scholars. In this case, the high reputation of al-Ḥājj Aḥmad, ancestor of this branch, and the extraordinary impact of Aḥmad Bāba, secured for the lineage a position of high prestige.[54] A difficulty, however, arises from the fact that the scholars alone are usually featured in the sources while their brothers and cousins, even though they may be wealthier merchants or plantation owners, are barely ever mentioned. Thus, among the sons of Muḥammad Gurdu, both Alfa 'Ali and Isma 'īl Yoro are known only from the pedigrees of their descendants who, in their own time, deserved mention in the chronicles because they were scholars.[55] At an earlier time, we may perhaps assume that the illustrious sons of Maḥmūd b. 'Umar had a whole array of non-learned brothers. One of these brothers, Alfa 'Abdu, is mentioned in connection with the uprising against the Moroccans solely because a fire which was put to a part of the city by the Maghsharen chieftain Awsanbu reached his home. This Awsanbu had grown up among the Aqīt brothers and al-Sa'di mentions the incident simply to illustrate how he treacherously turned against them.[56] Similarly, we learn only incidentally that Ibrāhīm b. 'Abdullāh b. Ibrāhīm b. Aḥmad Baghayughu al-Wangari, *imām* of Sīdi Yaḥya in the mid-eighteenth century, had a brother in a certain Alfa Aḥmad who was apparently a merchant who traded between Timbuktu and Jenne. The detail in this case is mentioned because Aḥmad's boat, with everything in it, sank on one of the return journeys to Kabara. It seems that many people died in the incident, including Aḥmad himself, his son, his concubine and his slaves.[57]

The work ethic which permeated Timbuktu society saw nothing wrong with the accumulation of personal wealth and often looked upon it as a sign of *baraka*. However, this basic orientation was surrounded by numerous qualifications, especially insofar as the conduct of scholars was concerned. Traditions which flourished some two centuries after the death of Sīdi Yaḥya al-Tadulsi, for example, recalled that he began his career as a merchant of some sort who derived his livelihood, while already a scholar, from participating in commercial transactions (*mu'āmalāt*). Later, in his middle years, he forsook such transactions altogether and apparently relied on his previous earnings. We are told that at this time he came to be favoured by numerous apparitions in which the Prophet Muḥammad, in the conventional psychological mystic sense, visited him very frequently. Later in life still, his limited means forced him to return to *mu'āmalāt* and, as a result of this, the apparitions became less frequent. This story projects an ethic whereby participation in the day-to-day affairs of commerce deprives the scholar of some of the benefits of his piety. Nonetheless, when Sīdi Yaḥya was asked why he would not give up his commerce, he said: 'I would not like to be needful of other people's aid'.[58]

Somewhat similar to the case of Sīdi Yaḥya was that of al-Mukhtār b. Muḥammad Zankanu. This scholar could not have been very wealthy for, although he patronized the *muddāh* on a yearly basis, he personally had to undertake the journey to Jenne on the occasion of each Ramaḍān in order to purchase the necessary supplies at favourable prices. In old age, we are told, his sons urged him to give up these journeys as they themselves would provide the supplies. The old man repeatedly refused, it seems, and he actually died on one of his journeys. Of the sons themselves, only one is specifically named in our sources; he is Muḥammad b. al-Mukhtār who became *Qāḍi*.[59]

Wealthier than al-Mukhtār, though not necessarily among the wealthiest, was al-Ḥājj al-Amīn Kānu (or Gānu). This scholar virtually had to force his hand against al-Qāḍi al-'Āqib so as to contribute his share towards rebuilding and widening the mosques. The practice, its seems, was that each notable would contribute the expenses of one day's work. Al-Amīn contributed the expenses of three days, amounting to a total of some 250 *mithqāls*.[60] Most of the expenses at that time appear to have been borne by the Aqīts themselves: Al-'Āqib 'spent sums on the building of the three mosques which God alone can count'.[61] We have no reason to doubt that the Aqīts in their heyday were the wealthiest in the city, though perhaps equalled by the Ḥājj family and the And-Agh-Muḥammads. Descriptions of the audiences of al-'Āqib, surrounded by his *shuhūd*, his retinue and his servants, invoke an image of great wealth. Similarly, we learn that among those who fell in the struggle against the Moroccans were two *harraṭīn* (client farmers) 'who belonged to Awlād Sīdi Maḥmūd'.[62] Besides participating in agricultural projects and, as we shall see, in the raising of cattle, the Aqīts almost certainly had a hand in the salt-trade and the trans-Saharan commerce. We learn incidentally, for example, that Aḥmad Bāba was born in the then-growing Saharan settlement of Arwān. At that time, in 1556, his father, still in his early thirties, probably secured a small fortune for his family, before rising to the top ranks of scholar–notables.[63] Aḥmad Bāba indicates that some of his Aqīt kinsmen were people of 'high finance' (*mutamawwilīn*), but this seems mainly to refer to the sons of Maḥmūd b. 'Umar.[64]

The wealthy scholars, like other notables, probably exhibited their wealth in terms of aggrandizing and embellishing their homes. There is no evidence of sumptuous dwellings being built or of virtual palaces staffed by domestic servants. The stone quarries in the area were far from the trade-routes and, besides being soft, they cost a fortune upon arrival in the city. We know from as late as the nineteenth century that the lime which was used for whitewashing the houses of the rich cost four times as much at Timbuktu as at Jenne.[65] In any case, the fragile nature of the building materials have left us little or no evidence as to what the old houses and mosques used to look like.[66] We know, for example, that Aḥmad Maghia fell well inside the city and the house near which he was killed was transformed to become his tomb. Yet, today the tomb is represented by a small structure standing at quite a distance from the city with barely any evidence of previous habitation around it.[67] A trace of the previous wealth is found in the copies of voluminous books, extant in Morocco, which used to belong to the Aqīts and And-Agh-Muḥammads. We are inclined to believe, in fact, that investment in books was one of the most socially accepted media for exhibiting one's wealth. Furniture, besides valuable cloths, and even silver cutlery, were luxuries which were also imported for local consumption by the wealthy. Thus, when the Aqīts were arrested, before being exiled,

> The Pasha Maḥmūd entered their homes and carried away everything that was in them, including funds, goods and furniture. God alone could assess their properties at the time and those of the people who had deposited their goods for safety with them.[68]

An indication of the wealth involved is evident from the statement that Maḥmūd sent the Moroccan sultan only a fraction, amounting to 100 000 *mithqāls*, from the value of the goods thus plundered.[69] Strangely enough, Askia Isḥāq had almost succeeded in buying off the entire Moroccan expedition for an equal sum, even though he made the offer rather too late after the first Songhai defeat by the Ruma.[70]

Our sources sometimes tend to confuse us concerning the reconcilability of learned piety and the acquisition of wealth. Thus, we are told that Makhlūf b. Ṣāliḥ al-Balbāli was a merchant who had little interest in learning until, at an advanced age, he started studying the *Risāla* of Ibn Abi Zaid under 'Abdullāh b. 'Umar Aqīt. The latter allegedly urged him 'to take up learning and to forsake commerce' when he saw that he was gifted with special intelligence.[71] Yet, as we know from elsewhere, 'Abdullāh himself was a wealthy person who indirectly participated in the local commerce. It seems that he owned a rather large number of milk cows whose daily produce was taken to the market by his slaves or servants. Aḥmad Bāba mentions that on a certain day the servants were late in selling the milk and continued to do so after sunset. 'Abdullāh objected to this practice as contrary to Muslim law and, since the money earned in the daytime was mixed with that which was collected in the evening, he felt obliged to distribute the whole income of that day to the poor. Aḥmad Bāba mentions the episode solely to illustrate the old Shaikh's strict adherence to the letter of the law. We learn incidentally in the process, however, that the Shaikh was a large-scale cattle owner whose income on a daily basis from the sale of milk alone was a 'consequential sum'.[72]

Ownership of cattle and camels was one among several sources of wealth which were open to scholars in the vicinities of Timbuktu, Arwān and Walāta. Up to recent times, cattle have continued to be exported on a large scale both to Hausaland and to various regions southwest of Massina.[73] Another important source of wealth was ownership of plantations at the outskirts of Timbuktu and along the Niger. Our evidence on this point, as on many other economic factors, is not detailed. We have from the mid-eighteenth century two contracts concerning the transfer of plantations from one owner to another. One of these was sold by the Ruma notable Abu Bakr b. al-Qā'id Bāḥaddu al-Drāwi, for a sum of 10 000 *mithqāls*, to a certain Hungudu b. al-Murdu. It is remarkable that the contract in this case took the form of a proclamation by both parties addressed to 'the attention of the judges, the jurists, the *tulba*, and the generality of Muslims'.[74] The other plantation was sold to al-Qāḍi Bāba b. al-Qāḍi al-Bakr (or Abkar) by the heirs of a certain Alfa Juma b. 'Abṭallāh. Unfortunately, we have no definitive clue to the identity of al-Qāḍi Bāba even though the document is dated 1174 A.H. (1760/61 A.D.).[75] There is a strong possibility, however, that the contract, which is extant only in a secondary copy, involves a scribal error. The purchaser would seem to have been al-Qāḍi Abkar b. al-Qāḍi Bāba al-Mukhtār, of the Zankanu family, who formally became Judge in 1764/5 A.D.[76]

Considering the emphasis which has always been placed on the question of slavery in the Niger bend area it is rather tempting to consider that ownership of slaves was a major source of wealth for scholars and other notables. This subject is surrounded by an extraordinary set of complications however. First, although assertions that slaves were exported from Timbuktu in large numbers across the Sahara have continued to be made up to the present century, these have rarely been based on substantive information.[77] René Caillié, the earliest European to leave a first-hand account of Timbuktu had little to say on the subject of slaves besides the following:

> In general, the slaves are better treated at Timbuctoo than in any other countries. They are well clothed and fed, and seldom beaten. They are required to observe religious duties, which they do very punctually; but they are nevertheless regarded as merchandise, and are exported to Tripoli, Morocco and other parts.[78]

Henry Barth was equally non-committal in his information except to say that reports which were current in his time concerning the extensiveness of the trans-Saharan slave-trade generally were 'certainly mistaken'. So far as he could ascertain, 'Ivory and slaves . . . seemed not to be exported to any considerable amount' from Timbuktu itself.[79] His evidence and that of Caillié together left open the possibility that slaves were taken by the Saharan warrior clans, both Tuareg and Hassāni, sometimes via Arwān, to North Africa. This same impression is, in fact, created by the queries sent to Aḥmad Bāba from Tuāt concerning the whole question of sub-Saharan slavery. It seems that slaves were taken by various routes to Tuāt and, there they often proved to be Muslims, not subject according to Māliki Law to enslavement. Pious Muslims, at Tuāt as at Timbuktu, feared retribution for the sale or purchase of anyone who claimed to be Muslim and could perform the prescribed prayers. Other views, however, maintained that the practice was lawful provided that the person was non-Muslim at the time of his original capture and enslavement. This, it seems, a rather legalistic question, formed the basis of Caillié's remarks as quoted above.[80]

Our sources do not help us to assess the role of the trans-Saharan slave-trade in the economy of Timbuktu with any sort of precision. The restrictions imposed by the rulings of scholars and judges may have discouraged slavers altogether from bringing their trade to Timbuktu. We know, for example, that one of the officials of Askia Isḥāq dealt heavily in the slave-trade besides being a merchant in horses. Al-Qāḍi Maḥmūd b. 'Umar warned him on one occasion, 'Why do you sell free people? Are you not afraid they will sell you?'[81] It seems, however, that during the periods of politico-military upheaval captives were brought in large numbers to Timbuktu to be sold as slaves. This happened in 1591 to the Zaghrānis of Yurwa when the Moroccan commander Māmi, after defeating them, sold them at Timbuktu for as little as 200–400 cowries each. This was a tiny fraction of the normal price of a slave; merchants were probably not inclined to purchase the captives.[82] The recent uprisings in Jenne and Timbuktu had made the prospects for the Ruma rather uncertain at this point and there was always the fear of retaliation from the Zaghrānis. Indeed, shortly after the reduction of Yurwa, the Zaghrānis became a junior partner in a campaign led by the Western Maghsharen and the Sanḥāja of Massina. The warriors fell upon the Ruma garrison at Rās al-Ma' and killed all its members, 70 in all.[83] It is almost impossible to ascertain the fate of the Zaghrāni captives, mainly women and children, at Timbuktu. However, the activities of the scholar Muḥammad 'Aryān al-Ra's in purchasing slaves to free them seem to pertain to this period. Subsequently, some of the Ruma commanders themselves perceived the public opinion advantage of freeing their captives and, in time, Muḥammad attained the status of a *walī* whereby the Pashas themselves visited him most frequently for blessing.[84]

We may perhaps safely conjecture that the scholars and notables of Timbuktu, much as at Jenne, Walāta and the Hausa towns, saw no particular interest in the depopulation of villages within the range of their commercial contacts simply to satisfy the demands of slavers.[85] Other captives, originating in areas remote from Timbuktu, often passed through the local market on the way to North Africa, but this appears to have been a sporadic rather than a constant, or economically dependable, factor. Perhaps we are deceived by the sources, for they tend to cover only the controversial cases. One such case was the sale at the market of Timbuktu in 1075 A.H. (1664/5 A.D.) of certain descendants of the ancient scholar Mūr Hukār. That this was an exceptional case is evident from the fact that it is the only piece of information dating to the seventeenth century which is included in the authentic copies of *Tārīkh al-Fattāsh*. With one minor exception, all other events mentioned in this source date prior and up to 1599 A.D.[86] Indeed, an opening paragraph included in one of the authentic copies (MS A) mentions among the policies of Askia Muḥammad the following:

> He established for the Muslims certain rights, taking upon himself that their inviolability would be observed. He ordered that the people of Mūri Kuyra would marry anyone they wished and that their sons [even from slave or servile wives] would inherit those rights [as free men]. These rights are still observed to this day and have not changed because of his (Askia Muḥammad's) *baraka*.[87]

It seems that violation of the special rights of Ahl Mūri Kuyra invited the first additions to the text of *Tārīkh al-Fattāsh*, a work which so far as we can tell was drawn from the notes of Maḥmūd Ka't by his son Isma'īl.[88] Subsequently, in the early nineteenth century, numerous additions were made (known from MS C) which tried to justify the servile status of several groups along the Niger on the basis of alleged historical precedent. The text of the original document which was drawn by Askia Muḥammad for the benefit of the grandsons of Mūr Hukār, a document now extant in separate copies besides being originally included in *Tārīkh al-Fattāsh*, became the centre of a controversy, as we shall see further in Chapter 6.

The presence of slaves at Timbuktu itself tended to be minimal as a result of a practice whereby their owners tended to free them or free their sons while retaining them as clients and protégés among the ranks of the Ghabibi (including the Haddādin = Smiths) and the Ḥarrāṭīn. These semi-servile ranks included some who were fully independent and others, impoverished though originally free, who actively sought a prestigious patron. It is remarkable that the same Gurdu scholar who, as we shall see, allegedly stopped the slave-trade, is also remembered in connection with a legend which suggests that scholars actively sought to enhance the interests of their Ghabibi. The legend concerns a Ghabibi who belonged to Gurdu and another who belonged to an unnamed *imām* of Sankore. The story need not be related in full except to say that while the two clients competed over the hand of a maiden the main actors in the competition were actually their masters.[89] The legend in the defective MS C of *Tārīkh al-Fattāsh* that the Ghabibi are descended from slaves originally belonging to al-Qāḍi al'Āqib suggests that scholars during Songhai times were the principal patrons. By the eighteenth century, however, Ruma and other notables joined the ranks of urban patrons.[90]

It seems that similar patterns of patronage characterized the relations between urban-based scholars and notables and the servile agriculturalists who worked their plantations along the Niger. The agriculturalists enjoyed a customary right to working the land, in return for a portion of the produce, and there are indications indeed that the rights of absentee owners often lapsed. The Ḥarrāṭīn, for their part, were principally urban-based and they do not seem to have carried the bulk of the agricultural work, even in the immediate vicinity of Timbuktu. For, as Barth observed, 'All the people of the town who did not belong to any trade or profession, together with the inhabitants of the neighbouring districts, were . . . employed in the rice harvest'.[91] It is possible that the Ḥarrāṭīn acted as agents for their masters in providing seeds to the agriculturalists and in overseeing the harvest. At the outskirts of Timbuktu, where the seasonal inundations were extensive enough to allow limited agriculture, vegetable and melon gardens were planted which sometimes were owned by the Ḥarrāṭīn themselves.[92]

An important source of wealth, and perhaps the most important for scholars, was ownership of urban property which was used for storage. As already suggested, the wealth of Timbuktu as a whole rested on its being a depot for the transit of goods between the peoples of the Niger and the Sahara. One arm of this depot was Arwān in the north, while the other was Kabara which adjoined Timbuktu on the Niger. Of Kabara, Barth wrote:

> While traversing the village, I was surprised at the many clay buildings which are to be seen here, amounting to between one hundred and fifty and two hundred; however, these are not so much the dwellings of the inhabitants of Kabara themselves, but serve rather as magazines for storing up the merchandise belonging to the people of, and the foreign merchants residing in, Timbuktu and Sasandi.[93]

The remains of buildings well to the north of Timbuktu suggest that the city itself had a considerable storage capacity in Songhai times. Later, however, Arwān became a major centre for the distribution of goods and some of the commerce went from there directly to Walāta and Sasanding.[94]

It is important to emphasize that the Saharan crossing itself had, as a result of a gradual development, lost much of its initial profitability. Thus, one of the late-eighteenth-century invoices published by Jackson shows that 200 loads of gum arabic fetched some 4500 Mexican dollars in Morocco though their original cost at Timbuktu was only 800. However, fully 3600 dollars was expended for the hire of the camels alone.[95] This had always been an immense expense for merchants because the Saharan crossing taxed the life-span of these beasts of burden. In the salt-for-grain commerce between the Niger and the Sahara, the bulkiness of the merchandise meant also that the greatest expense went to the owners of boats and keepers of the camels. In 1917, the French established a commission of enquiry concerning the trans-Saharan trade; its findings tend to confirm the evidence preserved by Jackson. It was discovered that six loads of tobacco cost only 240 francs at Tuāt and fetched as much as 2700 francs at Timbuktu. The sum could then be used for purchasing goods which fetched 5400 francs at Tuāt; however, the camel wear was estimated at 1050 francs for such a journey, while the upkeep and losses amounted to 1000 francs. In other words, the net profits for a small caravan accompanied by two persons barely exceeded 3000 francs. The round-trip journey lasted fully five months and very few people could pursue the arduous career of caravaneering across the Sahara for very long.[96]

By contrast, the merchants at Timbuktu who owned good storage depots and were aware of developments in the markets could amass virtual fortunes without any great physical exertions on their part. The arrival of small caravans at various seasons was a feature which perhaps began in the seventeenth century with the growing importance of clerical clans. This tended to reduce the scale of the price fluctuations but not their frequency. Thus, Barth observed during his extended stay that the price of a piece of *khām* (unbleached calico) rose from 5700 to 7200 cowries all in a matter of a few days between January and February. One of the causes for this, so far as we can tell from the traveller's account, was that the rise of the Niger had brought the merchants from Jenne and elsewhere with their boats. They had already unloaded their boats and were ready, it seems, for their return journey. For, as Barth recorded:

> It was on January 4th, that the first boat from Kabara approached close to the walls of the town of Timbuktu; and, as the immediate result of such a greater facility of intercourse, the supply of corn became more plentiful and, in consequence, much cheaper.[97]

'Meanwhile', as we read elsewhere, 'the price of the merchandise from the north went on increasing', despite the arrival of two small caravans, one from Tuāt carrying dates and tobacco, and 'a small group of Tajakant traders with 80 camels' who carried tea and sugar, besides even pomegranates and other products. To Barth also we owe the detail that the average price of a slab of salt fluctuated between 3000 and 6000 cowries in a short period, 'the price always rising towards Spring'. The main Azalai (salt caravan), usually including 10 000 or more camels, used to arrive at Timbuktu during May and sometimes as late as June. The prices then fell but they rose gradually again until the appearance of the first small caravans in November or December. The fluctuations became 'the profit of the merchants, who buy their supplies on the arrival of a caravan and store it up'.[98]

From more recent evidence we know that a load of salt, or four slabs per camel, cost five times as much at Timbuktu as at the mines of Taoudenni. The profits of the transporters were, however, consumed in the upkeep and the wear and tear to the camels, whose value was equivalent to 100 slabs of salt each or more. By contrast, a merchant who was able to store up 1000 slabs could turn these over, under favourable circumstances, at a profit of 1000 *mithqāls* in one season. It is this factor perhaps which led one of the early French administrators to conclude from a distance that the population of Timbuktu was 'parasitic'. The city, in fact, was crucial for the economy of the Sahelo–Sahara and the risks of losses were always great. Naturally, the local notables diversified their investments to include gold and grain from the south, cattle and hides from the north, besides cloths from North Africa and Hausaland, and sometimes even guns from the Asante trade.[99] Goods exported to Tuāt included such ephemeral products as incense (*bakhūr*), herbal medications and female make-up products, besides wooden utensils, basketry, Tuareg cheese, rugs, sandals (manufactured especially by the Ruma) and hides of all sorts.[100] The imports from North Africa, ranging from dates to European cutlery, have for the most part already been mentioned. These were traded further south in return for the kola nut, vegetable butter, pepper, ginger, cotton, limes, silver (cheaper at Sasanding) and numerous other items.[101] The main balance of the north–south trade, however, rested on the exchange of cloths, salt and cattle in return for grain and gold, allowing an undetermined role for the passage of slaves through Timbuktu. Today, the exchange of cattle and salt for grain (the latter on the scale of 2000 tons per year) lies at the backbone of the local economy.

The economic system which prevailed in Timbuktu made it possible for scholars to participate in the commerce of the area without occupying a visibly prominent role as merchants. We may recall that the wholesale exchange of goods at Timbuktu was largely an 'invisible commerce' which was carried through the agency of the hoteliers and *teifa* who acted as commercial brokers. We are inclined to believe that the scholars invested primarily in the ownership of urban property at Timbuktu and Kabara and in the storage of goods. At the very least, they were able to purchase the yearly supplies for their own families and for their clients in bulk quantities at favourable prices. Additionally, the wholesale storage of goods could serve as a basis for setting up a son in business or for financing a student or a *protégé* who acted as a small merchant or a retailer. We know, for example, that Sīdi al-Mukhtār al-Kunti al-Kabīr himself resided for some time at Timbuktu in his youth and was patronized there by a local notable who was not exceptionally wealthy.[102] An indication of how the system operated is provided by René Caillié who made his appearance at

Timbuktu in the guise of a Muslim returning from European slavery. Being nearly destitute on arrival, the French traveller was well received and patronized by a certain Sīdi-Abdallahi Chebir (presumably al-Kabīr), a notable who is otherwise unidentifiable. Caillié later wrote:

Sidi-Abdallahi daily lavished on me marks of his kindness; he even went so far as to urge me to remain in Timbuctoo. He said he would give me merchandise to trade on my own account; and, observed, that when I should have accumulated sufficient profit, I might return to my own country without assistance from any one.[103]

It seems that a complex system of patronage permeated the whole society and linked, by various means, the wealthiest to the very poorest. This explains Marc-Shrader's assertion that the profits of the salt-trade, for example, diffused to the entire population of Timbuktu. Similarly, diffusion of profits from the cloth trade helped sustain an extraordinarily large number of tailor–alfas. Even the trade in hides had an important impact because the Ruma commoners tended to specialize in the manufacture of sandals.[104] According to Dupuis-Yakouba, fully two-thirds of the population derived their livelihood around the turn of the century from commerce.[105] The system of patronage extended to the long-distance trade as well as to the local retail market. The retailers were for the most part drawn from Ghabibi clients and slaves who received their supplies from their patrons and masters but nonetheless traded on their account. The participation of a slave in the market, and especially if successful, raised him and his sons to the status of a free Ghabibi protégé.[106]

In some cases it is possible to find evidence of direct participation by scholars in commerce. Thus, in the 'spiritual' chain of transmission of the Kunta Qādiri *wird* we find reference to al-Sayyid 'Urwa b. Sīdi Muḥammad who was a man 'of finance' at Arwān. Another scholar, al-Shaikh Sīdi al-Amīn, enjoyed ownership rights at the salt-mines of Taghāza and apparently resided at that place in the middle of the Sahara. A third scholar yet, Sīdi al-Ḥājj Abu Bakr, 'used to organize the Azalai himself [at Arwān] and used to travel to Taghāza and Tuāt'.[107] The Kunta merchant–scholars were perhaps the most dynamic that ever flourished in the Sahara, but a similar role, with more extensive contacts in Massina and the rest of the Niger bend area, appears to have been characteristic of the al-Ḥājj family, the Aqīts and the And-Agh-Muḥammads at a much earlier time.

The families which traded with Jenne and further south during the seventeenth to the nineteenth centuries are not as well documented as the Saharans who traded via Arwān. Nonetheless, we find a representative though recent case in Muḥammad 'Umar b. 'Umar b. Alfa Sa'īd b. Bāba. Born at Kabara around 1848, this scholar became very influential at the time of the French conquest and, possibly because he was a descendant of the illustrious Gurdu family, he acquired the honorary title of *imām*. As Marty later wrote:

Mamadou Omar is intelligent, active and energetic. He is a large-scale merchant whose commercial affairs often require him to travel very far south. Other than that, he is at the same time a tailor, an owner of many buildings, an *imām* of the great mosque of Jinguerebir and chief of the Badyindi quarter.[108]

The combination of learning and wealth in the same family is attested at a much earlier time in the case of the chronicler 'Abd al-Raḥmān al-Sa'di himself. The Sa'di family is sometimes vaguely thought to be originally Moroccan while, for our part, we have identified it as principally southern Saharan Tuareg. In fact, the recorded kinship ties include Saharan Balbālis, Fulānis, Wangara, Anṣāris (presumably Kel Antasar), Hausa or perhaps Tuareg Kel Housa, besides Sharīfs from the Ṣaqali family.[109] Moreover, while the Sa'dis entertained strong relationships with the judges of Massina, they also had a permanent branch established at Jenne. This made it possible for 'Abd al-Raḥmān to attain the imamate of the Sankore Mosque of Jenne at an exceptionally young age; he was later dismissed from this post in a move which was equally as exceptional, and became *kātib* (or secretary) to the Pashas though no scholar of his calibre had previously accepted such a post. It is not clear to what extent the Sa'dis were representative of the Timbuktu–Jenne merchant–scholars. 'Abd al-Raḥmān himself, being a full-fledged scholar, did not play a pronounced role in the commerce of the family. In the autobiographical sections of his study however, he mentions certain events which indicate that he got embroiled both in the politics and in the commercial affairs of Jenne. For one thing, he acted for a long time in conjunction with the *Qāḍi* Aḥmad b. Mūsa Dābu as a mediator between the Ruma regime and the Ardo of Massina, Ḥammādi Āmina. Secondly, his dismissal from the imamate came in the wake of a disagreement between local governor and notables whereby 'all the merchants left Jenne to Bīna'.[110] We can assume that al-Sa'di's brothers played a leading role in precipitating this exodus, for we find them involved in a similar episode which took place two years earlier in 1043 A.H. (1633/4 A.D.). At that time, the reigning Pasha Sa'ūd b. Aḥmad 'Ajrūd al-Sharqi alienated the merchants of Jenne and became subject to charges that his conduct was 'ruinous to the country'.[111] Among other things, he had apparently extorted 200 *mithqāls* from Muḥammad Sa'di, brother of the chronicler 'Abd al-Raḥmān. Later, the Pasha complained to the same Muḥammad by saying: 'You, Alfa Sa'di, have no other work except assembling the merchants at your house every day . . . to discuss our [alleged] ills and misdeeds'.[112] At a later juncture, we find Muḥammad Sa'di being highly honoured on one of his visits to Timbuktu by a subsequent Pasha.[113]

The wealth of the scholars, whether owned individually or shared by kinsmen, gave strength to the influence which they otherwise exercised by virtue of their learning. Wealth on its own was not sufficient as a criterion of status, possibly because its owner could be stigmatized for his preoccupation with worldly affairs. Thus, we know that among the merchants who supported the rebellion of Muḥammad al-Ṣādiq, a leading position was held by a certain al-Gīd b. Ḥamza al-Sanāwi who was apparently one of the wealthiest in Timbuktu at the time. Yet, in retrospect, this non-learned person was looked upon as a 'poor and meddlesome merchant who had no influence and not to be heeded'.[114] By contrast, when al-Qāḍi 'Umar b. Maḥmūd Aqīt was implicated in the rebellion against the Moroccans a few years later, the Pasha Maḥmūd b. Zarqūn wrote him saying:

> How is it, when you are the *qudwa* (a man who is emulated) in this Sudanic region, and when your word is heeded throughout, that you allowed such disturbances to occur in your presence? . . . You allowed the commoners to carry out their desires despite the fact that you were able to put a stop to the strife . . . In short, you are the pillar upon whom this matter rests.[115]

The Aqīts dispensed not only of wealth and patronage of their own, but they also acted as protégés for the wealthy Ghadāmsi and Tuāti merchants established in the city. A similar role is documented for the Kunta in the nineteenth century; they acted as spiritual protectors for the Saharan and North African merchants as well as for the Tuareg Kel Inkundar, a fraction of the Kel Idnan, who encamped in the region of Timbuktu.[116] It is almost certain that the main scholar families of the intervening period, namely the Maghia, Guidādu, Baghayughu and Gurdu, also protected the rights of lesser merchant families from both north and south. For although we find reference to Ruma families who adopted a similar posture, the properties of their protégés were far from inviolable. The Dara'is, Tazarkīnis, Tilimsānis and Mas'ūdis, the main Ruma families, sometimes plundered each other and each other's protégés.[117] By contrast, the position of the Baghayughus, for example, was never threatened. Their monopoly over the imamate of Sīdi Yaḥya was no doubt a very important factor which gave them a highly venerated status. Additionally, any threat against them might have caused them, in conjunction with their kinsmen further south, to divert a substantial portion of the gold-trade away from Timbuktu. For it seems that the Baghayughus, probably in conjunction with the Guidādus and Gurdus, predominated in the southern commerce. Additionally, the boatmen and merchants from the south probably looked to the latter three families as spokesmen and as representatives of their interests, much as the Saharan caravaneers and northern merchants looked to the Aqīts and Maghias and, later, the Kunta.[118]

Although the scholars were in a position to intervene in the daily affairs of the military–fiscal hierarchy, and in the selection of Pashas and Ḥukkām (provincial governors), the evidence on this point is essentially lacking except in the above-mentioned case of the Sa'di family. The reticence of the chroniclers, and even al-Sa'di himself, pertains to two factors which are closely related. First, the attitude of the scholars was always reserved and they seem to have exercised their political influence through the agency of non-learned (or less-learned) kinsmen. Thus, it was only at times of the gravest crises that scholars came to the forefront of political events. Secondly, the ideological orientation of scholars, which forms the subject of the following discussion, fully distinguished them from all temporal authorities. This meant, in turn, that direct influence over the rulers, through constant interaction, was not necessarily desirable. For it threatened to rob the scholars of the image of neutrality which they projected throughout the Sahelo–Sudan.

Ideological factors

Perhaps the most important criterion which influenced the status of scholars was their own ideological emphasis on their distinctiveness from state hierarchies. Seen in conjunction with the potential bearing of Muslim jurisprudence on matters of state organization and policy, this ideological emphasis tended to exert an enormous pressure upon the rulers. We need only note that, as a result of this, several rulers, both Songhai and Ruma, sought to enhance their image by adopting even if only partially the posture of scholars.

The ideological emphasis on the distinctiveness of scholars may to an extent have been inherited from across the Sahara and, especially, in the wake of the strong fifteenth-century contacts with Egypt. There, the position of scholars was strengthened by the fact that the Mamluk military elite was foreign and somewhat marginal to the organization of urban society. In Morocco, the distinction was not as clear-cut, but the state and military hierarchy, partly modelled along Ottoman lines in the sixteenth century, was increasingly made up of Christian renegades, Andalusian fugitives and recruits from the East.[119] This factor requires being emphasized because of its bearing on the role and status of the Moroccan Ruma who conquered the Sudan. Their differentiation from the rest of the urban population, in the earliest stages at least, was perhaps predetermined by their previous standing in Morocco. In the Sudan, they tended to adopt most of the practices of their Songhai predecessors, who indeed became their partners. Together, the two groups amounted to a military class or even caste which continued to acknowledge the separate religio-legal authority of the scholars.

In the Sahelo–Sudanic region generally, there were two important local factors which sharpened the distinction between military and religio-legal elites. The first was the tradition of Muslim autonomism, already discussed in Chapter 2, which was rooted in the fact that Muslims were in the earliest times foreign to Sudanic society and quite marginal. An outcome of this tradition, which outlived the processes of conversion and intermarriage, was the special status accorded to Muslim communities, first within the state capitals and later in their own settlements and towns. We have mentioned the case of Zāgha, but it seems almost certain that the first Wangara towns along the way to the Akan gold-fields were also autonomous. We have a glimpse of the first appearance of the Wangara in the city–states of Hausaland and, there too, the norm appears to have been communal autonomy for Muslims.[120] In the Bambuku region, Sālim al-Suwāri is associated with the establishment of several exclusively Muslim settlements which were centred around a town given the name of Diakha (a variant upon Zāgha).[121] Finally, we might mention that in the Futa regions of present-day Senegal there existed a town named Kunjur (which may have given its name to the later state of Kajoor) where *qāḍi* and scholars were fully autonomous.[122]

At a later stage the distinction between Muslims and non-Muslims in all the above-mentioned regions tended to give way to a more technical one between literati (clerics and clerisy) and between various shades of Muslims and Islamized groups in the Sudan. What concerns us in this development is that the special status accorded to the clerics tended throughout to carry pseudo-ethnic connotations. Thus, we often speak of the Dyula merchant clerics as descendants of the Wangara, but while the Wangara themselves were of mixed Soninke and Mālinke origins, the Dyula have over the centuries absorbed recruits into their clerical tradition from a multitude of other groups as well. In the Upper Volta Basin, for example, the clerics have been seen more or less as an ethnically differentiated middle estate which stood in an intermediate status position between the 'nobles' or rulers on the one hand and the commoners relegated to an inferior status.[123] This model is sometimes also extended to the Torodbe clerisy of the Futa regions, though a series of religious movements there often gave actual rulership to scholars beginning perhaps with the early fifteenth century.[124] Willis has emphasized the mixed ethnic origins of this 'Fulāni' clerisy, but the tendency to identify the clerics of the Sudan with a rather limited set of ethnic entities remains an important consideration.[125] It means that initiation into the circles of the clerics amounted, especially insofar as the non-learned could perceive it, to a separate way of life.[126] This perhaps helps explain why we have no specific reference to Songhai scholars in Timbuktu, Jenne or Gao. This did not mean that the ethnic group did not contribute to the ranks of the learned; we know of many scholars whose ethnic identity is not specified. Rather, it seems that Songhai, like Ruma at a later time, became synonymous with a profession, namely the military. The scholars, by contrast, were not ethnically differentiated in Timbuktu from the mass of free and respectable citizenry. Nonetheless, the earliest French observers tended to look upon them as a class on its own and sometimes even described them as a *caste* of *alfas*.[127]

The second factor is not much different from the first, but it pertains especially to the southern Saharan region, an area which ultimately had greater influence on Timbuktu than the rest of the Sahelo–Sūdān. Here there arose a distinction nearly everywhere among the nomadic populations of the

Saharan fringes whereby whole clans identified themselves on the basis of the preoccupations of their chiefs either as 'warrior clans' (Imoshagh among the Tuareg) or as 'scholar clans' (Ineslemen, Zwaya, Tulba or Fuqaha). In a recent article C. C. Stewart has related this development to transformations which took place in the Sahara during the second half of the seventeenth century.[128] This view finds some support in the fact that our first reference to the Kel al-Sūq as 'Fuqaha' dates to 1106 A.H. (1694/5 A.D.).[129] The model had much earlier roots, however, and it is not clear that the warrior clans, or their ruling lineages, were the ones who 'carefully preserved it'.[130] We know, for example, that Muḥammad b. Muḥammad b. 'Ali Sili al-Tunbukti al-Walāti, who died in 1050 A.H. (1640/41 A.D.), ruled it permissible to take interest on credit (or practise usury, *riba*) from the warrior clans of the Sahara who 'were steeped in unlawful practices (*dhimam*)'.[131] At an even earlier time, Aḥmad Bāba made a distinction between due observance of the law (*shar'*) and its manipulation through *siyāsa*, or politics. He insisted on the preferability of the former but had recourse nonetheless to a law all on its own which he described as the 'law of warriors' (*ḥukm al-muhāribīn*).[132] It seems almost certain that the orientation of the scholars themselves was a contributing factor to the distinction between warrior and learned clans.

The distinctions, though emphasized by the clans themselves, were never as clear-cut or stable as some modern scholars have viewed them. Certainly, they did not give rise to a class system as such, whereby Imoshagh lorded over Ineslemen who, in turn, enjoyed higher status than the dependent Imghad clans.[133] The noble status of Imoshagh among the Tuareg, recently extended only to the Tingeregif, a fraction of the Kel Tadmekkat, defined their relationship to their Imghad clients but not to the Ineslemen. Indeed, it is possible that the term Ineslemen corresponds to the 'Muslimi' *nisba* which appears in the nomenclature of a specific group of Saharan scholars.[134] Among other groups it seems almost certain that the fragmentation of Tuareg society into warrior and scholar clans, and possibly the earlier distinctions between Tuareg and other Berber Sanhāja, resulted from the conflict between the matrilineal and patrilineal systems of succession. Recently, H. T. Norris has recorded certain traditions which indicate that the split of the Wulmdān from the rest of the Kel Tadmekkat resulted from such a conflict in the seventeenth century.[135] In this case, as later among the Tingeregif, the 'secessionists', so to speak, became the dominant force and gained over the majority of the Imghad clans. Similar criteria might have caused the split earlier on between the learned Kel al-Sūq and the rest of the Kel Tadmekkat. We observe the conflict among members of the chief lineage of the Maghsharen in the early seventeenth century, though the scholars in this case probably lost their Tuareg identity and did not become the founders of scholar clans.[136] Elsewhere, the traditions of Arwān are overshadowed by a constitutional legend surrounding a certain Aḥmad b. Adda (or Aḥmad Ag-Adda, sometimes simply Agadda).[137] This scholar–chieftain appears to have had intermarriage links with the chief lineages of Maghsharen, the Kel Idnan and the Kel Antasar. He is alleged to have been a Sharīf 'beyond the shadow of a doubt' but, as he is associated with al-Sūq, 'before its ruin', he probably belonged to the Kel al-Sūq.[138] His sons and grandsons inherited two chieftaincies, one vested in the judgeship of Arwān, while the other was a temporal one, possibly based upon matrilineal descent from a chief lineage of either the Maghsharen or the Antasar-Idnan.[139] Ultimately, the judgeship reigned supreme in Arwān, especially under al-Wāfi b. Ṭalibna b. Agadda and his son Sanbīr. The sources somehow lose track of the temporal chieftaincy which perhaps later merged through intermarriage with an already existing patrilineal chieftaincy among the Barābīsh.[140]

The warrior chieftaincies sometimes looked down upon the scholar clans and especially the term *tulba* acquired a low-status connotation. While scholar–chiefs had their own clients among the *tulba* fractions however, they regarded the warrior chiefs as 'tyrants' and 'thieves' and generally represented them in a derogatory light. This was rationalized in terms of the abhorrence among scholars of all authority based on military might and brute force. Thus, concerning a sequence of Kunta chieftains, themselves matrilineally linked to the Tuareg, we read:

> All of these were not sultans but, rather, people of virtue, *baraka* and good organization. The kings or sultans (*ahl al-mulk*) among the Wulmdan, the Massina, the Futa, the people of Air, and the Fulani of Sokoto, kinsmen of 'Uthman b. Fūdi, honored them greatly. They themselves gave presents to some of the tyrants such as the Wulmdān. These presents they called *al-baraka* and were given to them to ward them off. Sometimes they gave presents also to the Huggār, for the same purpose, but to no other group.[141]

It is notable that the Kunta who acquired a reputation for scholarly and even 'saintly' status did not refrain from military undertakings.[142] More interestingly yet, the Kel Antasar, a Tuareg clan held to be descendant from the Ansar (companions of the Prophet), at one point evolved a separate military chieftaincy, besides its traditional Ineslemen chieftaincy, in order to defend itself against the encroachments of the Kunta.[143] The Kel Antasar may perhaps be the Yantasar mentioned by al-'Umari in the fourteenth century among the independent Berber clans north of the empire of Mali.[144] Oral tradition suggests strong links between them and the warlike Kel Idnan, including intermarriage and cross-over of chiefs, resulting it seems from differences in their succession systems. Among the Barābīsh, who partly absorbed the Maghsharen and succeeded them as the main regional power in the seventeenth century, the scholars of Arwān acted in lieu of an Ineslemen chieftaincy. These scholars, though led by descendants of Agadda, were diverse in origins and generally tended to lose their specific clan or ethnic identity.[145]

The status of scholars in Timbuktu, therefore, must be viewed against a much wider configuration which distinguished the learned elites throughout from the military elites. Warlike clans did not rely for their livelihood on plunder or on the tributes which they imposed upon clients and semi-clients. Likewise, the scholar clans, excepting in recent times the case of the Kel al-Sūq, were not uniformly learned and could not rely on teaching or alms.[146] In both cases, raising cattle and participation in long-distance trade were the main sources of wealth. The status distinctions, however, imparted a sense of order upon the relationships between clans and with the commercial centres. The Wulmdān, for example, were held supreme among the Tuareg who interacted with Timbuktu from the seventeenth century onwards, though the Kel Tadmekkat were at times probably more powerful. The Wulmdān exacted a tribute from the Barābīsh which, however, originated as 'blood-money' given to them after the defeat and massacre of one of their raiding parties.[147] The scholar clans held their own against the warriors by virtue of a much more dynamic and organized participation in commerce. Partly because of this, they were held in high esteem in the commercial centres and acted as mediators and settlers of disputes throughout the Sahara.

In Timbuktu itself, the scholars consciously set themselves apart from the temporal authorities of the area. They stood somewhere in the middle between the organized states of the Niger bend and the confederations of nomadic chieftaincies of the southern Sahara. Depending upon the circumstances at any one given time, they leaned towards one or the other of these forces. Their general preference was for the organized and stable state, and this ultimately determined their acceptance of the Ruma. For, as al-Mukhtār al-Kunti expressed their view, they believed for example that:

> The dynasty of the Arma (Ar-Rūma) was better than that of the Tuaregs because they adhered to the policy of a kingdom. As for the Tuaregs, they conquered without knowledge of the policy of a kingdom and the establishment of offices according to the Sharīʿa. They ruin and do not build and construct.[148]

This view is representative of the prevalent attitude among scholars but should not be understood to be the last word on the subject. Thus, when al-Ḥājj 'Umar threatened the autonomy of Timbuktu in the mid-nineteenth century, al-Bakkā'i argued that 'Timbuktu could not have any prosperity without the [cooperation] of the Tuareg'. The jurist in this case was alluding to economic besides political factors, for he added: 'People of the deserts and of cattle are important for the prosperity of towns and villages'.[149]

The ambivalent attitude of scholars towards the Saharan warrior clans extended with some reservations to politico-military elites generally. This is illustrated by numerous anecdotes concerning Songhai and early Ruma times. But the best expression of this attitude comes from Aḥmad Bāba's *Jalb al-Niʿma wa-Dafʿ al-Naqma bi-Mujānabat al-Wulāt al-Ẓalama.*[150] This treatise, described by the North African al-Maqqari as one of the best on its theme in Muslim jurisprudence, is levelled against rulers and state officials generally and calls upon Muslims (and, implicitly, the scholars) to avoid all dealings with them.[151] Since Aḥmad Bāba and his Aʿqīt kinsmen were exiled to Morocco by al-Sulṭān al-Manṣūr, it has always been tempting to see this composition as a retaliation: it may have been intended to stigmatize al-Manṣūr in Morocco and to warn local scholars in the Sūdān against cooperating with his officials.[152] Alternatively, the document may have some indirect bearing upon the civil war which erupted in the Songhai empire at the time of Muḥammad al-Ṣādiq's rebellion. The involvement of some scholars, along with Timbuktu merchants and tailor-alfas, in al-Ṣādiq's rebellion might have inspired a reassertion of the distinction between learned and military elites in retrospect. All copies which mention the date of this composition assign it to 997 A.H. (1588 A.D.).[153] This corresponds to some two years after the Songhai civil war and three years before the Moroccan conquest. The chronological factor is somewhat obscured, however, by the fact that Aḥmad Bāba returned to the same theme in a treatise entitled *Ma Rawāh al-Ruwāt fi Mujānabat al-Wulāt*. This document has survived only in a truncated form but enough remains to show that it was written ten years after *Jalb al-Niʿma*, while the author was in exile in Morocco.[154]

Aḥmad Bāba documented his views with reference to the Qur'ān, the Ḥadīth and the authority of the earliest Māliki jurists but he did not offer a systematic treatment of the relations between scholars and state. Citing incidents from Ibn Khaldūn's history and elsewhere, he prefaced his *Jalb al-Niʿma* as follows:

> This is a work in which I have brought together some of what has come down to us by way of warnings against being close to tyrants and befriending them or seeking them out and entertaining companionship with them. Such quest after the rulers of this passing world and its lowly and waning rewards is reprehensible.[155]

It is interesting that Aḥmad Bāba's 'tyrannical rulers' are designated as *wulāt*, a term which applies to officials of high rank but is rarely applied to supreme rulers in Islam. Since the author does not distinguish any ruler of his time as being other than tyrannical, however, his treatise could be construed as levelled against state hierarchies in general. As we know from another one of his works, Aḥmad Bāba did not go as far as to deny the need for sovereignty in the organization of Muslim society. On the contrary, he advised that a Muslim community governed autonomously by its own *Jamāʿa* should of necessity acknowledge the sovereignty of a *sultān* to satisfy the full requisites of Māliki law.[156] Beyond this highly theoretical premise, however, he relegated state authority to an extremely marginal position in the affairs of Muslim society. Muslims in general, but by implication especially the scholars, should shun state service and refrain at all costs from court life. Gifts and wages should never be accepted from any official other than the *khalīfa* himself or the deputy-*khalīfa* who is lawfully qualified to dispense revenue at his own discretion. Even then, Aḥmad Bāba sought to bypass this technicality in Muslim Māliki law. He surveyed a whole spectrum of early Māliki opinion which, as he saw it, allowed that the Judge alone could, like governors (*hukkām*), lawfully receive wages from the state.[157] The main implication of this argument, of course, is that the relationship between Muslim society and the Muslim state should be channelled almost solely through the judgeship.

It is rather difficult to see any specific relationship between the views expressed by Aḥmad Bāba and the circumstances surrounding Muḥammad al-Ṣādiq's rebellion against Askia al-Ḥājj. That was a case in which some scholars, and especially the merchants, supported a royal candidate against the reigning monarch. As we know from al-Maghīli's answers to Askia Muḥammad, the prevalent view was that no one could contest the sovereignty 'of an *amīr* who discharged the affairs of his subjects to the best of his abilities'.[158] Askia al-Ḥājj had essentially alienated the scholars, while Aḥmad Bāba is more concerned with a situation in which the scholars allowed themselves to become clients patronized by the monarch. This, more than anything else, suggests implicit reference to the court in Morocco where al-Manṣūr indeed enhanced his image by drawing to his audiences some of the most prominent scholars of the time.[159]

Whatever the case may be, the relationship between Timbuktu and the Songhai state, channelled primarily through the judgeship, certainly lies at the background of Aḥmad Bāba's thought. The scholars had recognized Askia Muḥammad as a true *khalīfa*, or alternatively as a deputy-*khalīfa*, and this recognition more or less extended to his successors. As mentioned in Chapter 2, the chronicles give the impression that an ordered and mutually satisfactory relationship emerged from the beginning of Muḥammad's reign. This, as we should point out here, partly reflects the biases and constitutional legends of later times and is not altogether true. In his queries to al-Maghīli, Askia Muḥammad went as far as to accuse his scholars of 'ignorance' and further complained:

> They have books which they study and traditions which they relate, and among them are to be found judges and interpreters who expound God's religion. They claim that they rank among the scholars who are the heirs of the prophets and that we are obliged to follow their views. God help me support this burden which the heavens and the earth could not support.[160]

So far as we can tell, this pertains to an early period of tension, shortly after Muḥammad's accession, prior to his pilgrimage, after which, as

Tārīkh al-Fattāsh puts it, the Askia 'changed all that and started asking the scholars about the *sunna* of the prophet and following their views'.[161] The main factor which distinguished Muḥammad's reign was an earnest attempt evidenced from the very beginning to reconcile the interests of scholars and state. It was this which ultimately transformed him into a legend, and especially at the time of the nineteenth century *jihāds*. His successors, however, and certainly the first two, who usurped the throne in his old age, did not gain the proper recognition as *khalīfas*.[162] The role and influence of scholars in Gao gradually became restricted and this differentiated the Songhai capital both from Jenne and Timbuktu.

The custom which emerged was one in which the state and the scholars, in Timbuktu, observed a mutual distance from each other. Thus, when the Askias visited Timbuktu, they came accompanied by their grandees, and struck camp outside the city at a place called Balma'a Jindi, possibly to the west of Badyindi.[163] Then, after a short while, as *Tārīkh al-Fattāsh* describes the formalities of a visit by an Askia:

> He would proceed to the house of the *qāḍi* and find him in the presence of his *shuhūd*, the aids of the *shar'* and his servants. They met at the door, and then the *qāḍi* played host, providing food and drinks and called blessings according to custom. Then they all went to the Main Mosque where the prominent scholars of the city and the *imāms* greeted him . . . Afterwards at Balma'a Jindi the merchants of Timbuktu and its grandees came to him and played host to him by giving him many presents in the evening. He usually spent only one night there.[164]

The most striking feature of this formality is that the monarch came to the scholars while merchants and other grandees came to *him*. And, indeed, we know of only two cases of scholars who visited the Songhai court. One was Maḥmūd Ka't who is encountered at the court at the crucial moment when measures for confronting the Moroccan expedition were being discussed. Maḥmūd was *Qāḍi* of Tindirma, the capital of the eastern provinces, whose forces had been decimated during the Songhai civil war. Being informed of the true state of affairs north of the Niger, he counselled that the whole population of Gao should be immediately evacuated across the river to preempt a full collapse of the state under the impact of Moroccan firearms. His opinion was snubbed by one of the generals, and the measure was not taken until it was too late.[165] Maḥmūd Ka't probably acted as counsel to the Askias at other times but he did so through the intermediacy of Aski Alfa Bakr Lunbari, long-time *kātib* (secretary) at the Songhai court.[166]

The only other scholar who is specifically recorded to have visited the Songhai court was himself teacher of Maḥmūd Ka't, the illustrious Aḥmad b. Muḥammad Sa'īd. There exists a treatise, extant in at least one copy at Dakar, which deals with the difference between appeasement of rulers (*mudārāt*), to avoid conflict with them, and the pandering to their wishes (*mudāhana*) to gain favours from them. This treatise bears the name of our scholar but, although the nomenclature in this case should not be too common, we can only tentatively associate him with its authorship.[167] He travelled to Gao only on one occasion to intercede on behalf of his ex-students, the brothers Muḥammad and Aḥmad Baghayughu. Askia Daūd had called upon one of them to take over the judgeship of their native Jenne, apparently at the death of their father, but neither would accept the post. Significantly, the two accompanied their Shaikh to Gao but did not proceed with him to court. Rather, they stayed at a house by the port where, eventually, the Askia himself came to greet them. Al-Shaikh Aḥmad, on the other hand, used the occasion of his visit to chide Daūd for practices at court which humiliated the monarch's retainers.[168] A parallel is found in the case of Aḥmad Bāba who, though in exile, virtually defamed al-Manṣūr for his court practice in Morocco of addressing his visitors from behind a veil.[169]

As will be seen in Chapter 6, the Ruma Pashas fell under the same type of pressure as the Askias, and especially during the first few decades of their regime. Ultimately, certain conceptions of continuity between Songhai and Ruma became part and parcel of local Songhai legend. Traditions, for example, affirm that the commander of the Moroccan expedition, Pasha Jūdār, never defeated the Askias until he received samples of the traditional Songhai charms from one of their youths.[170] As if to confirm the differentiation of the Ruma into a military class, there arose a custom whereby they were for a long time prohibited from donning the turban, the traditional headdress of scholars. Indeed, it is sometimes asserted by popular legend that Aḥmad Maghia was killed by the Ruma because 'he stole their turban'.[171] This might pertain to a ruling by the celebrated *mufti* which rejected the claim by al-Manṣūr that he conquered the Sūdān to unify the realms of Islam.[172] The 'martyrdom' of Aḥmad Maghia made a strong impression upon traditionists because, as already mentioned in Chapter 3, he ranked very high among the leadership of the scholars at the time of the Moroccan conquest. The 'Ulūj, who were responsible for his death, came to be seen as the vilest and the lowest in status among the Ruma. Popular legend still asserts that the 'Ulūj cannot come anywhere near the tomb of Aḥmad Maghia, just outside the city, or else they would lose their sight.[173] The Alfas today offer a variant on this tradition and maintain that all evil people cannot visit the *walī's* tomb, even if they wished to do so, because something would come up to hinder them.[174] Interestingly, the integration of Ruma leaders among the ranks of notables is expressed in terms of a legend in which the turban also makes an appearance. It is alleged that, at a time unknown, the leaders of the Ruma were assembled in one spot for the purpose of choosing one of them as *Amīr* of Timbuktu. A turban was thrown in the air and, since it fell on a representative of the Mas'ūdis, the choice fell upon him. This legend, outside the circles of the scholars, is usually offered to explain why the Mas'ūdis were the last Ruma to contribute to the chieftaincy of Timbuktu before the French conquest.[175]

Not all the historical legends which are extant in Timbuktu are reconcilable with the documentary evidence. It is held, for example, that Gurdu (*sic*) put a stop to the slave-trade in Timbuktu with the aid of supernatural powers which he enjoyed. The story goes that he sent the youngest and the brightest of his *'ifrīts* to the Moroccan sulṭān and made him sign a document in which the sulṭān undertook never to ask again for yearly dispatch of slaves from Timbuktu. This may somehow hark back to the policy of Mawlāy Isma'īl and his successors in the eighteenth century of raising an imperial guard from West African slave recruits.[176] Accordingly, it may hinge upon a *fatwa* by Muḥammad Baghayughu b. Muḥammad Gurdu, or else by his son Muḥammad, concerning the always-controversial problem of slavery. So far as we can tell, Timbuktu may still have sent an occasional tribute to Morocco up to somewhere around 1700 both in gold and slaves. Thus, the hypothetical Gurdu ruling may have formalized and finalized the revocation of Moroccan sovereignty which actually began in the mid-seventeenth century.[177]

The views and writings of scholars from the mid-seventeenth to the early nineteenth century are almost fully obscured by the scarcity of extant documents. We have no reason to doubt that local *fatwas* and legal compositions continued to be written, though never as prolifically as in the case of Aḥmad Bāba. The latter's ruling on the lawfulness of tobacco was apparently made a subject of commentary some two generations later by al-Sharīf al-Shāb, but this influential scholar is himself ill-documented and none of his writings have survived.[178] What has survived is a collection of writings on the subject of tobacco and tea by al-Imām Sa'd b. al-Ḥabīb Bāba b. Muḥammad al-Hādi al-Waddāni. This document is more literary than legal and is extant in a copy from Tuāt which also bears the name of Aḥmad b. 'Abd al-Raḥmān b. Aḥmad al-Mujtahid.[179] The author, Sa'd b. al-Ḥabīb Bāba, was almost certainly an *Imām* of Sankore: his father or uncle, Santā'u b. al-Hadi b. al-Waddāni, was in occupation of that post when al-Sa'di completed his chronicle in the mid-seventeenth century. The sons of Sa'd and his grandsons are known from later times as *Imāms* of Jāmi' al-Hanā' and Sankore.[180] The family, originally from Tuāt and having probably a branch there, seems to have participated in the important trans-Saharan tobacco trade.

We know also that the ruling by al-Qāḍi Muḥammad Sili which legalized the practice of usury with warrior clans was endorsed a generation later by Muḥammad al-Mukhtār al-A'mashi al-'Alawi. Such rulings probably helped integrate some of the Tuareg clans into the Saharan commerce and gave them a stake in it for some time. They were contested, however, and probably superseded by a *fatwa* which objected to the practice. The author of the new *fatwa* was a certain al-Ḥājj Ḥasan, who may be al-Ḥasan b. Aghbid al-Zaidi, author of several works who died in 1123 A.H. (1711/12 A.D.).[181] Unfortunately, all the known writings on this and related subjects are no longer extant. Indeed, we know that Aḥmad b. Muḥammad b. Mūsa b. Ijil al-Zaidi composed a biographical dictionary in verse which covered the obituaries of many prominent scholars. This composition became one of the main sources for al-Bartīli's *Fath al-Shukūr* but no copy of it has survived.[182] The tendency for new compositions to supersede earlier ones may be responsible for the loss of a treatise on the prerogatives of judges and governors (*Fi'l-Qudāt wa'l-Ḥukkām*) by Muḥammad b. Muḥammad Baghayughu b. Muḥammad Gurdu.[183] Though this scholar (also known as Muḥammad Baghayughu) occupies a central position in the chains of transmission of learning, his career remains rather obscure. He is noted in *Tadhkirat al-Nasyān* for his absence from a hearing in a murder case which was called for by the Pasha in 1126 A.H. (1714/15 A.D.).[184] This may suggest that he objected to the procedure altogether as an infringement by a *hākim* on the prerogatives of a judge. So far as we can tell, his politico-jurisprudential views fell within the bounds of the traditions known in detail from the writings of Aḥmad Bāba.

The views of Aḥmad Bāba are echoed to a remarkable degree in the writings of Aḥmad al-Bakkā'i. The attitudes of al-Bakkā'i pertain to a context in the mid-nineteenth century when the jihādists of Hausaland had for a long time exerted pressure on scholars in various parts of the Sudan to take the initiative in resolving the polarization between military and learned elites in favour of a purely theocratic state. Our scholar, for his part, held firm for a long time to ideas which must have been characteristic of scholars in such stable urban centres as Jenne, Walāta and Timbuktu: namely, that the duality between moral and political power was as inevitable as it was undesirable. He argued against *jihād* during his visit to Sokoto and later in his correspondence with al-Ḥājj 'Umar on the grounds that it leads to unmitigated political power. It was implicit, furthermore, in his views that rulership and temporal authority had a corrupting effect on the individual. He seems to have felt that the instruments of political power were not necessarily the means for reforming society. He based his ideas on a critical, though broad, view of Muslim history whereby he observed that it was only in rare cases, such as under the earliest four caliphs and the Omayyad 'Umar b. 'Abd al-'Azīz, that political power and true Muslim rulership were combined. 'The exceptional [or rare] can serve as no basis for generalization', he concluded in a formalistic jurisprudential vein.[185] This statement is all the more remarkable because its author subsequently got involved in politico-military undertakings and actually assumed the symbols of Muslim sovereignty towards the end of his career.

Learning and status

Over and beyond the factors of wealth and ideological orientation, the extensiveness of the body of scholars in Timbuktu gave them an influence which has no parallels elsewhere in the Sahelo–Sūdān. Thus, even in the early years of the present century, Marty observed:

> The Alfas, or the body of literati in Timbuktu, constitute the aristocratic class which is the most numerous in the city. They are perhaps also the most influential, especially if we include among them the Shurfa who are naturally linked to the group.[186]

Among the 'aristocrats' specifically listed by Marty there were, in fact, only a few Ruma and Ghabibi merchants who ranked among the notables without being scholars. At that time, the body of scholars amounted to some 30–50 individuals, including some whose learning was rather limited in comparison with earlier times. As already estimated in Chapter 3, the numerical strength of the scholars stood at some 200–300 in the sixteenth century. During that period, the tailor-*alfas* alone may have numbered in the thousands and it seems that most merchants acquired some learning beyond the simple stage of literacy.

The extensiveness of the body of scholars, in a relatively small city, serves as a basis for synthesizing the various factors which affected their status. Firstly, as we have noted elsewhere, the vocation of teaching, though highly regarded, could not itself have stimulated the extraordinary growth of learning which took place in Timbuktu, for it was a profession in the full sense of the word only among the lesser *alfas*, the *mu'allims*, who taught in the elementary Qur'ānic schools. Secondly, the personal benefits which could be derived from training in jurisprudence in terms of enhancing one's ability in commerce or in terms of attaining a salaried religio-legal post were largely by-products of the learning process rather than being its main purpose. Thirdly, as we may observe in contrast to other societies, hierarchical positions to which scholars could aspire were almost totally absent, while government service was not desirable among scholars in any case. Finally, as we may recall, state support of scholarship was rather minimal and, indeed, the sustenance of needy students and lesser literati often devolved on the scholars themselves or on their wealthy kinsmen and associates rather than on the rulers.

The problem then is to explain why Timbuktu nurtured such a broad category of accomplished jurists when the sole posts to which their learning qualified them were few in themselves and each was normally a lifetime appointment. This, to our mind, emphasizes more than anything else the pure status criteria which attached to the acquisition of learning. Very few scholars could realistically hope to attain the post of *Qādi*, but the comparable education which they received placed them in the same status stratum as the Judge. Since the Judge, moreover, often interacted on equal terms with rulers, becoming a learned colleague had immense status and influence ramifications.

The criteria of pure status which attached to learning are of course complicated by the religious component and by the belief system which affected the public outlook towards literati and scholars. Among the illiterate, mere command of literacy was associated with magical or supernatural powers which naturally gave special status even to the least-learned literati. This, among other things, gave rise to a lucrative trade in the writing and manufacture of charms which catered mainly for the visiting Tuareg and was based in the Abaradyu suburb.[187] We need not suggest that this was a principal source of income for the rank-and-file literati, though such a model may conceivably be applicable elsewhere. In Timbuktu, the setting aside of the tailoring craft specifically for the *alfas*, coupled with participation in retail commerce, tended to minimize the reliance of literati on such remuneration or on alms. Nonetheless, it seems almost certain that many *alfas* utilized their literacy by going out to the lesser Saharan clans and the small villages of the Niger where their special skills were conceived mainly in magical terms. In such cases, the *alfa* became a sort of *imām* and *kātib*, combined in one, besides often acting as an advisor or a spiritual *protégé* to a chief.[188] In Timbuktu itself, and especially in the Abaradyu and the Bela Farandi quarters, many literati no doubt also applied their talents to magical and semi-magical spiritual concerns,[189] but the main factor which encouraged the growth of literacy among commoners was the element of social respectability which knowledge of the Qur'ān afforded.

At a higher level of learning, it seems that many medium-ranking scholars acquired high status among their specific ethnic groups, or among their clans or sub-clans, without being prominent in the city-wide affairs of Timbuktu. Thus, today the traditionists boast of a legend that 333 *walīs* from various periods are buried in the city and around it. Indeed, even the list of thirteen *walīs* whose graves are well known and visited includes seven who are not readily identifiable in the chronicles. Among them, we find the names of al-Shaikh Sīdi Muḥammad al-Mik, al-Shaikh Muḥammad Tanba-Tanba, al-Shaikh Sīdi Muḥammad Bukka and al-Shaikh Muḥammad Sankara, who almost certainly were prominent only in their own quarters and among their own kinsmen.[190] When we take into consideration the fact that some of the earlier *walīs*, duly mentioned in the chronicles, are no longer remembered, it becomes apparent that the city's conceptions of learned and venerated status differed from one quarter to another, from one generation to another, and moreover, from one stratum of learning to another.[191]

Among the most learned, the concept of *wilāya* was essentially a posthumous honour which combined in varying degrees all the elements of status sought after by scholars during their lifetime. Moral rectitude and piety, to the point of blamelessness, formed as much a part of this concept as the ability of a scholar to settle disputes justly. Learning was the fulcrum around which the whole ideal revolved, but Sufi-related *ma'rifa*, or gnosis, also had a place. Veneration could likewise be derived from charitable acts. To Aḥmad Bāba, erudition was paramount and, on that basis, he raised his teacher posthumously to the rank of a *mujaddid* or Renovator of the Faith.[192] The pragmatic author also mentioned apparitions he had seen which told him that his father, after his death, had risen to a status, in the mystic sense, which even surpassed that of the celebrated master Aḥmad b. Muḥammad Sa'īd.[193] Society was willing to reward the scholars by holding them in the highest veneration and respect, but over and beyond that, it was willing to concede that God rewarded them directly by special gifts, or *karāmāt*. Muḥammad al-Kāburi, the Master of Masters, could walk upon the water because 'his feet had never once trod on an unsure path'.[194] Mūsa 'Aryān al-Ra's could attend the Friday congregation in old age, in the mystic sense, though physically remaining at home.[195] By a reversal of the same principle, al-Qā'id Ba Ḥasan Farīd was jerked off his camel and fell to the ground with a broken neck because, while escorting the Aqīts across the Sahara to exile, he committed the outrage of kicking 'the *walī* of God, the ascetic al-Faqīh 'Abd al-Raḥmān'.[196] To the extent that the *karāmāt* of departed scholars were universally accepted as statements of fact, society accorded a high and inviolable status to those living scholars who could potentially become *walīs* as well. Furthermore, the less rigid and defined were the criteria of *wilāya*, the more generally they extended to the body of scholars, and by association to their kinsmen, students and disciples as a whole.

The Chinese case provides a comparative model for our study, though on a limited scale, because some of the salient features of learned role and status in the Sūdān were explicit and formalized among the Mandarins. The strongest component of Chinese formalism lay in the fact that ascent from the rank-and-file literati (*sheng-yuan*) into the intermediate learned status of *chu-jen* and *kung-shen*, and later into the ranks of full-fledged erudites (*chin-shih*), took place primarily through a series of examinations which were held successively at the district, provincial and metropolitan levels.[197] Though certain degrees could in fact be purchased, nonetheless the distinctions between the various grades, ideally based on learned status, were clear-cut. By contrast, the distinction between lesser *alfas*, scholars and jurists, and ultimately among the leadership of scholars at Timbuktu, is an implicit one which is arrived at principally through inference. Indeed, in many cases it is impossible to decide whether an individual, such as Caillié's host, Sīdi Abdallāhi, was seen by his colleagues primarily as a merchant–notable or as a scholar. Among the poor, the acquisition of a modest level of learning, with the concomitant title of *Alfa*, was an important event because it could eventually pave the way, in later life at least, towards full recognition as a scholar. Among the wealthy, on the other hand, patronage of needy *alfas*, or pious acts in general, could serve as an alternative avenue towards learned notability status. The ambiguity of the term notable in this case, designating literally 'a man in the public eye', seems to bear comparison to the Chinese term *shen* which often referred vaguely to the 'gentry', especially in the provinces, without specific implications of personal learned status.[198]

The ambiguity of the questions of learned status among the wealthy is illustrated in the case of the chronicler al-Sa'di's brother Muḥammad. Judging from the few notices available on this merchant–notable, he was not especially learned and did not identify closely with the circles of scholars. Yet, while his brother quotes one of the Pashas as describing him as an '*alfa*', clearly a lesser title at the time, he himself assigns him the title of *faqīh* at a later juncture.[199] Similarly, we have a reference to Aski Alfa Bakr Lunbāri, the last secretary at the Songhai court, being addressed as *faqīh* by his monarch at a critical moment when the *kātib's* advice was being sought. This, however, is an isolated reference which is counterbalanced, among other things, by the absence of an obituary notice on Alfa Bakr Lunbāri. The evidence suggests that he was a lesser *alfa* who was not accorded the status of scholar, and certainly not by the erudites themselves.[200] By and large, the *Kātibs* or the secretaries to the rulers, excepting al-Sa'di in the seventeenth century and Sān Sirfi in the nineteenth century, belonged to the tolerably learned but did not quite rank among the full-fledged scholars.[201] A third example of the ambiguity concerns the father and uncles of Abu Bakr al-Ṣiddīq, a Timbuktu–Jenne literatus who fell into slavery at Buna in one of the Asante wars and has left us a most interesting account of his background. Abu Bakr's family, which boasted of a Shirfi identity, enjoyed an extraordinary set of links throughout the Sūdān. In this case, preoccupation with commerce seems most pronounced, but the merchants in question seem all to have been scholars of some calibre or another.[202]

In the absence of any formal standardization of the various grades of learning, Timbuktu served for a long time as the learned metropolis in which the status of a scholar, if acquired elsewhere, could be most fully confirmed. That is presumably why al-Qāḍi Maḥmūd Baghayughu of Jenne (father of the two illustrious settlers who founded the Baghayughu Timbuktu family) sought an *ijāza* in *Mukhtāsar Khalīl* from Maḥmūd b. 'Umar Aqīt. The scholar clearly had other prominent masters but his certification by 'the foremost scholar of Takrūr' ('Ālim al-Takrūr) would have left no doubt about his learned status. Even in the late eighteenth century, a period of comparative decline in learning, we find that Ṣāliḥ al-Fulāni of Futa Toro found it advantageous to reside some time in Timbuktu and study there before proceeding to the East where he achieved widespread veneration and fame.[203] Scholars must have come in droves to Timbuktu to acquire further learning and confirm their learned status so that in the late nineteenth century, the *tulba* (or potential scholars) in the town by far outnumbered the 30–50 established scholars estimated above. Our evidence for the most part concerns those who stayed behind and especially the few, such as Ṣiddīq b. Muḥammad Ta'alla al-Kāburi, who made a special impact, but it is clear that others returned to their towns, villages and clans and introduced or strengthened the status criteria which attached to scholarship in Timbuktu.

Recent studies have tended to see the Confucian tradition of learning in China in terms of giving the scholars what has broadly been described as 'a knowledge of the management of human affairs'.[204] This recalls the very wording of one of our sources which describes the leaders of the Kunta as people of 'good management' (*tadbīr*).[205] More generally, as Willis has pointed out in his study on the scholars or clerisy of Futa Jallon:

> Every community has its clerisy – its poets and philosophers – in short, its learned men. It is the clerisy which frames the nation, lays down its canons and interprets them; it is the clerisy which embodies the nation, inspirits its courage, rouses its fury.[206]

Despite the emphasis on ritual and belief in the Muslim tradition of learning, the factor which distinguished the full-fledged scholars from lesser literati in Timbuktu was precisely their knowledge of legal matters which affected the affairs of the public as a whole. Theoretically, the more purely religious studies took precedence over others and, indeed, stood at the very beginning of most legal commentaries and *hadīth* compendia. In practice, however, the training of the modest *alfa* never went beyond reading, and sometimes memorizing, the first sections of each book. The completion (*khatm*) of a major jurisprudential work was an important event duly noted in the biographies. It signified that the scholar had delved into the more controversial aspects of the Muslim laws, including those pertaining to market, tax and land laws, which were often as open to interpretation as the elusive principles surrounding the relationship between society and state. The central role which had been set aside for analogy (*qiyās*) in the jurisprudential method gave the full-fledged scholars, and especially the jurists (*fuqahā'*), a rigorous training in the established norms of logical deduction. The deductive method was carried to extremes in the academic debates known under the name of *nawāzil* which came into vogue especially in more recent periods at Walāta and Arwān.[207] By the same token, however, the scholars were seen as especially equipped to deal with conflicts by virtue of their measured and persuasive approach.

The strongest basis for contrast with the highly formalized Chinese case lies in the fact that scholars there were strongly identified with officialdom. Recent studies have tended to de-emphasize this factor by showing that only a small fraction of the overall body of Chinese literati were in fact officials. Indeed, in the provincial and district capitals the presence of officials was restricted and administration often devolved *de facto* upon the gentry, and especially upon scholars of the *chu-jen* intermediate grade.[208] Nonetheless, the *chu-jen* enjoyed a semi-official capacity along with certain legal privileges which were far more pronounced than in the case of scholars in the Sahelo–Sūdān. More importantly yet, those who were automatically qualified to the status of officials or potential officials in China were the *chin-shih*, or the holders of the highest academic grade. Additionally, while participation in commerce was considered almost reprehensible, Chinese society associated the highest honours with qualification for official post.[209] In sharp contrast to this, we find that al-Bakkā'i ranked the highly honourable position of Judge, along with supreme rulership in Islam, among temporal state functions which were not necessarily desirable nor to be actively sought after by scholars.[210]

The Sudanic states, including the Ruma, with which Timbuktu interacted, did not evolve the centralized bureaucratic machinery which might have afforded a basis for routine participation of scholars in matters of administration. Rather, beginning with the Malian empire, the tendency was to preserve the older chieftaincies and posts and integrate them only loosely with the agencies of the central state. As a result, tensions which led to strife were a sporadic feature which required the intercession of parties least liable to be involved in the conflicts. The distance of the scholars from politics, which amounted almost to a ritual at all but the times of greatest crisis, naturally made them the best suited for this role. We have an interesting example of this feature in the case of the Ardo of Massina, Ḥammādi Āmina, who in one instance insisted that he would accept no mediator other than the chronicler al-Sa'di, at that time *imām* at Jenne. When some Ruma officials were sent to him as mediators, he refused to see them and said:

> What caused these [emissaries] to enter this road which is not their road? This is not a matter to be handled by the people of the sultanate. Rather, it falls only among the functions of the *tulba*, because it involves establishing peace and goodwill (*islāh*) between people.[211]

As already indicated in Chapter 4, all scholars in Timbuktu acted as mediators in the disputes which arose in their own quarters and the market. Indeed, al-Bartīli goes as far as to single out one scholar for the fact that he refused to mediate between people though he was quite learned and erudite.[212] In such cases, under the influence of a pronounced mystic orientation, the scholars carried their reserve to its ultimate extreme. More commonly, they exerted their influence through disciples or lesser associates, or through personal intervention, while maintaining as much as possible a disinterested and neutral posture.

In its formative period, Timbuktu had the greatest need for the moderating influence exerted by scholars. At that time, there was little in common between the various groups of Tuareg, Sanhāja, Soninke and

Mālinke settlers besides common subscription at one level or another to Islam or Islamic learning. Erudition, therefore, became the most acceptable means for the assignation and sharing of status. Much as in the Chinese case, in the provincial context at least, the rise of an individual to learned status transformed the image of his whole family and sometimes even of his whole clan or ethnic group.[213] Under the circumstances it became advantageous for each group to raise as many members as possible to the prestigious ranks of scholars. Indeed, in a pattern which was much more formalized in the Chinese case, the prestige accruing to a scholar could be passed on to his descendants, for a few generations at least, even if they did not especially distinguish themselves in learning.[214] Ultimately, of course, the learning of a few scholars in each case, or the special erudition of a single ancestor, determined the identity as *tulba*, Zwaya or Ineslemen of entire Saharan clans. Prestigious status inherited in this way tended to be diluted from one generation to another much as, in the economic sphere, the greatest fortunes could become fragmented in a matter of two or three generations under Islamic law. Nonetheless, the greatest honour attached to that individual who first raised his family or clan to the status of scholars. Henceforth, a moderate emphasis on learning could sustain the family in its inherited position of prestige.

The factor of upward mobility through learning essentially lies beyond the reach of controlled investigation. The chroniclers simply do not record the background or descent of an emerging scholar unless it was prestigious. Furthermore, the rise of an individual to high erudition raised the status of his ancestors as well. Once again, we find a parallel in the Chinese case whereby scholars of the *chu-jen* grade and above were entitled to have their forebears mentioned alongside their names in the local histories. This privilege did not extend to the modest-ranking literati of the *sheng-yuan* grade 'because as scholar–commoners they had no valid reason to honour their forebears'.[215] In our case, the pedigree of a rank-and-file literatus, such as Mu'allim Takariyya and Alfa Kunba'ali, rarely forms part of his nomenclature. By contrast, some of the Bartīli and Muslimi scholars of Walāta are identified by a long and elaborate nomenclature, though their pedigrees do not terminate in any historically prominent individuals. This phenomenon pertains to the emphasis on lineage among Saharan nomads, but it also attests to the patrician tendency in the towns. The main Ruma notables, along with the Songhai descended from Askia Muḥammad and his brother 'Umar Kumzāghu, also boasted of their descent until the late eighteenth century. The scholars were seen as especially qualified to trace their lineage, however, and this feature remained a live factor up to the French conquest. In some cases, such as that of al-Qāḍi Muḥammad b. al-Faqīh al-Mukhtār b. Muḥammad Zankanu b. Abkar al-Maddāḥ, it is possible to find evidence of upward mobility in the nomenclature. While Abkar and his son Muḥammad Zankanu seem to have been lesser literati, al-Mukhtār was probably the first in his family to achieve recognition as a full-fledged scholar, and this no doubt paved the way for his son's ascent to the highest ranks.[216] In other cases, such as that of the anonymous author of *Tadhkirat al-Nasyān*, the pedigrees, which are only partly recorded, suggest that the family ranked among the lesser *alfas* for several generations and never rose beyond that grade.[217] By and large, the evidence suggests that upward mobility into the ranks of scholars became more and more rare after the sixteenth century. Indeed, even in the sixteenth century, it appears to have been a difficult and protracted process which took place in stages over a period of two or three generations. So far as we can tell, it was simply inconceivable for a poor, servile or semi-servile individual to rise directly to the ranks of scholars. At best, he could attain a modest education as a preliminary for sending one of his sons to one of the accomplished masters.

The numerical decline of the body of scholars after the sixteenth century was not strictly the product of growing disinterest in the cause of learning. The infusion into the population of Timbuktu of a large unlettered body of Ruma and Songhai soldiery was certainly an important consideration. More importantly, however, the corresponding emigration of merchant–scholars to Walāta, Arwān and even to Ghadāmis, reduced the importance of Timbuktu as a learned metropolis while eventually making possible the extraordinary flowering of Muslim scholarship in the Sahara. Traditionists today maintain that the Aqīts actually migrated to the region of Walāta during and sometime after the eighteenth century. We also have it on record that some Shurfa migrated to Tuāt in the eighteenth century.[218] More specifically affecting the scholars was a migration southwards towards Jenne and beyond, as well as to Hausaland, which began before the Moroccan conquest. The first appearance of members of the Sa'di family at Jenne probably came in the wake of the Moroccan conquest and, indeed, the chronicler 'Abd al-Raḥmān himself ventured further into Shibla where he almost settled, after marrying a daughter of al-Faqīh Abu Bakr San'atar, at the invitation of the reigning Sana Koy 'Uthmān.[219] We can assume quite safely that the emigration of Wangara scholars from Timbuktu, as from Jenne, was a constant factor from the seventeenth century onwards. The growing importance of trade-routes which linked the West African interior with the Atlantic ports stimulated an acceleration in the growth of a number of towns where Muslim scholars had a presence. That includes Sasanding and Segu, to the southwest, as well as Kong, Buna and Salaga, due south and southeast. Traditions of Yendi associate the growth of Islam in the kingdom of Dagbon with the arrival there of al-Shaikh Sulaimān b. 'Abdullāh Baghayughu of Timbuktu sometime during the seventeenth century.[220] Similarly, traditionists of Bubu Dioulasso recall a certain Muḥammad al-Muṣṭafa, an important scholar recorded to have died in 1108 A.H. (1696/7 A.D.), as having originally migrated from Timbuktu. The latter was apparently nephew of a certain Aḥmad who 'in his travel from Timbuktu settled in the town of Dag, between Ghuna and Massina, where a group from the people of Dafi received him respectfully, so he stayed amongst them and they surrounded him, becoming his students'. As if to confirm the wide travels and migrations of these scholars, a son of the above Muḥammad al-Muṣṭafa is remembered for saying: 'Fear God alone and do not give a heed to where you might die'.[221]

It should be emphasized, therefore, that the decline of learning in Timbuktu was for a long time a numerical rather than a qualitative factor which went hand in hand with the growth of scholarship elsewhere in West Africa. The process continued well into the eighteenth and early nineteenth century when the father of the above-mentioned Abu Bakr al-Siḍḍīq, for example, went to Hausaland where he married the daughter of a local scholar, before finally settling to trade in gold and cloths at Buna. Of his uncles, Abu Bakr recalled:

> Idriss went to the country of Massina where he dwelt in Diawara, and married a daughter of Mar al-Qa'id Abu Bakr: her name was Umuyu. 'Abd al-Raḥmān travelled as far as the land of Kong. He married the daughter of Abu Thauma 'Ali, lord of that country, and dwelt there. The name of his wife was Sarah. Maḥmūd travelled to the city of Buna and settled there. His wife's name was Zuhra. Abu Bakr remained at Timbuktu with the rest of the family. He was not married at the time I left our country.[222]

The family of Abu Bakr al-Siḍḍīq is no doubt representative of generations of scholars and lesser literati who contributed to the diffusion of learning from Timbuktu. The extensive migrations of such scholars are fabled, both in living memory and in older records, throughout the Sudan. On balance, Timbuktu was a beneficiary of these movements in its earliest periods, and in its golden age it became a sort of Mecca visited by all, but even in its period of decline, the city, through the dispersal of its scholars, persisted in its role as the main centre for the diffusion of learning in the Sudan.

In short, we may perhaps explain the extraordinary extensiveness of the body of scholars in the sixteenth century as a result of a common quest on the part of diverse ethnic groups to share in the high-status criteria which attached to learning. These same criteria had existed elsewhere in the Sudan before the rise of Timbuktu and, under its influence, they were further strengthened and extended. This meant that although the city itself could not sustain a broad body of erudites and literati in the periods of its slow economic decline, ample opportunities existed both north and south, in the Sahara and throughout the Sudan. In fact, the very migrations which accompanied the economic and demographic decline of Timbuktu from the seventeenth to the nineteenth centuries resulted in wide diffusion of the city's scholastic and social traditions in various parts of West Africa.

Naturally, the diffusion of Muslim learning in other parts of the Sahelo–Sūdān tended to widen the sphere of Timbuktu's affiliations. Indeed, insofar as these affilations were pedagogical besides being mercantile, they continued to provide the city and its leadership with a source of strength. Indirectly, this made it easier for Timbuktu to preserve its tradition of autonomous leadership by scholar–notables, despite the transformative impact of the Moroccan conquest. Some of the relevant considerations have already been discussed in the previous three chapters – though more in analytical rather than a narrative framework. In the process, we have looked at the varied factors of social stratification, administration and status which affected the standing of scholars in Timbuktu. Together, these factors amounted to what we have described as a *social tradition*. In the next chapter, we shall essentially deal with the persistence of the social tradition in a narrative devoted more directly to the three centuries following the Moroccan conquest.

CHAPTER 6

Persistence of the patriciate

The social tradition which we have introduced and further described in the preceding chapters gave the scholars certain roles, along with elements of status and influence, which are more or less characteristic of an urban patriciate. In seeking now to outline chronologically the persistence of the patriciate from the seventeenth century onwards we are confronted with two major problems pertaining both to methodology and sources. Firstly, the later history of Timbuktu, and especially from the eighteenth century onwards, was undeniably one of economic, demographic and cultural decline. To be sure, the period of the *jihāds* restored to the city some of its earlier importance, but in the second half of the nineteenth century this was followed by an exceptionally accelerated pace in the process of decline. It has become almost customary to correlate economic factors somewhat exclusively to politico-military events. This approach is valid to an extent and may, indeed, attribute the special decline of the late nineteenth century to the militarization of the Kunta and, ultimately, to the ascendency of the Tuareg Kel Tingeregif. By all accounts, or judging primarily by French accounts, the policies of the Tingeregif were predatory in nature and their exactions taxed what had remained of the local commerce. Other economic transformations, however, beginning with the resurgence of Walāta and, later the rise of Sasanding and Segu, deprived Timbuktu of a large share of its earlier sources of wealth. Recent studies have shown that the trans-Saharan trade continued to be an important factor in the nineteenth century. Such studies are, however, generally documented by reference to Hausaland, an area which had its own direct links to North Africa and which contributed marginally to the commerce of Timbuktu.[1] The same is most certainly true of Walāta which had its own direct links northwards, among other things via Shingīt, and southwards via Segu. In other words, while the Saharan trade was itself in general decline, the share which Timbuktu received declined most dramatically. The city retained its basic social traditions and modes of organization, but its patriciate by the time of the French conquest was no longer as powerful and wealthy as it used to be even in the early nineteenth century.[2]

Basing his anthropological study upon observation of Timbuktu society in the 1940s, Horace Miner has found in that society an example of what he considers to be 'the primitive city'. For our part, in a historical study, we have to contend with the factor of change over the centuries. At best we see an element of stability in the fact that the decline of Timbuktu was commensurate with the contribution of its emigrant merchants to the growth of commerce elsewhere. The period following the French conquest is of great interest in itself but it lies beyond the scope of this study. It may well be that, at some point, the composition of Timbuktu was seen in terms of Arabs, Tuaregs and Ruma–Songhai, each group with its own slaves or servile clients, as Miner observed.[3] Historically, however, we find no strong basis for this categorization and we may even doubt its validity in recent times. Miner, for example, describes the *imāms* of the mosques as drawn from the Songhai, while their *mu'adhdhins* he ranks among the Ghabibi.[4] Yet, as known by their specific lineages, the *imāms* of Jinger-ebir, Sīdi Yaḥya and Sankore are identifiable, allowing for intermarriages, as, respectively, Fulāni, Wangara and Sanḥāja. The role of scholars or *alfas* appears minimal in Miner's study, but from our vantage point it is almost impossible to understand the historical integration of the diverse ethnic groups in the city without recourse to the social tradition which evolved around the status and influence of scholars.

Secondly, the problems of interpretation are exacerbated by the difficult nature of the sources which are available for the period from the seventeenth to the nineteenth centuries. Beginning with the death of al-Sa'di around 1655, or at least the completion of his chronicle at that time, we have to rely almost exclusively upon the lists of the Pashas in *Tadhkirat al-Nasyān* and *Dīwān al-Mulūk*, both dating to around 1750. Besides reproducing the information of al-Sa'di on the early Ruma, these sources share the same materials between them and are almost certainly of common authorship. The *Dīwān al-Mulūk*, which lists the Pashas according to the sequence of their reigns, was probably the original source from which the *Tadhkira* was drawn. However, while the only extant copy is quite disordered and defective, the *Tadhkira*, with its awkward alphabetical listing, is a more complete source. The two might appear substantial, but they supply only indirectly the type of information which is sought after by the social historian. They are taken up with listing the nomenclature and regnal durations of 97 Pashas who alternated over the Tibshāsha fully 157 times in nearly as many years.[5] Indeed, if we take into account the fact that the first 25 Pashas reigned on the average for a period of slightly over two and a half years each, it becomes apparent that the overwhelming majority of later reigns lasted less than one year. Succession over the post of Farma at Kabara and over the post of Ḥākim at Jenne, much as over the command of the main military divisions, was almost equally as rapid. If tenure of these posts and honours was to be indicative of the actual configurations of power, then it would seem that some 30–50 individuals shared control of the Ruma regime in each generation. In fact, as we shall see, the actual reins of power rested in the hands of a few Ruma families which contributed the largest numbers of Pashas, Farmas and Ḥākīms, and wielded the greatest power in any case, irrespective of who held the main offices at any one time. The competition between the main families, coupled with the inability of any one among them to achieve dominance, accounts more than anything else, for the swift sequence in which Pashas and other officials were elected and deposed. In short, a wide latitude of interpretation is necessary for the purpose of adequately utilizing the evidence of the *Tadhkira* and the *Dīwān*.

The Ruma regime in Timbuktu, with considerable emphasis on the background of events in Morocco preceding the conquest of the Sudan, has been the subject of a recent study by Michel Abitbol.[6] The author covered in detail the structure of the military hierarchy, including close attention to the chronology and sequence of reigns, besides tracing the fluctuations in the territorial extent of the Ruma empire. Our own study, therefore, need not dwell at length on these subjects, some of which indeed have been covered by more general studies as well.[7] Abitbol has, however, attributed the rise of 'an oligarchy of descent' among the Ruma to the first half of the eighteenth century. For our part, we recognize that a restricted number of Ruma families contributed the largest numbers of Pashas during the same period from 1700 to 1750,[8] but this was the culmination of an earlier development which, indeed, laid the basis for future configurations in the nineteenth century. This development will be one of the main themes in this chapter of our study, because it reveals the *modus vivendi* which regulated the relationship between military elite and scholars.

Seen against the background of inadequate sources, the most extraordinary feature of the seventeenth and eighteenth centuries in the Niger bend area is the phenomenon whereby foreign conquerors are fully integrated into, and absorbed by, local society. The Ruma retained a special status, to be sure, and this is exemplified by the fact that, while the rank-and-file literati specialized in the tailoring craft, the Ruma commoners came to specialize in the manufacture of sandals and presumably other leatherwork. When Caillié reached Timbuktu in the early nineteenth century however, he could not distinguish between the 'Ruma' governor at the time and the majority of the Songhai-speaking population.[9] The 'naturalization' of the Ruma, as it were, began some 30 years after the Moroccan conquest, with the rise to military rank of many born locally, principally from Songhai mothers. Awareness of actual descent in the male line was strong only among the notables and chiefs, both Ruma and Songhai. Ultimately, even these distinctions tended to disappear, and among the common soldiery we may safely assume that distinctions based on patrilineal descent gave way in the face of common usage of the Songhai language as early as the seventeenth century.[10]

The social traditions of Timbuktu, exhibiting an extraordinary capacity for assimilating and absorbing ethnically diverse newcomers, no doubt constituted an important factor. Ultimately, the Ruma were thoroughly integrated into Jenne society as well, and at Gao all the inhabitants claimed a Ruma identity by the nineteenth century.[11] In the earliest phase, however, it seems that Pasha Jūdār, commander of the Moroccan expedition, felt that the position of his forces would be tenuous at Gao and this determined the choice of Timbuktu as the capital of the new state. In rationalizing his decision, evidently against the wishes of al-Sulṭān al-Manṣūr, Jūdār pleaded that Gao was ill-built and was not as suited for quartering the main army as Timbuktu.[12] Al-Manṣūr retaliated by dismissing him from his post, though leaving him in the administrative-fiscal governorship of the conquered territories (*ḥukm al-arḍ*), while sending Maḥmūd b. Zarqūn to replace him in command of the army. Later, Maḥmūd b. Zarqūn was killed on one of his campaigns against the forces of Askia Nūḥ, now reigning in the main Songhai homelands at Dendi, and the seat of the Ruma state remained at Timbuktu. The city offered the conquerors the advantage of already having a large number of North-African settlers, though paradoxically, it was these settlers who were most displaced by the conquerors. More importantly perhaps, the Arabic language spoken by the conquerors was widely known in Timbuktu on account of the extensiveness of the body of literati and scholars.

A second important factor, much more crucial in the long-run, was the absorption of a Songhai military elite as part and parcel of the Ruma state. Recent studies have emphasized the survival of the independent Askiate at Dendi as an expression of Songhai patriotism, but have erroneously underestimated the comparable influence of the Askiate at Timbuktu.[13] After the first defeats of the Songhai armies, which by far were the most devastating, Askia Isḥāq was deposed in favour of his brother Muḥammad Kāgh in the hope that the latter might be in a better position for reaching an acceptable settlement with the Moroccans. The ill-advised Askia Kāgh, however, trusted his fate and that of his followers to the Pasha Maḥmūd b. Zarqūn under the most precarious terms. The Moroccans later fell upon them and arrested all who could not flee, and subsequently, as many as 60 were murdered in cold blood.[14] From then on, the leadership of the Songhai split into two factions, with the majority joining Askia Nūḥ at Dendi. The other faction was led by Askia Sulaimān, a son of Askia Daūd who had been arrested along with Muḥammad Kāgh, but was spared his fate.[15] Sulaimān was later invested as Askia at Timbuktu, and the posts of Kurmina Fari, Balma'a Farma and Banku Farma were likewise revived and entrusted to Songhai military commanders. *Tārīkh al-Fattāsh* claims that 'those who came with Askia Sulaimān b. Daūd to Timbuktu from among the original soldiers of the Askias were few and did not exceed forty-seven men, both horsemen and footmen'. According to this source, Sulaimān later brought together remnants of the Kurmina, Balma'a and Banku armies, till at last he assembled a force of 100 men.[16] And, indeed, we learn that even the Khaṭīb of Gao discouraged some of the sons of Askia Daūd from joining the defectors.[17] Ultimately, however, an implicit peace was struck between the Ruma and the independent Askiate at Dendi, and, by gaining new recruits, the Askiate in Timbuktu became an important factor.[18]

Incorporation of the Songhai system, even if only partially, into the new regime suggests an awareness on the part of the Moroccan Ruma that their position in the Sudan, and even at Timbuktu, would be tenuous unless reinforced by the presence of sons of the Askias among them. The first Askia at Timbuktu, Sulaimān b. Daūd, probably exercised little real power, though the Ruma honoured him highly. When 13 years later he was caused to be succeeded by Askia Hārūn, however, the latter proved unacceptable to the Songhai and after four years they used the occasion of their presence in a campaign at 'Unkubu to depose him. The Moroccan commander of the expedition at that point, 'Ali b. 'Abdullāh al-Tilimsāni, could do little more than restrain the Songhai soldiery from deposing their Askia until the expedition had safely returned to Timbuktu.[19] Henceforth, the Askiate devolved primarily on sons and descendants of the once-loved rebel, Muḥammad al-Ṣādiq, though the descendants of 'Umar Kumzāghu and of Askia al-Ḥājj II also had a share. The Pashas occasionally resorted to deposing the Askias, but in appointing successors they did not have full freedom of choice. The Askias enjoyed their posts for a far longer period (some ten years on the average) than the Pashas themselves. Like the chiefs of the Maghsharen and the Ardos of Massina, they enjoyed an independent source of power, though not nearly as independent as the chiefs of the Wulmdān. By the mid-seventeenth century, the Pashas also interfered, though with limited success, in the selection of Askias at Dendi as well. The two Askiates interacted rather closely with each other, a factor which furthered the independence of those who reigned at Timbuktu.[20] In 1076 A.H. (1665/6 A.D.), the Songhai soldiery arose against the reigning Askia al-Ḥājj b. Muḥammad Bankanu b. Muḥammad al-Ṣādiq, again on their return from an expedition.[21] Some 50 years later, we learn of an internal struggle among the Songhai over the Askiate in which the Pashas did not seemingly interfere.[22] This type of evidence suggests rather strongly that the Askiate was governed by internal criteria of power and influence, independently of the Pashas. Indeed, in 1151 A.H. (1738 A.D.), the reigning Askia al-Ḥājj rescued the remnants of the Ruma army when it was virtually decimated in open battle by the Kel Tadmekkat.[23]

Besides their merger with the Songhai military elite, a factor which facilitated the assimilation of the Ruma was the presence of southern Moroccan Saharan troops among them. Al-Manṣūr's main *kātib*, or Wazir al-Qalam, ʻAbd al-ʻAzīz al-Fishtāli, even claimed in his chronicle that the soldiers who conquered the Sudan, mainly Andalusian and ʻUlūj, were recalled back to Morocco and replaced by Saharan troops from the Sūs, the Ḥāḥa clans and the Maṣāmida.[24] This, in fact, appears to have been al-Manṣūr's original plan when he envisaged the conquest, but it was never carried out. Certainly, we know that Maḥmūd b. Zarqūn never returned to Morocco, as al-Fishtāli claimed, but was killed in the Sudan. Later, Mawlāy Zaidān complained with some exaggeration to Aḥmad Bāba that his father had sent 23 000 soldiers, from the country's choice forces to the Sudan, but only 500 returned.[25] The returnees might have included a large number of ʻUlūj (Christian renegades) whose division in Morocco, under the command of Maḥmūd b. Zarqūn, had been considered the most loyal.[26] Similarly, many of the Andalusians, who appear to have been numerically dominant in the original force which conquered the Sudan, must have returned with Jūdār. The latter had been commander of the Andalusian division in Morocco and he returned somewhat reluctantly after repeated orders from al-Manṣūr that he should do so.[27] A few subsequent Pashas, appointed directly from Morocco, came in the company of northern Saharan forces, including both Shrāqa and Māsa. These were more familiar to the nomadic and semi-nomadic inhabitants of the Timbuktu–Gao region and were thus in a better position to be assimilated, as Abitbol has suggested. Indeed, their presence might have influenced the obscure but important transformations which began taking place in the southern Sahara sometime around 1600.[28]

A change in the composition of the Ruma forces is also suggested by the reorganization of the army in the Sudan. In Morocco, the Sūsi and Shrāqa divisions enjoyed ceremonial precedence, but the bulk of the army was made up of the ʻUlūj on the right wing and the Andalusians on the left wing.[29] Shortly after the conquest, this system was reversed whereby the main two divisions became the Fāsiyyīn, including apparently eastern Moroccans, and the Marākishiyyīn, including mainly western and south-western Moroccans. The ʻIlji and Andalusi divisions were made subsidiary to these two and were later absorbed by them. The Shrāqa division apparently retained its identity for some time and its presence was necessary for formalizing the investment of a Pasha.[30] It was mainly the commanders of the Marākishi and Fāsi divisions who alternated over the Tibshāsha. These included ʻIlji, Andalusi, Ḥāḥi, Māsi and Shrāqa commanders, but power devolved primarily on the descendants of a few early commanders. The top ranks in the Marākishi division were enjoyed by the Shrāqi descendants of ʻAli b. ʻAbdullāh al-Tilimsāni and by the Drāwi descendants of ʻAli al-Mubārak al-Daraʻi. In the Fāsi division, on the other hand, the Zaghāri descendants of Pasha Masʻūd and the Tazarkini descendants of Pasha ʻAli b. Bashūt Muḥammad were predominant. Others who at various times contributed to the main posts were Shrāqi descendants of Pasha Maḥmūd b. Muḥammad b. 'Uthmān al-Ya'qūbi, and their in-laws, the 'Ilji kinsmen of Pasha 'Ammār besides especially the descendants of Pasha Nāṣir b. 'Abdullāh al-A'mashi al-Dara'i, al-Shaikh 'Ali al-Dara'i and Pasha Muḥammad Buwa al-Shuṭūki. One Andalusi family, descended from Pasha Yaḥya al-Gharnāṭi, was also prominent, but the *nisbas* on the whole suggest that the Ruma who were of native Moroccan background became most influential. The Dara'is, including three separate families, stood in an especially favoured position probably because merchants from Wādi Dir'a had settled in the Sudan before the Moroccan conquest.[31] An additional factor may lie in the fact that scholars bearing a Dara'i *nisba* had achieved veneration and fame in Morocco and one Dara'i scholar, indeed, occupies an important position in the southern Saharan chains of transmission of learning.[32]

Perhaps the most important factor which accelerated the assimilation of the Ruma was their dissociation from Morocco, under the conditions of an intense pressure from scholars, at a relatively early date. As we shall shortly see, the conquest of the Sudan received bad propaganda even in Morocco itself, and in Timbuktu it was represented as an ominous act. It is not clear to what extent the Timbuktu scholars could at that time exert an influence on public opinion in Morocco. It seems, however, that they somehow succeeded in discrediting al-Manṣūr without necessarily holding his commanders, excepting Maḥmūd b. Zarqūn, directly responsible. We have, for example, an 'Anonymous chronicle of the Sa'did dynasty', written during the seventeenth century in Morocco, which claims that al-Manṣūr had sent a whole army across the Sahara, before Jūdār's expedition, simply to get rid of its rebellious troops.[33] Under the impact of such stories, and especially in view of the strife that swiftly followed upon the death of al-Manṣūr in Morocco, the pressures exerted upon the Ruma to forsake their Moroccan connection must have been immense. In any case, the sequence of events, as we shall see, gave the Ruma regime the basic structure of an independent state very early in its history.

Pressures against Morocco and the Ruma

We have not tried in this study to give a detailed account of the Moroccan conquest and its immediate circumstances because that subject has been treated in many recent studies. The broad outline of events is already quite familiar, but certain peculiarities in the Timbuktu chronicles need to be put in perspective. As we may recall, al-Sa'di's main *Tārīkh* was written over half a century after the Moroccan conquest. It reflects the collective interpretations of two generations of scholars and traditionists besides providing a factual account of the events. No doubt some of the same interpretations entered the *Tārīkh al-Fattāsh* as well, especially since, as is generally believed, the work was edited with modifications sometime around or after 1665 anonymously by Ibn al-Mukhtār. A few years before that, the Sa'did dynasty in Morocco had given way to the nascent 'Alawi dynasty and, in Timbuktu, even the formal acknowledgement of Moroccan sovereignty during the Friday *khuṭba* had been discontinued. In any case, it is clear that al-Sa'di, even at an earlier juncture, had unreservedly condemned the Moroccan conquest and had freely expressed his contempt towards a series of Pashas under whom he served as *Kātib*.

At an earlier time, it seems that traditionists had evolved a more neutral or conciliatory interpretation of events. Thus, the lost chronicle *al-Durar al-Ḥisān*, which was probably written early in the seventeenth century, is quoted *verbatim* in a rather perplexing passage of *Tārikh al-Fattāsh* which claims that the Moroccan conquerors were well received on their first arrival at Timbuktu. According to the quoted passage, when Jūdār and his army rode towards Timbuktu after defeating the Songhai and entering Gao, they approached the city rather cautiously:

> They encamped outside the city of Timbuktu, to the east, on Thursday, the first of Rajab, in the year 999 (25 April 1591). The notables of the city received them with welcome and they obeyed [Jūdār] in rendering the *bī'a* [acknowledging the sovereignty of al-Manṣūr]. They made a reception to receive him (*dayyafuhu*) and then he arranged to obtain the Qaṣba inside the city. He obtained it and then entered it with his soldiers.[34]

Remarkably enough, the *Fattāsh* proceeds to contradict this passage, and the evidence of al-Sa'di does not confirm it either. Indeed, a consistent pro-Moroccan bias in the *Durar* may conceivably account for the fact that no copies of this work have survived. Al-Sa'di makes a point of indicating that al-Qāḍi 'Umar received Jūdār quite discourteously. The Moroccan Pasha had entered Gao after defeating Askia Isḥāq's forces and the Khaṭīb there had raised a banquet to receive him. 'Umar, on the other hand, did not make a reception for the Moroccans (*ma-ḍayyafahum bi-shay*') and at first merely sent the Mu'adhdhin to greet Jūdār. Subsequently, on learning that Jūdār was enraged, he did raise a banquet, and this change of heart 'caused people of intelligence to question the wisdom of that'.[35] As we know from Moroccan sources, Jūdār brought with him a letter to al-Qāḍi 'Umar in which al-Manṣūr praised him highly while threatening him at the same time with dire consequences if he should refuse to cooperate. The text of the letter, which is still extant, treated al-Qāḍi 'Umar as though he was already a subject of al-Manṣūr on the grounds that the Sharīfian descent of the Sa'dis automatically entitled them more than the Askias to the allegiance of Muslims in the Sudan.[36] We do not know what was 'Umar's response to the letter, but the initial contact between him and Jūdār set the pace for what happened afterwards.[37]

The claim originating in the *Durar* that the Moroccans entered Timbuktu gracefully is repeated in the letter, already mentioned above, which

Maḥmūd b. Zarqūn addressed to al-Qāḍi 'Umar in the aftermath of the uprising against the conquerors. The Pasha claimed that the people of Timbuktu had no cause for grievance against the Ruma because on entering the city they had not harmed them in any way. According to Maḥmūd, they had paid for all the supplies which they received and had consciously sought to avoid conflict. Yet we know from *Tārīkh al-Fattāsh* that the Ruma had exacted 1200 *suniyyas* of grain from the merchants of Timbuktu each month. The same source indicates that they entered the Ghadāmsi quarter, which they soon demolished to raise their citadel, virtually by assault: 'There was never a calamity which befell the people of Timbuktu greater or more bitter than this'. People were driven away from their homes before they could even move away their goods and their furniture, just as the Moroccans proceeded to pull the houses down. Furthermore, the same people, along with rich merchants from other quarters, were required to send their servants and slaves, along with their daily supplies, to work on building the Qaṣba. The detailed information of *Tārīkh al-Fattāsh* and of al-Sa'di contrasts sharply with the brief statement above-quoted from *al-Durar al-Ḥisān*.[38]

The chroniclers have not left us a straightforward account of the immediate circumstances which led up to the uprising. We know that al-Qāḍi 'Umar had pleaded with Jūdār to postpone the building of the fort until people had a chance to find accommodation for their families and their properties, but the Pasha, soon joined by Maḥmūd b. Zarqūn, wanted to quarter a garrison in Timbuktu before resuming his campaigns against the Songhai. According to *Tārīkh al-Fattāsh*:

> It is impossible to exhaust the list of calamities which befell Timbuktu when the [Moroccans] first entered it. Nor is it possible to enumerate the various acts of deception which they committed. The worst thing was that they pulled out the doors of the houses in the city and cut down the trees in it to use the timber for building their boats. Then they ordered the boats to be dragged from Timbuktu to the Niger.[39]

It is only reasonable to assume that, as soon as the main Ruma army left the city, the notables sought to arrange a Songhai re-entry to Timbuktu, much as happened at Jenne. Al-Qāḍi 'Umar was alarmed when his colleague in Jenne, al-Qāḍi Banba Kanati, was arrested and imprisoned. In that case, a Songhai detachment was able to enter the city and free the Judge. Similarly, north of the Niger, the Timbuktu Mundhu, Yaḥya walad Bardam, who had fled the city upon the entry of the Moroccans, had in the meantime assembled a small force, apparently near Tindirma, which was supported by Zaghrāni warriors from Yurua. Al-Sa'di blames Yaḥya for his recklessness whereby he charged against the Ruma fort quite heedlessly and was the first to be shot and killed. Later, al-Qā'id al-Muṣṭafa al-Turki had the satisfaction of cutting off Yaḥya's head and parading it through the streets. His soldiers mocked the citizens by telling them 'this is the head of the Mundhu of your town'. Strange as it might seem, this very sequence of events precipitated the rebellion a few weeks later.[40]

It seems that the fall of the Timbuktu Mundhu encouraged the Ruma soldiery to commit daily outrages against the citizens. Some of the notables pressed al-Qāḍi 'Umar at this point to issue an order, or more formally a *fatwa*, condoning an armed uprising. Other notables, however, feared the consequences of a retaliation and advised restraint. Finally, one night, the *Qāḍi* found it necessary to act, and sent the Ashra' Mundhu with a message to the Shaikh of the Sharīfs, 'Umar al-Ṣaqali, to the effect that the citizens, presumably in the Sarekeina quarter, 'should take precautionary steps' against the Ruma. According to al-Sa'di, the Ashra' Mundhu changed the message and told the Sharīfs: 'The *Qāḍi* orders you to rise in *Jihād* against them'.[41] Whatever the case may be, the next morning the people of Timbuktu all rose up in arms and the fighting lasted for two months. One of the first to be killed was a certain Walad Kuzunful, a previous Songhai official who, after falling out with Askia Isḥāq, had fled to Morocco and returned with Jūdār's expedition. A total of 76 Ruma soldiers were killed and the rest of the garrison was besieged inside the newly built fort.

It seems almost certain that the purpose of the uprising was to drive the Ruma out of the city altogether and to pull down the fort. At the very least the notables hoped to impress upon the Ruma the fact that they commanded a source of power of their own. It is tempting to conjecture that some contact between the Aqīts and the main Songhai forces south of the Niger was still taking place. From Zarqūn's letter to 'Umar Aqīt, we get the impression that the *Qāḍi* of Timbuktu was in a better position to be informed about the various developments than the Pasha himself. The chronology of events outside Timbuktu in the years 1591–2 is most uncertain however. In the throes of the crisis Timbuktu may have been still unaware of the overthrow of Askia Isḥāq and of the ensnarement of Askia Muḥammad Kāgh who pointlessly replaced him. In retrospect, the chroniclers were favourable to the memory of Askia Isḥāq and they were certainly partial towards Askia Nūḥ who ultimately led the resistance. We may mention, for example, that the Moroccan Sulṭān had postured as a scholar and, among other things, had obtained an *ijāza* from Muḥammad al-Bakri in Cairo. The *Tārīkh al-Fattāsh* makes a point of mentioning that Askia Nūḥ had had a correspondence with al-Bakri's son, Zain al-'Ābidīn.[42]

Besides counting on a possible Songhai comeback, the Aqīts probably expected some support from the Maghsharen as well as the Zaghrānis. The Maghsharen, however, proved to be disunited, whereby the Eastern branch sided with the Ruma while the Western branch stood against them. The former, though led by Awsanbu who had grown up with the Aqīts, treacherously turned against them. For, as soon as the Ruma were pinned in the fort at Timbuktu, Awsanbu rode in with his clansmen and started putting the peripheral quarters to fire. A great battle apparently took place at the Jingerebir quarter but its outcome is uncertain. It may have reopened contact between the Ruma garrison and the Niger at least, while Awsanbu controlled the southwestern quarters surrounding the fort. The Sankore quarter, and probably the adjoining wards, remained under the control of the citizens for the most part until the arrival of Ruma reinforcements sent by Maḥmūd b. Zarqūn.

So far as we can tell, Timbuktu could count on the support of the Western Maghsharen, allied to the Zaghrānis and the Fulāni-Sanhāja, but their help proved ineffective. They did not intervene directly until al-Qā'id Māmi, who was sent to reinforce the garrison at Timbuktu, marched against Yurua and reduced its inhabitants to slaughter and captivity. Returning to Timbuktu with the main army afterwards, Maḥmūd b. Zarqūn made conciliatory gestures towards the Aqīts and the notables, while proceeding to reinforce his position for a showdown. He sent a garrison to be stationed at Rās al-Mā' in order to forestall any intervention from the Western Maghsharen. The latter and their allies were able to storm the fort there and kill all members of its garrison, but they proved no match in open battle for any large Ruma force.[43] At best, they prevented the Ruma from extending their power westwards and, thus, helped insure the future autonomy of Walāta. Many citizens had fled to that place on hearing of the approaching reinforcements of al-Qā'id Māmi, and the Aqīts may themselves have considered that option. However, the deceptive actions taken by Maḥmūd b. Zarqūn led them to believe that a reconciliation was possible.

Tārīkh al-Fattāsh includes the dubious story that when Maḥmūd heard of what had happened at Timbuktu he sent Māmi at the head of 700 *rumāt* instructing him to put the people of Timbuktu to the sword for seven days. The latter allegedly objected on the grounds that 'the people of Timbuktu cannot withstand an hour of that sort of action. They are the kindest of people and the softest of heart. If you kill three of them, seven would die out of fright.'[44] Once again, we are dealing here with a controversial interpretation of events, possibly quoted *verbatim* from *al-Durar al-Ḥisān*. The *Fattāsh* goes on to show that the citizens of Timbuktu were far from meek and feeble. Thus, when Māmi eventually went to the house of al-Qāḍi 'Umar, he found the inhabitants, in the Sankore quarter at least, braced for battle. As our source says:

> When the warriors of Timbuktu saw al-Qā-id Māmi going to the house of the Qāḍi, they thought him going there for an evil purpose. They therefore assembled and went up to the roof of the Sankore mosque with their spears and arms. Others stationed themselves over the roofs of the nearby houses. Then when Māmi talked gently, kindly and submissively, the Qāḍi sent al-Faqīh Muḥammad Baghayughu to call the men down . . .[45]

The *Fattāsh* claims that Māmi went as far as to kneel before al-Qāḍi 'Umar and kiss his knees and feet. We may perhaps doubt this, but nonetheless, the letter which Māmi brought with him from Maḥmūd b. Zarqūn projected similarly deceptive signs of respect. The Pasha held 'Umar responsible for the uprising only on the grounds that he was the acknowledged leader of the city. He added: 'However, the true state of affairs has become clear to us and we have accepted your excuse on that basis. We need nothing from you except your good blessings. May your *baraka* accompany us.'[46]

The Aqīt's acceptance of these gestures, whereby the citizens laid aside their arms, apparently proved to be their downfall. As a first step, al-Qā'id al-Muṣṭafa, who had been besieged at the citadel, executed the two main leaders of the warriors as soon as the city calmed down. The 'martyrs', as they came to be seen, were Bāba b. 'Umar al-Ṣaqali, apparently son of the above-mentioned al-Shaikh 'Umar, and his cousin al-Shaikh Muḥammad b. 'Uthmān.[47] Later, when Maḥmūd b. Zarqūn returned and secured the position of the Ruma, he treacherously put most of the scholars under arrest. Under the pretext of asking them to renew their *bī'a* to al-Sulṭān al-Manṣūr, he caused all to assemble at the Sankore Mosque, where they were seized. All, excepting al-Qāḍi 'Umar, were led in chains towards the fort. When one of those arrested, a Wangara notable, struck one of the Ruma soldiers, a carnage ensued. Fourteen men were killed, including Aḥmad Maghia, Muḥammad al-Amīn b. Muḥammad b. Maḥmūd b. 'Umar Aqīt, al-Faqīh al-Muṣṭafa b. Misir And-'Umar and other scholars and non-scholars. The event left an indelible mark upon the conscience of Timbuktu for a long time thereafter.

In exile in Morocco the Aqīts had a greater influence upon public opinion than would be expected. It appears almost certain that al-Manṣūr brought them to Marākish so that, after breaking their spirit, he could use them to strengthen his position in the Sudan. That might explain why his official historian, al-Fishtāli, describes 'Umar Aqīt as al-Manṣūr's *Qāḍi* over the Sudan without indicating that the old scholar actually perished in prison during his exile.[48] Some recent historians have been inclined to believe that the Aqīts were accommodated in comfortable quarters and were merely placed under house arrest. Recent evidence, however, suggests that they were sent to the common prisons of the Sa'did capital and were probably at first not allowed any contact with the outside. The poor conditions of the prison might explain why most of them died during the plague which hit Marākish in 1005–6 A.H. (1596–8 A.D.). Moroccan sources indicate that they had been released in 1004 A.H., an event which 'brought happiness to the heart of Muslims', but as al-Maqqari points out few survived besides Aḥmad Bāba.[49] It seems that the Aqīts were released, though prohibited from returning to the Sudan, under pressure from the local scholars. For, already in 1002 A.H., Aḥmad Bāba used the opportunity of embarking on his commentary on *Al-Sanūsiyya* in prison to indicate the conditions under which he and his relatives lived. He said:

After ordaining that I should enter Marākish in that way . . . , God made it possible for me to have access to a number of marvellous books which I had not seen before. Despite the conditions of restriction and imprisonment that I am in, students have been frequently coming to me, and bringing books with them, on account of their love of strangers of their own kind.[50]

In the colophon, Aḥmad Bāba indicated that he completed the work in 1004 A.H. 'in the city of Marākish, where I am now in prison with a group of my people, may God speed our relief'. This plea, as it were, in a work which was probably well circulated, may account for the release of the Aqīts in that year. We know that the other Aqīts also made an impact, judging by the survival of a short poem by a grandson of Aḥmad Bāba, a son of a daughter named Muḥammad who released a rhymed expression of homesickness to Timbuktu. Al-Maqqari in his work quotes this poem, while al-Wufrāni quoted another one by Aḥmad Bāba which was addressed to the people of Timbuktu on the occasion of the death of 'Abd al-Raḥmān Aqīt during the plague.[51]

Aḥmad Bāba spared no effort to defame al-Manṣūr and to praise the scholars of his own family and of Timbuktu generally. In his biographical dictionary of the Māliki scholars, and in other writings, he acquainted the Moroccan literati with the careers and works of Maḥmūd b. 'Umar Aqīt, al-'Āqib al-Anṣamuni and, most especially, Muḥammad Baghayughu. Indeed, he set aside a rhymed composition on the subject of the *mujaddidīn*, the renovators of the faith, in which he advanced the novel idea that these appeared in different regions at the end of each century. In the tenth century of the Hijra the *mujaddid* appeared in the Sudan, he claimed, and the candidate for that honour was none other than his master, Muḥammad Baghayughu. We have no reason to doubt that Aḥmad Bāba's views were well received in Morocco, and he seems well aware of that factor. In writing the biography of Khalīl b. Isḥāq al-Jundi, he indicated that before his exile he had embarked on a compilation of the various commentaries on *Mukhtasar Khalīl* which was not completed because 'the tribulation fell upon us, dispersing our ranks, and scattering our best books'.[52] Even as late as 1609 A.D., he recalled in a commentary on the important passages of *Khalīl* 'the difficult circumstances and worries and the mastery of evil people over us'.[53]

The strongest evidence of an influence on the part of Timbuktu exiles over public opinion in Morocco comes from the 'Anonymous chronicle of the Sa'did dynasty' which we mentioned above. For while the official history of the conquest, written by al-Fishtāli, praises the conduct of the conquerors in glowing terms, the 'Anonymous chronicle' portrays them as faithless marauders who abused the advantage of their superior arms. It is rather clear that the author, whoever he may be, was most inimical to al-Manṣūr himself. For he accuses him of having first sent a rebellious army towards the Sudan and arranging for it to be lost and to perish in the Sahara. Otherwise, he describes the victory of Jūdār's own expedition against the Songhai as the result of stratagem and treachery rather than the outcome of an honourable military contest in open battle. Further, he indicates in no uncertain terms that Maḥmūd b. Zarqūn slaughtered the Songhai who came to him peacefully though during the carnage they raised their arms and repeatedly declared, 'We are your brothers in the faith'. Finally, as the chronicler sarcastically states, when Manṣūr heard of what happened in the Sudan:

He ordered a feast to be held for three nights and days in order to celebrate the killing of God's Muslim worshippers. The commanders and the superficial *'ulamā'*, who have no clear sight, along with the *umana*, who do not deserve the name, came to congratulate him for fighting the people of Islam, for seizing their properties and enslaving their families and their children. He attained great happiness from all that.[54]

We do not know what was the position of the Moroccan scholars *vis-à-vis* the conquest of the Sudan in the first place. According to al-Manṣūr's official chronicler, they objected to the project only on the grounds that they did not believe it realizable. However, the sympathy towards the Aqīts which is expressed by all the Moroccan chroniclers, except al-Fishtāli, suggests that the scholars had been dubious about the merits of the conquest from the beginning. Mūlāy Zaidān, who succeeded his father after a series of family struggles, probably expressed the views of others as well when he said that the conquest drained the military resources of the kingdom in vain.[55] Though further research may be necessary on this point, it seems that the loss of some of the most disciplined forces to the Sudan contributed to the deterioration and, ultimately, the collapse of the Sa'did dynasty.

Al-Manṣūr's public rationalization of the conquest is known to us, among other things, from a dialogue he had with Aḥmad Bāba after the latter's release from prison. As quoted by al-Wufrāni:

Abu'l-'Abbās [Aḥmad Bāba] said to him: 'What purpose did you have in plundering my properties, scattering my books and bringing me in shackles from Timbuktu so that I fell from my camel and broke my leg?' Al-Manṣūr answered: 'We wanted to unify the word of Islam, and in your country you are among its masters. If you submit, others will submit.' Abu'l-'Abbās retorted: 'Why then do you not unify the word with the Turks of Tlemsen, and the countries lying beyond? These places are nearer to you than we are.'[56]

From the fact that this celebrated dialogue is quoted in a number of sources, it seems that many Moroccan scholars shared Aḥmad Bāba's view. At first, their opposition might have been softened by the promise, or at least by the propaganda, that the conquest would further the expansion of Islam in the Sudan. The appearance of the accomplished Timbuktu scholars in chains, however, soon convinced them that the conquest was more liable to damage than advance the cause of Islam.[57]

Aḥmad Bāba was in a position to influence the public in Morocco because he taught some of the most outstanding scholars of the time. He himself says that queries on legal questions were addressed to him from various regions, including Egypt, and we have no reason to doubt him. Certainly, his *Nayl al-Ibtihāj*, with the variant *Kifāyat al-Muhtāj*, attained the widest readership, and al-Qādiri at first wrote his biographical dictionary as an appendix to the *Kifāya*. The even more influential al-Maqqari boasted that he received from Aḥmad Bāba the rough draft of *Nayl al-Ibtihāj*.[58] Among his students, Aḥmad Bāba counted Muḥammad al-Marrākushi, who praised him in his *Fahrasa*, Aḥmad al-Hashṭūki al-Sanḥāji, who wrote the widely quoted *Badhl al-Munāsaha*, Aḥmad al-Zanāti (better known as Ibn al-Qāḍi), who was author of two biographical dictionaries and became Judge of Meknes, and Muḥammad al-Qaṣṣār, who became Mufti of Fez.[59] Yet, despite all the honour which he attained in Morocco, Aḥmad Bāba wished for nothing better than to return to his hometown. It is related that when Mulāy Zaidān, on becoming king, allowed him to return to Timbuktu, some scholars who came to bid him farewell expressed the hope that he would return so they might see him again one day. At that point the old scholar withdrew his hand from the man who was greeting him and said: 'May God never return me to such a rendezvous, nor bring me back to this land again'.[60]

The fact that such details were quoted and requoted by Moroccan authors suggests widespread misgivings about the conquest of the Sudan. These misgivings were apparently given further circulation during the strife and calamities which followed upon the death of al-Manṣūr. Even before al-Manṣūr's death, one of his sons rose up in arms against him and later the struggles between the royal contenders reached such bloody dimensions that Abu'l-Maḥalli, who launched a religious movement against them, repeatedly declared that 'the sons of al-Manṣūr have killed each other over the throne and have caused many people to perish between them. Properties have been plundered and sanctities have been violated and, therefore, their power must be broken.'[61] We need not suggest that the Aqīt survivors could have had strong influence on these events. Nonetheless, it is interesting that Mūlāy Zaidān, according to one Moroccan source, promised Aḥmad Bāba that he would allow him to return to the Sudan, should he become king.[62] More interestingly yet, Abu'l-Maḥalli, whose forces drove Zaidān for a time out of Marākish, is counted by al-Wufrāni and later Moroccan chroniclers among the students of Aḥmad Bāba.[63]

Our interest in Abu'l-Maḥalli's rebellion lies in the fact that it gave Timbuktu its first opportunity to revoke the sovereignty of the Sa'dids. Indeed, locally al-Sa'di considered the entry of Abu'l-Maḥalli's forces into

Marākish as the culmination of a series of events which were viewed as signs of divine vengeance against al-Manṣūr and his sons for the plight of the Aqīts. The people of Timbuktu were especially impressed when property which had been plundered by Abu'l-Maḥalli's forces from the palaces of the Sa'dids in Marākish reached the Aqīts as part of the trans-Saharan trade. This apparently confirmed the local belief that al-Qāḍi 'Umar had invoked God's wrath against Marākish when he was led to that town in chains.[64]

We find it most extraordinary that Abu'l-Maḥalli himself was aware of similar beliefs which were current in Morocco well before the launching of his religio-military movement. For in his little-known work *al-Aslīt* he mentioned a legend which held that the conquest of Timbuktu was an eschatological sign that the world was nearing its end. The legend was allegedly based upon a prophecy by an unknown Timbuktu sage who once declared:

> Oh, people of Timbuktu, if it should come to pass by God's ordinance that you will go out of this town, whereby it will be ruined, and some of its people will die in chains, after having been dispersed from it, prepare ye then for meeting your lord with evidence of good deeds, for that is one of the signs of the end of the world.[65]

It is possible that this legend came to North Africa with fugitives who had been displaced from the Ghadāmsi quarter where the Moroccan fort was built. The fugitives no doubt later learned that some of the Aqīt exiles, and certainly al-Qāḍi Abu Ḥafs 'Umar, died in prison. Abu'l-Maḥalli did not endorse the credibility of the legend insofar as it heralded the end of the world. He mentioned a variant upon the same prophecy, however, which said that the conquest of Timbuktu would be followed by 'a drought in the extreme Maghrib (Morocco), along with evils and enmities which would result in an absence of security . . . all of which has happened in our own time just as the [sage] predicted'.[66] This is precisely what al-Sa'di in Timbuktu claimed too, namely that the persecution of the Aqīts 'opened the door' for a series of misfortunes in Morocco which were an expression of divine revenge.

It goes without saying that such legends left a great impression upon the Ruma in Timbuktu itself. Judging from al-Sa'di's *Tārīkh* especially, the city subscribed to a highly moralistic interpretation of history: even the ancient empire of Mali, according to local legend, had succumbed as a result of divine vengeance for oppression which its rulers had committed during the last heyday of their power.[67] Similarly, the Songhai empire collapsed, not so much under the force of Ruma arms, but in retribution for immoral practices which were introduced at Gao as early as the reign of Askia Muḥammad. Even the founder of the Askia dynasty did not escape the judgement of moralistic traditionists, for it is alleged that when he defeated the sons of Sunni 'Ali he seized 73 men from among their sons and servants and killed them at a place called Tansha. It was at that same place that Maḥmūd b. Zarqūn seized a similar number with Askia Muḥammad Kāgh from among the descendants of Askia Muḥammad and their followers.[68] To mention only one more example, traditionists believed that the reduction of Shenengu by the Ruma brought vengeance upon its townsmen for having once aided a Bambara campaign which crossed the Niger and devastated the land of Jenne.[69]

Dramatization of the fall of the Aqīts served Timbuktu in lieu of a constitutional legend which would emphasize the moral sanctions against violating the persons or property of scholars. Much like Sunni ʻAli, Maḥmūd b. Zarqūn, and the ʻUlūj more generally, came to be held most responsible for the atrocities committed during the conquest. Al-Qā'id al-Muṣṭafa likewise suffered in reputation, and it is stated that on the day when the two Shurfa were executed by his order 'the sky became clouded and a red dust arose in the air'. The Ḥākim of Timbuktu at the time, who was directly responsible for executing the order, is alleged to have been stricken by paralysis of the hands immediately after the event.[70] Almost all the commanders who were prominent at the conquest suffered from bad propaganda and their descendants did not feature prominently in the subsequent history of Timbuktu. By contrast, ʻAli b. ʻAbdullāh al-Tilimsani, who is praised for his moderation, became the founder of the earliest family of Ruma notables. As we shall shortly suggest, he was also essentially the founder of the Ruma state in its stable form which was to survive for generations to come.

Independence from Morocco

Even in its briefest outline, the story of Ruma independence from Morocco begins in the first year of the conquest when Jūdār Pasha favoured a peaceful accommodation with Askia Isḥāq. The events of the next decade or so, up to the death of al-Manṣūr in 1603, indicate that the Moroccan Sulṭān's control of his forces south of the Sahara was a tenuous one. By 1608, when Aḥmad Bāba returned to Timbuktu, it became clear to the Ruma locally that a *modus vivendi* with the Songhai Askiate at Dendi, the kingship at Jenne and the Fulāni sultanate of Massina would alone ensure the survival of their state. Four years later, in the wake of the Abu'l-Maḥalli rebellion in Morocco, ʻAli b. ʻAbdullāh al-Tilimsāni became the first Pasha to hold the post without authorization from Morocco. When Mūlāy Zaidān was restored to Marākish, by the help of Sīdi Yaḥya al-Sūsi, he sent a small force with orders to execute ʻAli. Nonetheless, the Pashas continued to be selected locally from then on, and the sovereignty of the Sa'did, and later the ʻAlawite, sulṭāns was reduced to a formality.

Recently, the Moroccan writer Muḥammad Aḥmad al-Gharbi suggested that Jūdār conceived the project of carving a state of his own on arrival at Timbuktu after having defeated Iskia Isḥāq and entered Gao. According to this view, Jūdār struck an agreement with the Aqīts whereby the Songhai empire would be split into two states, one centring upon Timbuktu, ruled by the Ruma, and the other under continued Songhai rule, centring upon Gao.[71] This bold thesis, if true, might explain al-Manṣūr's anger against his Pasha and his dismissal in favour of the more loyal Maḥmūd b. Zarqūn. However, it is equally possible that al-Manṣūr was merely angered by Jūdār's reluctance to lead his army in pursuit of the Songhai across the Niger. Whatever the case may be, it is clear that the Ruma commanders immediately aligned themselves into opposing factions with minimal recourse to the orders of al-Manṣūr.

We know that Jūdār was strongly associated in his decision to seek a peaceful settlement with al-Qā'id Aḥmad b. al-Ḥaddād al-'Umari, the fifth ranking commander in the expedition, who in Morocco had been in charge of the Makhaziniyya force. It seems that Aḥmad was instrumental in sending a letter to al-Manṣūr which emphasized the advisability of accepting Isḥāq's terms. The Sulṭān was so angered by this that he immediately sent orders to have Aḥmad executed, though later, at the intercession of his courtiers, he sent another letter reversing his own order.[72] In the meantime, Aḥmad acted swiftly in conjunction with Jūdār to safeguard his position in any case. He assembled the lieutenants (*al-kawāhi*) and the sergeants (*bashūts*) and distributed to them 100 *mithqāls* each during a banquet in which they all undertook that no harm would befall him. This move, which became characteristic of the actions of future commanders when in trouble, ensured that Maḥmūd b. Zarqūn would not be able to harm Aḥmad beyond demoting him. It seems that Maḥmūd himself likewise distributed large sums to the soldiery to secure his own position. Thus, we learn that Aḥmad retaliated for his demotion by fleeing secretly to Morocco and telling al-Manṣūr that Maḥmūd had seized enormous sums from the houses of the Aqīts and had dissipated most of the funds. The Aqīts on their arrival in exile apparently confirmed the truth of this, and the Sulṭān sent al-Qā'id Manṣūr b. 'Abd al-Raḥmān to replace, and presumably punish, Maḥmūd b. Zarqūn. The latter seemingly heard of his imminent downfall and proceeded, though with inadequate forces, to campaign against Askia Nūḥ in difficult terrain. He took the recently-appointed Askia Sulaimān with him, but the latter refused to follow him in the end. The outcome was that Maḥmūd was killed and his head was sent by Askia Nūḥ to the Sulṭān of Kebbi.[73]

The sending of Maḥmūd's head to Kebbi might provide a clue perhaps to the territorial extent of the state which al-Manṣūr had hoped to carve out in the Sudan. We know that the then-reigning Sulṭān of Bornu had sent a formal act of allegiance to al-Manṣūr well before his conquest of the

Sudan. Though the text of the *bī'a* is still extant, the circumstances which brought it about are quite obscure.[74] Nonetheless, it had helped encourage al-Manṣūr to plan his conquest of the Sudan, whereby his realms would stretch past Dendi into Kebbi and the rest of Hausaland. This grand design seemed to Jūdār rather impractical, but Maḥmūd was more willing to try and carry out his master's order. His fall, therefore, in the contest against Dendi, fully put an end to any further hope of Moroccan expansion.

Subsequent events further weakened al-Manṣūr's control of the increasingly independent Ruma. Indeed, every Pasha who was sent directly from Morocco, beginning with Maḥmūd b. Zarqūn himself, had to be dispatched with a force of his own to ensure that his position would not be undermined. It was this which caused Mūlāy Zaidān to complain to Aḥmad Bāba that his father had dissipated the strength of the Moroccan army. Indeed, when Abu'l-Maḥalli's forces entered Marākish, Zaidān could not marshal a sufficient army to confront him. His reliance on the Sūsi forces of Sayyid Yaḥya to quell the rebellion contributed further to the territorial disintegration of the Sa'did state.[75] We learn, among other things, that the above-mentioned al-Qā'id Manṣūr, who replaced Maḥmūd b. Zarqūn, had served as commander of the Aṣbāḥiyya elite force in Morocco, an honour which raised him to the status of commander-general (Qā'id al-Quwwād) of the Moroccan army. The man died under mysterious circumstances in the Sudan amidst rumours that Jūdār poisoned him. His successor, Maḥmūd Ṭābi', who came with a force of 1000 men, seized the army from Jūdār and went in the company of the locally-unloved al-Qā'id al-Muṣṭafa al-Turki to resume Maḥmūd's campaigns against the Songhai. He too died amidst rumours of being poisoned by Jūdār, however, while al-Qā'id al-Muṣṭafa was strangled upon his return from the campaign to Timbuktu. Eventually, Jūdār returned reluctantly to Morocco, after repeated threats from al-Manṣūr against him, and much later fell in one of the succession struggles.[76] The last Pasha sent by al-Manṣūr was a certain Sulaimān who actually took the precaution of establishing himself at the outskirts of Timbuktu rather than at the fort. He was recalled on al-Manṣūr's death by Mūlāy Bū-Fāris, but was sent again towards the Sudan when Mūlāy Zaidān became Sulṭān. However, on his second journey he was killed in southern Morocco by Shrāqa clansmen who had apparently supported the claims of Bu-Fāris.[77] Actual power in the Sūdān devolved unofficially from then on upon al-Qā'id 'Ali b. 'Abdullāh al-Tilimsāni.

We have no direct evidence that Jūdār had established any special links with the Aqīts or any other local notables. It is possible, however, that he sought to ingratiate himself with the people of Timbuktu after the initial upheaval caused by his entry. Al-Sa'di makes a point of emphasizing his enmity to Maḥmūd b. Zarqūn, who was most directly responsible for the fall of the Aqīts. Moreover, we have some evidence that his close associate, the above-mentioned Aḥmad b. al-Ḥaddād, won some sympathy from the Timbuktu notables. For, besides testifying against Maḥmūd b. Zarqūn, we encounter one of his brothers on the side of the scholars during the carnage which resulted in the 'martyrdom' of Aḥmad Maghia. The brother rode up to the scholar Muḥammad b. al-Amīn Gānu just as he was about to be struck down by one of the Ruma. He lifted him to his horse and thereby allowed him to proceed safely to his house. This act almost certainly created a bond of friendship between the Gānu family and al-Qā'id Aḥmad, and also perhaps between the family and Jūdār. That might explain why the quoted passage from the lost chronicle *al-Durar al-Ḥisān* paints Jūdār's entry into Timbuktu in favourable light. The author of the *Durar* is known to us as Bāba Kūr (or Gūr) b. al-Ḥājj Muḥammad b. al-Amīn Gānu. This makes him the son, though possibly simply a nephew, of the scholar who was thus rescued.[78]

Before exiling the Aqīts, Maḥmūd b. Zarqūn apparently sought to confer some legitimacy upon the act. He drafted a letter to al-Manṣūr in which he said:

> We did not arrest these *fuqaha*', al-Qāḍi 'Umar and his brothers and followers, until their enmity to the sulṭān became clear to us, and we became sure that their sympathies were towards the Askias and that they were assembling men for them so that they might fight us, after having already killed from the army of the sulṭān seventy-three men, and we have the testimony of most of the notables and grandees of Timbuktu on that, including the corroboration of al-Qāḍi Muḥammad.[79]

The reference to al-Qāḍi Muḥammad may conceivably implicate Muḥammad b. Aḥmad b. 'Abd al-Raḥmān, of the al-Ḥājj family, who succeeded 'Umar Aqīt to the judgeship. Maḥmūd b. Zarqūn took the letter to Muḥammad Baghayughu, however, and tried to force him into signing it. The controversial text of the *Fattāsh*, which is our only source on this detail, reads quite ambiguously. It is open to the conclusion that Maḥmūd implied that he would recognize Muḥammad Baghayughu as *Qāḍi* should he prove willing to testify against the Aqīts. The old scholar was adamant in his refusal, however, though Maḥmūd threatened to expose him as a secret ally of Askia Nūḥ. He said: 'A testimony can be based either on witnessing an event or on learning firmly of it or on receiving the testimonies of others about it. As for me, I have neither personally witnessed nor learned about this, nor am I willing therefore to testify.'[80]

We do not know when Muḥammad b. Aḥmad b. 'Abd al-Raḥmān accepted the judgeship, and the reticence of the sources might further suggest that he complied with Maḥmūd b. Zarqūn in compromising the Aqīts. Al-Sa'di tells us little more than that the old enmity between the two families had persisted till towards the end of the Songhai period.[81] It seems to us doubtful that Muḥammad could have accepted the judgeship immediately after the arrest of the Aqīts in late 1593. Rather, he was probably invested after their exile, which dates in the spring of 1594, some five months later.[82]

At first, it seems, the Ruma offered the judgeship to the erudite Mufti 'Abdullāh b. Aḥmad Boryo, of the And-Agh-Muḥammad family, but this scholar declined the post, probably pleading on the basis of his old age. The Ruma apparently availed themselves of a stipulation in Māliki Law that it was incumbent upon a scholar to accept the judgeship should he be considered the most qualified for the post. They subsequently offered the position to Ḥabīb b. Muḥammad Bāba, son of the illustrious commentator on al-Suyūṭi. We have been inclined to recognize the father of Ḥabīb, namely Muḥammad Bāba b. Muḥammad al-Amīn, as none other than the above-mentioned al-Hājj Muḥammad b. al-Amīn Gānu. The coincidence may suggest that Pasha Jūdār's party, rather than that of Maḥmud b. Zarqūn, eventually determined the choice of the Judge. Ḥabīb once again declined the judgeship and we even learn that his father, Muḥammad Bāba, paid a sum of 400 *mithqāls* to relieve him of the responsibility. Nonetheless, it seems that Ḥabīb was instrumental in nominating Muḥammad b. Aḥmad b. 'Abd al-Raḥmān who accepted the post.[83] The latter's tenure lasted for 14 years, till shortly before his death in 1016 A.H. (1607/8 A.D.) he apparently abdicated upon the return of Aḥmad Bāba. According to *Tārīkh al-Fattāsh*:

> This *qādi* was one of the most noble and most generous of people. He was the kindest of heart, may God have mercy upon him. When Sīdi Aḥmad Bāba returned from Marākish he found him still alive. The *qādi* went to greet him and to congratulate him upon his return. Then he went back to his house and did not go out again during the remaining days of his life until he died.[84]

It is almost certain that Aḥmad Bāba could have become Judge at this juncture had he wished to discharge the function. As things turned out, the judgeship went to the And-Agh-Muḥammad family for some time and was later taken over by sons and grandsons of Aḥmad Maghia.

The return of Aḥmad Bāba coincided with a series of revolts which seriously threatened the position of the Ruma throughout the Sudan. It is almost certain that agitation in Timbuktu was a major precipitating factor. The Ruma in the meantime had remained disunited whereby the leadership of the peaceful party was inherited from Jūdār by 'Ali b. 'Abdullāh al-Tilimsāni while the aggressive party was now led, among others, by Ḥaddu b. Yūsif al-Ajnāsi. After an ambush and defeat of the Ruma in 1018 A.H. (1610 A.D.) at the hands of the Songhai, the latter returned to Timbuktu and virtually imposed a state of emergency upon the city:

> Al-Qā'id Ḥaddu and his companions wore the hides of tigers against the people of Timbuktu and prohibited them from holding their normal meetings and assemblies. The town remained for a long time whereby two people could not talk together in

any [of the customary places of] meeting. Even before the arrival of the [defeated] force at Timbuktu, the Pasha had ordered that the *Maddāhūn* should not meet after the afternoon prayers, as was customary in Ramaḍān, but rather after the evening prayers.[85]

A few years earlier, the Fulāni Sulṭān of Massina, Ḥammādi Āmina, had annihilated with Bambara support a force which was sent against him from Jenne, and now 'the whole land of Jenne rose up in arms' against the Ruma. Even the Songhai at Timbuktu had recently asserted some independence by overthrowing Askia Hārun in favour of Askia Bakr Kanbū' following a campaign led by 'Ali b. 'Abdullāh al-Tilimsāni in Massina. It seems doubtful that the new Askia was sympathetic to the rebels, for he was later instrumental in having the Jennekoy, Kal Shā' Muḥammad, against the wishes of 'Ali b. 'Abdullāh al-Tilimsāni, dismissed and executed. However, the Massina, Jenne and Dendi rebels were probably in contact with each other, and possibly with opponents of Ḥaddu b. Yūsif al-Ajnāsi in Timbuktu. By and large, it seems that the events of 1608–10 A.D. brought the newly established Ruma state to the verge of collapse. The Maghsharen allied to the Ruma had for various reasons ceased to be an important force, and their decline in the seventeenth century was rapid. In Morocco, Zaidān was in anything but a strong position, and the prospects of reinforcements arriving from that quarter were remote.

Without formally being Pasha at this point, 'Ali b. 'Abdullāh al-Tilimsāni stepped into the breach and secured an acceptance of the Ruma state on a lasting basis. Al-Sa'di indicates that 'Ali had occupied a position of prestige in the Moroccan state but had fallen in status on account of his drunkenness. He seems to have arrived in the Sudan as a commander in Jūdār's first expedition but he was not among the highest ranking *quwwād*. He rose locally in rank very rapidly however, and much of the campaigning after the death of Maḥmūd b. Zarqūn devolved upon him. In 1006 A.H. (1597/8 A.D.), Jūdār had sent him on a campaign led by al-Qā'id al-Muṣṭafa al-Turki which resulted in a slaughter at Shenengu wherein many captives were taken, including men and women and even some scholars. 'Ali and his companions distinguished themselves by releasing all captives who fell to their lot.[86] Later, on the accession of Mūlāy Bū-Fāris in Morocco, he had secured from him exclusive right to the revenues of Tindirma. He repelled a force led against him by Ḥaddu b. Yūsif al-Ajnāsi and essentially established an independent power for himself based at Tindirma. It seems that the conflicts between the sons of al-Manṣūr in Morocco had their reflections on the alignments and realignments which arose in the Sudan. Since this subject is too complex to be treated here, however, we need only mention that 'Ali probably belonged to a party which opposed the enthronement of Zaidān.

During the widespread rebellions against the Ruma, 'Ali endeared himself to the people of Jenne by sparing and honouring the rebellious

Jennekoy Kal Sha'.[87] Subsequently, his decision was reversed by the then-reigning Pasha Maḥmūd Lunku (or Lungo). Nonetheless, he was determined to pursue a conciliatory policy and was apparently in contact with some of the notables in Timbuktu. Thus, when his independence at Tindirma was challenged by the Pasha and the Amīn, Sayyid 'Ali al-Tuāti went to him and told him not to retaliate. The notable said to him, 'Do not risk losing this army because it is coming to your hands soon, God willing'.[88] The climax of 'Ali's conciliatory policies took place shortly after the pacification of Jenne when he led virtually the whole Ruma army into a confrontation with the forces of Dendi, then led by the Dendi Fāra, Sayyid Kara Iji (Idye). According to al-Sa'di:

Each detachment stood opposite its counterpart in the two armies facing each other. Then they parted without fighting. One went this way and the other went the other way. It is related that Askia Bakr [of Timbuktu] declared: 'I have never seen two parties who rode to each other in state and then their state disappeared as happened to these two'.[89]

We learn that the Dendi Fāra, Kara Iji, was nephew of Bakr Kanbu' b. Ya'qūb b. Askia al-Ḥājj b. Askia Daūd, who had been raised to the chieftaincy by the Songhai at Timbuktu. 'Ali had arranged through the latter for the confrontation to be peacefully resolved without bloodshed. This angered Askia al-Amīn who was reigning at Dendi and, after being accused of accepting bribery from 'Ali, Kara Iji actually committed suicide. Nonetheless, the above event essentially put an end to the bitter struggle between Ruma and Songhai which lasted two decades.[90] 'Ali, for his part, returned to Timbuktu and assumed the Pashalik after deposing the reigning Maḥmūd Lunku.

The reign of 'Ali b. 'Abdullāh, the first Pasha to attain the post without authorization from Morocco, corresponded with the growth of the Abu'l-Maḥalli rebellion against Mūlāy Zaidān and the entry of the rebels in triumph into Marākish. It is rather obvious that the notables, and certainly the Aqīts, were pleased at this turn of events. If indeed Abu'l-Maḥalli had been a student of Aḥmad Bāba, then the old scholar probably counselled that the Ruma should endorse the *bī'a* of the rebel and revoke that of Zaidān. All we know is that the people of Timbuktu, including the Pasha, acknowledged the sovereignty of Abu'l-Maḥalli and were followed in that by the Ruma at Jenne, though not by those at Gao. Unfortunately for the Pasha, Zaidān was restored after his flight from Marākish by the clansmen of Sīdi Yaḥya al-Sūsi who marched against Abu'l-Maḥalli and defeated him. At this point, the people of Timbuktu, under pressure from Jenne, reversed their decision and reacknowledged the sovereignty of Zaidān. A few years afterwards, Pasha 'Ali was overthrown, and the following year, in 1618, a force of 400 Ruma sent by Zaidān brought orders which secured his execution. This, in fact, was the last force ever to be sent from Morocco and its members were dispersed in the various detachments and garrisons of the Ruma state.[91] Choice of the Pashas henceforth devolved upon the Ruma locally, and was to be held in alternation between the commanders of the Marākushi, Fāsi and Shrāqa divisions. It is most interesting that the Ruma army was reorganized along these lines, for in Morocco itself, Fez remained for a long time under the rule of its notables, independent of Marākish.

Concerning the sequence of Pashas who succeeded 'Ali b. 'Abdullāh, little need be said except that most died violently, after reigning some two to three years, amidst intense succession struggles. The struggles did not affect the population at large, nor indeed the Ruma soldiery, but were restricted to the top ranks in the army. The administration at Timbuktu rested primarily upon the *Qādi*, for the governorial post of Ḥākim, much like the post of Farma at Kabara, increasingly served as an avenue towards attaining the Pashalik or Tibshāsha. The Pashas sought to ingratiate themselves with the local population so that even Ḥaddu b. Yūsif al-Ajnāsi, on finally gaining his turn to the Pashalik after a period of drought and famine, distinguished himself by abolishing some of the taxes.[92] Already in 1035 A.H. (1625/6 A.D.), a certain al-Shaikh al-Munīr was sought after by the Ruma commanders to mediate between them. Other scholars, beginning with Muḥammad Baghayughu and Ṣāliḥ Takun, set themselves apart from the dynastic struggles but interceded with the Pashas on matters affecting the civilian public.[93]

One Pasha who deserves special mention is a certain 'Ali b. 'Abd al-Qādir who may conceivably have been one of the first Ruma to be born locally in the Sudan. The factor which most strongly suggests partial Songhai descent is his attempt to emulate certain aspects of the career of Askia Muḥammad. The man must have been the son of one of the earlier lieutenant-commanders (*kāhias*) for he too held that rank shortly before attaining the Tibshāsha. He enjoyed the advantage of succeeding a rather weak Pasha whose troops took advantage of the situation to commit various extortions from the people of Timbuktu. At his accession, according to al-Sa'di:

> He appeared like the sword of God unsheathed against the villains and extortioners of the days of Pasha Ibrāhīm al-Jarāri. He insulted, humiliated and killed them until they started seeking refuge in the mosques and at the houses of the virtuous, hiding in fright from him . . . He reigned four years and five months.[94]

It seems that at the beginning of his reign (1628–32) 'Ali b. 'Abd al-Qādir duly observed the sovereignty of Mūlāy 'Abd al-Malik who had recently attained the throne in Marākish. He soon started contemplating the establishment of a new dynasty, however, fully independent of Morocco. As a first step, al-Sa'di associates him with the building of Jāmi' al-Hanā' in the northern sections of Timbuktu, the same mosque which traditionists identify as having been built for the exclusive use of the virtuous.[95] As a second step, he used the occasion of campaigning towards Dendi to ask Askia Daūd b. Muḥammad Bān b. Askia Daūd for one of his daughters in marriage. This event finally sealed the peace pact which in practice had existed between Timbuktu and Dendi since the days of 'Ali b. 'Abdullāh al-Tilimsāni. Finally, the Pasha conceived the project of making the pilgrimage while leaving his brother Muḥammad al-'Arab as his deputy, much as Askia Muḥammad had entrusted the rulership of Songhai to his brother 'Umar Kumzāghu during his absence in the East and at Mecca.

Al-Sa'di tells us that the *Qādi* and the *Fuqaha'* in Timbuktu assembled with the Pasha at the Sankore Mosque before his departure across the Sahara and warned him of possible dangers during the journey. The wording of the chronicler may remotely suggest that the scholars opposed the project in principle but it seems that they mainly questioned its feasibility under the circumstances. First of all, al-Qāḍi Sayyid Aḥmad b. And-Agh-Muḥammad, who occupied the judgeship at the time, was remembered by later traditionists for contrasting the 800 soldiers who accompanied Askia Muḥammad on the pilgrimage and the small force of 80 men which went out with 'Ali b. 'Abd al-Qādir.[96] And, indeed, we learn that 'Ali had requested a reinforcement of 50 men from the Ruma garrison at Gao but this was denied him. The Pasha nonetheless set out towards Tuāt with an inadequate force, while leaving his brother facing the threat of a possible rebellion inspired by the Ruma of Gao.

Secondly, the scholars were certainly aware of the political implications of a pilgrimage by a ruler and of the fact that his passage might require prior contact with the Ottoman authorities. Whatever the case may be, it is probable that some scholars still favoured the project and saw in it an opportunity for formally revoking Moroccan sovereignty. The Pasha was accompanied on his journey by none other than a son of Aḥmad Bāba, a factor suggesting continued influence on the part of the Aqīts. Another scholar who accompanied the caravan was a certain Sayyid Aḥmad b. 'Abd al-'Azīz al-Jarrāri, possibly a Ruma elder who had joined the ranks of scholars.[97] 'Ali's caravan halted apparently a long time at Arwān, where it presumably negotiated for Tuareg–Barābīsh escort across the Sahara. Nonetheless, it was pursued to Tuāt by al-Filāli b. 'Īssa al-Raḥmāni, chief of the Raḥāmina Barābīsh, who prevented the Pasha from proceeding any further. The scholars and the rest of the caravan continued their journey, but the soldiers were sent back to Timbuktu and the Pasha was likewise forced to follow them.

It is quite conceivable that the Barbūshi chieftain was acting in the interest of Morocco, though his father, 'Īssa b. Sulaimān, had given refuge to one of the Aqīts who had managed to escape the grip of the Moroccans in 1594. Alternatively, the chieftain may have concerted his efforts with the Ruma garrison at Gao, which since the days of 'Ali b. 'Abdullāh al-Tilimsāni began asserting its independence from Timbuktu. Upon his return, the Pasha sent his brother, Muḥammad al-'Arab, against Gao, but its Ruma arrested Muḥammad and did not release him until Muḥammad Bankānu b. Muḥammad al-Ṣādiq b. Askia Daūd, who was the reigning Askia at

Timbuktu, interceded on his behalf. Indeed, we learn that the Ruma of Gao sought to persuade Muḥammad Bankānu to remain with them 'so that they may have his blessing', presumably in the hope that that would strengthen them against Timbuktu. Later, when 'Ali b. 'Abd al-Qādir led his army in a campaign towards Gao, his forces deserted him and he was overthrown. Strangely enough, 'Ali sought refuge with the Barbūshi chieftain in his flight, but he was turned over to the newly elected Pasha who had him killed.[98]

The independence of the Ruma from Morocco was henceforth a gradual process which culminated in the rendition of a *bī'a* to the locally reigning Pasha in 1657 A.D. The occasion for that was the fall of the last Sa'did king and the rise of the 'Alawite dynasty, though still in embryonic form, in Morocco. At the completion of his chronicle, al-Sa'di had recorded with inexplicable satisfaction the accession of Mulāy al-'Abbās in Marākish after the death of his father Muḥammad al-Shaikh in 1655. Yet from Moroccan sources we learn that the Sa'dids could not have controlled much territory beyond their capital by this time and, even earlier, events in southern Morocco would have made contact between the Sa'dids and the Sudan logistically tenuous.[99] Further research may perhaps be necessary on this point especially since Abitbol in his recent study has tended to overemphasize the factor of continued Ruma subservience to Morocco.[100]

The crucial step in formally revoking the sovereignty of the Sa'dids at Timbuktu was taken by al-Qā'id Muḥammad b. al-Ḥājj b. Daūd al-Shuṭūki. The *Tadhkirat al-Nasyān*, which for reasons to be mentioned below is not favourable to this Ruma commander, describes him as 'an understanding *tālib* who had acquired somewhat of learning'.[101] Our source indicates that his Marākushi division advanced his candidature to the *tibshāsha* because, being a man of wealth, they hoped to be generously remunerated. At that point he stipulated that he wished to be recognized as 'Sulṭān, Commander of the Faithful, Calīph of the Muslims'. And, indeed, as we read:

> During this period [1657–60], the *khutba* in favour of the sons of Mulāy Aḥmad [al-Manṣūr] al-Dhahabi ceased in Takrur. That is because al-Shuṭūki made himself Sulṭān, with the agreement of all the town. The *qādi*, the *imāms* and the merchants rendered *bī'a* to him, and all the army agreed on that except the Fāsiyyīn. The *khutba* was in his name at Timbuktu and Gundam only, while elsewhere it was in the name of Pasha Ḥammu.[102]

The *Tadhkira* includes these details under the biography of Ḥammu b. 'Abdullāh al-'Ilji, who overthrew the Pasha and succeeded him, rather than in the biography of Muḥammad al-Shuṭūki himself. Elsewhere, the author betrays a bias in favour of the Fāsiyyīn, and most especially in favour of the Tazarkīni family. It would be tedious to discuss the various subtle details which indicate this bias, but we may mention that although the chronicle terminates with the reign of a Pasha from the powerful

Mubārak al-Dara'i family, the recapitulation of the list of Pashas ends somewhat awkwardly with 'Ali b. Manṣūr b. al-Qā'id 'Ali al-Tazarkīni. From the later chronicle, *Dhikr al-Wafayāt*, we learn that this Pasha reigned only five months during the year 1178 A.H. (1764/5 A.D.) and was later succeeded by Baḥaddu b. Bakr b. Alfa Manṣūr al-Dara'i, who had preceded him to the *tibshasha* and now became dominant among the Ruma for a long time to come.[103] It is possible that several hands contributed to the making of *Tadhkirat al-Nāsyān* but it has not been possible to draw any firm conclusions from comparisons between this document and the variant *Dīwān al-Mulūk* because of the incompleteness and defectiveness of the latter source.

There are some indications which have been mentioned by Abitbol which may suggest that Timbuktu acknowledged the new 'Alawite dynasty in Morocco in 1669/70 and that the *khutba* was recited in the name of Mūlāy Ismā'īl from sometime around 1688–90.[104] After al-Shuṭūki's reign however, this became a thoroughly theoretical issue, for we have a copy of a letter addressed by Isma'īl to Timbuktu which suggests that his dynasty had fully lost contact with the Ruma. The extant copy, which is not dated and which is lacking its prolegomena, seems to have been made by a son of Aḥmad b. 'Abd al-Raḥmān b. Aḥmad al-Mujtahid, possibly al-Qāḍi Maḥmūd whose tenure of the judgeship in the early eighteenth century is not precisely dated.[105] In any case, we know that the factor which revived Ismā'īl's interest in the Sudan was the occasion of his victory over the Spaniards at al-'Arīsh in 1708. As we may now mention, al-Manṣūr had conquered the Sudan in the wake of his victory against the combined Portuguese–Spanish invasion, at the battle of Alcazar (Wādi al-Makhāzin), and it seems that a similar exploit against non-Muslims encouraged Ismā'īl to believe that his sovereignty would be welcomed by the people of Timbuktu. For, as he wrote them, 'Since your city has virtuous and elect men, and you are neighbours to pagan blacks, we conveyed to you the good news of our victory'. He implicitly threatened to send an army against Timbuktu but, recalling the experience of al-Manṣūr, he said:

> If we send an army to you from here it might do more harm than good. It would disperse you and destroy your system (*dīwan*) . . . The army itself which we might send would be lost to us and would not return to its proper place here . . . However, if you request from us such an army, and accept it voluntarily so that it might strengthen you against your enemy, we would be willing to reinforce you with it in the shortest space of time.[106]

Ismā'īl mentioned in the letter that an emissary had returned to him from Timbuktu bringing presents from the city along with an instrument acknowledging his sovereignty. He expressed his satisfaction at this turn of events, but the details surrounding the embassy suggest that it was of dubious credentials. The emissary was a certain Muḥammad b. al-'Asri al-Jakani who first appeared at the court of Ismā'īl to complain that the people of Timbuktu had plundered his goods. The *bī'a* which he subsequently brought back from across the Sahara may have been a rather shabby document because the extant beginning of the letter mentions 'very few words indeed, not amounting even to a page'.[107] Subsequently, Ismā'īl allowed the same Muḥammad al-Jakani to purchase supplies at state expense so that he might take them as presents to Timbuktu, but the man went away and never returned, and the monarch enquired, among other things, concerning his whereabouts. Locally, in Timbuktu, the *Tadhkirat al-Nasyān* mentions an emissary of Ismā'īl who arrived in 1121 A.H. (1709 A.D.) and indicates that the reigning Pasha arranged a military parade to entertain him. The source suggests, however, that the visit made no impact on Timbuktu's relations with Morocco and, indeed, it adds, 'It has been said that the visitor was an emissary of one of the commanders of the Sulṭān [rather than of the Sulṭān himself]'.[108]

Recent research, as partly also the above-mentioned letter, suggests that Mūlāy Ismā'īl extended his influence southwards in the Western Sahara towards Walāta. Indeed, in 1151 A.H. (1738 A.D.), as the author of the *Tadhkira* relates:

> News reached us from people in the West who said that the Maḥalla (Moroccan force) which had been there from the past had approached the people of the West [possibly of Walāta] and arose from there heading towards our town of Timbuktu.[109]

This proved to be a false alarm, but it is interesting that the reigning Pasha Aḥmad b. Alfa Manṣūr al-Dara'i called for an assembly of the merchants on hearing the news and requisitioned a sum of 1000 *mithqāls* which was given to him in full. This suggests that both Ruma and notables were opposed to renewed intervention from Morocco. It is doubtful that Ismā'īl's influence was perceptible at Walāta itself, though here as in Timbuktu some of his sons and grandsons were well received when they visited the Sudan in an unofficial capacity.[110] These visits, duly recorded south of the Sahara, may have given currency to the legend that it was Ismā'īl rather than al-Manṣūr who originally conquered the Sudan. The legend is featured in a history of the Wulmdān (Ouillimiden), thereby possibly reflecting the acceptance by this Tuareg confederation of Ruma sovereignty during Ismā'īl's reign.[111] Otherwise, Ismā'īl's alleged conquests circulated primarily in Morocco where, in the late eighteenth century, the English consul Jackson heard about them. By that time, clearly, Morocco had barely any official contact with Timbuktu, though the citizens held on to the idea of theoretical 'Alawite Sharīfian sovereignty for a long time to come. Thus, when the French eventually approached the city at the end of the nineteenth century, the notables sent an embassy to Morocco and asked the reigning Mūlāy al-Ḥasan to aid them. The monarch, no doubt surprised by this, asked them for documentation to prove that they had historically acknowledged the sovereignty of his state or dynasty.[112]

The emergence of Ruma notables

The growth of Ruma families of notables was a gradual process which began sometime in the mid-seventeenth century when the sons born locally to the earliest Ruma commanders attained seniority in the ranks of the army. The various factors which affected this process are rather obscure, but we are inclined to believe that the attitudes of scholars, with their exceptional influence in matters of public opinion, contributed greatly towards determining the patterns of precedence and prestige among the Ruma. This is strongly suggested by the fact that 'Ali b. 'Abdullāh al-Tilimsāni, who had distinguished himself by his conciliatory policies, became the founder of the earliest family of Ruma notables. Though he himself fell in the wake of acknowledging the sovereignty of Abu'l-Maḥalli against Zaidān, he was succeeded as early as 1056 A.H. (1646 A.D.) by his son Aḥmad. The occasion led the chronicler al-Sa'di to observe that 'Aḥmad was a man of generosity and wisdom; he was noble of descent and was the like of his father in virtue'.[113] Statements such as this indicate that the patrician tendency among the scholars themselves was already being imparted upon certain select segments of the Ruma. We have already observed that Ḥaddu b. Yūsif al-Ajnāsi ingratiated himself with the people of Timbuktu during his short reign, though previously his conduct had alienated them. His son Aḥmad (also Ḥamad, Ḥammadi), who reigned in 1651–54, further sought to strengthen his family's standing among the city's notables. Al-Sa'di indicates that 'he was kind to people and was highly respectful towards the virtuous and to all people of merit'.[114]

Though the Ajnāsi family did not ultimately occupy a position of any special precedence, the Tilimsānis remained prominent among the top ranks till the early eighteenth century. Aḥmad b. 'Ali b. 'Abdullāh was succeeded by at least one brother, namely Nāṣir, who reigned in 1667–69, and both were eventually succeeded by their sons Aḥmad al-Khalīfa b. Aḥmad and 'Abdullāh b. Nāṣir. Indeed, 'Abdullāh enjoyed the royal honour four or five times between 1698 and 1712, but was not able to pass his prestige to his sons al-Qābily and Muḥammad.[115]

We have already mentioned above another Pasha who became the founder of a very influential family. This is Muḥammad al-Shuṭūki, also known as Muḥammad Buwa, who adopted the posture of scholar and had himself proclaimed as sovereign Sulṭān. Indeed, Muḥammad was the first Pasha to reign twice, for after his initial dismissal in 1660 he was again briefly invested in 1667. He owed his second reign, it seems, to a certain Pasha 'Ammār b. Aḥmad 'Ajrūd al-Sharqi (Shrāga) who, upon his dismissal, insisted that Muḥammad should succeed him. This 'Ammār was allied by intermarriage to Muḥammad b. Muḥammad b. 'Uthmān al-Shārqi. The latter had reigned in 1643–46 and was responsible for appointing the chronicler al-Sa'di to the post of Katīb. His descendants included a line of three Pashas down to his great-grandson. Among them was al-Qā'id 'Ammār b. Sa'ūd Bakarna (Bagarna), the last to serve as commander of the Shrāga division before its absorption by the Marākushi and Fāsi divisions. He boasted of two grandfathers who occupied the Tibshāsha, including his father's father and his mother's father.[116] His son 'Ali flourished as late as 1172 A.H. (1758/9 A.D.), but the descendants of Muḥammad al-Shutūki remained important till even later. Initially, they contributed many members to the office of Kabara Farma and four among them, besides the founder, attained the rank of Pasha. The evidence on other lesser lineages suggests that a great proportion of Pashas, of whom many reigned two or three times, were drawn from a total of some ten families. Among these, the Shuṭūkis and Sharqis were prominent but, unlike the Tilimsānis in their heyday, they did not quite occupy the positions of top rank among the Ruma.

Throughout the eighteenth century, top rank among the Ruma devolved on the Tazarkīnis and Mas'ūdis and, primarily, upon the family of Mubārak al-Dara'i. The Tazarkīnis, in fact, were responsible for weakening, and almost destroying, the Tilimsāni family. The initial cause for what later gave rise to a bloody upheaval was the convergence of a number of families around 1700 all staking their own claims to the Tibshāsha. In the process, it seems, the claims of the Tilimsāni family were bypassed for some time. In 1106 A.H. (1694/5 A.D.), Aḥmad al-Khalīfa went as far as to post himself at Wīki on the way to Jenne, and taxed the passage of the merchants there, in order to reassert his family's rights to the Pashalik. It seems that he amassed a fortune in the process and the whole Ruma army gradually defected and went over to him at Wīki. His enthronement at that place, with all the pomp and ceremony which had come to characterize the investment of Pashas at Timbuktu, was an unprecedented event in the history of the Ruma period. According to the *Tadhkira*, which is not favourable to the Tilimsāni Pashas, 'the grandees (*al-kubarā'*) could no longer support his actions and they sent to him the army so that it might take from him the funds which reached his hands before he could cause even greater harm to them and to the generality of Muslims'. Aḥmad al-Khalīfa returned as Pasha to Timbuktu, but he was soon deposed and banished to Kūna. Later, both he and his sons had occasion to repeat similar actions which were directed especially against the Tazarkīnis and other affiliates of the Fāsi division.[117]

The Tazarkīni family was relatively a newcomer which strengthened its position among the Ruma in a very short period. The founder was a certain Muḥammad b. 'Abdullāh al-Tazarkīni, described as a *bashūt* or a lower-ranking officer. His son 'Ali rose to the Tibshāsha in 1072 A.H. (1661 A.D.) and, although he reigned briefly without distinguishing himself by any actions, four of his sons became Pashas between 1696 and 1735. The eldest of these sons, namely Aḥmad, reigned three times, and at his death in 1703

A.D. he left a clan of Tazarkīnis behind him, including several sons who became Pashas. This earned him the title of 'father of sulṭāns' in *Tadhkirat al-Nasyān*. During his second reign, he distinguished himself by leading a campaign against Aḥmad al-Khalīfa al-Tilimsāni when the latter once again established an independent authority, this time at Ankabu. According to the *Tadhkirat*, Aḥmad al-Tazarkīni was specifically elected Pasha so that he might lead an army against Aḥmad al-Khalīfa and, indeed, after the campaign he was duly deposed. In the meantime, he defeated the Tilimsāni contender and, at the advice of al-Qā'id Sanībar (also San Ber) b. Mas'ūd al-Zaghari, he had him executed. This further intensified the enmity between the Tilimsānis, leaders of the Shrāga division, and between the Tazarkīnis and Zagharis, leaders of the Fāsi division.[118]

The Zaghari family was older than the Tazarkīnis in importance but, owing to a confrontation with the scholars and, later, with the Tuaregs, it fast declined in prestige during the mid-eighteenth century. The first member of this family to become Pasha was Mas'ūd b. Manṣūr al-Zaghari who enjoyed a relatively long reign in 1637–43, but at a time of famine at Jenne and Timbuktu. Even before that, at the dismissal of al-Sa'di from the imamate at Jenne, Mas'ūd was already exercising the foremost influence among the Ruma from behind the scenes. It seems that he was one of several persons who secured the dismissal of Aḥmad b. Ḥammu b. 'Ali al-Dara'i from the governorate of Jenne after the latter had committed the exceptional act of demoting an *imām*. During his reign, however, Manṣūr did not distinguish himself in any particular way and, after his deposition in the wake of opposition from Jenne, he spent the rest of his life in prison.[119]

The family was raised to an exceptionally high status by Mas'ūd's son, Manṣūr, nicknamed Sanībar, who paved the way for the accession of four sons to the Tibshāsha. As in most other cases, we know very little about Manṣūr's career other than his two reigns in 1688–89 and 1698–1700. We learn indirectly, however, that he married a daughter of Pasha Muḥammad b. Shaikh 'Ali al-Dara'i. This is mentioned incidentally to illustrate the fact that his eldest sons Mas'ūd (also sometimes confused with Manṣūr) and Muḥammad Buḥ were grandsons of a Pasha on their mother's side as well. The event must have been very significant, for under the biography of Mas'ūd, known as Pasha Kūri, we find an obscure reference to the fact that he was 'the son of the daughter of the King (*ibn bint al-mālik*)'.[120] The 'King' in this case, namely Muḥammad b. Shaikh 'Ali al-Dara'i, is given a very short biography in connection with his brief reign during 1682. On genealogical grounds, however, this Pasha seems to be none other than Muḥammad b. 'Ali al-Mubārak al-Dara'i whose biography shows him to have reigned previously in 1672–3.[121] More importantly yet, Muḥammad was the first of a long series of Pashas from the Mubārak al-Dara'i family who emerged dominant in Timbuktu during the second half of the eighteenth century.

The origins of the Dara'is, or Drāwis as they were collectively called in Timbuktu, are obscured by the existence of several families bearing this *nisba*. Thus, we know of a few Pashas who are distinguished from other Drāwis by their descent from 'Abdullāh al-A'mashi al-Dara'i. Even before the Moroccan conquest, we learn that a certain Ḥammu b. 'Abd al-Ḥaqq al-Dara'i was arrested and imprisoned at Gao by Askia Isḥāq after being accused of spying for al-Manṣūr. This same Ḥammu was later appointed *Amīn*, to represent al-Manṣūr's fiscal interests, but was discredited and imprisoned after Aḥmad b. al-Ḥaddād accused him and Maḥmūd b. Zarqūn of dissipating the wealth plundered from the Aqīts. Later, a certain Ḥammu b. 'Ali al-Dara'i became Pasha in 1621, without however adopting the title. A son of Ḥammu, namely Aḥmad, was the governor of Jenne who was responsible for dismissing the chronicler al-Sa'di from the imamate of Sankore there. This governor subsequently met a violent death at the hands of Mas'ūd b. Manṣūr al-Zaghari, and his kinsmen did not retain any influence. We learn of a series of Kabara Farma, however, including one who later became Pasha, who were descended from a certain Ibrāhīm Jāmi' al-Dara'i. These might somehow be related to the Mubārak al-Dara'is, for indeed the latter inherited their predominant position at Kabara.[122]

Though other particulars are obscure, it seems certain that the Mubārak al-Dara'i family was raised to prominence by 'Ali and Manṣūr, sons of Mubārak, who occupied the governorships of Jenne and Gao, respectively, at one time or another in the mid-seventeenth century.[123] By the mid-eighteenth century, the sons and descendants of 'Ali had contributed no less than 12 Pashas, of whom one reigned as many as four times. The Tazarkīnis contributed an even greater number of Pashas but they gave way in influence to the Dara'is, in the wake of stronger acceptance for the latter among scholars. By the late eighteenth century, and well into the nineteenth, the Dara'is enjoyed full mastery among the Ruma.

The growth of Ruma families of notables was accompanied by a series of transformations which changed the character of the Ruma state. One of the most immediate results of the process was a growing moderation between the Ruma notables themselves in their struggles over the Tibshāsha. For, while most of the early Pashas met a violent end after the *coups d'états* which overthrew them, from the mid-seventeenth century onwards the deposed Pashas increasingly retained their influence. The deposition of a Pasha came to be secured by a rather simple process, whereby a fragment of the army would go to him and declare publicly 'there is no well-being (or felicity – *hanā*') under him'. It is peculiar that this phrase was chosen, in view of the legends mentioned above concerning Jami' al-Hanā'.[124] In any case, the system enabled the deposed Pashas from each family to regain the post or, alternatively, to be eventually succeeded in their own lifetime by brothers and cousins and sometimes by nephews. This meant that the sources of power became more stable, being lodged in the family rather than in the individual. However, the same system soon generated an intense competition between the various families and their respective protégés among Ruma commoners. Thus, by the second quarter of the eighteenth century, the struggles over the Tibshāsha were no longer between individual commanders but, rather, they often involved pitting whole sectors of the Ruma population against each other. At times, they took the form of virtual battles between quarters of the city or at least some of the wards of the Sarekeina and Jingerebir quarters. This trend had a paralysing effect upon commerce and, while contributing to the decline of Timbuktu, it gradually ushered in the end of the Ruma state.

Another development which accompanied the above transformation was the fact that direct taxation of the wealthy gradually superseded the imposts on the passage of goods as a source of revenue for the state. The system was almost certainly preferred by the scholars and notables for it gave them a voice in determining the amount and frequency of the taxation. The custom was that each Pasha, or at least those who commanded sufficient influence, would request a specific sum usually upon his accession. The sums requested varied greatly, though generally within the range of 1000–3000 *mithqāls*. Some Pashas requested even a lesser amount, the evidence in such cases suggesting that the notables were not predisposed to deliver a larger sum. In other cases the Pashas received less than they requested, and this seemingly had a bad reflection on their prestige. The *Tadhkirat* praises 'Abd al-Ghaffār b. Usāma b. 'Ali b. Muḥammad al-Tazarkīni for requesting a sum of 4000 *mithqāls* and for receiving that amount in full. According to our source: 'They gave it to him without discussion because of the prestige and gravity of stature which God gave him'.[125] This Pasha apparently distributed the whole sum equitably among the army, giving the various grades of officers 50–200 *mithqāls* each. It transpires, however, that the Tibshāsha had been vacant for two years previously at that time in 1748, and the later chronicle *Dhikr al-Wafayāt* barely mentions 'Abd al-Ghaffār's short reign.[126]

The system of direct taxation, though it sustained the Ruma army for a long time, deteriorated in the face of patronage by Ruma notables during the eighteenth century. Many Pashas withheld most of the funds for themselves so that they might patronize only their followers. A practice also arose whereby the main Ruma families acted as protectors for foreign merchants who did not dispose of an independently strong position in Timbuktu. We learn, for example, that at one point in 1723 the Tazarkīnis plundered a house belonging to the merchant Bel-Ḥasan Jaḥshi who was a *protégé* of the Dara'is. The merchant, it seems, had left the town and taken most of his possessions with him. Al-Qā'id Baḥaddu al-Dara'i had asked him whether he should post some soldiers at the house to protect it but the latter replied: 'We are not leaving much in it, and I will post my slaves to guard it'. Strange as this might seem, the *Tadhkirat* nonetheless states that when the Tazarkīnis entered the house 'they plundered great amounts from it, including cloths, salt and Leghbu'.[127] The story suggests that the Ruma families of notables were not wealthy at this juncture, and the same impression is created by other evidence. At the deposition of Mas'ūd b. Manṣūr al-Zaghari, following a major upheaval to be discussed below, it was found that he had accumulated a fortune of 12 000 *mithqāls* at a time when no other Ruma owned more than 1000 *mithqāls*. In this case, however, we know that Mas'ūd drew part of his wealth from plunder, whereby his slave-troops even entered the houses of the Mujtahid family of scholars and the Aqīts.[128] At his fall, his fortune seems to have been taken over by the Dara'is who helped overthrow him and this indeed, dating to 1719, may have invited the retaliation of the Tazarkīnis, aided by the Zagharis, in the above-mentioned attack on the house of Bel-Ḥasan Jaḥshi. In the long run, plundering the merchants did not play an important role in sustaining the Ruma families for we know of only one additional case, at least insofar as merchants at Timbuktu are concerned, in which such plunder was practised. This took place in 1743 when the Dara'is attacked merchants arriving from the north at Abaradyu and plundered, among others, a merchant affiliated to the Tazarkīnis.[129]

Eventually, each Ruma family established an independent source of income and wealth. The Zagharis, beginning perhaps during Manṣūr b. Mas'ūd's career (*c.* 1700), raised huge herds of cattle on the Niger at Yindibugh, the same place where the Ḥājj family of scholars were once strongly represented. It is possible that the original herds were plundered from the Tuareg, for the Zagharis contributed more than anybody else towards alienating the Kel Tadmekkat against the Ruma. The Tazarkīnis, on the other hand, seem to have increasingly participated in the commerce of Jenne, where its members contributed a large number of governors. Finally, the Dara'is almost certainly owned many storage buildings both at Kabara and in the Sarekeina quarter. In both places, they and their Drāwi kinsmen and followers established numerical dominance.

The first few decades of the eighteenth century, and perhaps up to *c.* 1750, could be characterized as a period of showdown between the main Ruma families. The deterioration of the Ruma system began in 1716, a year when, according to the *Tadhkira*, a number of innovations entered the life of Timbuktu. A virtual civil war broke out whereby the southern quarters of Timbuktu became the battlefield. A leading figure in the conflict was a certain 'Abdullāh b. al-Ḥājj b. Sa'īd al-'Amrāni, a commander who without belonging to any of the main Ruma families controlled the Tibshāsha more frequently than any other notable. By playing the main families against each other, it seems, he managed to reign fully seven times during the period between 1713 and 1730. It was during his third reign that the Ruma civil war broke out and, lacking strong support from kinsmen, he brought Bambara troops, led by a certain Maru, to help sustain him in office. This action may have given rise to the stories later current in Morocco which claimed that Timbuktu fell under the sovereignty of one of the Bambara states.[130] More importantly, 'Abdullāh's action invited further outside intervention in Timbuktu, for Mas'ūd b. Manṣūr, who led the campaign for deposing the Pasha, brought the Tuareg Kel Tadmekkat to help him. According to the *Tadhkira*, this was the prelude for the later supremacy established by the Kel Tadmekkat over the Ruma.[131]

Unlike al-Sa'di, the author of the *Tadhkira* rarely reflects upon the details which he narrates. Accordingly, it is impossible to assess the various factors which contributed to the intensity of the conflict. All we know is that the opposing camps polarized virtually the whole city between supporters and opponents and the fighting took the form of exchanging sniper fire from rooftops. It seems that 'Abdullāh was established at Sarekeina while Mas'ūd and his followers were based in the Jingerebir quarter. Many people, it seems, died in the crossfire and the main market was deserted throughout the four months of fighting. The bulk of the army, including Tazarkīnis and Dara'is, appeared to have remained neutral until, at the end, they abandoned Pasha 'Abdullāh. He was replaced by Mas'ūd b. Manṣur, who apparently capitalized on a promise of restoring law and order but ended by alienating the scholars. They apparently showed weakness during the conflict, and this eventually encouraged Mas'ūd's men to commit outrages against some of them.[132]

The reign of Mas'ūd b. Manṣūr b. Mas'ūd in 1716–19 witnessed the first and only serious case of conflict between Ruma and scholars since the banishment of the Aqīts in 1593–4. It is most remarkable that the Pasha in question was one among very few Ruma who adopted the posture of scholars and yet was the one who most alienated the scholars. Before attaining the Tibshāsha, Mas'ūd 'spent some time studying under the *Fuqahā*' and he sat among the *tulba* to acquire learning . . . claiming in those days that he has quit the Ruma and left their ways'. Subsequently, however, it seems that he began using his learning for the purpose of self-aggrandisement:

> He talked good Arabic and was almost as eloquent in that language as some Arabs. He made friendship with the '*urban* and often visited their encampments and married among them. Whenever he saw a scholar he honored him highly and asked him about legal questions, and he acted in the same way whenever he saw a *tālib*. He would keep discoursing with him and would not leave him until he would find out his stature in learning and knowledge. If he found him unable to answer his queries he would laugh at him and take pride over him in knowledge.[133]

This conduct was probably itself reprehensible to the scholars and perhaps especially to the Shurfa who often enjoyed the same stature as scholars, on the basis of their acknowledged descent from the Prophet, without being particularly learned. And, as we shall see, the leaders of the upheaval against Mas'ūd, after a relatively long reign of over three years, devolved primarily on the Shurfa.

Mas'ūd b. Manṣūr (or simply Manṣur, as he is sometimes called) came to the Tibshāsha from a position of exceptional strength in the wake of the above-mentioned civil war. His learning no doubt enhanced his image and, as already mentioned, he boasted of dual descent from Pashas on his father's and his mother's side. Moreover, it seems that he inherited from his father a body of client and slave-troops, identified as the Legha or Leghat of al-Qā'id Manṣūr, which served him as a personal army. As a result of this, he could act far more independently than other Pashas of the main Ruma families and the main troops. Indeed, his initial policy, which was probably encouraged by scholars, was systematically to reduce all the various factions of Ruma soldiers and officers and restore among them the strict discipline of a professional army. In a short time, it seems, he put a stop to the variety of avaricious acts which the soldiers had been accustomed to and prohibited all but the grandees (*al-kubarā'*) from participating in any types of commerce or escort of merchants. The text is somewhat ambiguous on this point but it states that he allowed the Ruma 'none of their habitual sources of income, except what came to them from him, by way of salaries, supplies and gifts'.[134] These policies would probably have been welcome to the civilian population, but while the Legha of Mas'ūd soon started plundering the humiliated Ruma soldiery, they eventually extended their outrages to civilians and even to the descendants of scholars.

The first outrage committed by Mas'ūd's personal troops implicitly alienated Sayyid Aḥmad b. Ibrāhīm b. 'Abdullāh b. Aḥmad Maghia who, since 1698/9, had occupied the judgeship of Timbuktu. The Legha beat Alfa 'Abdullāh b. al-Imām Ibrāhīm b. Muḥammad Wangarab and later apparently whipped the chief of the muleteers, the Arukoy Bilāl b. Arukoy Mūsa, though the latter's actions probably fell under the jurisdiction of the Judge. Whatever the case may be, a confrontation with the muleteers led one of them to flee and seek immunity at the tomb of Aḥmad Maghia. The fugitive was nonetheless violently arrested, after some hesitation on the part of the Legha, and this naturally gave rise to rumours that divine punishment would be inflicted upon the Pasha. And, indeed, a few days later Mas'ūd fell down while riding and his horse dragged him for a distance. The humiliation, coupled with whatever agitation surrounded it, caused Mas'ūd not to venture much out of his home until the day of his actual overthrow.

In the meantime, the Legha became even more bold in their conduct and actually plundered houses which belonged to descendants of the still-venerated Aqīts. One night they entered the house of Alfa 'Abdullāh

b. Muḥammad b. 'Abd al-Raḥmān b. Aḥmad al-Mujtahid. The family discovered them and fought back, but an infant was killed in the incident. The climax took place when the Legha killed a Shurfa notable identifed as Mūlāy Hāshim b. Mūlaȳ Aḥmad Būdiyya. This caused the chief of the Shurfa, a certain Mūlāy 'Abdullāh b. Mūlāy Ḥamad b. Mūlāy Muḥammad, to take an oath that he would never again wear his cap, the symbol of the Shurfa, until the action was avenged. Mas'ūd was frightened at this point but he ordered one of his lesser slaves killed, a boy who had nothing to do with the murder. Mūlāy 'Abdullāh was not satisfied with this gesture and, after some skirmishes it seems, he forged an alliance with Baḥaddu b. Yaḥya b. al-Mubārak al-Dara'i.

> Then there arose a struggle between the Pasha and all the people of Timbuktu in their entirety. It has even been said that al-Qā'id Bahaddu sent someone up to the minaret of the Jazuli mosque to declare a *jihād* against him.[135]

Mas'ūd fought back for a time, but when the Shurfa and the Drāwi Ruma besieged the ward of the Jingerebir quarter in which he lived, he made his escape via Kabara to Yindibugh. It is stated that the Shurfa gave Baḥaddu 500 *mithqāls* for his support, but the Qā'id was probably willing to participate in a popular cause in any case. For one thing he was able to succeed Mas'ūd, though this was no great honour, for he had reigned twice previously. More importantly, Mas'ūd had given over to his Legha full control of Kabara, though the Drāwis had been predominant there. Now Baḥaddu, in alliance with the Shurfa, proceeded to destroy the Legha systematically. Thirdly, and most importantly, the alliance of the Drāwis with the Shurfa and the scholars raised them above everybody else in prestige. Today, while the traditionists consider the 'Ulūj the lowest-ranking among the Ruma, they hold the Drāwis to be the most noble.[136] And in practice, the Mubārak al-Dara'i family emerged predominant out of the internal struggles of the eighteenth century among the Ruma.

The decline of the Zagharis after this incident was a slow rather than a dramatic one and, in the long run, it was not as complete as that of the Tilimsānis. The resourceful Mas'ūd, reappearing under the name of Manṣūr after his flight from Timbuktu, managed to rehabilitate himself by various means and, although he never again became Pasha, three of his younger brothers attained the post. It seems that after the flight of Manṣūr the persecution of his followers was so intense that captured Legha from Timbuktu and Kabara were executed on a daily basis for over two months. The chief of the Legha, a certain Buru Kandi, sought refuge in the house of Bāba al-Mukhtār b. al-Qāḍi Muḥammad of the Zankanu family, later to become Judge, but he was nonetheless seized and executed. This detail might suggest that there were differences between the Maghias and the Zankanus who alternated over the judgeship. Whatever the case may be, it seems that Mas'ūd feared reprisal against his immediate kinsmen and, riding with Agashīkh b. Karidanna, Chief of the Wulmdān, marched against Timbuktu:

> The Ruma went out to them, along with the Shurfa and their slaves, accompanied by the men of Timbuktu, all of them, without exception that day. They drove them back and they, in turn, did not stand to them, but fell back towards the woods in flight.[137]

Manṣūr and his allies made another attempt at forcing an entry into the city from the north, at a later juncture, but they were driven back by Baḥaddu and his army alone. In a third attack, however, Mas'ūd brought with him the Tuareg of Houssa and Gurma, along with the Ruma of Banba, besides presumably the Wulmdān. No attempt was made upon the city itself, but an escort accompanying the muleteers to Kabara was attacked and dispersed on arriving at the port, whereby many travellers were killed. Among the dead was al-'Abbās b. Muḥammad Baghayughu b. Gurdu, besides a few other notables and eleven Ruma. Subsequently, Agashīkh rode with Mas'ūd to the tomb of Aḥmad Maghia, already then outside the city, and sought a peaceful settlement. The Wulmdān chief was given a generous 3000 *mithqāls* by Baḥaddu, clearly from funds left behind by Mas'ūd in his flight, and although Mas'ūd himself was not immediately repatriated, this turn of events later enabled him to enter Timbuktu at a time of strife between Dara'is and Tazarkīnis. The brother of Mas'ūd subsequently stood between the two main warring factions and this enabled them to have several turns at the Tibshāsha.[138]

One of the results of the internal struggles among the Ruma was the virtual destruction of the Tilimsāni family a decade or so after the upheavals involving Mas'ūd. The conflict in this case began building up in 1708 when, after his fourth reign, 'Abdullāh b. Nāṣir b. 'Ali al-Tilimsāni was deposed. At that time, supporters of the Tilimsānis in the army once again closed the route to Jenne and, although 'Abdullāh was later enthroned once more, for one day, they resolved to revenge themselves for their exclusion from the Tibshāsha. The magnitude of the upheaval is apparent from the fact that the Tazarkīnis mounted a force of over 700 *rumāt* (men carrying firearms), besides numerous auxiliary forces, against the sons of Aḥmad al-Khalīfa at Wīki. The latter had been stopping all boats headed towards Jenne and imposing their own taxation upon them. Moreover, they apparently destroyed some boats as well, and especially those belonging to kinsmen and associates of the Tazarkīnis. By 1730, it seems, there was a general condemnation of the actions of the Tilimsānis and possibly even a *fatwa* accepted by the *Qāḍi* and scholars that these actions amounted to 'closing the roads of Muslims'. In any case, it is recorded that the salt merchants supplied 40 of the 100 or so boats which carried the force to Wīki and that 300 of the *rumāt* who attacked the town were drawn from among the merchants or their clients.[139] The result was a total defeat of the Tilimsānis and, besides the fact that their town of Wīki was destroyed, most of their notables were killed in the battle. The family henceforth essentially disappeared from the ranks of Ruma notables while the Tazarkīnis, who were seen as having accomplished a great feat on behalf of 'Muslims', gained considerably in prestige. Their triumph was, indeed, one of the factors which helped restore the Zagharis, as both families were closely associated with the Fāsi division and, ultimately, with the Alfasin Kunda, in the Jingerebir quarter.

In the wake of the above events, almost all the 30 or so tenures of the Tibshāsha between 1730 and 1760 were held by Zagharis, Tazarkīnis and Dara'is. With the passage of time, the leaders of these three families joined the ranks of urban notables, irrespective of whether or not they adopted a military career, while the rest of the Ruma, excepting a few representatives of the Shuṭūki family, were being assimilated among the commoners. The process was accelerated after 1737 when the Kel Tadmekkat finally broke the power of the Ruma. The origins of this conflict are obscured by the alignments and realignments between various Ruma and Tuareg factions. The Zaghari family, however, which first invited Tuareg intervention in Timbuktu, was also historically responsible for alienating the Kel Tadmekkat.

The Tadmekkat had settled in the Hausa area north of the Niger, between Timbuktu and Gao, during the mid-seventeenth century. They arrived in a humbled state and accepted Ruma sovereignty after being defeated and driven away by the Wulmdān who had split from them. By 1688, they might already have started challenging Ruma authority in the region of Gao, for Manṣūr al-Zaghari, father of Mas'ūd, is recorded to have conducted a campaign against the Tuareg in that region. The Pasha in that case 'killed their grandees, enslaved their youths, women and children, and drove their cattle away with him'.[140] Indeed, Mas'ūd also campaigned against the Tadmekkat in 1716/17 A.D., apparently after having already obtained their help, under the leadership of Alāl, against 'Abdullāh b. al-Ḥājj b. Sa'īd al-'Amrāni and his Bambara allies. The *Tadhkira* does not comment upon this peculiar turn of events but states that legends were already in circulation that Mas'ūd or one of his brothers would lead the main Ruma army against the Tadmekkat and would suffer utter defeat at their hands. In any case, it appears almost certain that the Tadmekkat, led by Alāl's brother Aghmir, determined to avenge themselves upon the Ruma generally and the Zagharis in particular. When Mas'ūd fled from the Shurfa and Baḥaddu they did not come to his aid, and he therefore had to seek reinforcements from the perhaps more powerful but distant Wulmdān. The latter's ascendency was more or less acknowledged throughout the Saharan fringes of the Niger bend area, as well as further north and west. Their presence in the region of Timbuktu, however, was restricted to the arrival of their chiefs upon their accession to power so that they may be formally invested by the Pashas.[141] The arrival of Aghashīkh in actual support of Mas'ūd, and especially his receipt of 3000 *mithqāls* from Baḥaddu, threatened the Tadmekkat with a real Wulmdān predominance in the area.

On the accession of Muḥammad Buḥḥu b. Manṣūr al-Zaghari, in the wake of the Tazarkīni triumph over the Tilimsānis, the Tadmekkat fell upon his kinsmen at Yindibugh and seized their cattle and clients.[142] A period of extreme insecurity ensued under the following few Pashas, though al-Qāḍi Bāba al-Mukhtār arranged for a peace agreement with Aghmir. A drought was ravaging the area at this time and many Saharans had come to Timbuktu for relief from strife and famine. The climax took place in 1737 when Ḥammādi b. Manṣūr al-Zaghari, after a brief initial reign which witnessed a confrontation with the Tadmekkat, was again restored to the Tibshāsha. He sent out detachments to check the movements of Aghmir's clansmen and this angered the Saharan chieftain. He now assembled his entire confederation, including women and children weakened by the famine, and marched with them past Timbuktu. Most of the Ruma had already left the town by this time, and when the merchants came out with their clients to defend the northern outskirts, he counselled his clansmen to ride on. Later, on being contacted by a Kunta settler, he declared:

> There has remained [in Timbuktu] today only the *Fuqaha'*, the *Ṭulba*, the merchants, the poor and weak, and the women. We know all of them and we know that those who have gone out are men like us. They have come out in the open to challenge us and if they stand up to us we will meet them. Otherwise, we have nothing against the people of Timbuktu nor any purpose in the city itself except dealing with its thieves and warriors.[143]

Ḥammādi committed the error of taking Aghmir fully up upon his challenge and ventured his forces into unfavourable Saharan terrain against the advice of his officers. The result was a total defeat for the Ruma at Tuwa in which 300 *rumāt* were killed, besides innumerable auxiliary (or lesser armed) forces. Among the dead were a number of Zaghari, Tazarkīni and Shuṭūki notables, besides Ḥammādi himself, while the Dara'is also suffered appreciable losses. The decline of the Zaghari family shortly thereafter was one of the lesser consequences of this event. The main consequence was Tadmekkat control over the region of Timbuktu mitigated only by the continued theoretical (and potential) ascendency of the Wulmdān and by the increasing influence of the Kunta on both confederations.[144]

It is remarkable that even in the immediate aftermath of the defeat the internal Ruma struggles did not cease. It seems that the Dara'is had not put their full weight behind Ḥammādi al-Zaghari even though Aghmir had seemed to threaten the whole Ruma. The sons of Baḥaddu b. Yaḥya, who had allied himself with the Shurfa and with the whole city in driving away Ḥammādi's brother Mas'ūd, had remained behind in Timbuktu, along with the scholars and merchants, and did not venture into the open against the Tadmekkat. Baḥaddu's eldest son, Muḥammad, indeed acted conjointly with the *Qāḍi*, in arriving at a settlement with Aghmir after the battle. This was apparently interpreted as some sort of treason by the survivors of the battle of Tuwa who assembled south of the Niger and dared not return to Timbuktu for months. When Muḥammad b. Baḥaddu went over to bring them back they actually killed him 'lest he should cause us all to perish'.[145] When his cousin 'Ali b. Ḥamad al-Jasīm heard of this event, he marched against them but, for a reason which is not fully known, he could not venture any further than Kabara. Ultimately, it devolved upon none other than the reigning Askia al-Ḥājj to arrange a compromise and escort the fugitives back to Timbuktu. This chief was son of Askia Bakr b. Muḥammad Ṣādiq b. Askia al-Ḥājj b. Muḥammad Bankanu b. Muḥammad al-Ṣādiq b. Askia Daud b. Askia al-Ḥājj Muḥammad. Being preoccupied with listing the Pashas, the *Tadhkira* supplies very little information about the Askias who reigned at Timbuktu besides delineating their lineages. It is clear from this episode however, that, while they stayed away from the internal Ruma conflicts, they acquired a position of particular veneration and prestige. Askia al-Ḥājj's leadership of the defeated Ruma back to Timbuktu apparently became a memorable event in the annals of the city:

> He rode before them out of the island after the conciliation which they reached amongst themselves at the hands of Askia al-Ḥājj himself. They walked after him in the manner of walking behind a Pasha with the flag of the Pasha, his drum and his armour beside him.[146]

At Kabara, the procession was joined by 'Ali b. Ḥamad al-Jasīm, and on arrival at Timbuktu a great lamentation arose over those who it was learned had died at Tuwa. By that time, the distinction between Songhai and Ruma, as between the two and the population generally, had gradually eroded owing to constant intermarriages between the various groups. The main families of scholars had, to an extent, retained a separate identity, and the same was true among the top leadership of Ruma and Songhai. Among the Songhai, two lineages descended from Askia Muḥammad, besides a third descended from 'Umar Kumzāghu, probably retained notability status till the nineteenth century and contributed almost as many members to the overall body of notables as the Ruma.[147]

It would be tedious to go into the details of the subsequent struggles between Dara'is and Tazarkīnis over the Tibshāsha. Suffice it to say that while we leave the two families intermittently in conflict at the completion of *Tadhkirat al-Nasyān* around 1750, their petty disputes are taken up in the opening pages of the later chronicle, *Dhikr al-Wafayāt*. In the meantime, the city remained during frequent interludes without a Pasha, and in 1741, one was briefly appointed simply to invest the visiting Ghamān b. Aghāshikh b. Karidanna, who had succeeded to the chieftaincy of the Wulmdān.[148] The Amenokals received presents on such occasions, and their visits reminded the local Kel Tadmekkat of their continued interest in at least a nominal Pashalik at Timbuktu. Locally, as well as among the Kunta, the scholars too had evolved a vested interest in sustaining a small Ruma army, which would keep the Saharan arrivals in check during the caravan seasons.[149] The Dara'i and Tazarkīni Pashas, for all their squabbles, somehow managed to keep remnants of the Marākushi and Fāsi divisions in the semblance of a disciplined urban-based force. The Songhai askiate, for its part, increasingly based itself outside the city, and may even have merged by the mid-eighteenth century with the chieftaincy at Dendi.[150] From *Dhikr al-Wafayāt* we learn that the Dara'is emerged predominant around 1766, under the leadership of Baḥaddu b. Bābakr b. Alfa Manṣūr b. Muḥammad b. 'Ali b. al-Mubārak al-Dara'i. This Ruma notable had first reigned in 1163 A.H. (1750 A.D.) but now he enjoyed the Tibshāsha fully for nine years, and hence longer than any other Pasha, till his death in 1775. Subsequently, the Tibshāsha remained vacant for 20 years, but it is clear that Baḥaddu's sons, and especially Bābakr, were implicitly recognized as the chiefs of the Ruma and, theoretically, of Timbuktu. Bābakr was formally invested for one year in 1794 and, three decades later, the first European visitor, Caillié, gained the impression that his son 'Uthmān was 'King of Timbuktu'.[151] It is interesting that the lineage which led the Dara'is was descended from Alfa Mạnṣūr (also Manṣūr), a previous Kahia rather than a Pasha, for his title suggests that he acquired some learning. Subscription to the Muslim tradition of scholarship, besides support of the Shurfa and scholars in 1719, may indeed have paved the way for the precedence of the Dara'is. We know at least that Alfa Manṣūr's cousin, Aḥmad (Ḥammadi) b. Kabara Farma 'Abd al-Raḥmān b. 'Ali b. al-Mubārak al-Dara'i, had been a literatus. The earliest extant copy of al-Maghīli's answers to Askia Muḥammad was written by him in 1715.[152]

The resurgence of scholars

It should be apparent from the above that a continuous though subtle influence on the part of scholars was a permanent feature of the Ruma regime. Indeed, immediately after the Moroccan conquest, the accession of a judge from the ancient Ḥājj family, followed by And-Agh-Muḥammads, affirmed the old order whereby the affairs of the civilian population would be discharged by the religio-legal administration dominated by scholar–notables. The accession of 'Abd al-Raḥmān b. Aḥmad Maghia in 1651/2, later to be succeeded by other kinsmen, further asserted the independence of the civilian administration from the Pashas. For it implicitly honoured the memory of the fallen Aḥmad Maghia, whose martyrdom had come to symbolize the rejection of the Ruma regime in its initial brutal form. Moreover, traditionists tended to see the precedence given to the Maghias as partly shared by the Aqīts on basis of an undetermined kinship relationship between them. Today, the *imām* of

Sankore, Alfa Sālum, is believed to be descended from a lineage owing its ancestry to both families and to the Zankanus. The basis for this seems to be the fact that the earlier Zankanus were descended from a daughter of al-Qāḍi al-'Āqib b. Maḥmūd Aqīt, while the first Zankanu Judge, al-Qāḍi Muḥammad, was half-brother to al-Qāḍi Ibrāhīm b. 'Abdullāh b. Aḥmad Maghia, through a common mother.[153]

The dynastic factor in the inheritance of the judgeship no doubt strengthened the hands of the judges and minimized the possiblity of influence by the Pashas on their succession. Unfortunately, however, we do not have much by way of substantive detail concerning the careers and policies of the Maghia and Zankanu judges. We know that seven of these judges administered the civilian population for well over a century, at an average of some 18 years each, up to *c.* 1780. This means that each of them saw the rise and fall of numerous Pashas and, although they were themselves invested by the Pasha reigning at their accession, it is probable that they indirectly influenced the succession to the Tibshāsha at all times but the period of serious strife in the early eighteenth century. At that time, the judgeship was held by Sayyid Aḥmad b. Ibrāhīm b. 'Abdullāh b. Aḥmad Maghia who reigned for fully 38 years till death at the age of 94 in 1734/5. This old Judge is known only for mediation attempts between the various Ruma factions which, however, were mostly unsuccessful. In 1712, the Ruma deposed Mas'ūd b. Manṣūr, after a brief first reign by this Pasha, without even telling him of the fact. He suffered the humiliation of appearing at Mas'ūd's house for the customary recital of *Bukhāri* in Ramaḍān, later to be told that the man was no longer Pasha.[154] Soon afterwards, in 1714, he allowed a virtual trial to take place in his presence, presided over by the reigning Pasha Baḥaddu al-Dara'i, in which his was not the dominant voice. The occasion was a murder of a Drāwi and a Filāli in which four Shurfa were implicated. At the call of the Pasha:

> Al-Qāḍi Sayyid Aḥmad b. al-Faqīh al-Qāḍi Ibrāhīm came with all the Fuqaha' of the town excepting al-Faqīh Muḥammad Baghayughu [b. Gurdu] to the Qaṣba. The Pasha asked them what is to be done, and he repeated his question several times till he called each by name but they did not reply . . . Then al-Imām al-Faqīh Sāliḥ b. al-Imām Aḥmad b. al-Imām Sa'īd b. al-Imām Muḥammad Gidādu rose and said to the Pasha: 'Kill the [Shurfa culprits], all of them, because retaliation is more lawful than compensation in such a case, and the spilling of their blood is my responsibility'.[155]

As it turned out, the Pasha executed only one of the implicated Shurfa, but the weakness of the *Qāḍi* in this instance further eroded the prestige of scholars and of Shurfa. This probably was one of the factors which encouraged the Legha of Pasha Mas'ūd to extend their excesses to scholars and Shurfa, as already mentioned above, in 1718–19. Indeed, it seems possible that al-Qāḍi Sayyid Aḥmad lost his universal recognition as Judge, for we have one independent reference to Maḥmūd b. Aḥmad b. ʿAbd al-Raḥmān b. Aḥmad al-Mujtahid as Judge.[156] We have already seen that the latter's kinsmen fought back the Legha of Manṣūr when they assaulted one of their houses. Moreover, we learn that the chief of the Legha in his flight from Shurfa and Drāwis sought refuge with Bāba al-Mukhtār b. Muḥammad b. al-Mukhtār b. Muḥammad Zankanu, who was later to succeed Sayyid Aḥmad formally, rather than with the Judge himself. Altogether, it seems that Sayyid Aḥmad's indecisiveness during a long tenure of the judgeship, was partly responsible for the bloody dimensions of the internal Ruma struggles in the early eighteenth century.

Relying almost exclusively on records of the Tibshāsha, the anonymous author of *Tadhkirat al-Nasyān*, born in 1700 as he tells us, left no appreciable details on any judges other than Sayyid Aḥmad and Bāba al-Mukhtār, who occupied the judgeship during most of the author's lifetime. Bāba al-Mukhtār proved a formidable *Qāḍi* who, judging by various indications, helped put a stop to the arrogance of the main Ruma families. He formally attained the judgeship in the year 1147 A.H. (November 1734), the same year in which the Ruma, led by Ḥammadi b. Manṣūr al-Zaghari, were decimated by the Tadmekkat. We learn, incidentally, that the Judge had no sympathy for Ḥammadi, and for none excepting perhaps the Daraʿis among the other Ruma families. Ḥammadi came to the Tibshāsha shortly after Bāba Mukhtār's formal assumption of the judgeship and he proceeded to enhance his image by presiding at a restoration of a section of the Jingerebir Mosque though such a privilege was a prerogative of *Qāḍis*. The *Tadhkira* is ambiguous on this point, saying that the *Qāḍi* 'may have given him permission' (*sic*) to do so, but it goes on to record that the *Qāḍi* and two of the *imāms* absented themselves from the ceremony.[157] Besides amounting to a subtle power struggle, this probably gave a signal to the Tadmekkat chieftain, Aghmir, that the leadership of the scholars, and hence the civilian population, dissociated itself at this point from the leadership of the Ruma. As already mentioned above, the chieftain reciprocated by declaring that his warlike moves were strictly directed against the warrior Ruma.

The fact that the *Qāḍis* commanded the allegiance of the entire civilian population is best illustrated by the events immediately following the defeat of Ḥammadi's army at Tuwa. When news of the defeat first reached Timbuktu on the evening of the battle, as we read in the *Tadhkira*:

> Al-Faqīh al-Qāḍi Bāba went out to the courtyard of the Sankore mosque and sent for the Shurfa and the main merchants to come to him. He said to them: 'What are we to do at this time, after what has happened, by way of arranging for ourselves, our children and our families tonight'. They answered: 'You are our Judge, our Faqīh and our Shaikh. Whatever you order us to do, we will obey.' He said to them: 'Go back to your houses and post guards [around the city] for the night, and we will look into the matter tomorrow morning'.[158]

For all this, the author of the *Tadhkira*, apparently a lesser literatus who did not rank among the notables, leaves us only an indirect impression that the *Qāḍi* reached a settlement with Aghmir. This might further suggest that prior agreement existed between the two and had been reached through the good offices of ʻAbd al-Mu'min b. Sayyid Muḥammad al-Muṣṭafa b. Aḥmad b. Gāda al-Kunti. The ancestor in this case may be Aḥmad Agadda, the founder of the Ṭālibna lineage of scholars in Arwān.[159] However, even the patrilineal Wulmdān have a certain Aḥmad b. al-Adda in their ancestry and it is possible that the Kunta, whatever may be their origins, were matrilineally related to both Wulmdān and Arwānis. Their influence on Timbuktu, which began at this time, or perhaps slightly earlier in the eighteenth century, was to become a very strong feature in the nineteenth century.[160]

Al-Qāḍi Bāba al-Mukhtār did not put a final stop to the internal struggles among the Ruma, now mainly between Daraʻis and Tazarkīnis, but he certainly moderated the effects of these struggles. The rise of the Shurfa as an urban-based military power, coupled with the fact that the body of notables as a whole could marshal an army of their own if the need arose, contributed towards humbling the Ruma notables. By 1743, when a struggle broke out between Daraʻis and Tazarkīnis, they brought their case to be settled in court before the *Qāḍi*.[161] This was a step towards bringing the whole population again, with the distinction between civilian and military gradually eroding, under the religio-legal authority of the Judge. Bāba al-Mukhtār was succeeded by ʻAbdullāh Bābīr b. Sayyid Aḥmad b. Ibrāhīm b. ʻAbdullāh b. Aḥmad Maghia, whose accession in 1750 is the very last event recorded in the *Tadhkira*. The source apparently compensated for its inadequacy on the careers of judges by including an extraordinarily elaborate praise of ʻAbdullāh and his ancestors.[162]

The system which evolved in Timbuktu by the end of the eighteenth century essentially survived intact up to the French conquest at the end of the nineteenth century. As known initially from the collection of obituaries in *Dhikr al-Wafayāt*, and later from European records and other sources, the system bore essential similarity to the period of Maghsharen Tuareg ascendency in the mid-fifteenth century. Indeed, in one respect, it recalls the brief observations made by Ibn Baṭūṭa during his visit in the fourteenth century when Timbuktu was under Malian sovereignty. The traveller had occasion to observe that the native governor, bearing a Malian title, invested the chieftains of the nearby Saharan clans. The privilege at the time was probably shared by Timbuktu and Gao, and later under the Songhai empire, it became an exclusive right of the Askias. The Pashas at Timbuktu inherited that right, by first investing the chiefs of the Maghsharen, and possibly the Barābīsh, and after 1690 by investing the chiefs of the predominant Wulmdān. This system survived five centuries after Ibn Baṭūṭa until at least 1796, when Kāwi Ag-Amma Ag-Agashīkh b.

Karidanna came for his ceremonial robes and horses like his great-grandfather.[163] It just so happened that Bābakr b. Baḥaddu b. Bābakr b. Alfa Manṣūr al-Dara'i had been named Pasha two years previously. Though now deposed, he served as *de facto* chief of the Ruma for many years. Kāwi was therefore ceremoniously invested according to tradition and this preserved a much older sense of order in the relationships between the city and the Sahara. For reasons not entirely known, the Kel Tadmekkat often stayed beyond the reach of this theoretical order of relationships and, indeed, in 1770 when their chief Habtīt was killed by the Ruma, they placed Timbuktu under a state of siege. Al-Mukhtār al-Kabīr al-Kunti interceded at this point and secured a peaceful settlement. Not long thereafter, a split began taking shape among the Tadmekkat themselves whereby eventually one of the two fractions, known as the Tingeregif, became predominant.[164] Under the leadership of Awwāb, in the mid-nineteenth century, the Tingeregif (still at times calling themselves Tadmekkat) were under the influence and direction of the Kunta while implicitly recognizing the superior power of the distant Wulmdān.[165] Towards the very end of the century, they helped the Kel Antasar in reducing the Kunta and, for a brief period, enjoyed an undetermined sort of sovereignty over Timbuktu.

The role of Pashas, or Kāhias or Amīrs as they came to be known, became very similar to that of the Timbuktu-Koy Muḥammad Naḍ, of the fifteenth century. The Dara'is were dominant among the sector of the population which still identified itself primarily as Ruma, and especially in the Sarekeina quarter. Other than that, however, their leader at any one point was looked upon by the notables as first among equals. Indeed, it is more than probable that the later Maghia and Zankanu judges stood before the Dara'i Pashas on many occasions in precedence. Certainly this was true of the Shurfa judges, beginning with 'Abd al-Qadīr al-Sanūsi and Sān Sirfi, especially since the former combined the emirate with the judgeship at the rise of the Massina Caliphate of Ḥamdullāhi. In any case, it seems that the precedence given to the Amīr increasingly bore the same elements of veneration which extended to elders, scholars and judges. Even in the old days, the Pashas had increasingly been drawn from the ranks of middle-aged persons and elders. Now, notability became contingent upon seniority in terms of age and descent, besides a moderate level, at least, of learning. Beginning perhaps as early as 1760, and all the way up to 1894, rulership of the city essentially devolved upon the *Jamā'a* of Timbuktu, already discussed in Chapter 4, which was made up primarily of scholar–notables. This, of course, was a reversion to the older tradition which crystallized under Malian rule and the Maghsharen ascendency and had been characteristic of the Songhai period as well.

Local sources of the nineteenth century are numerous, but their information is almost as fragmentary as that of the European sources. Altogether, the combined evidence suggests a proliferation of power and influence among notables from the late eighteenth century onwards. Thus the Astrakhāni merchant Wargee, after visiting Timbuktu in 1821, left us a second-hand account which was written by his English interviewers at Cape Coast. Besides describing the houses belonging to a certain 'Sulṭān Muḥammad', Wargee observed that 'the houses of the rich people are built in the same style as that of the Sulṭān'. This already suggests that there was no 'royal palace' of any particular distinction at the time in Timbuktu. Furthermore, we read that:

Sulṭān Muḥammad is . . . independent, although not powerful; for he (Wargee) says, that his control does not extend much beyond Timbuktu itself. Muḥammad succeeded Sulṭān Abu Bakr, who, he heard, died about eight years ago, but he is ignorant who was his predecessor. Abu Bakr was extremely rich. Wargee remained at Timbuktu five weeks, during which time he lived in Sulṭān Muḥammad's house, and was treated by him with the greatest kindness.[166]

We know, of course, that Abu Bakr (Bābakr b. Baḥaddu b. Bābakr al-Dara'i) had become Pasha in 1794, but he simply had had no predecessor because the Tibshāsha had been vacant for two decades previously. The administration of Timbuktu had devolved primarily upon the Judge, Abkar (Abu Bakr) b. Bāba al-Mukhtār b. Muḥammad b. al-Mukhtār b. Muḥammad Zankanu up to 1779/80. The latter's death apparently left the judgeship *de facto* in the hands of one or more of the Maghia and Zankanu scholars until one of them, identified only as al-'Āqib (possibly Muḥammad al-'Āqib), was formally invested at the accession of Pasha Bābakr. The *Qāḍi* probably outlived the Pasha who, as we know independently, died in 1230 A.H. (1814/15 A.D.), and it is remotely possible that the same al-Qāḍi al-'Āqib was Wargee's Sulṭān Muḥammad.[167] We know that Pasha Bābakr had a brother named Muḥammad who, however, died in 1792. He also had a son named 'Uthmān who was later believed King, several years after Wargee's visit, by Caillié. At this juncture, 'Uthmān may have acted as Kahia, theoretically a military post which by this time combined the prerogatives of the Timbuktu-Mundhu and Ashra' Mundhu of Songhai times. Wargee specifically associates Sulṭān Muḥammad with judicial functions and mentions no instrument of power other than a prison manned by a few guards during his visit to Timbuktu.[168]

Alternatively and more probably, Sulṭān Muḥammad was none other than Sīdi Muḥammad b. al-Mukhtār al-Kabīr b. Abu Bakr al-Kunti. Actual control of the area of Timbuktu, and certainly the management of its relations with the Tuareg, devolved primarily on the Kunta scholars well before Wargee's visit. The first Kunta intercession between the Tuareg and Timbuktu dates back to 1720 when a certain al-Ṣiddīq al-Kuntāwi was prominent in the area. It has been suggested by Marty that this Ṣiddīq was none other than Abu Bakr, grandfather of Sīdi al-Mukhtār al-Kabīr.[169] The Kunta enjoyed strong links with the learned Kel al-Suq, besides the scholars of Arwān and Walāta, and shared reference to Timbuktu scholars, especially the sons and grandsons of Muḥammad Gurdu, as their direct or ultimate masters. Al-Mukhtār al-Kabīr consolidated a position which he partly inherited from his father and his other kinsmen whereby the Kunta virtually *managed* the affairs of the southern Sahara, besides strongly influencing some of the clans of the northern Sahara. They did so by establishing for themselves a middle position between the Ahoggār and the Wulmdān, the two greatest Tuareg confederations. The Ahoggār, far to the east and northeast, could not directly influence the state of affairs in the region of Timbuktu but they kept the Wulmdān in check and the latter, in turn, checked the power of the Tadmekkat and, later, of the dominant Tingeregif fraction of the Tadmekkat. Al-Mukhtār al-Kabīr al-Kunti strengthened this order of relationships, and extended it to other Tuareg, Barābīsh and Hassāni clans, so that by his death in 1811 recognition of the special role of the Kunta was universal. He did not, except in youth, reside at Timbuktu, but his son Sīdi Muḥammad established himself at the city in 1234 A.H. (1818/19 A.D.) in a move mentioned by several sources which became celebrated.[170] Sīdi Muḥammad no doubt immediately established an ascendency over all other notables, though still as first among equals, until his death in 1241 A.H. (1825/26 A.D.).

Insofar as the nineteenth-century history of the Timbuktu area has already been researched, the greatest emphasis has been placed on the role of the Kunta.[171] This is quite justified by the fact that the clan, or at least the lineage descended from al-Mukhtār al-Kabīr, controlled the relations between Tuaregs and between the Jihādist state of Massina. Indeed, just before the death of Aḥmad al-Bakkā'i, grandson of Sīdi Muḥammad, the Kunta established some sort of sovereignty over Massina which, though quite ephemeral, lasted till towards the end of the century. It would be impossible to cover adequately these events, which are the main focus of attention in the local sources, and we will therefore essentially restrict our discussion in this final section to the configurations of power and influence which pertained at Timbuktu itself.

The rise of the Jihādist state of Ḥamdullāhi in Massina was a momentous event for the scholars, or at least it was seen as such in retrospect, though it did not accomplish the desired hope for a stable state modelled after an idealized version of the Songhai empire. The Timbuktu scholars found favour in Aḥmadu Lobbo's claim to be the spiritual successor of Askia Muḥammad and, in the person of al-Mukhtār b. Ṭāhir, a student of Sīdi al-Mukhtār al-Kunti, they introduced this legend into the text of *Tārīkh al-Fattāsh*. Indeed, a son of Sān Sirfi, who does not fully identify himself, also incorporates into one of his compositions the claim that Askia Muḥammad had prophesied the future advent of Aḥmadu Lobbo, or at least a Mujaddid from the Sanqara Fulāni clan who would revive the faith and establish a virtuous Muslim state.[172] The scholars of Timbuktu may have adhered to this constitutional legend throughout the sovereignty of Aḥmadu Lobbo

(1825/6–1844/5) but, especially during the reign of Aḥmadu's grandson, Aḥmad b. Aḥmad, elements which were closely related to the emendations in *Tārīkh al-Fattāsh* were rejected.

Aḥmadu Lobbo's triumph over the Ardo of Massina, and his control over Jenne and Massina by 1818, were welcomed by the scholars of Timbuktu, but the extension of his control to their city did not entirely go unchallenged. Our sources are somewhat reticent on the sequence of events, but it seems that the Jihādist seized the opportunity of the death of Sīdi Muḥammad b. al-Mukhtār al-Kabīr in 1825/6 to request formal recognition of his sovereignty. He sent al-Amīr al-Ḥājj Mūdu, at the head of a large army, as an emissary to al-Qā'id 'Uthmān b. Bābakr who, as already suggested, had been Kahia in charge of a small force at Timbuktu. According to Sān Sirfi's son, who is our only source on the subject, Mūdu merely requested 'Uthmān to give up the use of the drum and other ceremonials and 'they entered under his *bi'a* and he agreed to give up the wax (candles?) and the drum'.[173] The visit of Caillié took place shortly after this but, in confusing the scholars for Moors and describing 'Osman' as king of the Kisoor, the French traveller hardly adds anything to our information. From elsewhere, we learn that several years later, in 1249 A.H. (1833/34 A.D.), 'Uthmān revoked the sovereignty of Massina and, supported by the Kel Tadmekkat, led a small Ruma army in a march against Ḥamdullāhi. The force was intercepted by a greater one and was decimated, but Timbuktu was spared direct rule through the intercession of Sīdi al-Mukhtār al-Ṣaghīr, son of Sīdi Muḥammad b. al-Mukhtār al-Kabīr, who established himself at Timbuktu a year later.[174] Aḥmad al-Bakkā'i, who later succeeded al-Mukhtār al-Ṣaghīr to the leadership of the Kunta, and hence to precedence among the notables at Timbuktu, recalled this event simply as follows: 'I found that my brother had entered between [the Tuareg] and al-Shaikh Muḥammad Aḥmad b. Aḥmadu Lobbo and made peace between them for the benefit of the country and for the sake of its security'.[175]

The resistance to Lobbo rule, followed by the 'conquest' of the city, did in fact result in some political realignment coupled with a measure of retaliation. For we read that a third of the property of each Ruma who participated in the campaign with the Tadmekkat was confiscated.[176] Indeed, there has survived a copy of a letter addressed to Aḥmadu Lobbo by a scholar who pleads against sequestration of a third of the property of his own kinsmen.[177] This might suggest that the notables as a whole backed 'Uthmān and the Tadmekkat. We know, at least, that the Lobbos prohibited throughout the new state the use of tobacco, a commodity which had an important place in the commerce of Timbuktu. This and other legislation introduced by the Jihādist state were to remain a permanent bone of contention between Timbuktu and Ḥamdullāhi.

One action taken by Aḥmadu Lobbo which had an effect on later configurations of power was the appointment of 'Abd al-Qādir b. Muḥammad al-Sanūsi, a member of the Shurfa, as Qāḍi and Amīr of Timbuktu. This took place immediately after the defeat and capture of 'Uthmān, who was taken to imprisonment for two and half years at Ḥamdullāhi. Subsequent events are rather obscure, but Sān Sirfi, who acted as *kātib* under 'Abd al-Qādir, continued to do so when the latter was deposed in favour of al-Qāḍi Alfa Sa'īd b. Bāba Gurdu. 'Abd al-Qādir had studied under the Gurdus and, therefore, his dismissal in favour of Alfa Sa'īd is not easily explained. However, Sān Sirfi outlived both, and emerged as the most powerful figure, closely allied to Aḥmad al-Bākka'i, in the mid-nineteenth century.[178]

The Lobbo dynasty sufficiently enforced a stable regime in the Niger bend area so that the commerce of Timbuktu became a major beneficiary. At a later time it was even claimed that the city attracted so many merchants and settlers that it was restored to its previous size under the Songhai.[179] This does not seem true, but a measure of growth is certainly evidenced by Barth's observations concerning the extensiveness of storage buildings at Kabara. In the late eighteenth century that port-town had been under constant threat of depredation by Tuaregs, and even the Sankore quarter at Timbuktu had to be walled in one case, after being evacuated in a conflict with the Tuareg.[180] Now, thanks partly to the Kunta, the Tadmekkat, under the leadership of Awwāb, were integrated as cattle producers into the economy of the region. The rise of a new Jihād led by Ḥājj 'Umar, who overthrew Aḥmad b. Aḥmad b. Aḥmad Lobbo in 1862, plunged the region once again into a state of even more extreme strife.

Though a working relationship had secured unusual stability for Timbuktu throughout the period of Lobbo sovereignty, the extremely puritanical interpretation of Islam by the monarchs, and especially by the less-learned Aḥmad III, was a cause of constant complaint on the part of Timbuktu scholars. The best known example of the tension surrounds the visit of Henry Barth whose stay at Timbuktu as a guest of al-Bakkā'i was opposed on the grounds that he was a Christian by Ḥamdullāhi. We have also already mentioned the prohibition of smoking tobacco, though the jurists of Timbuktu had long legalized it. A third complaint which al-Bakkā'i specifically lodged against the Lobbos was their insistence that Islam required women to be fully segregated from the men throughout the state. This ran counter to Tuareg–Hassāni custom and, indeed, al-Mukhtār al-Kabīr had issued several *fatwas* against it.[181]

Unfortunately, the views of al-Bakkā'i are known mainly from a letter by Aḥmadu III himself which he addressed to his commander Ghūru b. Sa'īd. The most serious cause of complaint, as far as we can tell from the letter, is that the Lobbo state reduced many tribes and villages in their realms *de jure* to slave status. The emendations introduced into *Tārīkh al-Fattāsh* along with the claim that Aḥmadu Lobbo was the long-awaited twelfth true caliph, attributed the enslavement of many groups to historical precedent which was allegedly set by Askia Muḥammad. The defective manuscript C of *Tārīkh al-Fattāsh*, which alone is a complete copy, mentions the groups by name and alludes by various means to their original alleged slave status. Yet, no document had survived from the time of Askia Muḥammad, aside from al-Maghīli's *Risāla*, other than the privilege already mentioned elsewhere in this study which was issued by the monarch in favour of Ahl Mūri Kuyra. That had clearly formed part of the original text of the *Fattāsh* and, in giving the impression that some groups were relegated to slave status, it served as a basis for further embroidery on the subject. Even the Ghābibi of Timbuktu, who were free though lower status traders and craftsmen, were assigned a slave origin. We do not know what were the motives of Aḥmad al-Bakkā'i nor to what extent he reflected the views of other Timbuktu scholars, but he apparently objected that the non-Muslim villages and tribes in the Massina state were subject to the *Kharāj* (special tax in Muslim jurisprudence) but not to enslavement. Aḥmadu III simply countered the argument by saying, 'We have owned them by the right of their ownership by Askia Muḥammad, as we saw in *Tārīkh al-Fattāsh*'.[182] It is almost certain that his appeal to the same groups enabled al-Ḥājj 'Umar to overthrow the Lobbos swiftly when he launched his *Jihād* against them.[183]

So far as we can tell, the embroilment of Timbuktu against Ḥājj 'Umar in a struggle which thoroughly disrupted the entire commerce of the Niger bend area was primarily the result of the conflict between the Kunta-led Qādiriyya Sufi Ṭarīqa, on the one hand, and the Tijāniyya Tarīqa which was now being disseminated by the disciples of Ḥājj 'Umar. In ways which require to be researched further, the Qādiriyya brotherhood had gradually built strong links between scholars and literati throughout the southern Sahara, and now it was threatened by the rising force of the more closely knit Tijāniyya brotherhood. Another factor was an attempt by Ḥājj 'Umar, after the initial acceptance of his sovereignty, following his entry into Ḥamdullāhi, to establish more direct rule than his predecessors had accomplished over Timbuktu. After having captured Aḥmadu III and executed him, he demanded that the notables of Timbuktu, led by Bakkā'i himself and presumably Sān Sirfi, along with the chiefs of the Tuareg, or at least Awwāb, should present themselves at his court for a formal act of allegiance. Al-Bakkā'i responded by withdrawing from Timbuktu on the innocent plea that Ḥājj 'Umar's agents in the city were committing unlawful acts which he did not want to witness. This withdrawal, in fact, symbolically amounted to a Hijra such as preceded the *Jihād* of 'Uthmān Dan Fodio in Hausaland and Aḥmadu Lobbo in Massina. Sān Sirfi then acted on behalf of all the notables in drafting a *bī'a* in favour of al-Bakkā'i should he wish to lead a struggle against Ḥājj 'Umar. At the same time, it seems, the kinsmen of the fallen Aḥmadu III in Massina drafted a similar *bī'a*. After throwing Ḥājj 'Umar's agents out of the city, the combined forces of the Kunta and the Tuareg

Tadmekkat (now more commonly known by the name of the Tingeregif fraction) marched on Ḥamdullāhi and brought down Ḥājj 'Umar.[184]

Under the influence of later conciliation between the Tijāniyya and the Qādiriyya, the chroniclers have not left us much information concerning some important details of the conflict. From letters addressed to him by his supporters, we learn that Aḥmad al-Bakkā'i was recognized as Muslim sovereign, including the title Commander of the Faithful, but the old scholar barely lived one year after the triumph to enjoy the honour.[185] The death of Ḥājj 'Umar, after his flight from besieged Ḥamdullāhi, is surrounded by controversy and legend, while it seems possible that Sān Sirfi also met a violent death in the conflict.[186] To exonerate other Kunta, Tijāni accounts sometimes claim that most of Bakkā'i's warriors were Tuaregs of ill-repute, but it is obvious that Kunta clansmen stood foremost in the Massina campaigns and were principally allied to the Fulāni supporters of the fallen Lobbos rather than the Tuaregs. The Timbuktu citizenry no doubt also contributed a substantial portion of the warriors, and they continued to do so for two decades thereafter. Beginning even before the untimely death of al-Bakkā'i, the victors were divided amongst themselves between Lobbos and Kunta. Conflicts between the allies ensued and this enabled Ḥājj 'Umar's son, Aḥmad Tijāni, to wrest some victories and, after a long and bitter struggle, to preserve a 'Umarian state based at Segu. The Kunta's claim to sovereignty, or at least to leadership in Massina, somehow survived until 1880 when the *bī'a* of 'Ābidīn b. Bakkā'i b. Muḥammad al-Amīn b. Sīdi Muḥammad b. al-Mukhtār al-Kabīr was revoked in favour of the Lobbo Muḥammad b. Aḥmad b. Abu Bakr.[187] By that time, the militant stance of the Kunta had eroded their special prestige, and in 1876/7 a struggle had escalated between them and the clerical Kel Antasar in the southern Sahara. The Tuaregs as a whole, it seems, led by the Tingeregif, supported the Antasar, with the result that the Kunta were defeated and some of their encampments were plundered.[188] It is possible that the Wulmdān, once again, checked the Tingeregif from pursuing their victory and that this preserved some of the influence of the Kunta. Visiting Timbuktu in 1880 in the wake of this conflict, Oscar Lenz still gave precedence to 'Ābidīn over the chief of the Tingeregif, Ed Fandagoumou, in listing the most important persons of the region. However, the traveller could not have gained an accurate picture of the new configurations of power, for he assigned to the Kahia of Timbuktu, whom he does not name, a position of unspecified special importance.[189] In practice, for the next 13 years till the French conquest, the Timbuktu region was essentially under the control of the Tingeregif who now came to be distinguished as the noble–warrior class (Imoshagh) among the Tuareg.

Current tradition holds somewhat vaguely that the last *amīrs* of Timbuktu belonged to the Mas'ūdu branch of the Ruma. The group is a rather large one which is believed to be descended from Mas'ūd b. Manṣūr al-Zaghari, the very first Pasha of that nomenclature who flourished at the time of the chronicler al-Sa'di in the mid-seventeenth century. No details are cited to confirm these traditions, however, nor are they supported by the few available sources. At best, the traditions suggest a fuller assimilation of a few Ruma and Songhai families, besides the Dara'is, into the ranks of urban notables. Hacquard mentions that a certain Bourahim son of Amar was *Amīr* of Timbuktu till his death in 1884. And, indeed, in the same year of 1884, the French at St. Louis received an embassy from Timbuktu accompanied by a letter from 'Kahia Ibrāhīm, Amir of Timbuktu', but the language of the letter, which is almost illiterate, is one of several indications that the ambassador, a certain al-Ḥājj b. Bābakr (Bakkā'i) al-Jaibar, did not enjoy strong credentials.[190] Hacquard states that Ibrāhīm had been appointed by Ḥājj 'Umar (presumably *c.* 1862) but another French document which describes the same as Ould el Kahia or Sidi el Aya (*sic*) says that he was appointed by al-Bakkā'i.[191] *Dhikr Waqāi'* mentions the *Amīr* of that time as a certain Sīdi b. Aḥmad 'Umar who died in 1283 A.H. (1866/67 A.D.).[192] If Sīdi was the honorific title of Ibrāhīm, as appears to be the case, then he could not have reigned more than a few years. His successors are not known by name, but it seems that two of his sons were recognized as *amīrs*, one replacing the other briefly in 1893, as the French were approaching Timbuktu. The Drāwis, for their part, had an influential notable around the turn of the century in the person of Sān wuld al-Qā'idi Bābakr. According to one traditionist this was Sān b. al-Qā'id Bābakr b. al-Khalīfa Sān b. al-Qā'id Muḥammad b. Bāḥaddu al-Dara'i.[193] In a letter to the French by al-Qāḍi Aḥmad Bāba b. Abu'l-'Abbās, however, the same notable makes an appearance as Sān b. al-Qā'id Bābakr b. 'Āl b. Mas'ūd.[194] As in most cases, we are dealing here with a copy rather than the original text of the letter. Scribal errors cannot, therefore, be ruled out, but the combination of two lineages by the same man may suggest a putative kinship between the later Dara'is and Zagharis. In any case, it seems certain that other factors besides descent, and perhaps principally wealth and patronage, determined the criteria of precedence among the Songhai–Ruma. Holding the emirate or chieftaincy of Timbuktu, coupled with alternation over the chieftaincy of the main four quarters, afforded a basis for the non-learned to share honour and influence with the scholars.

Among the scholar–notables, the element of descent, though always reinforced by learning, remained important up to the present century. The ancient Gidādus, who dominated the imamate of the Main Mosque for over a century, essentially disappeared from the picture after the eighteenth century. Recollection of their importance, however, if not direct lineal descent, is exemplified by the nomenclature of Alfa Sa'īd b. Gidādu. This scholar was widely enough respected throughout the city to be elected chief or *Amīr* of Timbuktu during the crisis which was occasioned by the

French conquest. At that point, the scholars dissociated themselves and the city from the resistance which the French had met at Kabara and from the massacre of the Bonnier column at Tacoubao. As a result, the Tingeregif, who certainly led the attack, bore the brunt of French retaliation, but the scholar–notables continued to entertain good relations with Kunta, Barābīsh and Kel Antasar rebel clansmen for many years to come. Ultimately, with the outbreak of the First World War, the scholars issued a voluntary act of support and allegiance to the French. At that point, many towns in the Sudan were requested to do so, but in all cases the statement of support was in the form of a brief letter. The scholars of Timbuktu, on the other hand, drew up an elaborate jurisprudential treatise in which they almost surveyed the whole history of their city. They pointed to Moroccan support of the French as a factor favouring their own stance with the allies, not so much because they had once owed allegiance to Morocco, but rather because the 'Alawite dynasty was Sharīfian in descent and because, according to *hadīth* which they cited, supreme leadership in Islam belonged to the Prophet's clan, Quraish, and hence to the Shurfa. Further, as they might have explained with implicit reference to Askia Muḥammad's pilgrimage, leadership in the central lands of Islam did not devolve on the Ottomans but rather upon the Sharīf of Mecca: 'We are bound by God and the Prophet to recognize the religious supremacy of the Sharīf of Mecca. It is he who has the right in truth to command our obedience, and no one else has that right.' Since the Sharīf at the time was concerting his efforts against Turkey with the Allies, the people of Timbuktu would support the French and the Allies also.[195]

Among the families of scholar–notables which had historically been prominent, the Gurdus had been closely related to the Gidādus, as both were originally Fulāni. Indeed, according to current information, the Amīr Alfa Sa'īdu b. Gidādu was descended from the Gurdus at least on his mother's side. The Gurdus had contributed at least one Judge, in the early nineteenth century, and had inherited the imamate of Jingerebir. In turn, they passed on the parochial leadership of the city to in-laws under the following circumstance. 'Abd al-Raḥmān (nicknamed Suyūṭi) b. al-Imām Bāba b. Ismā'īl Yoro b. Muḥammad Gurdu married his daughter, Yaya, to Alfa Bānia b. 'Ali b. 'Abdullāh b. Muḥammad al-'Irāqi, a scion of an ancient family. The offspring of the union, Muḥammad Baghayughu, became ancestor of several *imāms*, the present-day *imām* of Jingerebir, Alfa Humal, being his fourth-generation descendant. In the early part of this century, the family had a prominent scholar–notable in the person of Imām Suyūṭi b. Muḥammad b. Imām Suyūṭi and Alfa Humal is his nephew.[196]

We do not have much information concerning the Maghia and Zankanu scholars but their continued importance is evidenced from the elaborate nomenclature of their descendants as recorded in French sources. Very prominent as a notable and as a teacher in the present century was Sīdi Aḥmad b. Bābīr b. 'Abdullāh b. Muḥammad b. Ibrāhīm b. Bābīr b. 'Abdullāh b. Aḥmad Maghia. Sīdi Aḥmad's father was *imām* of Sankore in his own time, and so was Aḥmad's brother, Maḥmūd. The present-day *imām* of Sankore is Maḥmud's son, the widely respected elder Alfa Sālum.[197] A contemporary of Sīdi Aḥmad, in the early part of this century *imām* of Sankore, was Saifu b. Bāba Mukhtār Aita b. 'Abdullāh b. Abu Bakr. Saifu's great-grandfather, Abu Bakr (also Abkar) was brother of the illustrious eighteenth-century Judge known to us above as Bāba al-Mukhtār b. Muḥammad b. al-Mukhtār b. Muḥammad Zankanu.[198] The stability of the patriciate formed by scholar–notables is in no case as evident as in that of the Baghayughu Wangara scholars. Beginning with Muḥammad Baghayughu in the sixteenth century, the scholars of this family have uninterruptedly held the prestigious imamate of Sīdi Yaḥya down to the present *imām*, Alfa Aḥmad Banio b. al-Ḥasan b. Aḥmad Baghayughu b. al-Imām Muṣṭafa. We know nothing about Aḥmad Banio's great-grandfather, namely al-Imām Muṣṭafa, but the latter's brother, al-Imām Ibrāhīm, who died in 1258 A.H. (1842/3 A.D.) is known to us from a short composition by Sān Sirfi as the maternal uncle of this powerful Judge.[199]

Finally, the chronicles confront us with a minor though indicative difficulty in outlining the sequence of events in the late nineteenth century. For while they show that Sān Sirfi was succeeded by two sons to the judgeship, they do not specifically indicate the duration of their tenure of the post. That is because sometime after 1880, the Tingeregif claimed formal sovereignty over Timbuktu, apparently after a disagreement with the Sirfis, and named their own Judge in the person of a certain Dumna Koy (sometimes Duwana Koy) al-Madān. According to the information of Alfa Humal:

> The Tuareg brought a man from the people of Buna named Alfa Douanakoy, but he did not really discharge the judgeship because people did not hold him in respect as he was not from among them. Subsequently, Aḥmad Bāba, who was later to become Judge, helped him strengthen his position, and he married a sister of Aḥmad Bāba. Then Aḥmad Bāba himself became Judge under the French.[200]

Aḥmad Bāba b. Abu'l-'Abbās b. Mūlāy 'Umar b. Zayyān is the only Shurfa notable in Timbuktu whose descent is traced for more than two or three generations. Otherwise, we know virtually nothing about the origin of the powerful Shurfa who in the eighteenth century helped overthrow Mas'ūd b. Manṣūr. Likewise, we do not know the descent of al-Qāḍi 'Abd al-Qādir al-Sanūsi and Sān Sirfi. We are inclined to believe, however, that the Shurfa in Timbuktu, beginning with Bāba b. 'Umar and Muḥammad b. 'Uthmān, who fell in the wake of the Moroccan conquest, descended from the early sixteenth-century settler Aḥmad al-Ṣaqali. Certainly, Aḥmad Bāba traced his descent in the male line to Aḥmad al-Ṣaqali though we have no confirmation that the original settler had any offspring other than daughters.[201] Whatever the case may be, the Shurfa had always occupied an important position as some sort of middlemen between scholars and other non-learned notables. The rise of 'Abd al-Qādir and Sān Sirfi reflects a later stage whereby, under the influence of the Gurdu scholars especially, they increasingly joined the ranks of the learned. Aḥmad Bāba was himself a scholar and he derived his prestige from close association with the Kunta, for we learn that, besides presumably studying under them, he participated in their campaigns in Massina.[202] This made him more acceptable than Douana Koy and it is probable that Sān Sirfi's sons gradually relinquished their judicial functions to him. By the arrival of the French, he was to all practical purposes already the Judge of Timbuktu, and his sons subsequently succeded him.

Under the French regime, Aḥmad Bāba was theoretically second in rank to Alfa Sa'īd b. Gurdu, a scholar who was elected *Amīr* of Timbuktu. After only a few years of colonial rule, however, the French observed a fact which had always been characteristic of Timbuktu: although the Judge did not necessarily enjoy ceremonial precedence, he was nonetheless effectively the man in control of the city. The Pasha or the Kāhia, or later the *Amīr*, much like the Timbuktu Mundhu of Songhai times, was understood to be the highest post, at least insofar as part of the populace was concerned. Among the scholar–notables, however, the Judge embodied their views and saw to the implementation of their collective interests. In short, the primacy of the judgeship – along with the idea of collective leadership by the '*Jamā'a*', was a legacy of the earliest periods which exerted its influence on the organization of Timbuktu even after the establishment of French colonial rule.

CHAPTER 7

Summary and conclusions

It may perhaps be said that any historical study is shaped (and should be shaped) by the nature of the existing evidence. This is particularly true in research on the history of cities because in the absence of any established methodologies, the approach which might be adopted in any one case must rest upon substantive findings which are derivable from the available data. This means that some of the findings – in practice the most important findings – have to be presented from the beginning either in the format of an hypothesis or as part of a broad framework of analysis. In this case, we were confronted with two central findings which were closely related to each other and which, therefore, provided the basic synthetical framework of analysis in this study. Both of these findings had to do with the prominent position occupied by scholars, first in the sources and ultimately, in the history of Timbuktu.

One finding pertained to the factor of autonomy as a recurrent though variable theme in the history of Timbuktu. Even the barest outline of the city's political history (as presented in our introduction) suggested a certain primacy for the theme of autonomy and autonomous urban leadership by scholars. Nonetheless, the autonomous status of Timbuktu could not in itself be the central focus of attention in this study. Indeed, it would be misleading if we said that the autonomy of Timbuktu under its scholars and notables is the major conclusion which derives from our study; rather the role and status of scholars and notables, in relation to the rest of Timbuktu society, was the main subject of investigation. Regrettably, it is not possible to offer any single conclusion on this theme without running the risk of overstatement or oversimplification. More specifically, we cannot say that the scholastic establishment occupied a position of 'predominance' throughout the history of the city. The very concept of autonomy is itself relative in any context and, in this case, it is a variable rather than a constant or unchanging factor. Historically, the autonomy of Timbuktu was subject to external factors in each period. Hence, it had to be viewed within the framework of the broader history of the region. Nonetheless, the phenomenon of autonomy did have a base in the internal organization of the city – a base which was relatively stable and constant. This base is to be found in the elaborate structure and affiliations of the learned hierarchy.

A second finding which amplified the need for detailed social structural analysis was also introduced at the beginning of this study when we described Timbuktu as a 'city of scholars'. This proposition was not merely an hypothesis which could be verified or otherwise rejected. Instead, it was a proposition which we encountered in the sources. Indeed, it pertained to Timbuktu's own conception of its experience. The scholars simply occupied a pronounced role – not only at Timbuktu, but in other Muslim communities in the Western Sudan which came to be viewed as 'communities of clerics'. Insofar as Timbuktu gained a reputation as the 'city of scholars' *par excellence* in the Sudan, its internal organization and social structure was especially interesting. In other respects Timbuktu exemplified a social tradition which is encountered elsewhere in the region: namely, a tradition whereby a whole society came to be characterized by the status and role of its scholars.

Basically, the project which confronted us was to find a synthetical framework for examining (and eventually describing) the significance and meaning of this phenomenon. This could not be done through exclusive examination of the role and status of scholars. Such an approach would presuppose, in itself, total differentiation of scholars from the rest of society. Instead, it was necessary to examine the internal criteria of status and prerogative which made for close identification between scholars and society. In the administrative sphere, these criteria gave the city some of the characteristics of an autonomous 'polity'. Nonetheless, the factor of autonomy was only a part (though an important part) of this phenomenon. Another part was the accessibility of learned status to at least the leading sectors of society. But this in itself would not have been sufficiently significant had it not been for the diffusion of literacy (and more modest levels of learning) to the rest of the urban population. The parochial and religious aspects of Muslim learning were also important – especially as they pertained to subtle criteria of moral, legal and social order which were subject to adaptation in different societies. In the end, the factors involved were as much 'historical' as they were embodied in 'academic' (or pedagogical), administrative and status criteria. Indeed, the relevant factors were sufficiently varied as to be encompassed only by the concept of a *social tradition*.

Regrettably, the idea of a social tradition is not as familiar as it should be. More frequently, we speak of an 'intellectual tradition' or a 'religious tradition', or otherwise of 'traditional societies'. In so doing, we essentially overlook the fact that in every society traditions tend to have their own history. The intellectual, religious, sociological and other facets interact with each other rather than strictly being separate. Indeed, it is the interaction between various facets of tradition which tends to characterize each society. In theory, it should be possible to speak for example of an urban tradition (or a tradition of urbanism) or a 'mercantile tradition' (or a tradition of mercantilism) in the sociological sphere. In other words, the concept of 'a tradition' need not be exclusive to the intellectual or religious spheres; nor should we view it as a 'residue' from the past which characterizes a 'traditional society'. Quite to the contrary, traditions have a dynamism and history of their own whereby they supply the framework for development and change, besides stability.

The social tradition which characterized Timbuktu was a legacy of older cities in the area and, to an extent, it was a legacy of the earliest periods of Islamization in the Western Sudan. Inasmuch as Islam first diffused to mercantile communities and market-towns, the legacy (and the social tradition) had a 'mercantile' along with an 'urban' dimension. Its origins are to be found in the twin-cities of the Western Sudan which had been mentioned by the mediaeval Arab geographers. Later, the tradition was exemplified by a number of 'clerical towns' and 'clerical communities', but it is only at Timbuktu that the entire history of the tradition is documented in appreciable detail and across a period of several centuries.

Our study has essentially dealt with the history of this tradition, both in narrative form and in terms of an analysis of the social structure. The tradition was one which conditioned the character of Timbuktu while also conditioning the role and status of its scholars. The unifying link between city and scholars, therefore, was at the level of a local tradition of mercantilism and/or urbanism. Insofar as the tradition of autonomous leadership by scholars had roots and influence elsewhere, our study also had to follow the broader outlines of the history of the Western Sudan. Indeed, the relative stability of Timbuktu as an 'urban' entity supplied us with a framework for surveying the history of its region generally at a time when no complete history of the area had been written.

Regrettably, there was no scope in this study to compare Timbuktu adequately to other Muslim cities outside West Africa. At most, it was possible to refer to common themes, especially in the spheres of administration, law and jurisprudence. At other times, however, the very topics which arose in connection with the traditions of Timbuktu and its region had not been raised in the existing Islamicist literature outside West Africa. Indeed, the central theme of adaptation (change within tradition) has rarely been the subject of adequate discussion in the North African or Middle Eastern context. We do possess some interesting generalizations about the 'Islamic city', but no study which justifies recourse to a specific 'tradition of Muslim urbanism' which could embrace the West African Sudan equally as it could embrace the cities of Indian Islam or those of Indonesia. Hence, it appeared quite hazardous to present any definitive view concerning either the distinctions or parallels between Timbuktu and other Muslim cities outside West Africa. At most, as indicated in the introduction, the role of scholars in Timbuktu and its region presents itself as a more pronounced feature than in the Middle Eastern and North African cities.

Our study of Timbuktu yielded an important finding which may conceivably be encountered in the sources on other Muslim cities. The finding has to do with the existence of a 'patriciate' which was relatively stable over several centuries. The 'patrician' dimension has certainly been encountered in other cities, both Muslim and non-Muslim. For the most part, however, this has been the subject of theorization rather than the subject of both narrative *and* social-structural analysis over an extended period. The patrician dimension was most significant in the history of Timbuktu for supplying a modicum of stability. Elsewhere, a similar dimension was encountered by Bulliet in mediaeval Nishapur (itself a 'Muslim city') but during a restricted period. In other instances, however, the patrician factor has remained merely a subject of restricted conjecture, largely on the basis of the views of Max Weber.

In the case of Timbuktu, the chronicles laid bare sufficient detail so as to show the existence of a small patriciate which dominated the affairs of the city, beginning from at least around 1400 onwards. The evidence on later periods pertained, to a large extent in fact, to the persistence of this patriciate down to the late nineteenth century. Hence, the narrative sections of this study (Chapters 2 and 6) may be seen as a history of the patriciate of Timbuktu. At times, most especially in the earliest periods, the centrality of the patriciate gave it an autonomous position of authority in the city. Later, following the Moroccan conquest, the city (and its patriciate) virtually had to conquer its conquerors. In subsequent periods, on the other hand, the city had to contend with pressure from the nearby pastoralists – much as it had done in earliest periods of its history.

If we were to subject our evidence to the full rigours of socio-economic analysis, we might perhaps say that Timbuktu was a city of large-scale merchants rather than a city of scholars. Indeed, we might go further and speak of the dominant class in Timbuktu as a 'mercantile bourgeoisie' in the conventional sense of these terms. But the factors of familial status and kinship affiliation were always important. In the earliest periods, Timbuktu must have been made up principally of an aggregate of 'patrimonial estates', each represented by a major merchant family with its own dependants and clients. With the passage of time, however, large fortunes tended to be diluted through inheritance and, hence, the patterns of class and status differentiation became more complex. Over the long run, the large mercantile fortunes were repeatedly transformed into stable patrimonies shared on familial basis by many heirs. Accordingly, the factor of long establishment in the city, along with evolving notions of prestigious descent, supplemented the factor of wealth as a major determinant of status and prerogative. Indeed, it is the combination of wealth with established prestige which accounts, in the socio-economic sphere, for the 'patrician' character of Timbuktu.

The patrician factor in the history of Timbuktu presented itself, from the beginning, in terms of subscription (and access) to the social, legal and administrative dimensions of Muslim learning and jurisprudence. The humanistic and literary facets of Muslim learning could not be ignored any more than could the religious and parochial aspects. They helped cement the communal texture of a highly diversified society while supplying, at all levels of literacy and learning, a common universe of cultured discourse. The social dimension – and the impact of literacy and learning on status and prerogative – is a theme which admits greater scope for investigation and analysis however. It pertains more closely to the self-perception of Timbuktu as a city of scholars and it also has to do with the theme of urban autonomy.

In a sense, we had to ask why it is that the wealthy merchant families of Timbuktu, its notables and patricians, found it advantageous to subscribe to the tradition of Muslim learning or else patronize it. At a broader level of analysis, the question applies equally to the city as a whole as to the patricians. After all, even the most modest citizens, among the stable population at least, sought and acquired a minimum of Qur'ānic literacy. Timbuktu was a city of modest *alfas* besides being a city of accomplished jurists. Especially, during the Songhai period, Timbuktu was 'a place of kindness and support to students'. Nonetheless, the initiative of the leading families could not be ignored. We had to ask at least why it was that the merchant classes of Timbuktu, itself a merchant-city, gave a leadership position to the scholars among their ranks. In practice, this was equivalent to asking why it is that the topmost ranks of the notables gave themselves (and their sons) the rigorous religio-legal education which raised them to the status of scholars and jurists.

Perhaps the above questions may be posed more advantageously to the much more detailed sources of the larger Muslim cities in the Middle East and North Africa. Nonetheless, it would be useless to pretend that the answers would be the same or that they pertain solely to 'city' or urbanism. In all cases, the answer must be sought in historical factors of evolution and adaptation rather than solely in terms of the bearing of jurisprudence or ideology upon questions of social structure. In Timbuktu, at least, the concerns of scholars can be related partly to the interests of the leading classes, while in another part they pertain to questions of integration in the city as a whole. The historical background to the rise of 'scholar–notables' in the Western Sudan differs substantially from its equivalent in the Middle East and North Africa. In essence, we must not be misled by reference to 'classical Islam'. The phenomenon of an extensive body of 'scholar–notables' belongs far more visibly to the 'post-classical' period (or 'middle period') of Islam. Its development in the Western Sudan was therefore *parallel* to its development in the Middle East and North Africa.

Basically, we have focused upon historical factors which are primarily relevant to the Western Sudan. Indeed, the main theoretical factor which is applicable elsewhere in Islam – namely the contingency of status upon learning – is also applicable in other non-Muslim societies and civilizations. At Timbuktu, shared subscription to a learned tradition essentially supplied a common means for the assignation and sharing of status and prerogative. Naturally, the wealthy and established families enjoyed greater access to the higher levels of learning. By the same token, they also had a greater access to an elusive *de jure* sort of participation in the legal and administrative affairs of the city. But insofar as learning itself was a matter of status, it could serve on its own as an avenue to influence, an avenue which was available in various gradations to various sectors of the population.

In the relatively small world of West African Islam, the status of Muslim scholars, clerics and literati (*alfas*, *marabouts*, *tulba*, *fuqahā'*, *etc.*) presents us with as much variety as any other Muslim region. Nonetheless, a measure of commonality is evidenced by the designation of whole clans in the southern Sahara as 'clerical clans'. Similarly, a clerical feature characterized entire merchant communities, especially in the Dyula market-towns in the Sudan. In the small kingdoms or 'city–states' of Hausaland, the scholars were perhaps drawn from a sort of 'middle class', principally mercantile. Indeed, perhaps an erosion of the status of scholars there, along with a decline in the mercantile interests of their class, may lie at the background of the nineteenth-century *jihāds*. In Futa Toro, a militant scholastic tradition had earlier roots, while in Massina this was a feature of the early to mid-nineteenth century. In Timbuktu, the dominant position of scholars was a legacy and feature of much earlier periods – a feature which was a matter of resurgence and reaffirmation in the eighteenth and nineteenth centuries. In essence, the prominence of scholars and scholar–notables was a more constant and stable feature at Timbuktu than elsewhere in the Muslim regions of West Africa.

One factor which distinguished Timbuktu from other cities and communities in the Western Sudan was the existence of a stratified hierarchy of learned status. At the top of the hierarchy, the scholars conceded precedence to a few individuals who were seen as exceptionally learned and erudite in each generation. Indeed, in many cases of succession, the Judge and the main parochial leaders or *imāms* were drawn from the ranks of these highly venerated scholars. Secondly, there appeared to be a distinction between the full-fledged jurists (*fuqahā'*) and between the rest of the body of scholars. Thirdly, there was a distinction between the body of scholars as a whole and a much wider stratum of lesser *alfas* or literati led by the tailor–*alfas* and the *muddāh*. Finally, the evidence on the enrolment and number of literacy schools, along with other indications, suggested that the whole stable and respectable citizenry of Timbuktu, including the client status Ghabibi and sometimes even the slaves, enjoyed one level of literacy or another, depending on their means and their affiliations. Hence, it was clear that leadership by scholars rested on a widely based subscription to the criteria of respectability, status and prestige which attached to literacy, learning and erudition.

Indeed, just as the existence of a patriciate made it possible for us to present the 'internal' history of the city in narrative form, so the existence of an elaborate hierarchy of learned status provided us with a framework for arriving at an adequate analysis of the social and status structure of the city. Admittedly, the data on the structure of the hierarchy pertained primarily to the turn of the sixteenth–seventeenth centuries, the best documented in the entire history of the city. Moreover, the evidence correlating learned status to wealth was often indirect. At the lowest levels of the social or status stratum, this was largely a matter of inference. Judging by the available evidence on the topmost ranks, it appeared quite probable that the lesser *alfas* (including tailor–*alfas*, lesser *kātibs*, *mu'adhdhins*, *etc.*) were drawn from a more modest stratum of small merchants and craftsmen. Similarly, the middle rank of scholars appears to have been drawn from the comfortable merchant families, but not from among the wealthiest families. The sons of the latter were sometimes non-learned while at times they joined the *muddāh* or else participated in the tradition of learning by either patronizing needy students or associating with the circles of scholars on the basis of fluid familial and other affiliations. Nonetheless, it was quite clear that the topmost ranks of scholars were drawn from the wealthiest strata in the city. Indeed, a single outstanding scholar often represented the interests of his entire merchant family (and even his clan) among the ranks of the learned. In fewer cases, a single nuclear family among the exceptionally wealthy and prestigious contributed a few or several scholars to the middle and topmost ranks.

Insofar as our study was concerned with both change and stability, it is not possible to project all our findings upon all periods of Timbuktu history. At times when the scholars enjoyed a position of definitive predominance, as during the sixteenth century, they appear to have been the leaders of the class of merchant–notables *par excellence.* Later, following the Moroccan conquest, there was unquestionably an erosion of the status of scholars, coupled with the admission of some non-learned notables (from among the propertied *musabbibīn*) into the ranks of civilian urban leadership. At that time, the civilian leadership stood in sharp distinction from the military leadership represented by a few Ruma and Songhai families. Later, with the integration of Ruma and Songhai into the civilian population, the leading families of both groups joined the ranks of notables. Nonetheless, and even as late as the time of the French conquest, the core of the leadership was still represented by scholars who were descended from the ancient families of Timbuktu.

Despite our emphasis on stability, we cannot present one single picture which could account for the organization of Timbuktu in all periods. Indeed, it is possible even to say that every phenomenon or institution in Timbuktu had its own history. In the earlier periods, for example, the institution of the judgeship was paramount. Though not necessarily the most learned himself, the judge was always drawn from the ranks of the most learned. He combined executive and judiciary authority with a quasi-legislative authority which was represented by the interpretation and adaptation of law or, more formally, the *futya*. During the Songhai period, and in earlier times, the judge came close to being the actual ruler of the city. Following the Moroccan conquest, the judgeship lost some of its authority, but judging by a number of indications, it remained the main 'urban institution' in the city. At all times the judge also shared his position of leadership with a few outstanding scholars as well as the *imāms*, and especially the *imām* of the Main Mosque, Jingerebir.

The religio-legal establishment witnessed a variety of leadership forms over the centuries. This makes it difficult to generalize about the 'organization' of Timbuktu (much as about the 'Muslim city'). At most, it is possible to say that the nature of the leadership revolved around the three criteria of parochial, judiciary and 'jurisprudential' authority. At times, an exceptionally erudite *mufti* (even when not specifically assigned this title) enjoyed the highest position of initiative and he shared it, in varying degrees, with other scholars who did not necessarily occupy any specific post. Despite this, the judiciary post was always important and often the forum for city-side leadership, shared by the *imām* of the Main Mosque. Other *imāms*, at Sankore, Sīdi Yaḥya and elsewhere, also stood in the topmost ranks of the '*Jamā'a*' (collective leadership) of Timbuktu.

The fluidity of the patterns of leadership and authority may seem somewhat confusing, but in fact this highlights the primacy of learned status over and above any administrative criteria of order. The hierarchy was given a strong institutional base in the judgeship and imamates, but ultimately its texture and structure was 'pedagogical'. The pedagogical links tended to correspond to familial and inter-familial affiliations – a factor which supplied an added basis for cohesion. The pedagogical links themselves amounted to the 'schools of learning' in the city and, indeed, they were themselves the 'schools of law'. Insofar as the pedagogical links extended in various ways from the highest levels of learning to the modest levels of literacy, they gave the learned hierarchy a strong and wide base in the city's social and status structure. In fact, they linked the hierarchy to a number of urban institutions ranging from the corporation of masons to the age-set organizations.

Perhaps the distinction between military and learned elites is a general theme in the history of Muslim urbanism elsewhere. We have alluded (in

Chapter 1) to Albert Hourani's view that Muslim civilization was characterized by a delicate sort of balance between military elites and 'bourgeoisie'. In the Sudan, this idea of a balance is quite relevant, though here as elsewhere, the factors which went into the making of the balance (and sometimes imbalance) are infinitely complex and varied. Our evidence, for example, suggests that the merchant classes of Timbuktu enjoyed economic and even fiscal resources which were comparable to those of the Songhai state, at least on the eve of the Moroccan conquest. Later, in the eighteenth century, the 'upper bourgeoisie' in Timbuktu appears to have had greater access to economic patronage than the Ruma leadership. Indeed, and except in the period immediately following the Ruma conquest, the Ruma had no monopoly of access to military action or firearms. Naturally, our evidence pertains to exceptional events since at all other times the economic and military facets of the balance are not covered by our sources. Nonetheless, it is possible perhaps to say that the city's power of collective action was contingent both upon the ability of the notables to mobilize the urban population and upon the economic and other resources which they could marshal.

Generalization about the theme of autonomy in the history of Timbuktu is obviously subject to qualifications. At times, the balance shifted in favour of the 'military elites' – or the major power in the area at any given period – while at other times the balance shifted in favour of the city. In some cases, the details of such shifts are infinitessimal, and we have tried to trace them as closely as possible. The theme of military *versus* economic power is only a facet of the balance. Another important facet was the access of scholar–notables to avenues of influence and control which were open to them at the level of law and adaptation of law through jurisprudence. This had an influence not only on the administrative and organizational affairs of the city, but also upon conceptions of legitimacy which affected the status of states and empires in the Sudan. Indeed, the parochial concepts which helped to legitimize the character of the state in Islamic terms were closely bound to the jurisprudential views which helped legitimize an autonomous parochial-type leadership in the city under judges, *imāms* and *muftis*.

Basically, we have emphasized the jurisprudential aspects of Muslim learning throughout this study. These, in turn, gave a special character to parochial, judiciary and legal facets of organization at Timbuktu. In essence, there was no scope for referring to any uniform body of precepts which might be characterized simply as 'Islamic' and could, therefore, be projected from a Middle Eastern stance (as is conventional) upon the Western Sudan. The very existence of a large body of scholars in Timbuktu had its significance in the sphere of adaptation. Yet, the adaptation of Islam is not solely contingent upon spatial, geographical or cultural differences. Rather, it is also a feature which is contingent upon changes from one period to another in *any* region, including the Middle East. Naturally, we must realize that adaptation and change takes place within the stabilizing framework of 'tradition', in this case a 'social tradition'. Nonetheless, traditions themselves do have history and we have for the most part traced the history of a tradition which belongs to Timbuktu and the Western Sudan.

APPENDIX 1:

Judges of Timbuktu, Fifteenth–nineteenth centuries

1)	Al-Qāḍi al-Ḥājj	Early 15th C.
2)	Muḥammad al-Kāburi	Early 15th C.
3)	And-Agh-Muḥammad al-Kabīr	(1446/7–1468)?
4)	Al-Qāḍi Ḥabīb b. Muḥammad al-Ṣāliḥ b. 'Abd al-Raḥmān al-Tamīmi	Died 1498/9
5)	Maḥmūd b. 'Umar Aqīt	Till 1509/10
6)	'Abd al-Raḥmān b. Abu Bakr b. al-Qāḍi al-Ḥājj (Deputy of Maḥmūd b. 'Umar?)	Till 1519/20
7)	Maḥmūd b. 'Umar Aqīt	Died 1548/9
8)	Muḥammad b. Maḥmūd b. 'Umar Aqīt	Died *c.* 1565
9)	Al-'Āqib b. Maḥmūd b. 'Umar Aqīt	Died 1583/4
10)	(Muḥammad b. Maḥmūd Baghayughu, Interregnum)	1583/4–1584/5
11)	'Umar (Abu Ḥafs) b. Maḥmūd b. 'Umar Aqīt	Exiled 1594
12)	Muḥammad b. Aḥmad b. al-Qāḍi 'Abd al-Raḥmān (grandson of no. 6)	Died *c.* 1609
13)	Muḥammad b. And-Agh-Muḥammad b. Aḥmad Boryo (descendant of no. 3)	Died 1611/12
14)	Sayyid Aḥmad b. And-Agh-Muḥammad b. Aḥmad Boryo (brother of no. 13)	Died 1635/6
15)	Muḥammad b. Muḥammad Kara	Died 1651/2
16)	'Abd al-Raḥman b. Aḥmad Maghia	Died *c.* 1660
17)	Maḥmūd b. Muḥammad b. And-Agh-Muḥammad (son of no. 13)	Died *c.* 1667
18)	Muḥammad b. al-Mukhtār b. Muḥammad Zankanu	Died *c.* 1683
19)	Ibrāhīm b. 'Abdullāh b. Aḥmad Maghia	Died 1698/9
20)	Sayyid Aḥmad b. Ibrāhīm b. 'Abdullāh b. Aḥmad Maghia (son of no. 19)	Died 1734/5?
21)	(Maḥmūd b. Aḥmad b. 'Abd al-Raḥmān b. Aḥmad al-Mujtahid)	1734/5?
22)	Bāba al-Mukhtār b. Muḥammad b. al-Mukhtār b. Muḥammad Zankanu	1734/5–1750
23)	'Abdullāh Bābīr b. Sayyid Aḥmad b. Ibrāhīm (Maghia, son of no. 20)	Died 1755/6
24)	Maḥmūd b. Sayyid Aḥmad b. Ibrāhīm (brother of no. 23)	Died 1764/5
25)	Abkar b. Bāba al-Mukhtār b. Muḥammad (Zankanu, son of no. 22)	Died 1779/80
26)	(Interregnum: several judges, beginning with Alfa Maghia, son of no. 24)	Till 1793/4?
27)	Al-Qāḍi al-'Āqib (parentage unknown)	1793/4–(1825/6?)

28) 'Abd al-Qādir b. Muḥammad al-Sanūsi	1825/6–1829/30?
29) Alfa Sa'īd b. Bāba Gurdu al-Fulāni	Died 1841/2
30) Sān Sirfi (Muḥammad b. Muḥammad b. 'Uthmān al-Kāburi)	1841/2–1863/4
31) 'Abd al-Raḥmān b. Sān Sirfi	1863/4–(?)
32) Aḥmad b. Sān Sirfi	(?)–*c.* 1880?
33) Douana or Dumuna Koy al-Madān	1880–1893/4?
34) Aḥmad Bāba b. Abu'l-'Abbās*	1893/4–1931

* Aḥmad Bāba was succeeded in this century by his sons Muḥammad al-Amīn and 'Umar Sirfi, respectively. A third son, Zubair, has been recognized by some as *Qāḍi* since the recent death of 'Umar, but he prefers to identify himself simply as a *'alim* or scholar.

APPENDIX 2:

Alternation of major families over the judgeship

The following table illustrates the monopoly of the judgeship by a few families, though direct succession of kinsmen was uncommon. The breakdown does not take into consideration the interregnum of Muḥammad Baghayughu (no. 10 in Appendix 1) nor does it consider in-laws as relatives.

	Directly succeeded relatives	Indirectly succeeded relatives	Total
Al-Ḥājj family	0	2	2
And-Agh-Muḥammads	1	3	4
Aqīts	3	2	5
Maghias	2	3	5
Zankanus	0	3	3
Sān Sirfi family	2	1	3
Other judges	0	9	9
Total	8	23	31

APPENDIX 3:

Known *imāms* of Jingerebir (Main Mosque)

1)	Kātib Mūsa	Early 15th C.
2)	'Abdullāh al-Balbāli	Mid-15th C.
3)	Abu'l-Qāsim al-Tuāti	Died 1516/17
4)	Manṣūr al-Fazzāni	Early 16th C.
5)	Ibrāhīm al-Zalafi	Early 16th C.
6)	Aḥmad Nāna Surgu	*c.* 1527/8
7)	Sayyid 'Ali al-Jazūli	*c.* 1528–1546
8)	Siḍḍīq b. Muḥammad Ta'alla	*c.* 1546–1569
9)	'Uthmān b. al-Ḥasan al-Tishīti	Died 1569/70
10)	Muḥammad Gidādu al-Fulāni	Died *c.* 1577
11)	Aḥmad b. Siḍḍīq (son of no. 8)	*c.* 1577–1596/7
12)	Maḥmūd b. Siḍḍīq (brother of no. 11)	Died 1619/20
13)	'Abd al-Salām b. Muḥammad Dikku al-Fulāni	Died 1625/6
14)	'Ali b. 'Abdullāh Siri b. Sayyid 'Ali al-Jazūli (grandson of no. 7)	Died 1642/3
15)	Muḥammad Wadī'at Allāh b. Muḥammad Sa'īd b. Muḥammad Gidādu (grandson of no. 10)	1642/3–(?)
16)	Bāba Sa'īd b. Aḥmad b. Muḥammad Sa'īd b. Muḥammad Gidādu (nephew of no. 15)	Died 1690/91
17)	Al-Imām (Anonymous) b. al-Imām Aḥmad (Possibly a certain al-Mukhtār, son of no. 11)	Died 1702/3
18)	'Uthmān b. al-Imām Aḥmad (also son of no. 11)	Date unknown
19)	Ṣālih b. al-Imām Aḥmad (also son of no. 11)	*c.* 1714
20)	'Abd al-Kāfi b. 'Abd al-Raḥmān b. Muḥammad Sa'īd (nephew of no. 15)	Date uncertain
21)	'Abd al-Raḥmān b. 'Abd al-Salām b. Aḥmad b. Muḥammad Sa'id (nephew of no. 19)	Mid-18th C.
22)	Siḍḍīq ('Atīq) b. Ibrāhīm b. Aḥmad b. Muḥammad b. Muḥammad Sa'īd (cousin of no. 21)	Died 1750/51
23)	Wadī'at-Allāh b. al-Ḥājj al-Amīn	Died 1758/9
24)	'Uthmān b. 'Uthmān (possibly grandfather of Sān Sirfi)	Died 1770/71
25)	Didar (?) b. 'Abd al-'Azīz	1771 (?)
26)	Bāba b. 'Atīq (probably son of no. 22)	1771–1793
27)	Sahl b. al-Ḥājj Ṣalīḥ	1792/3– (?)
28)	Sa'īd b. Bāba (of the Gurdus)	1816/17–1841/2
29)	Sān Sirfi (Muḥammad b. Muḥammad b. 'Uthmān)	Died 1863/4
30)	'Abd Al-Raḥmān al-Suyūṭi b. Bāba (possibly brother of no. 28)	Date uncertain

31) Gurku Mūdu b. Bābīr b. Bāba (of the Gurdus, possibly grandson of no. 28) — Date uncertain

32) Muḥammad b. 'Umar b. Alfa Saifu (of the Gurdu family)* — Early 20th C.

* Muḥammad b. 'Umar was succeeded by his brother, Gurku Mūdu ('the Old Man') who, however, was not sufficiently learned and did not enjoy the position for long. He gave way to a kinsman of the Gurdus by intermarriage, namely, Alfa Sān b. Muḥammad b. 'Abd al-Raḥmān Suyūṭi, of the Iraqi family. The latter was succeeded by Maḥmūd b. al-Mukhtār b. 'Abd al-Raḥmān al-Suyūṭi, his cousin, who in turn was succeeded by Muḥammad Bāba Alfa, son of Alfa Sān. This information comes from Alfa Humal, brother and successor of Muḥammad Bāba Alfa, who is now *imām* of Jingerebir.

APPENDIX 4:

Genealogy of the Ḥājj and Mujtahid families

(Dotted lines represent lines of descent which are inferred only tentatively from the sources.)

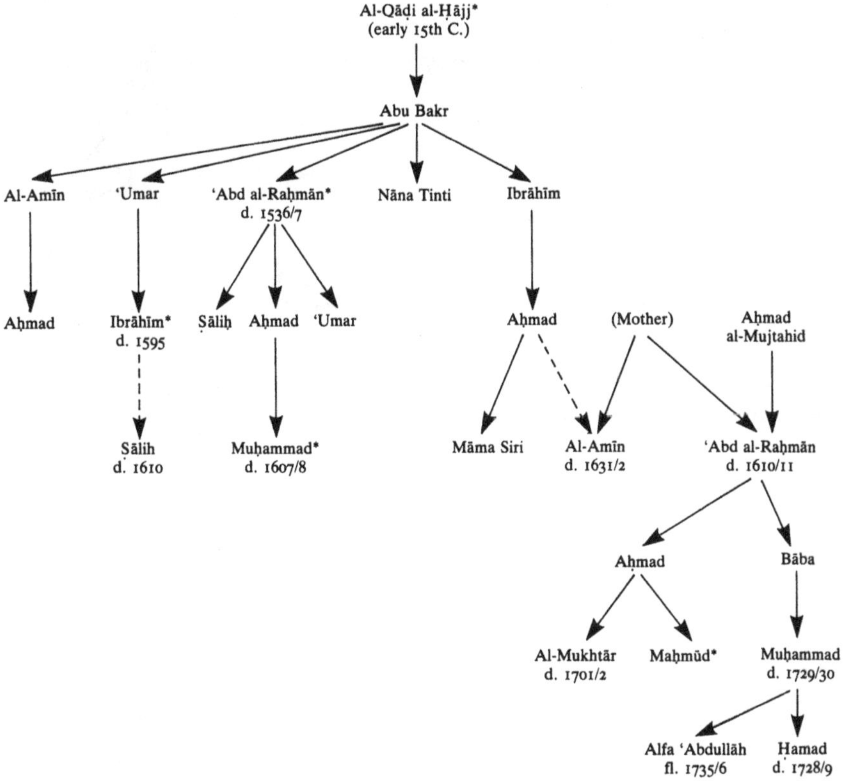

* These were *Qāḍis*. The case of Maḥmūd b. Aḥmad b. 'Abd al-Raḥmān b. Aḥmad al-Mujtahid (no. 21 in Appendix 1) is uncertain. Ibrāhīm b. 'Umar was Judge at Yindibugh.

APPENDIX 5:

Genealogy of the And-Agh-Muḥammads

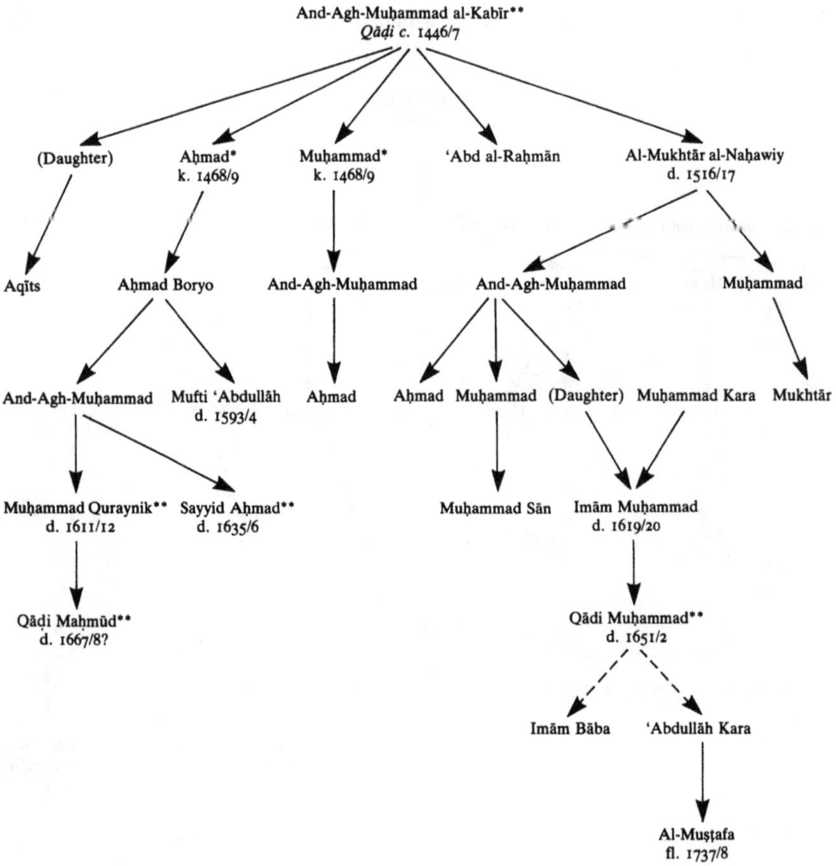

* Aḥmad and Muḥammad were killed by Sunni 'Ali.
** These were all *Qāḍis*.

APPENDIX 6:

Genealogy of the Aqīts

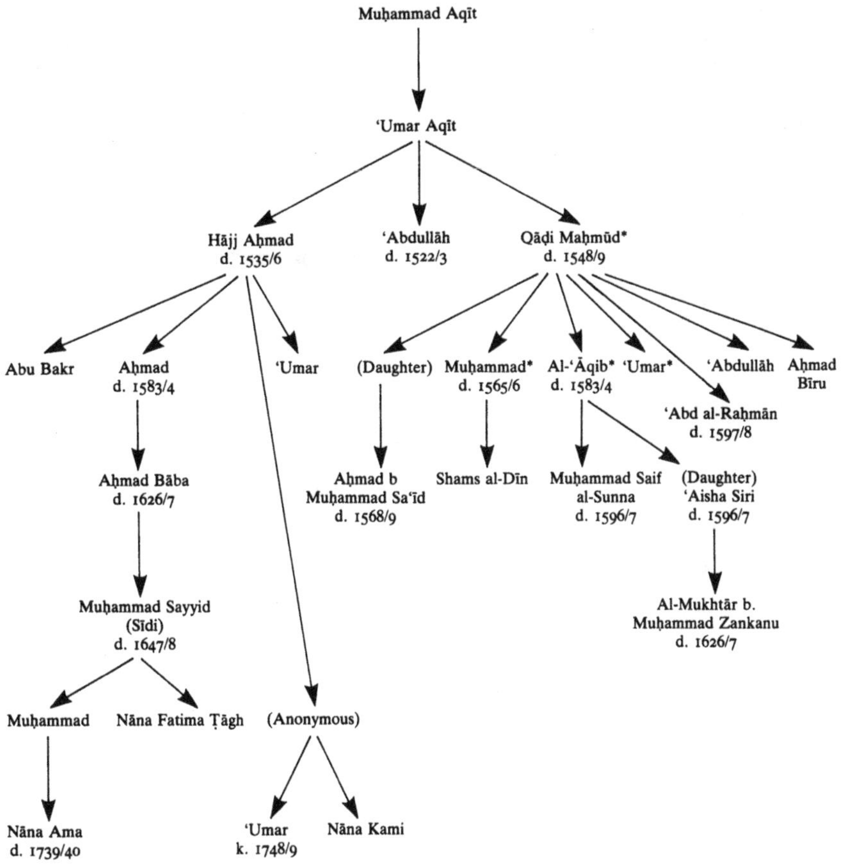

* These were *Qāḍis*. 'Umar was exiled in 1594 and died in 1597/8.

APPENDIX 7:

The Sa'di family and its affiliates

The horizontal arrows indicate cases of intermarriage. Owing to the details which the author supplies on his own kinsmen, this is the only genealogy which sufficiently illustrates the intermarriages between the various ethnic groups (al-Sa'di, *passim*).

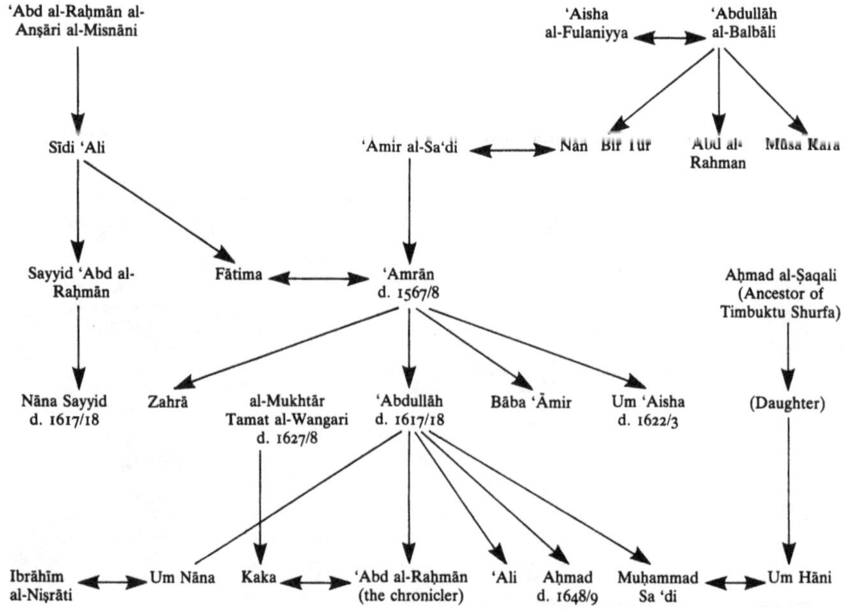

APPENDIX 8:

Genealogy of the Gidādu Fulānis

Scholars from this family for a long time monopolized the imamate of Jingerebir. The numbers correspond to the sequence of *imāms* as listed in Appendix 3. Dotted lines designate lines of descent which are established only tentatively.

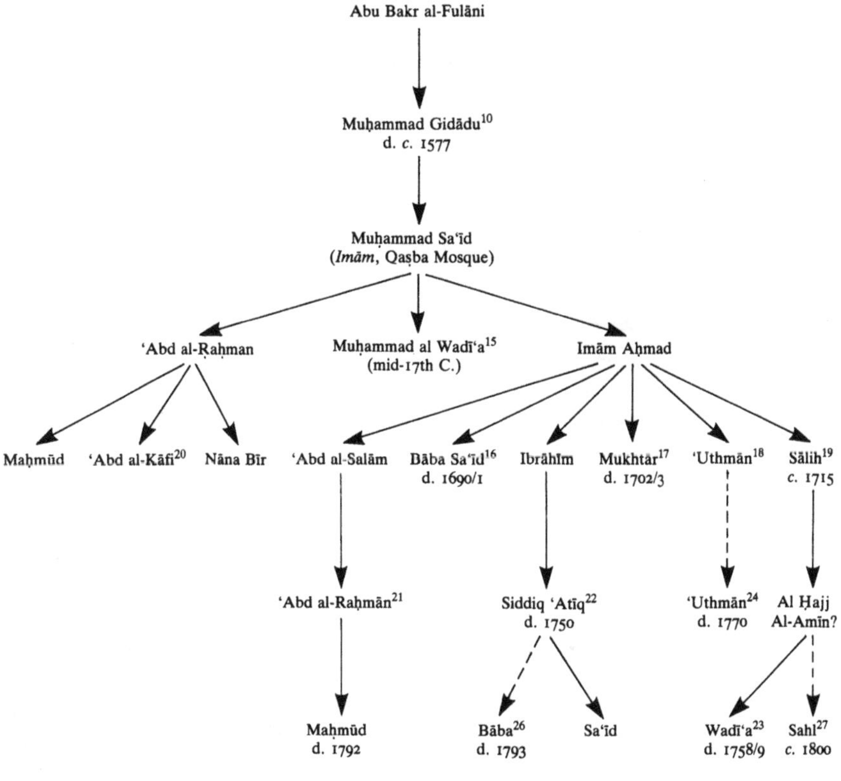

APPENDIX 9:

Genealogy of the Wangara Baghayughus

Those whose names are underlined were *imāms* of the Sīdi Yaḥya Mosque. The numbers in the last part of the genealogy indicate the sequence of the last *imāms*, down to Aḥmad Bānio, the present *Imām*. This genealogy, at least for the last few generations, is partly based on the information of Alfa Aḥmad Bānio.

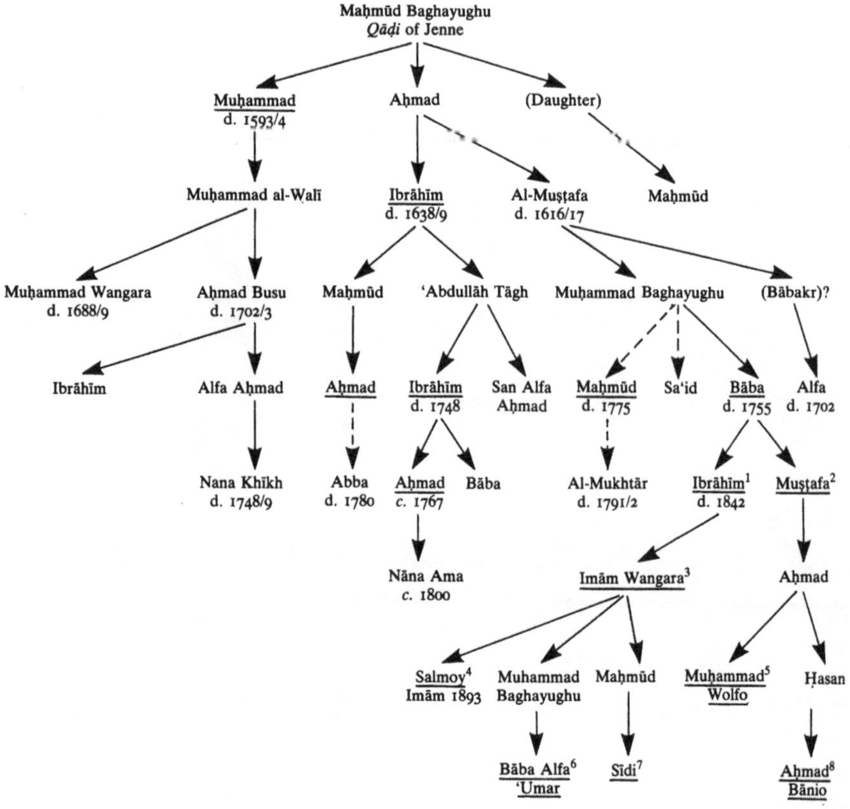

APPENDIX 10:

Genealogy of the Maghia and Zankanu families

Those whose names are underlined were *imāms* only (of Sankore). The present *Imām*, Alfa Sālum, is son of Maḥmūd b. Bābīr b. 'Abdullāh, hence nephew of Sanbīr and Aḥmad. Saifu's son, al-'Aqib, was also a recent *Imām* of Sankore.

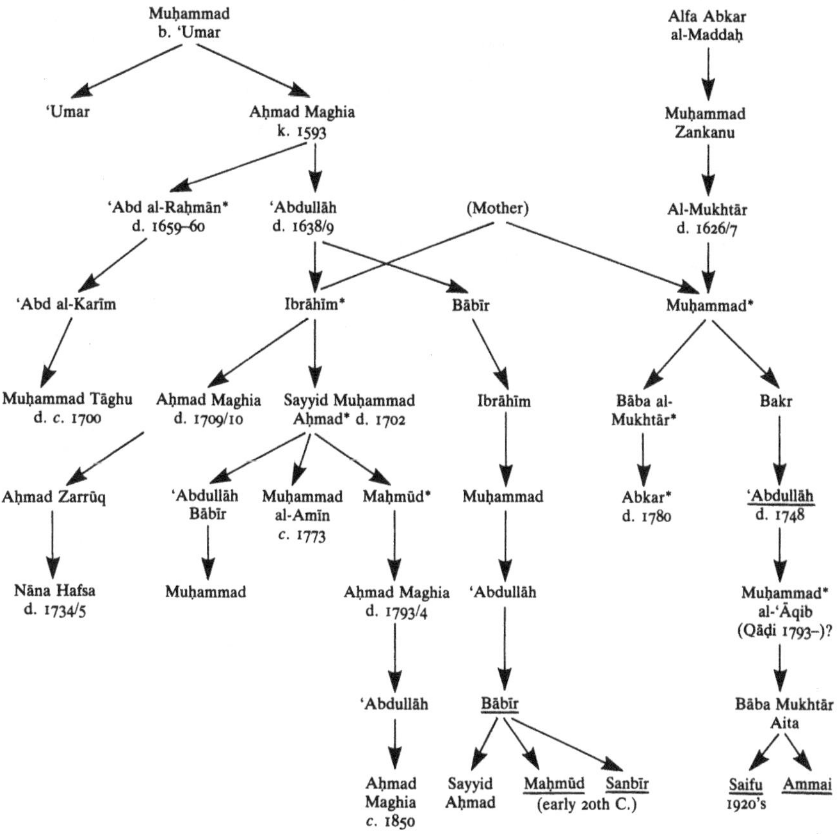

* These were all *qāḍis*, and sometimes also *imāms* of Sankore.

APPENDIX 11:

Genealogy of the Gurdus and Irāqis

The last part of this genealogy is based partly on the information of Alfa Humal, present-day *Imām* of Jingerebir. His brother Bāba Alfa, like his father Alfa Sān, had also been *Imām*. The identity of Mamadou Oumar (Muḥammad b. 'Umar) is uncertain, because he is also known as grandson of Saifu (rather than Sa'īdu).

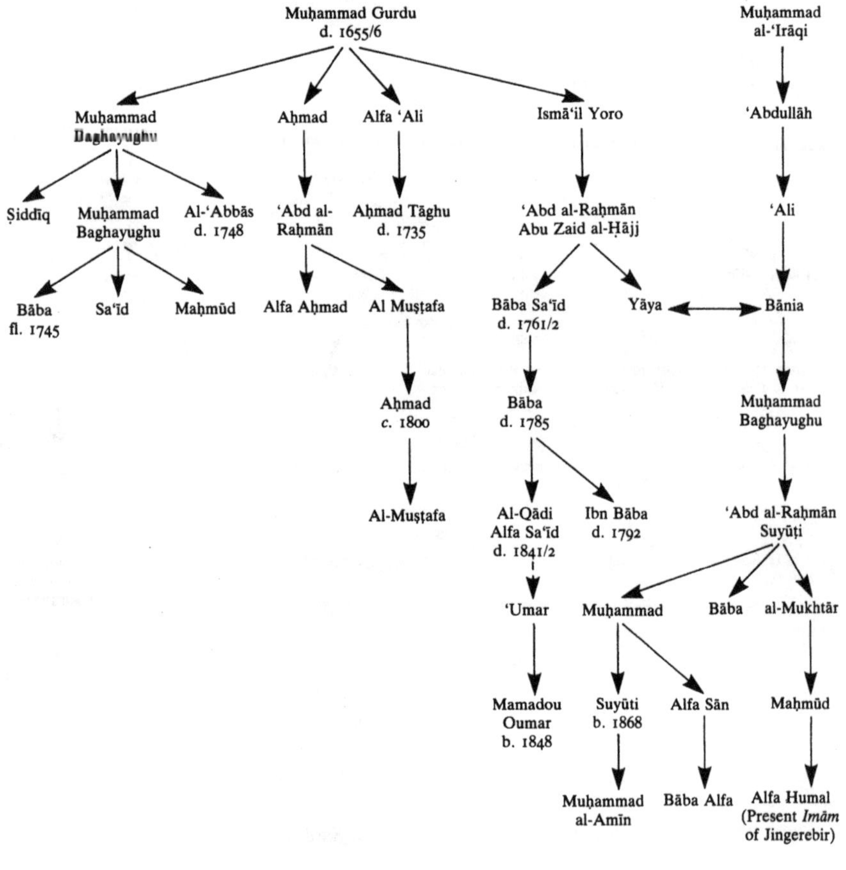

APPENDIX 12:

Selected lines of transmission of learning (A)

Double lines indicate descent besides transmission of learning. Dotted lines designate lines of transmission which are inferred.

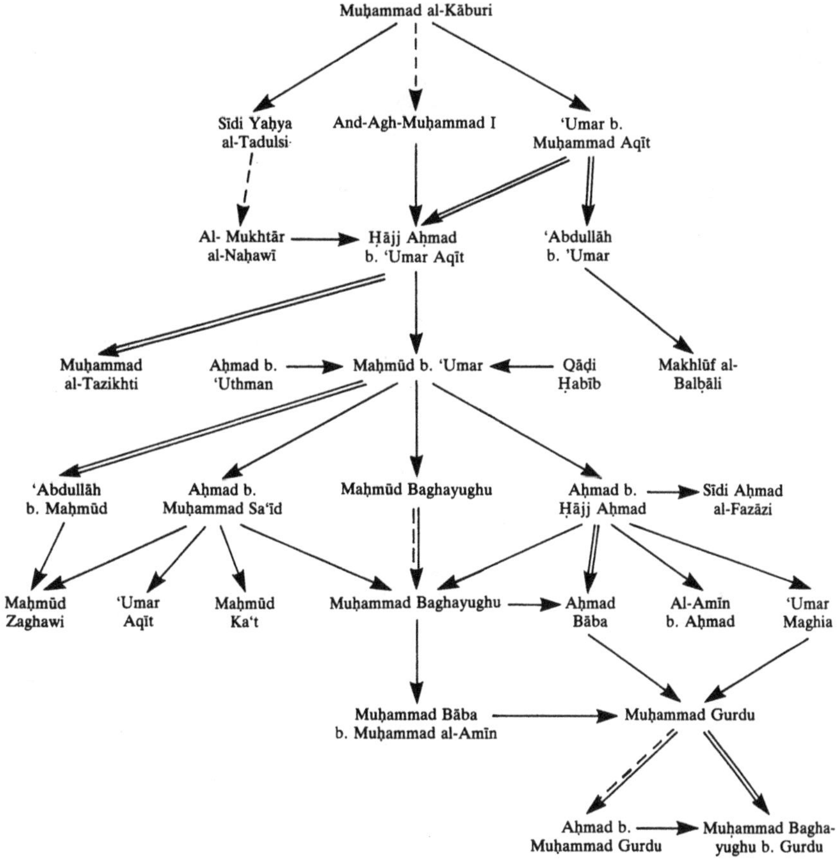

APPENDIX 13:

Selected lines of transmission of learning (B)

Double lines show actual lines of descent besides transmission of learning. The lines of transmission represented here lead back to other prominent Middle Eastern scholars besides al-Suyūṭi. Locally, these same lines became the most prestigious and the most frequently quoted after the seventeenth century. Most later *sanads* are traced backwards through Muḥammad Baghayughu b. Muḥammad Gurdu.

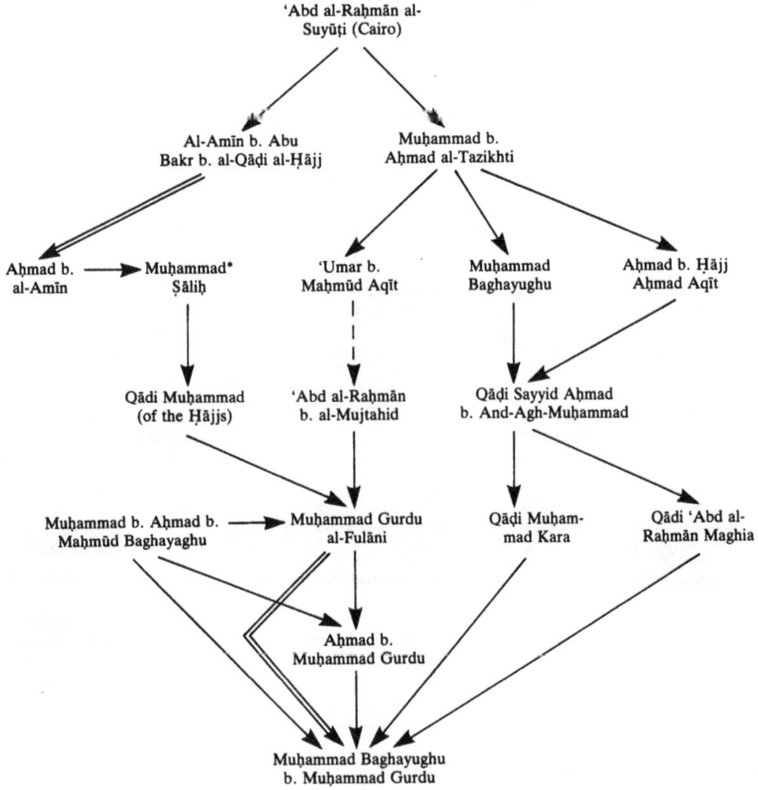

* is Muḥammad Ṣāliḥ b. al-Qādi 'Abd al Raḥmān b. Abu Bakr b. al-Qāḍi al-Ḥājj.

APPENDIX 14:

Selected lines of transmission of learning (C)

These are the main lines through which learning was diffused from Timbuktu to various groups in the Southern Sahara. Alfa Muḥammad Sanqara may have contributed to transmission of learning in pre-*Jihād* Massina.

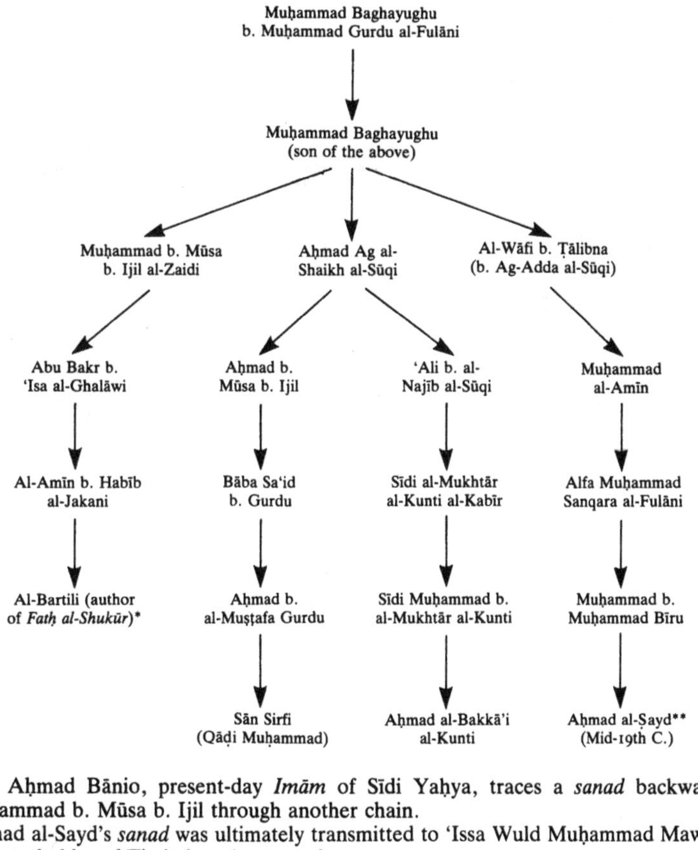

* Alfa Aḥmad Bānio, present-day *Imām* of Sīdi Yaḥya, traces a *sanad* backwards to Muḥammad b. Mūsa b. Ijil through another chain.

** Aḥmad al-Sayd's *sanad* was ultimately transmitted to 'Issa Wuld Muḥammad Mawlūd, a respected elder of Timbuktu–Arwān today.

APPENDIX 15:

Genealogies of the Tilimsānis, Zagharis and Shutūkis

Those whose names are underlined became Pashas. The numbers indicate how many times they reigned. Some confusion in nomenclature results from the fact that Manṣūr (Maṣuru) and Maṣ'ūd (Masudu) are interchangeable.

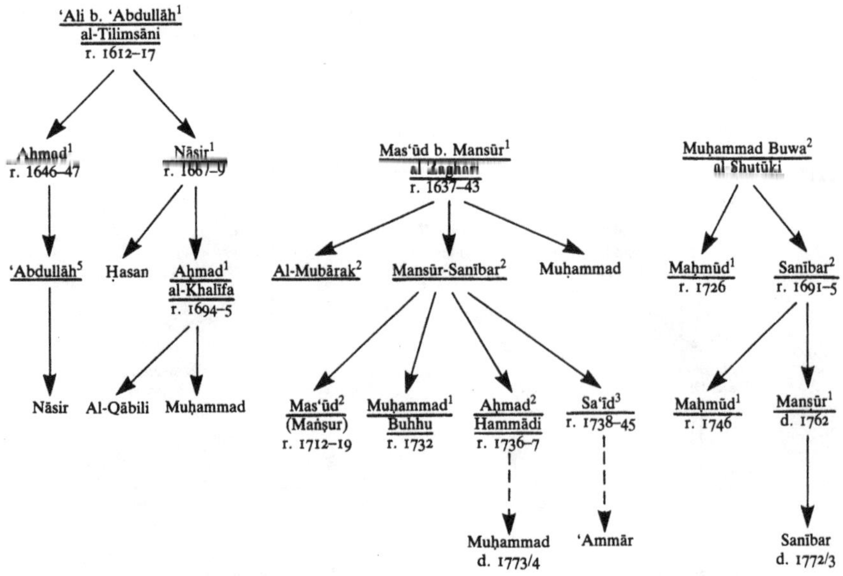

APPENDIX 16:

Genealogy of the Tazarkīnis

Those whose names are underlined were Pashas. The numbers indicate how many times each one of them reigned, at least for the period up to *c.* 1750. There is some confusion between the sons of Sa'īd b. Ḥammādi and those of Sa'īd b. Sanībar al-Zaghari (see Appendix 15).

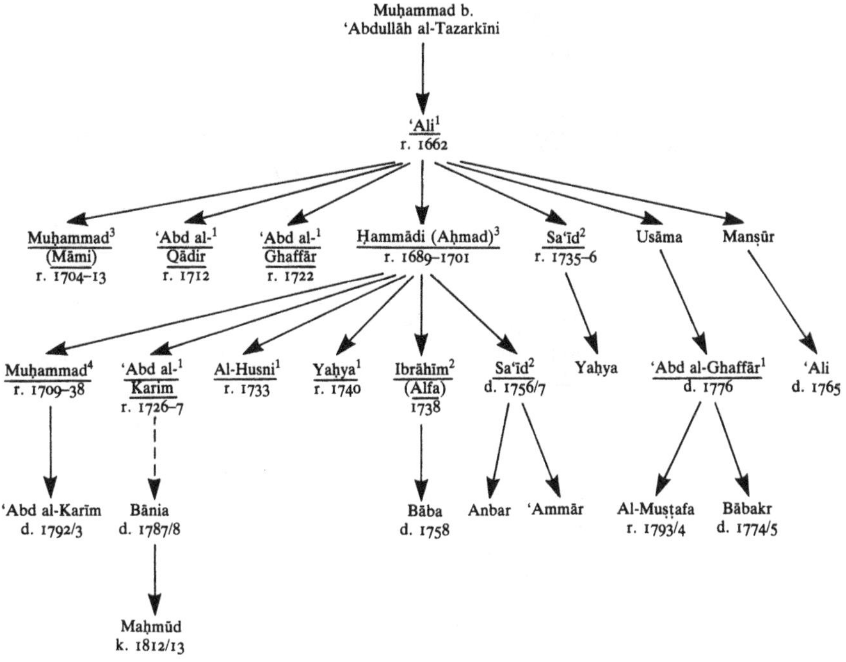

APPENDIX 17:

Genealogy of the Mubārak al-Dara'is

Those whose names are underlined occupied the Tibshāsha. The numbers indicate how many times each one of them reigned, at least up to 1750.

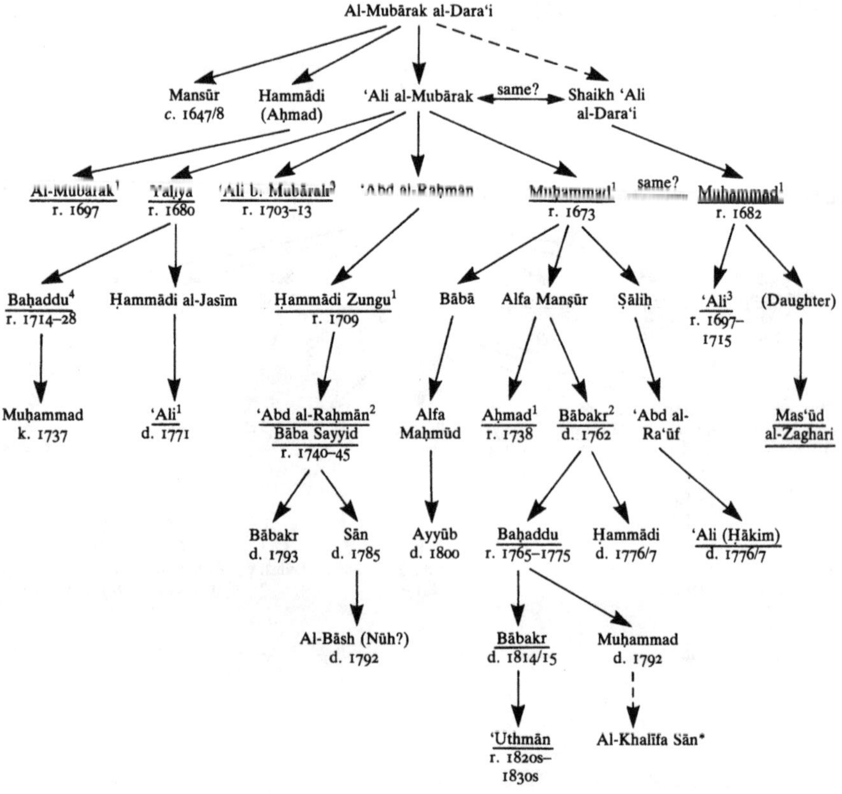

* The early twentieth century notable, Sān wuld al-Qā'idi, is identified by his nephew, the present-day Songhai elder, Aḥmadu Bādiji, as son of Qā'id Bābakr b. Al-Khalifa Sān b. al-Qā'id Muḥammad b. Baḥaddu. Otherwise, we have no reference to al-Khalīfa Sān in the extant sources.

APPENDIX 18:

Genealogy of the Askia dynasty

The numbers indicate the sequence of reigns, first at Gāo, during the empire period, and secondly at Timbuktu during the Ruma regime. The dates cited pertain to the durations of the reigns.

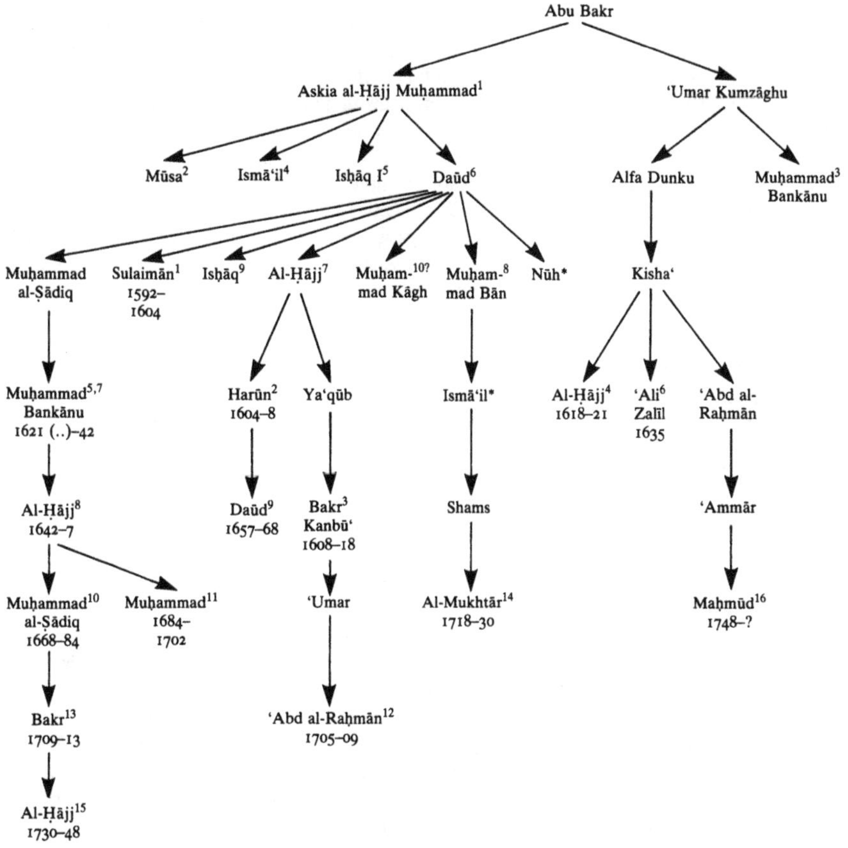

* These are two of several Askias who reigned at Dendi.

Notes

2. *Genesis of a social tradition*

1. Sekene Modi Cissoko, 'L'Intelligentsia de Tombouctou'. Also Cissoko, *Tombouctou et l'Empire Songhay*.
2. J. O. Hunwick, 'Aḥmad Bāba and the Moroccan invasion'.
3. As explained elsewhere in this study, the difficult nature of the eighteenth-century sources largely accounts for the underdevelopment of research on later periods.
4. See especially *Tārīkh al-Fattāsh* (*Tarikh el-Fettach*), attributed to Maḥmūd Ka'ti ben El-Ḥadj El-Motaouakkel Ka'ti. References throughout will be made to the Arabic text except where recourse to the French translation is necessary.
5. Various figures are offered in the French sources concerning the number of the schools around the turn of the century. See, for example, Mgr. A. Hacquard, *Monographie de Tombouctou*, p. 42. Cf. *Tārīkh al-Fattāsh*, pp. 180–1.
6. Al-Sa'di, for example, deplores the disinterest in history among members of his own generation in the mid-seventeenth century. Yet his work was not preceded by any chronicle of equal size and importance. See al-Sa'di, *Tārīkh al-Sūdān*, pp. 1–2. Again, references throughout will be made to the Arabic text.
7. See Paul Marty, *Etudes* pp. 89ff. The French established a 'Franco–Arab school' which, according to Marty, 'conquered professors and students in Timbuktu all in one stroke'.
8. *Ibid.*, p. 2. Marty seems to use the term *Jamā'a* technically to designate the body of notables who negotiated with the French at the time of the conquest.
9. Recent research on Muslim cities has tended to emphasize the role played by the schools of law in the absence of more formal criteria of urban integration. See A. H. Hourani, *The Islamic City*, especially the contribution by Ira M. Lapidus, pp. 195–205.
10. For comparison with Jenne, see J. Spencer Trimingham, *A history*, p. 39, n. 3.
11. See, for example, Oleg Grabar, 'The architecture', especially pp. 31–9.
12. See al-Bakri, *Al-Mughrib*, p. 172.
13. Authors who have suggested an Islamic impact for the Almoravids in the Sudan (besides the southern Sahara) have not seriously documented their viewpoint. At most, and as suggested by Hodgkin in another context, the Almoravid movement may have checked 'the spread southwards from the Maghrib of "deviant" forms of Islam'.
14. See al-Zuhri, *Kitāb al-Jughrāfiya*. Al-Zuhri's reference to the Islamization of Ghana led certain early French scholars (like Delafosse) to conclude that the old kingdom was conquered by the Almoravids. Although recent writers (like Levtzion) have followed this suggestion, we do not find much, if anything, to substantiate it.
15. As Trimingham emphasized (*A history*, p. 37), the adoption of Islam as an 'imperial cult' involved no attempt by rulers to propagate it in their domains. Nonetheless, the patronage of mosques by Mansa Mūsa and others, coupled with the facilities of travel extended to Muslims, positively encouraged the diffusion of Islam in commercial centres.

16. Al-Sa'di, pp. 20–21, 51. We are given this impression (concerning the early growth of learning) indirectly from an anecdote concerning the arrival of 'Abd al-Raḥmān al-Tamīmi in the early fourteenth century.
17. Separation was largely an outcome of the emphasis in Islam on the unity of ritual, law and belief. See J. S. Trimingham, *The influence of Islam*, pp. 53 ff.
18. See Paul E. Lovejoy, 'The role of the Wangara'.
19. Ibn Ḥauqal, *Configuration*, vol. I, p. 313.
20. Al-Bakri, (*Al-Mughrib*), pp. 164–83. Twelfth-century geographers continued to refer to twin cities, but the phenomenon seemingly disappeared during the age of the empire of Mali.
21. *Tārīkh al-Fattāsh*, p. 179. The reference there is to Ja'aba, presumably Jaghaba, a variant on Zaghaba. The same source identifies a Khaṭīb of Gao both as Muḥammad Jaghaiti and Muḥammad Zaghaiti. See also Lamin Sanneh, 'The origins', p. 59n; T. Lewicki, 'Un Etat Soudanais', on the interchange of Za and Ja.
22. Besides being identified as the merchant class among the Malinke, the Wangara are associated with the Soninke as ancestors both of the Songhai monarchs and of the influential Muri Kuyra clerics. See *Tārīkh al-Fattāsh*, pp. 38, 48. These and other traditions tend to complicate the questions of ethnic origins and ancestry.
23. Even the Mossi kingdoms must have facilitated the extension of Muslim Wangara commerce and settlement southwards. This gave rise to Bīghu as a major link towards the Akan goldfields. See Ivor Wilks, 'A medieval trade-route'.
24. The legend, recorded by al-Sa'di (p. 12), suggests that settlers owed a sense of allegiance to the kingdom.
25. Certainly, Muslim law never recognized a special status for cities, beyond the stipulation that the Friday congregational prayers could be held only in cities and large settlements. As will be seen in Chapter 4, scholars in Timbuktu were aware of this stipulation, but its significance to urban organization is rather an elusive problem.
26. This was a permanent feature in the history of Timbuktu and will therefore be discussed as we proceed, especially in Chapter 6.
27. Al-Sa'di (p. 20) praises the moral and economic advantages of Timbuktu all in the same breath. To him, it was 'a pure, blameless and splendid town, graced by *baraka*, liveliness and dynamism'.
28. Most pilgrim caravans from the Western Sudan used the Timbuktu–Gao–Tagedda route. See *Tarīq Ahl al-Maghrib*, fos 30–1.
29. An addition to *Tārīkh al-Fattāsh*, peculiar to the defective MS C, claims that the Ghabibi descended from a group of slaves sent by Askia Daud in a fit of generosity to al-Qāḍi al-'Āqib. (See p. 107). Current tradition affirms their mixed slave origins. Unlike the Bella, believed to have always been clients and protégés of the Tuaregs, the Ghabibi were slaves and clients of the settled population, including the body of scholars and notables. See Horace Miner, *The primitive city*, p. 21.
30. Internal struggles among the various Tuareg and Barābīsh clans often led elements of the defeated parties to settle in Timbuktu. Such settlers among the former, at least, usually lost their designation as Tuareg; at times they may have contributed to the ranks of the Bella.
31. See, for example, Raymond Mauny, *Tableau géographique*, pp. 495–503. For a more detailed treatment of the demographic factor, see Chapter 3 below.
32. The growth of Timbuktu was interrupted sometime roughly around 1400 by the Mossi conquest and, then again, towards the end of the fifteenth century, during the reign of Sunni 'Ali.
33. Fulānis from the Jingerebir quarter have been migrating for a long time towards Massina and the movement to Mopti continues to this day. However, a part of the Fulāni population has mixed with the Ruma, the Songhai and, to a lesser extent, the Wangara and Shurfa. If we exclude the 'whites', sometimes Tamashagh or Arabic

speakers in the Sankore quarter, the various groups which make up the total population are indistinguishable from each other and are all Songhai-speaking. Among the Songhai Ghabibi the distinction is one of status, rather than ethnic origin, and the same is true of the Bella.

34. Scholars from the Zaghaiti Wangara clan represented in sixteenth-century Gao are encountered at an even earlier time in far-away Kano. Comparė *Tārīkh al-Fattāsh*, p. 151, with *Aṣl al-Wangariyyin*, pp. 7–42. The Sanḥāja scholars, exemplified by the Aqīt association with Massina, present us with problems of origin equally as intense as those of Soninke and Wangara.
35. See Felix Dubois, *Tombouctou la mystérieuse*, p. 262.
36. Al-Bakri, *Al-Mughrib*, p. 183. Tadmekka, at nine-day's journey from Gao, is now generally believed to be safely identifiable with al-Sūq.
37. See H. T. Norris, *The Tuaregs*, pp. 22, 43.
38. A Tadmekka origin may perhaps be postulated for the Tuareg And-Agh-Muḥammad family. The strongest evidence of early Tuareg interest in Muslim learning in Timbuktu lies in the tradition recorded by al-Sa'di that the Sankore mosque was built by a wealthy woman from the Kel Aghlāl (Aghlāliyya). The relationship of And-Agh-Muḥammads and Aghlāl to the Maghsharen is obscure. See al-Sa'di, p. 62 and *passim*. On Tireqqa, see al-Bakri, *Al-Mughrib*, p. 182.
39. Al-Ya'qūbi's ninth-century information suggests that Gao was almost as important as the kingdom of Ghana. For Gao trade with Egypt, see T. Lewicki, 'A propos'.
40. It is becoming increasingly apparent that the dynasty represented by the steles at Sane, just north of Gao, is to be distinguished from the Za dynasty whose kings are listed by al Sa'di (pp. 2–5). See J. Sauvaget, 'Les epitaphes'. According to Hunwick, the transfer of the Songhai to Gao was a late (fifteenth-century) development. See J. O. Hunwick, 'The mid-fourteenth century capital', p. 204.
41. See Ibn Khaldūn, *The Muqaddima*, p. 119. Cf. Ibn Khaldūn *Histoire des Berbères*, vol. I, p. 267.
42. Ibn Baṭūṭa, *Voyages*, vol. IV, p. 437.
43. Compare al-Sa'di, *Tārīkh al-Sūdān*, pp. 11–15 with al-Zuhri, *Kitāb al-Jughrāfiya*, p. 125. Ghana is described as the capital city of Janāwa. Al-Sharīshi in the thirteenth century mentioned many 'houses of learning' in Ghana. See extract in al-Munajjid (ed.), *Mamlakat*, p. 11.
44. Al-Sa'di received his information on Jenne from the Jennekoy 'Abdullāh who had an interest in emphasizing the antiquity and power of his dynasty. Compare with al-'Umari, extract in al-Munajjid, *Mamlakat*, p. 45. 'No one under the Malian sovereign bears the title of king except the lord of Ghana . . .' (French translation: al-Omari, *Masālik al-Absār fi Mamālik al-Amṣār*, *L'Afrique moins l'Egypte*, translated by Gaudefroy-Demombynes (Paris, 1927), p. 59.)
45. Al-Sa'di, p. 12.
46. *Ibid.*, p. 21. Al-Sa'di goes on directly to say that, earlier, 'shopping' used to be at Bīru. This suggests an eastward shift in the main commercial route, a shift which was favourable to Timbuktu.
47. Al-Sa'di seems to suggest that Begho (Bīghu) was a town in a larger area called Bītu. 'Muḥammad Fūdi Sānu al-Wangari migrated from his town in *the land of Bīṭu*'. See al-Sa'di, pp. 16, 17. For the views of Delafosse and Houdas, see *Tārīkh al-Fattāsh*, tr., p. 68n. Cf. Ivor Wilks, *A medieval trade-route*, p. 338. Wilks assigned the Dyula (Wangara) colonization of Bīghu to somewhere around 1400. A much earlier beginning is justified by reference to people from Bīṭu (presumably already Muslim) among the settlers who gave Bīru or Walata its importance before the rise of Timbuktu.
48. Cf. Levtzion, 'The early states', p. 138. Levtzion, however, suggests later dates, while we believe that the growth of Timbuktu and Jenne began in the twelfth century.

49. Ibn Baṭūṭa did not visit Zāgha but heard of its people as 'ancient in Islam; they are people of religion who have a quest for learning'. See Ibn Baṭūṭa, *Voyages*, vol. IV, p. 395.
50. We know of two important Zaghawi scholars of nineteenth-century date. See Aḥmad Bāba . . . al-Zaghawi, *Anwa' al-Kufr fi'l-Sūdān*, fos 2–10. Also Muḥammad b. al-Ḥajj Ḥasan b. al-Ḥajj b. Sulaimān, *Shifā' al-Nās*, fos 37–50. Both treatises are levelled against superstition and, indeed, Marty (II, 1965) described Dia as a centre for the fabrication of amulets in which charges of charlatanism were frequent. A relatively early Timbuktu scholar is known as al-Faqīh Maḥmūd al-Zaghawi. But the strongest evidence of the influence of Zāgha comes from information about scholars from nearby Kābura. Cf. Ibn Baṭūṭa, *Voyages*, vol. IV, p. 395.
51. See Marty, *Etudes sur l'Islam*, vol. II, p. 164. 'For several centuries Dia has been the Islamic metropolis of Massina. It was, according to one legend, the mother of Jenne (Dienne), to which it gave its name, which had been Diana . . .'. For the introduction of masonry from Jenne to Timbuktu, see Dubois, *Tombouctou la mystérieuse*, p. 263.
52. See *Tārīkh al-Fattāsh*, pp. 61 ff. Presumably, the decline of Zāgha accelerated at the conquest of the town by the Songhai empire.
53. Al-Sa'di, p. 21. By '*al-mu'āmalat*' al-Sa'di actually refers to 'legal procedures of transaction'.
54. Cf. note 46 above. Al-Sa'di (p. 21) drops all further reference to Wagadu. *Tārīkh al-Fattāsh* (p. 119) mentions a campaign by Askia al-Ḥājj to Wagadu, but this occurs in an insert which is peculiar to MS C. As partly indicated elsewhere, we do not accept the association of Wagadu or Ghana with the tenuous Sahelian location of Kumbi Saleh. As Trimingham also noted (*A history*, pp. 49–50) that association, though widely reiterated in the current literature, 'rests on precarious grounds'. The Arab geographers consistently denote a riparian location for the capital of Ghana.
55. Al-Sa'di, p. 21. Among the places named, Bīṭu alone belongs to the Sudanic belt.
56. Mansa Mūsa went to North Africa by way of Walāta and Tuat, while returning via Gao. Ibn Baṭūṭa, on the other hand, went to Mali via Walāta, returning by way of Gao and Tagedda. Aside from these two itineraries, we have little information on the trade-routes at the time.
57. The excavations at Kumbi Saleh have neither been systematic, nor published systematically. Cf. Levtzion, *Ancient Ghana and Mali*, p. 25.
58. Ibn Baṭūṭa (*Voyages*, vol IV, p. 395), for example, mentioned the Saghanūghu as 'whites belonging to the Ibadite sect', but this is probably an error suggesting that both Soninke and Wangara may have intermarried with North African settlers from an early period. In later times, the Saghanūghu came to be seen principally as Wangara while Ibn Baṭūṭa specifically distinguished between the two at Zaghari.
59. Ibn Baṭūṭa's account does not indicate whether Walāta was more important than Timbuktu in his time, though it suggests that Gao was larger than both.
60. Miner, *The primitive city*, p. 47, says, 'While more homogenous towns defended their integrity against invaders, Timbuctoo capitulated without defense to one conqueror after another'. Our study shows that every conquest was met by one form of resistance or another.
61. The history of Massina prior to the nineteenth century *jihāds* is covered by a number of sources, but it is yet to be investigated or studied seriously. On the *jihāds*, see William Brown, *The Caliphate*.
62. See al-Sa'di, p. 22. The author's own family contributed settlers to Jenne.
63. The schema inherited from the early French writers (and especially Delafosse) was adopted by Levtzion in his *Ancient Ghana and Mali*, but with a most ambiguous set of results.
64. Cf. note 14 above. Al-Zuhri's text mentions that Ghana established an ascendency at Tadmekka with the help of the 'Almoravids'. Levtzion apparently understood this to mean that Ghana became a junior partner of the Almoravids in conquering Tadmekka

after having allegedly under obscure circumstances been conquered by the Almoravids. Compare Levtzion, *Ancient Ghana and Mali*, p. 45, with al-Zuhri, *Kitāb al-Jughrāfiya*, pp. 182–3.

65. Al-Sa'di, p. 65, suggests previous hardihood on the part of the citizens in connection with events dating to the conquest of Timbuktu by Sunni 'Ali. At that time, they regretted having previously withheld their children from military exercises.
66. The two posts of *imām* and judge were combined in the *khaṭīb* until the early sixteenth century at Jenne. See al-Sa'di, p. 18.
67. The tradition is attributed to Sīdi Yaḥya al-Tadulsi who flourished before Songhai times. See al-Sa'di, p. 18.
68. Ibn Baṭūṭa mentions that both were buried at Timbuktu. Al-Tuwaiḥin had built a sumptuous palace for Mansa Mūsa at his capital. His presence later at Timbuktu may attest to some need for his architectural skills in the growing town. Compare Ibn Kḥaldūn, *Histoires des Berbères*, vol. I, p. 265 with Ibn Baṭūṭa, *Voyages*, vol. IV, p. 431.
69. Al-Sa'di, pp. 8–9. The author has little information on the Mossi conquest beyond a quotation from Aḥmad Bāba (probably from a work no longer extant) on the extent of the damage. He says that after the Mossi conquest 'the Malians returned to Timbuktu and ruled it for a hundred years'. Since Malian rule altogether lasted about a century (see al-Sa'di, p. 72), an error in wording appears probable.
70. Al-Sa'di p. 7, assigns Mansa Mūsa's pilgrimage vaguely to the beginning of the eighth century of the Hijra. He nonetheless dates the beginning of Malian sovereignty to 737 A.H (1433/4 A.D.).
71. Ibn Khaldūn received contradictory information concerning the conquest of Gao. According to one version, this took place under Sakura, three reigns earlier than Mansa Mūsa. According to another version, Gao was conquered by a general of Mansa Mūsa called Saghamanja. The second version seems questionable because, among other things Saghamanja (possibly Sagha Mangha) may have been the title of a Songhai governor who was delegated authority by Mali over Gao. In any case, it seems doubtful that Mūsa would have returned from the pilgrimage via Gao had not the area been conquered for Mali well before his reign. See Ibn Khaldūn, *Histoires des Berbères*, vol I, p. 264.
72. See Dubois, *Tombouctou la mystérieuse*, pp. 265–6. The people allegedly invited Mansa Mūsa because they were tired of the exactions of the nearby Tuareg.
73. Al-Sa'di, p. 5. The mosques of Gundam and Dukurai were also believed to have been built by Mansa Mūsa but the seventeenth-century chroniclers treated these still earlier traditions with caution. See *Tārīkh al-Fattāsh*, p. 34.
74. Compare al-Sa'di, p. 8, with *Tārīkh al-Fattāsh*, p. 34. An extract is in Bernard Lewis (ed.), *Islam*, vol. I, p. 24.
75. In the appointment of governors at Walāta, the Malian monarchs were sensitive to local opinion. One governor, a certain Farba Husain, was discourteous to visiting white merchants, but his lieutenant in charge of imposts at Walāta, the Manshaju, was dismissed from his post on the basis of one single complaint from a Masufa merchant–scholar. See Ibn Baṭūṭa, *Voyages*, vol. IV, pp. 385, 416.
76. Norris, *The Tuaregs*, p. 45, sees the investment ceremony observed by Ibn Baṭūṭa at Timbuktu as typically Tuareg. See Ibn Baṭūṭa, *Voyages*, vol. IV, pp. 430–1.
77. Ibn Baṭūṭa omits reference to any Malian officials at Gao as well as Timbuktu. Ibn Baṭūṭa, *Voyages*, vol. IV, pp. 437–8.
78. On problems of the chronology of the Malian kings, see Nawal Morcos Bell, 'The age of Mansa Mūsa'.
79. Ibn Khaldūn, *Histoires des Berbères*, vol. I, p. 267. See also note 41 above.
80. *Ibid.*, p. 265. The evidence suggests that the power of Mansa Mūsa had been formidable in the Saharan fringes, including Wargala.

81. Al-Sa'di, pp. 9–10. The presence of the Malian garrison is recorded only in connection with the Mossi conquest.
82. Muḥammad Naḍ's clan, Ajir, is said to have been of Shinjīṭi origin. The emigration to Timbuktu, possibly after a residence in Massina, was probably of much earlier date. See al-Sa'di, p. 22.
83. See al-Sa'di, pp. 27–8, 47–8. The Kāburi *nisba* reappears in Timbuktu in the sixteenth century and, again, in the nineteenth century.
84. Ibn Baṭūṭa heard of Kābura but distinguished Zāgha alone as a centre of learning. However, he suggests a relationship between the two in saying, 'Kābura and Zāgha have two sultans in obedience to the king of Mali'. See Ibn Baṭūṭa, *Voyages*, vol. IV, p. 385.
85. Al-Sa'di, p. 48, mentions an anecdote indicating that Muḥammad al-Kāburi was black.
86. See al-Sa'di, pp. 27–8 and *passim*. Remotely, the present-day Keltina al-Ḥājj may be descendants of al-Qāḍi al-Ḥājj.
87. See al-Sa'di, p. 57. It seems doubtful that the title of *kātib* would have remained with Mūsa (the title of *qāḍi* being far more prestigious) unless at some point he had served in a secretarial capacity to the kings of Mali. Alternatively, traditionists may have confused him with al-Ḥajj Mūsa al-Wanjarati (al-Wangari) who had been ambassador of Mansa Sulaimān to Morocco. See Ibn Baṭūṭa, *Voyages*, vol. IV, p. 409. Al-Sa'di was certainly acquainted with Ibn Baṭūṭa's text.
88. Al-Sa'di, p. 57. Holding court at one's house implies limited jurisdiction, as will be mentioned in Chapter 4.
89. According to al-Sa'di, p. 57, 'He was one of the scholars of the Sūdān who travelled to Fez to acquire learning during the regime of the people of Mali by order of the just sultan, al-Ḥājj [Mansa] Mūsa'. Cf. note 85 above.
90. 'Abdallāh al-Balbāli allegedly first came to Timbuktu in the company of Kātib Mūsa (Al-Sa'di, p. 57). The *nisba* to which al-Balbāli refers is the oasis of Tabalbalat, west of Tuat. See also Levtzion, *Ancient Ghana and Mali*, p. 202.
91. The genealogy of Muḥammad ('Aryān al-Ra's) is our only guideline on this but the influence of this man suggests respected clerical descent. See al-Sa'di, pp. 15–16, 55, 56.
92. The rise of the Maghsharen at this time resembles the growing power of the Kel Tadmekkat who put an end to the Ruma ascendency in the mid-eighteenth century.
93. Al-Sa'di, p. 9.
94. Al-Sa'di, p. 23. Unfortunately, the text is somewhat ambiguous concerning the distribution of the revenue.
95. Apparently, Akil tried to forego 'Umar's share of the revenue and the latter responded by calling on Sunni 'Ali. See al-Sa'di, pp. 23–4.
96. Muḥammad's mother was daughter of Sum 'Uthmān, an important person who, however, is not otherwise identified. Since Muḥammad's father is not mentioned, there may be grounds for matrilineal succession among the Sanhāja and Masūfa of the city. See al-Sa'di, p. 22.
97. Al-Sa'di, pp. 22–3 and *passim*. The author relates that Muḥammad Naḍ and Sīdi Yaḥya died on the same night as further evidence of their close friendship. Since Sīdi Yaḥya became the *walī* of Timbuktu *par excellence*, the tradition attests to the high respect in which the memory of Muḥammad Naḍ was held.
98. Al-Sa'di, pp. 23–4.
99. The man is identified as And-Agh-Muḥammad b. Muḥammad b. 'Uthmān b. Muḥammad b. Nūḥ. The usage of Agh (son of) and And in the names of members of his family clearly attests to Tuareg descent. See al-Sa'di, p. 28.
100. See H. T. Norris, 'Sanhaja scholars of Timbuctoo', especially p. 637.
101. See al-Sa'di, pp. 22, 35–6. The author quotes Aḥmad Bāba, the celebrated descendant of Muḥammad Aqīt, to the effect that the latter hated the Fulānis (the dominant group in Massina) and feared that his sons would intermarry with them. Perhaps at some point prior to the mid-fifteenth century, the Sanhāja had been dominant over the Fulānis in

Massina. A biographical notice on Aḥmad Bāba, occurring on a Moroccan copy of one of his works, claims that he was originally from Walāta. However, the author of this notice seems ill-informed; among other things, he confuses between Aḥmad Bāba and his teacher, Muḥammad Baghayughu. See Aḥmad Bāba (Aqīt), *Mi'rāj al-Ṣu'ūd*, fo. 1.

102. The grandfather of Misir And 'Umar, an otherwise obscure scholar, interceded with Akil on behalf of Muḥammad Aqīt. At first, Akil objected, but upon hearing that Muḥammad had become a peaceful 'family man', consented. Al-Sa'di, pp. 35–6.

103. The intermarriage clearly enhanced the status of the Aqīts; al-Sa'di includes their biographies among the descendants of And-Agh-Muḥammad al-Kabīr. Al-Sa'di, pp. 28ff. 'There descended from him many of the *shaikhs* of learning and piety, some on their father's side and others on the mother's side.'

104. Ḥabīb and al-Ma'mūn were cousins; we have virtually no information on their fathers besides a reference to Ḥabīb in a much later source as son of Muḥammad al-Ṣāliḥ b. 'Abd a'-Raḥmān al-Tamīmi. See *Dhikr Fuqahā' Tumbuktu*.

105. The kinship relationship between Sunni 'Ali and Askia Muḥammad remains problematical and the problem would appear to bear on the significance of maternal descent. Songhai traditions suggest close kinship, holding Muḥammad to be a son of Sunni 'Ali's sister. *Tārīkh al-Fattāsh*, p. 48, points to a vague (Wa'kore–Wangari) origin. In his queries to al-Maghīli, Askia Muḥammad attributed Sunni 'Ali's pagan practices to his mother's people, inhabitants of Fara. See Hunwick, *Al-Maghili's replies*, pp. 163–71.

106. Triaud, *Islam et sociétés*, especially p. 155. Triaud speaks of 'the triumph of the Muslim party' at the accession of Askia Muḥammad.

107. Trimingham, *A history*, p. 94. If we may assume that the Songhai transferred their throne to Gao shortly before Sunni 'Ali, then accommodation with urban Islam led by scholars would indeed have been a major consideration.

108. Compare *Tārīkh al-Fattāsh*, pp. 45–6 with al-Sa'di, p. 76. Hunwick suggested an attempt on the part of Sunni 'Ali to maintain a distance between Islam and the indigenous Songhai cult. See J. O. Hunwick, 'Religion and state'.

109. The expansion of the Songhai kingdom had begun under Sunni 'Ali's immediate predecessor, Sulaimān Dama, who is said to have conquered the kingdom of Mīma in Massina, after the latter had established its independence from Mali. It is remotely possible that Sulaimān acted on behalf of Malian authority, unlike Sunni 'Ali, who sought no legitimization for his conquests. See *Tārīkh al-Fattāsh*, pp. 42–3.

110. The *Tārīkh al-Fattāsh*, though more detailed on Sunni 'Ali's campaigns than al-Sa'di's *Tārīkh al-Sūdān*, offers a confused chronology and sequence of events. See especially pp. 48–9.

111. When Sunni 'Ali ascended the throne, the cautious Muḥammad Naḍ wrote congratulating him and 'told him not to worry on his account as he counts himself among his relatives'. See al-Sa'di, pp. 64–5.

112. The chroniclers seem uncertain about the date of Sunni 'Ali's accession to the Songhai throne. What concerned them is the beginning of his conquests, it seems. For example, al-Sa'di quotes al-'Alqami, an Egyptian scholar, to the effect that 'he appeared in al-Takrur' in the year 869 A.H. (1464/5 A.D.). See al-Sa'di, pp. 64–5 and *Tārīkh al-Fattāsh*, p. 44.

113. The text of *Tārīkh al-Fattāsh* (see p. 48) is ambiguous; it dates the conquest of Timbuktu to 4 Rajab 873 A.H. (1468 A.D.), but assigns the return of Muḥammad b. 'Umar from Walāta (where his family had fled Sunni 'Ali) to that same year.

114. See al-Sa'di, pp. 24, 65. Unfortunately, we know nothing about Akil's subsequent actions.

115. *Ibid.* Quite possibly, the first evacuation, facilitated by Akil, merely transported the goods of the wealthy families out of fear of plunder.

116. These details are known only from al-Sa'di (pp. 65–7). The narrative of *Tārīkh al-Fattāsh*, based apparently on Songhai traditions, is more concerned with 'Ali's campaigns than with events at Timbuktu.
117. See al-Sa'di, p. 66. A second stage in the exodus caused 'those remaining in the Sankore quarter to flee to Walāta also'.
118. *Ibid.*, pp. 68, 75. In the initial appointment of Maḥmūd b. 'Umar to the judgeship, Askia Muḥammad acted on the advice of Abu Bakr.
119. *Ibid.*
120. See Norris, *The Tuaregs*, pp. 38, 53. It is possible that some of the refugees settled at Anṣamun, a settlement in the Tagedda complex which later produced outstanding scholars.
121. Al-Sa'di, p. 69. It would not be unreasonable to assume that the fugitives in Walāta sought the help of the Mossi king. The latter had entered Walāta after a siege in 885 A.H. (1480/1 A.D.) and was given a daughter of a certain And-Naḍ (son of Muḥammad Naḍ) in marriage, thereby sealing some sort of alliance, however temporary.
122. *Tārīkh al-Fattāsh*, pp. 48–9.
123. Quoting a certain Muḥammad Bāba b. Yūsif, the *Tārīkh al-Fattāsh* (p. 49) virtually scorns the people of Timbuktu for the haste with which they followed the orders to transfer to Hawīki. Cf. al-Sa'di, pp. 70–1.
124. See al-Sa'di, pp. 30, 70–1. Also Aḥmad Bāba (Aqīt), *Nayl al-Ibtihāj*, p. 88ff.
125. Al-Sa'di, p. 212. 'Abdullah's objections to returning to Timbuktu were levelled specifically against the Sankore quarter, but not Jingerebir. This suggests a disunited stand, among the scholars, at the time of Sunni 'Ali.
126. 'Abd al-Raḥmān al-Suyūṭi, *Al-Tanbi'a* fos 345–79, especially p. 375. See also E. M. Sartain, 'Jalal ad-Din', p. 196, n.2.
127. Al-Sa'di, p. 70. Al-Faqih 'Abd al-Jabbār Kaku may be 'Abd al-Jabbār b. 'Ali b. Muḥammad al-Akhṭābi al-Qāhiri al-Ṭūlūni, a student of al-Suyūṭi who resided in Mecca and was met there by al-Sakhāwi in 993 A.H. Al-Ḥājj Ahmad b. 'Umar Aqīt would have met this scholar when he made the pilgrimage in 890 A.H. See Muhammad b. 'Abd al-Rahman al-Sakhawi, *al-Daw' al-Lāmi'*, vol. IV, pp. 35–6.
128. See *Maghīli's replies*.
129. *Tārīkh al-Fattāsh*, p. 44. According to the defective MS C (p. 14), Sunni 'Ali had learned from the *kuhhān* that the twelfth true caliph was to arise (in the nineteenth century in the person of Aḥmadu Lobbo?) among the Sanqara. This allegedly turned him against them.
130. On the attitude of Ḥabīb and al-Ma'mūn, see al-Sa'di, p. 66.
131. Levtzion has suggested that the published first part of *Tārīkh al-Fattāsh*, which is peculiar to MS C, is a nineteenth-century emendation in its entirety. We, however, feel that the introduction up to p. 12 is authentic; the sections peculiar to MS C from then on are more readily identifiable as nineteenth-century additions. See N. Levtzion, 'A seventeenth century chronicle'.
132. *Tarikh al-Fattash*, p. 10.
133. *Ibid.*, p. 17. The reference in question is peculiar to MS C, but we believe that the date may be authentic. The author interrupts his narrative concerning the arrival of Aḥmad al-Ṣaqali in 925 A.H. and says: 'His arrival corresponded with the beginning of our composition. Since the pen has reached this point we have decided to give priority to the mention of his virtues before those of others . . .' It is difficult to see the wording here, though not the rest of al-Ṣaqali's story, as a nineteenth-century fabrication. The man's arrival at the beginning of the sixteenth century agrees with what we know of his grandsons at the end of that century.
134. See al-Sa'di, p. 211. The birth of Maḥmūd Ka't during the reign of Askia Muḥammad is obscured in MS C of *Tārīkh al-Fattāsh* (p. 82, n. 4), the name being changed there to al-Qāḍi Mahmūd b. al-Ḥājj al-Mutawakkil Sanba!

135. A full discussion of this problem lies beyond the scope of this study.
136. *Tārīkh al-Fattāsh*, pp. 12ff (MS C).
137. Jalāl al-Dīn al-Suyūṭi, *Al-Taḥadduth*, vol. II, p. 158.
138. It is quite clear that Ḥabīb remained *Qāḍi* under Askia Muḥammad up to his death in 904 A.H. See al-Sa'di, pp. 74–5.
139. Sartain ('Jalāl ad-Dīn', p. 96) indicates that al-Suyūṭi 'appears to have added no new material to his autobiography after about 896/1490'.
140. The possibility is quite remote; but if Askia Muḥammad gained a *taqlīd* (an investiture from the Khalīfa) before gaining power, then his struggle with Sunni 'Ali and his son Abu Bakr Dā'u, was more protracted.
141. See Ignatz Goldhizer, 'A contribution to the study of Jalāl al-Dīn al-Suyūṭi and his literary activity', translated from German by Michael Barry and edited with additional notes by J. O. Hunwick. I am indebted to Dr Hunwick for access to the translation of this article before its publication.
142. See J. O. Hunwick, 'Notes on a late fifteenth century document'.
143. 'Abd al-Raḥmān al-Suyūṭi, *Risāla*, fos 139a–140b.
144. Quoted in Sartain, 'Jalāl ad-Dīn', pp. 197–8.
145. Norris (*The Tuaregs*, pp. 56, 60) hesitantly suggests that al-Suyūṭi's reference is to a Sultan of Bornu.
146. See al-Sa'di, p. 217. The source assigns the birth of Muḥammad Bāba to 981 A.H., but judging by his age at his death, this is certainly a scribal error for 931 A.H.
147. Muḥammad Bāba b. Muḥammad al-Amīn b. Ḥabīb b. al-Mukhtār al-Tunbukti al-Māliki, *Al-Minaḥ al-Ḥamīda*, fos 3–4. J. O. Hunwick has made a search for *al-Aḥādīth al-Mutqana*, but did not find it though other short compositions by al-Suyūṭi on government are extant. In the composition, al-Suyūṭi is quoted describing Askia Muḥammad as 'the pious and just king, the *mujāhid* who upholds righteousness and truthfulness, the king of Takrūr, may God render the faith victorious at his hands . . . God has relieved his worshippers by his rule after the years of Sunni 'Ali, just as he relieved them with 'Umar b. Abd al-'Azīz after al-Ḥājjāj.'
148. See al-Sa'di, pp. 723–73. The author claims that 2500 soldiers accompanied Askia Muḥammad on the pilgrimage. This seems doubtful, since the pilgrimage went largely unnoticed in Middle Eastern chronicles of the time. *Tārīkh al-Fattāsh* (p. 34) quotes al-Qāḍi Aḥmad b. Aḥmad b. And-Agh-Muḥammad to the effect that the Askia's company included 800 men as compared to the 8000 in Mansa Mūsa's company.
149. Manuscripts A and B, which are free of nineteenth-century emendation, say Askia Muḥammad 'was accompanied by seven of the jurists of his country', but these are not named. See *Tārīkh al-Fattāsh*, p. 64, n. 1.
150. Al-Sa'di, p. 73. The author, though more reticent, provides essentially the same information as manuscripts A and B of *Tārīkh al-Fattāsh*.
151. See al-Sa'di, p. 73 and *Tārīkh al-Fattāsh*, pp. 86–7.
152. See al-Bakri, *Al-Mughrib*, p. 183.
153. See *Tārīkh al-Fattāsh*, pp. 86–7, 153–4. Apparently, the sword was inherited by one Askia from another until the defeat of the Songhai by the Moroccans when its fate became unknown.
154. The Maghsharen chieftaincy was incorporated into the new order and one Maghsharen-Koy married a daughter of Askia Daūd. See *Tārīkh al-Fattāsh*, p. 118.
155. There exists considerable doubt concerning Askia Muḥammad's campaigns in Hausaland (see al-Sa'di, p. 78). Although these are also recorded by Leo Africanus, they are not mentioned in the Kano Chronicle, nor in any other Hausa sources. See Humphrey J. Fisher, 'Leo Africanus'.
156. See Leo Africanus (Jean-Leon l'Africain), *Description de l'Afrique*, *passim*.

157. See al-Sa'di, p. 88 and *passim*.
158. Al-Mukhtār al-Naḥawī was absent at the time. On his return, he blamed Abu Bakr saying, 'Do you not have a son of your own who is qualified for the judgeship?' See al-Sa'di, pp. 76–7.
159. See *Tārīkh al-Fattāsh*, pp. 59–61. The defective MS C, which claims that Askia Muḥammad was the first to establish judges in Timbuktu, Jenne and elsewhere, omits this story which occurs in MSS A and B.
160. *Tārīkh al-Fattāsh*, pp. 75–7, is more explicit on the details of this story than al-Sa'di, pp. 76–7.
161. See al-Sa'di, p. 79. The text, in fact, speaks of ''Umar b. Abu Bakr, the Sultan of Timbuktu'. It is remotely possible that Askia Muḥammad had, in the meantime, appointed a grandson of al-Qāḍi al-Ḥājj ('Umar b. Abu Bakr b. al-Qāḍi al-Ḥājj) to the governorate of Timbuktu. Otherwise, a scribal error may account for the difference in the name.
162. See al-Sa'di, pp. 27–8, 76–7.
163. See, for example, al-Sa'di, pp. 82, 83.
164. Al-Sa'di, pp. 40, 98; and *Tārīkh al-Fattāsh*, p. 82. Aḥmad Bāba (Aqīt), in *Nayl al-Ibtihāj*, p. 340, says of Muḥammad b. Maḥmūd: 'Good fortune attended him and he obtained the degree of political power and leadership he desired, acquiring great benefit from it and profiting from this world extensively'. Quoted in Hunwick, 'Aḥmad Bāba', p. 314.
165. See *Tārīkh al-Fattāsh*, pp. 109–11, 121. According to al-Sa'di, p. 34, 'al-'Āqib filled the land with justice whereby he had no equal in that anywhere'.
166. Al-Sa'di, pp. 52, 60.
167. Aḥmad Bāba (Aqīt), *Nayl al-Ibtihāj*, p. 218.
168. See al-Sa'di, pp. 34–5. *Tārīkh al-Fattāsh*, p. 113, has Aḥmad b. Muḥammad b. Sa'īd. Nothing is known of this scholar's paternal descent.
169. Al-Sa'di, p. 19 and *Tārīkh al-Fattāsh*, pp. 88–90.
170. See al-Sa'di, p. 108 and *Tārīkh al-Fattāsh*, pp. 113–4.
171. Compare especially *Tārīkh al-Fattāsh*, p. 12 (MSS A and C) with pp. 74–5, both dealing with Ahl Muri Kuyra.
172. See *Tārīkh al-Fattāsh*, p. 70. Also Levtzion, 'A seventeenth century chronicle'.
173. See *Dīwān al-Mulūk fi Salāṭīn al-Sūdān*, fos 88v–153v, especially fos 104rv.
174. See genealogy of the al-Sa'di family in the Appendices.
175. The author of *al-Durar al-Ḥisān* was Bāba Kūru b. al-Ḥajj Muḥammad b. al-Ḥājj al-Amīn Kānu (see *Tārīkh al-Fattāsh*, p. 44). He is brother of Aḥmad b. al-Ḥājj Muḥammad b. al-Amīn Kānu, the last scholar whose death is recorded by al-Sa'di (p. 322), unless the two were the same. Their father might conceivably be the above-mentioned commentator on al-Suyūṭi's *Farīda*, Muḥammad Bāba b. Muḥammad al-Amīn b. Ḥabīb b. al-Faqīh al-Mukhtār, whose father is at one point identified simply as al-Faqīh al-Amīn. He had another son in Ḥabīb b. Muḥammad Bāba (al-Sa'di, p. 211). On al-Ḥājj al-Amīn Kānu, see *Tārīkh al-Fattāsh*, pp. 122–3.
176. See, for example, al-Sa'di, pp. 27, 36, on al-Qāḍi al-Ḥājj and on Aḥmad b. Ibrāhīm b. Abu Bakr b. al-Qāḍi al-Ḥājj. Al-Sa'di (p. 56) says al-Amīn's father had not been mentioned in his obituary, but one of the MSS describes the man as al-Amīn b. Aḥmad b. Muḥammad (p. 247). See genealogy of the al-Ḥājj family in the Appendices.
177. Al-Mukhtār b. Muḥammad Zankanu was a *sibṭ* (grandson through a daughter) of al-Qāḍi al-'Āqib. See al-Sa'di, p. 243. Cf. Marty, *Etudes sur l'Islam*, pp. 18ff.
178. Al-Sa'di, pp. 110–11. After Jingerebir, al-'Āqib renovated the Market Mosque and Sankore, but the Askia seems to have had no interest except in the Main Mosque.
179. *Tārīkh al-Fattāsh*, p. 110. The text speaks of 'the year of the dispute' (*munāza'a*) between Daūd and al-'Āqib.
180. *Ibid.*, pp. 109–11. The source mentions the episodes in a series of digressions on the virtues of Daūd and al-'Āqib.

181. Indeed, according to al-Mawardi, delegating the imamate or leadership of the prayers in the main mosques was a prerogative of the ruler. See al-Mawardi, *Al-Aḥkām*, p. 100.
182. Al-Sa'di, p. 118. Ṣāliḥ Takun was a nephew of Misir-And-'Umar, the Soninke scholar mentioned in note 102, above, whose grandfather had interceded with Akil on behalf of Muḥammad Aqīt. See Al-Sa'di, p. 170.
183. *Tārīkh al-Fattāsh*, pp. 124–5.
184. *Ibid.*
185. See Niamkey Georges Kodjo, 'La chutte', especially p. 10. Compare with *Tārīkh al-Fattāsh*, p. 125. Baghayughu had declined several posts, including the *Khutba*/judgeship of Gao, preferring his position as *Imām* of Sīdi Yaḥya. It seems doubtful that a competition could have arisen between him and the Aqīts on the judgeship. See Aḥmad Bāba (Aqīt), *Nayl al-Ibtihāj*, p. 340–2.
186. Muḥammad Baghayughu studied under Aḥmad b. Ḥājj Aḥmad b. 'Umar Aqīt and, in turn, taught the latter's son Aḥmad Bāba who, later, became teacher of al-Muṣṭafa b. Aḥmad Baghayughu. Even the ancestor of the Baghayughus in Jenne, al-Qāḍi Mahmūd, had apparently been accredited in *Mukhtasar Khalīl* by Maḥmūd b. 'Umar Aqīt. Aḥmad Bāba's biography of Muḥammad Baghayughu, one of the longest and most laudatory in *Nayl al-Ibtihaj* (pp. 340–2), indicates continued close ties between the two families up to the point when the Aqīts were exiled to Morocco. See also *Nayl al-Ibtihāj*, p. 114 (on the *Mukhtasar*).
187. Compare al-Sa'di, p. 118 with *Tārīkh al-Fattāsh*, pp. 124–5.
188. The fragment has been published by Houdas and Delafosse as an appendix to *Tārīkh al Fattāsh*. See p. 186. (Also translation 324; Muhammad Bankānu-Mar Bounkān). Compare with al-Sa'di, pp. 115–6.
189. Al-Sa'di, pp. 118–20.
190. *Ibid.*, pp. 121–2. See also p. 112 where, for some reason, al-Sa'di compares Askia AL-Ḥājj favourably with his earlier namesake, Askia al-Ḥājj Muḥammad I.
191. *Ibid.*, pp. 125–6. The *ṭulba* and *fuqahā'* led the campaign at Gao in defaming Muḥammad Bān because, according to al-Sa'di, this Askia claimed for himself the posture of a scholar. A drought during Muḥammad Bān's reign, coupled with a drastic rise in prices, helped to galvanize public opinion against him.
192. *Tārīkh al-Fattāsh*, p. 131.
193. See al-Sa'di, pp. 120–1. The source mentions the existence of several salt-mines which served as alternatives to Taghāza, but only *Tnurd* (possibly an error for Taoudenni) is named. The mines of Taoudenni later overshadowed Taghaza and the Barābīsh, associated with the new mines, largely replaced the Maghsharen as the main power in the area.
194. *Tārīkh al-Fattāsh*, p. 126. According to this source: 'The struggle between Askia Muḥammad Bān b. Askia Daūd and his brother Balma' al-Ṣadiq was the cause of the extinction of Songhai. It opened the doors of evil among them and led to the disruption of the system of their state from then on until the arrival of the Moroccan expedition.'
195. *Ibid.*, p. 138. The fact that Muḥammad al-Ṣādiq sought Muḥammad Baghayughu's house in his flight may suggest that this scholar had formally supported his bid for the throne. In any case, there is no evidence for Kodjo's claim that 'Umar Aqīt (in opposition to Muhammad Baghayughu!) was behind al-Ṣādiq's rebellion.
196. See al-Sa'di, p. 131.
197. *Tārīkh al-Fattāsh*, p. 131. This source, throughout, introduces numerous digressions which obscure the sequence and chronology of events. Cf. al-Sa'di, especially p. 126.
198. See al-Sa'di, p. 129; Kodjo, 'La chutte', p. 14.
199. See al-Sa'di, p. 313; also p. 131. The Maghsharen themselves actually split into two parties at the time of the Moroccan conquest.

3. *The scholars as a learned elite*

1. Al-Qāḍi al-Ḥājj allegedly administered a potion to the people of Banku and this enabled them to withstand the Mossi and drive them back. See al-Sa'di, *Tārīkh al-Sūdān*, p. 27.
2. See al-Sa'di, p. 51. A break in Timbuktu traditions is also suggested by the fact that al-Sa'di quotes Ibn Baṭūṭa to the effect that Abu Isḥāq al-Sāḥili, Mansa Mūsa's architect, was buried at Timbuktu, yet seems unaware of the place of burial nor does he supply any information besides quoting the traveller. *Ibid.*, p. 8.
3. Gao, for example, is referred to by Ibn Khaldūn as the birth-place of the Khārijite leader Abu Yazīd Makhlad b. Kaidād in 893 A.D. See Hunwick, 'Religion and state', p. 297. Cf. Ibn Baṭūṭa, *Voyages*, vol. IV, p. 395. Also Tom Hunter, *The development*, pp. 33ff.
4. See *Aṣl al-Wangariyyīn*, especially Arabic, p. 21 (fo. 5). Cf. *Kano Chronicle*, vol. III, pp. 92–132, especially pp. 104–13.
5. See Aḥmad Bāba, *Nayl*, p. 88; al-Sa'di, p. 37.
6. See Norris, 'Sanḥaja scholars' pp. 634–40. Aḥmad Bāba says that And-Agh-Muḥammad al-Kabīr was the first to serve the cause of learning among his family. See al-Sa'di, p. 28. However, we do not know if Muḥammad Aqīt was a scholar.
7. See H. T. Norris, *Saharan myth and saga, passim.*
8. *Tārīkh al-Fattāsh*, pp. 106, 151. The same person is referred to as Muḥammad Ja'aiti (or Jaghaiti) and Muḥammad Zaghaiti.
9. See E. N. Saad, 'Islamization in Kano'.
10. See Ivor Wilks, 'The transmission', pp. 173ff.
11. Ibn Baṭūṭa, *Voyages*, vol. IV, p. 395. On the itinerary of Ibn Baṭūṭa, see J. O. Hunwick, 'The mid-fourteenth century capital', pp. 195–208.
12. Ibn Baṭūṭa, *Voyages*, vol. IV, p. 395. Also p. 409 on Mūsa al-Wanjarāti.
13. See al-Sa'di, pp. 16–8. This scholar, originally from Bītu, was instrumental in eliminating a structure previously used for 'pagan worship' in Jenne. Wilks ('The transmission') p. 180, n. 5.
14. Wilks, 'The transmission', pp. 177–8; Sanneh, 'The origins of clericalism', *passim*, prefers a much earlier date.
15. Ibn Baṭūṭa, *Voyages*, vol. IV, p. 395.
16. The earliest known scholar from Jenne, Murmagh Kanki, apparently a Soninke, also received his education in Kābura, though he was originally from the town of Tay, between Bīghu and Kūbar. Al-Sa'di, p. 16.
17. In his childhood, Muḥammad al-Kāburi may have seen 'Abd al-Raḥmān al-Tamīmi. This, in the eyes of traditionists, may have made them contemporaries.
18. See Wilks, 'The transmission', *passim*. If Wilks is correct in assigning al-Suwāri to the fifteenth century, then his emigration to distant Diakha Bambuku may account for the fact that he is not mentioned in the Timbuktu chronicles.
19. Sunni 'Ali persecuted the al-Ḥājj scholars at Alfa Gungu. Al-Sa'di, p. 66; also, pp. 47–50. The earliest piece of literature extant from Timbuktu, a poem quoted by al-Sa'di, was composed by Sīdi Yaḥya al-Tadulsi in praise of Muḥammad al-Kāburi.
20. In the Dyula tradition, *Tafsīr al-Jalālain*, *Kitāb al-Shifa* and *Muwatta' Mālik* were the basic curricula for gaining the title of karamoko. See Wilks, 'The transmission', p. 168.
21. See Marty, *Etudes sur l'Islam*, vol. II, pp. 18–9.
22. Aḥmad Bāba says that, as a child, he attended the *durūs* of Aḥmad b. Muḥammad Sa'īd before his death in 976 A.H. Since Aḥmad Bāba was born in 963 A.H., his attendance was more that of an admirer than a real student. See *Nayl*, p. 95.
23. See, for example, al-Sa'di, p. 322 on Muḥammad Bāba.
24. See al-Sa'di, pp. 29, 31, 55, 65.
25. Makhlūf b. 'Ali b. Ṣāliḥ al-Balbāli took up learning under 'Abdullāh b. 'Umar Aqīt at

an advanced age. See al-Sa'di, p. 39. Previously, he had been a merchant. Aḥmad Bāba, *Nayl*, pp. 343–4.

26. See Aḥmad Bāba, *Nayl*, p. 114. The author studied *Mukhtaṣar Khalīl* at the three levels of *baḥth*, *taḥqīq* and *taqrīr* under Muḥammad Baghayughu.
27. See al-Sa'di, pp. 30–1, on his *mulāzama* to Muḥammad Sunni b. al-Faqīh al-Mukhtār.
28. Muḥammad al-Kāburi, for example, had a preference for teaching *Tahdhīb al-Barādi'i*, a work not known to have been taught by any other scholar of Timbuktu. See al-Sa'di, p. 47.
29. Aḥmad Bāba mentions a *ru'ya* he had which told him that Aḥmad b. al-Ḥajj Aḥmad, his father, received even higher recompense in the hereafter than Aḥmad b. Muḥammad Sa'īd. This caused him great surprise. See Aḥmad Bāba, *Nayl*, pp. 93–5.
30. Very few *ijāzas* are extant today which document the lines of transmission from the mid-seventeenth century onwards. Most of the extant *ijāzas*, though ultimately linking with Timbuktu scholars, are those of Saharan scholars from Arwān and the Kel al-Sūq.
31. See al-Sa'di, p. 65. Al-Bartīli has no specific entry for al-Imām al-Zammūri and indeed his biographies in *Fatḥ al-Shukūr* suggest a break in Walāta traditions sometime in the sixteenth century. See, for example, the biography of Muḥammad b. Muḥammad b. 'Ali Sili (Sali) b. Muḥammad b. Muḥammad b. 'Umar b. And-Agh-Muḥammad b. 'Umar b. 'Uthmān (Paris MS, fo. 17r).
32. The only known teacher of 'Abdullāh Boryo was Muḥammad Bāba Misir son of And-Agh-Muḥammad al-Muṣalli al-Dalīmi, who had been one of the *shuhūd* (probably also one of the students) of Maḥmūd b. 'Umar. See al-Sa'di, pp. 31, 212.
33. See, for example, Abu Bakr, 'Acte du vente passé à Tombouctou'. See also discussion of books and libraries below.
34. See al-Sa'di, pp. 29–30 and *passim*. The author lists the Aqīts as descendants (on the maternal side) of And-Agh-Muḥammad al-Kabīr.
35. The daughters of And-Agh-Muḥammad b. al-Mukhtār al-Naḥawī had prominent sons in Muḥammad b. Yumdhurghabīn and Aḥmad Mātini b. Asikala, besides Muḥammad b. Muḥammad Kara, who attained the imamate of Sankore. See al-Sa'di, p. 30.
36. See, for example, the biography of 'Umar al-Walī b. Muḥammad b. 'Abdullāh al-Maḥjūbi al-Walāti in al-Bartīli, *Fatḥ al-Shukūr*, Nouakchott MS, 81r–83v.
37. See al-Sa'di, p. 66. Of the sons of al-Qāḍi al-Ḥājj, none are known except Abu Bakr.
38. Al-Sa'di, pp. 27–8, 214. The author describes Ibrāhīm simply as a descendant of al-Qāḍi al-Ḥājj, but on genealogical grounds, he is identifiable as Ibrāhīm b. 'Umar b. Abu Bakr b. al-Qāḍi al-Ḥājj.
39. Aḥmad b. Muḥammad b. Muḥammad Bīru, *Ijāzas*.
40. See biography of al-Imām 'Umar Mamma b. Muḥammad . . . al-Walāti, in al-Bartīli, *Fatḥ al-Shukūr*, Nouakchott MS, fos 85v–88v.
41. Several descendants of Muḥammad Gurdu appear in the *sanad* of the nineteenth century Sān Sirfi. 'Abd al-Qādir b. Muḥammad al-Sanūsi, *Ijāza*.
42. Besides these scholars, 'Abd al-Raḥmān b. Aḥmad al-Mujtahid taught al-Muṣṭafa b. Aḥmad Baghayughu and Muḥammad Bāba b. Muḥammad al-Amīn, but his teachers are not known.
43. No students for Sīdi Yaḥya are mentioned though it is on record that *ṭulba* from the Sankore quarter repeatedly sought him at his mosque in the centre of the city. Al-Sa'di, p. 51.
44. See Aḥmad Bāba, *Nayl*, pp. 217–8, 343–4.
45. See al-Sa'di, pp. 47–50. Al-Kāburi's teaching of Sīdi Yaḥya could hardly have been forgotten by traditionists, since a poem by the latter in praise of his master is the earliest piece of literature extant for Timbuktu.
46. Indeed, most of the information on Muḥammad b. Muḥammad Kara is available from the biographies of his students rather than from a biography of him. Al-Sa'di, pp. 217–8, 238–9, 321–2. The title *Shaikh al-Shuyūkh* is reserved only for Muḥammad al-Kāburi and Muḥammad b. Muḥammad Kara.

47. See al-Sa'di, p. 322. Muḥammad Gurdu's father, a judge of Massina, is identified as Muḥammad (Mūdu) Sāj b. al-Faqīh 'Mālik b. Anas' b. 'Ali Sanba al-Saffūn b. Ibrāhīm b. Ibrāhīm Aḥmad al-Fulāni. Reference to his father as 'Mālik b. Anas' (the name of the founder of Malikism) suggests earlier subscription to Māliki studies. Muḥammad Sāj sent his son for study in Timbuktu on a temporary basis, but 'Abdullāh al-Sa'di insisted on allowing him to settle in the city. Later, the author 'Abd al-Raḥmān al-Sa'di was patronized by Muḥammad Sāj. See al-Sa'di, pp. 230–1 and *passim*.
48. Dying in 1066 A.H. at the age of 84, Muḥammad Gurdu was 34 years of age on Aḥmad Bāba's return to Timbuktu in 1016 A.H. See al-Sa'di, p. 322.
49. Al-Sa'di, pp. 321–2 and *passim*.
50. Al-Sa'di never directly refers to *Al-Durar al-Ḥisān fi Akhbār Mulūk al-Sudān*; his prolegomenon (pp. 1–2) may suggest that he was dissatisfied with this earlier chronicle.
51. Al-Sa'di, pp. 217–8. Unfortunately, none of the students of Muḥammad Bāba are mentioned, nor does his name appear in later *sanads*.
52. It is interesting that Muḥammad Bāba and Muḥammad Gurdu shared some of the same teachers. Al-Sa'di's text is inconsistent concerning the birth-date of the former, but in any case it seems that there was a great difference in age between the two. See al-Sa'di, pp. 217–8, 321–2.
53. See al-Sa'di, p. 217.
54. See al-Bartīli's biography of Aḥmad Bāba, (J. O. Hunwick, 'A new source', pp. 568–93.
55. Aḥmad Bāba, *Nayl*, p. 218ff. Also Aḥmad Bāba's *sanads*, in Aḥmad al-Maqqari *Rawḍat*, pp. 310–11.
56. Aḥmad Bāba, *Nayl*, pp. 217–8, 343–4.
57. Aḥmad Bāba's biography of al-Maghīli (in *Nayl*, p. 230), is not altogether complimentary. In Hausaland, al-Maghīli became a legend in his own right. See, for example, the references to Abdulkarimu Mukaila (presumably Muḥammad b. 'Abd al-Karīm al-Maghīli) in the Hausa history published by R. Sutherland Rattray, *Hausa folklore*, vol I, p. 2–34. Cf. 'Abd al-'Aziz al-Baṭrān, 'A contribution'.
58. See al-Maqqari, *Rawdat*, especially p. 311. Also, Aḥmad Bāba, *Nayl*, pp. 93–5, pp. 218ff.
59. Al-Maqqari, *Rawḍat*, pp. 304–12, includes the full texts of *ijāzas* received by the author from Aḥmad Bāba. Other Moroccan students of Aḥmad Bāba are quoted in *Fatḥ al-Shukūr*. See Hunwick, 'A new source', especially p. 578.
60. See 'Abd al-Raḥmān b. Muḥammad al-Jazūli al-Tamanarti, *Al-Fawā'id*, fo. 45.
61. See Aḥmad Bāba, *Nayl*, p. 335. Also al-Maqqari, *Rawḍat*, pp. 304–11.
62. Al-Bartīli, *Fatḥ al-Shukūr*, *passim*. See, for example, Nouakchott MS, fos 81r–83v, and 85r–88r.
63. See Muḥammad b. Sīdi al-Mukhtār al-Kunti, *Kitāb al-Ṭarā'if*, Paris: Gironcourt MS 2407, no. 21, fos 232–1 (pages numbered backwards). For other copies, see the Bibliography.
64. *Ibid*. Al-Mukhtār's principal teacher, Sīdi 'Ali, was student of Aḥmad Ag-al-Shaikh al-Sūqi, in turn a student of Muḥammad Baghayughu al-Fulāni. Confusing the latter with Muḥammad Baghayughu al-Wangari caused the author to insert the name of the latter's student, the illustrious Aḥmad Bāba, into the *sanads*. If the *sanads* indeed linked up with Aḥmad Bāba, the chain should have been considerably longer.
65. Al-Bartīli, *Fatḥ al-Shukūr*, *passim*. See also *infra*.
66. Verbal communication. See also Wilks, 'The transmission', *passim*.
67. Aḥmad Bāba, *Nayl*, pp. 340–2, and *passim*. Also, al-Sa'di, pp. 33ff. Muḥammad al-Bakri wrote a poem in praise of Aḥmad b. al-Ḥājj Aḥmad Aqīt. His son, Zain al-'Abidin, had a correspondence with Askia Nūḥ, who took over Songhai leadership after the defeat of Askia Isḥāq by the Moroccans. See *Tārīkh al-Fattāsh*, pp. 167–8.

68. Al-Sa'di, p. 61. Again, this scholar associated in Cairo with Muḥammad al-Bakri. Unfortunately, it was not possible to conduct a thorough search in the writings of the Egyptian for evidence on Timbuktu. See Carl Brocklemann, *Geschichte*, GII, pp. 334, 339; SII, pp. 463–4.
69. *Tārīkh al-Fattāsh*, which does not concern itself at all with the lines of transmission, mentions numerous *faqīhs* who do not fit in the known lines of transmission.
70. Muḥammad Baghayughu is praised, for example, for having virtually sacrificed his life (*afna 'umrahu*) to the cause of teaching. See Aḥmad Bāba, *Nayl*, p. 340.
71. Maḥmūd Ka't sought funds for his sons, besides his students, and for purchasing books, from Askia Daūd. See *Tārīkh al-Fattāsh*, pp. 108–9.
72. See, for example, Dupuis-Yacouba, *Industries*, p. 179.
73. Muḥammad Baghayughu b. Muḥammad Gurdu al-Fulāni was possibly born in 1002 A.H. (1593/4 A.D.), the year when Muḥammad Baghayughu al-Wangari died. It was customary to give new-borns the names of illustrious persons who died in the same year.
74. See 'Abd al-Qādir b. Muḥammad al-Sanūsi, *Ijāza to Sān Sirfi*. The *ijāza*, dated 17 Jumada II, 1079 A.H., was made it seems in the presence of a large audience.
75. Aḥmad b. Muḥammad b. Muḥammad Bīru, *Ijāza to Bāba 'Uthmān* . . . Al-Wāfi b. Ṭālibna b. Ag-Adda (Ag-Gin, also Ag-Gid) b. Sayyid Aḥmad b. Adda was great-grandson of Aḥmad b. Adda, who is alleged to have founded Arwān around 1600 A.D. As will be suggested (*infra*), however, Aḥmad founded the chieftaincy and judgeship traditions of Arwān, already a Maghsharen settlement at his time. On the students of al-Wāfi, see *Tārīkh Arwān*.
76. Already in 1106 A.H. (1694/5 A.D.), we have a reference to the clan as 'the Fuquha of Kel Sūq'. See *Tadhkirat al-Nasyān*, p. 63.
77. See al-Kunti, *Kitāb al-Ṭarā'if*, Paris: Gironcourt MS 2407, no. 21, fo. 232. The reference there is to Sayyid Aḥmad b. al-Shaikh (obviously Aḥmad Ag al-Shaikh). Cf. 'Abd al-'Aziz al-Baṭrān, 'An introductory note'.
78. 'Abd al-Qādir b. Muḥammad al-Sanūsi, *Ijāza* to Sān Sirfi.
79. Al-Bartīli, *Fatḥ al-Shukūr*, *passim*. The author counted among his Shuyūkh al-Amīn b. Ḥabīb al-Jakani, a student of al-Qāḍi Abu Bakr b. 'Issa al-Ghallāwi who, in turn, had studied under Muḥammad b. Mūsa b. Ijil. Moreover, the author's teacher, al-Amīn, had studied under Aḥmad b. Muḥammad b. Mūsa b. Ijil.
80. Al-Bartīli, *Fatḥ al-Shukūr*, Paris: Gironcourt MS, fo. 35r. A teacher of al-Bartīli's teachers, Sayyid Munīr (probably b. Ḥabīb al-Shamshāwi), associated with Sulaimān, but the latter's *floruit* remains uncertain.
81. For example, al-Mukhtār al-Kunti earned a rank among the scholars of Shinjīt (Shinqit). See Aḥmad b. al-Amīn al-Shinqīti, *Al-Wasīt*, p. 361.
82. See Al-Bartīli, *Fatḥ al-Shukūr*, Nouakchott MS, fos 85r–88r. A student of Muḥammad b. Mūsa was al-Imām 'Umar Mamma of Walāta who died in 1201 A.H. (1786/7 A.D.).
83. This is according to Aḥmad Banio, present-day *Imām* of the Sīdi Yaḥya Mosque. He traces his *sanad*, through Aḥmad b. Muḥammad Abba al-Wangari to Muḥammad Yaḥya b. Sālim. The latter studied under Babakr al-Maḥjūbi, a student of al-Imām al-Maḥjūb b. Sayyid 'Uthmān b. Muḥammad 'Abdullah b. 'Umar al-Maḥjūbi. The chain goes backwards among the latter four (from son to father) to Muḥammad b. Mūsa b. Ijil. Though recited to this author from memory, this chain seems to be confirmed by the evidence on some of the scholars involved in *Fatḥ al-Shukūr*.
84. 'Abd al-Qādir b. Muḥammad al-Sanūsi, *Ijāza to Sān Sirfi*. This discussion is also based on information from Alfa Humal, present-day *Imām* of Jingerebir.
85. See, for example, the biography of al-Bashīr b. Abu Bakr al-Bartīli (*Fatḥ al-Shukūr*, Nouakchott MS, fos 32r–33), a student of 'Umar b. Mūdu Ḥamad al-Fulāni.
86. Other 'jihādist' students of al-Mukhtār are mentioned in al-Baṭrān, 'A contribution', p. 350.

87. Several copies and fragments of *Tārīkh al-Fattāsh* exist, but none include the prolegomena except the defective MS C.
88. This according to Aḥmad Bāba's son Zubair, an elder currently viewed by some as *de facto Qāḍi* of Timbuktu.
89. See Marty, *Etudes sur l'Islam*, vol. II, pp. 13ff.
90. See *Encyclopaedia of Islam*, New Edition, I, p. 965. The scholar reportedly declared that the three sons of 'Umar Aqīt (Aḥmad, Maḥmūd and 'Abdullāh) were *walīs*. See al-Sa'di, p. 30.
91. According to his biography by Aḥmad Bāba (quoted by al-Sa'di, pp. 41–2), Abu Bakr was author of several compositions in Sufism. See also al-Sa'di, p. 32.
92. Muḥammad b. Aḥmad b. Maḥmūd Baghayughu, *'Aqīdat*.
93. See Aḥmad Bāba, *Tuḥfat al-Fuḍalā'*. An analysis of this composition, based on another copy, is to be found in Mahmoud A. Zoubeir, *Ahmad Baba*, pp. 162–9.
94. For the *silsila* of Sīdi al-Mukhtār himself see *Kitāb al-Tarā'if*. See also Marty, *Etudes sur l'Islam*, vol. II, pp. 18ff.
95. Marty, *Etudes sur l'Islam*, vol. II, pp. 13ff.
96. See Jamil M. Abun-Nasr, *The Tijaniyya*, especially p. 159.
97. Al-Sa'di (p. 293) mentions that his brother Muḥammad Sa'di was successfully operated on for an eye-ailment by a doctor identified as al-Ṭabīb Ibrāhīm al-Sūsi who, however, was a visitor to Timbuktu. We have no other reference to a physician in Timbuktu, though one of the late-eighteenth-century Walāta scholars, Aḥmad b. Abu Bakr al-Bartīli, is described as 'the *ṭabīb* of his time' and is praised for extending his services to everybody, including slaves. See *Fatḥ al-Shukūr*, Nouakchott MS, fos 26r–27v.
98. See, for example, Mohammed Ibrahim el-Kettani, 'Les manuscrits', especially p. 61 on a Timbuktu copy of Ibn Sīda's *Muḥkam fi'l-Lugha*.
99. Khālid al-Azhari's extant works are all in grammar. This scholar died in 1499 A.D. See Brocklemann, *Geschichte*, GII, p. 27; SII, pp. 22–3.
100. See al-Sa'di, p. 30.
101. See Dār al-Kutub al-Misriyya, *Fihrist*, II, p. 47. The copy at Dār al-Kutub (the Egyptian National Library) carries no. 5277H. The Bibliothèque Générale in Rabat has two copies: MS D 309 and MS no. 521.
102. The Archinard collection at the Bibliothèque Nationale is mainly from the royal library of Segu. The collection has three copies of the *al-Futūḥ al-Qayūmiyya* by Aḥmad b. And-Agh-Muḥammad; Fonds Arabes, MS 5709, fos 159–241; MS 4141; MS 5442, fos 195r–250v.
103. See Muḥammad b. al-Tayyib al-Qādiri, *Al-Iklīl*. Much the same information is in *Nashr al-Mathāni* by the same author.
104. See for example, Charles Monteil, *Djenné*, p. 156. (Hadjarouna=Ajerrūmiyya.)
105. Muḥammad b. al-Ṭayyib al-Qādiri, *Nashr al-Mathāni* (Moroccan facsimile edition, n.p., n.d.).
106. *Ibid*. See also al-Bartīli's biography of Aḥmad Bāba. Translation in Hunwick, 'A new source', pp. 580, 582. Also Aḥmad Bāba, *Al-Nukat*. Zoubeir (*Ahmad Baba*, pp. 98–9) lists other compositions on the same subject which have been preserved at the Zāwiya of Tamghrout.
107. *Tafsīr al-Jalālain*, recurrently published in the last century, reads more like a grammatical than an interpretative text. However, advanced students often studied it in conjunction with one or another of the works (one being by al-Suyūṭi) which delineated early verses in the *Qurān* superseded by later ones.
108. See, for example, the list of works studied by al-Mukhtār al-Kunti in *Kitāb al-Tarā'if*.
109. See Aḥmad Bāba, *Kifāyat al-Muḥtāj*, fos. 290–2. Also, Aḥmad Bāba, *Nayl*, pp. 93–5. For another Timbuktuan commentary in *Tawḥīd*, see also note 92 above.
110. Al-Kunti, *Kitāb al-Tarā'if*, fos 231–2.

111. See Aḥmad Bāba's biography in *Fatḥ al-Shukūr*, translated in Hunwick, 'A new source', pp. 581–90.
112. See, for example, *Kano Chronicle*, p. 113.
113. See al-Sa'di, pp. 21, 31, 65. Also, *Tadhkirat al-Nasyān. Kitāb al-Shifa fi Ta'rif Huqūq al-Muṣṭafa* was one of three books which were central to the Suwarian tradition further south. See Wilks, 'The transmission', p. 168.
114. The *Risāla* and the *Tuḥfa* have been repeatedly published in Egypt and Morocco during the past century.
115. See Aḥmad Bāba, *Nayl*, pp. 113–4. The author of the *Mudawwana* was 'Abd al-Salām (Ṣaḥnūn) b. Sa'īd b. Ḥabīb al-Tanūkhi (d. 854).
116. See al-Bartīli's *Fatḥ al-Shukūr*, Nouakchott MS, fos 19v–21v. In fact, Aḥmad Bāba was merely paraphrasing his father's teacher, Nāṣir al-Dīn al-Laqqāni of Cairo. See Aḥmad Bāba, *Nayl*, p. 113.
117. Al-Sa'di, *passim*. The Royal Library in Rabat, Morocco, boasts of no less than seven volumes of commentaries on Khalīl attributed anonymously to al-Shaikh al-Sudāni. Some of these, we believe, may be the works of Maḥmud b. 'Umar or of Muḥammad Baghayughu. See MSS 4338–9, 7027, 4708, 4341, 8745, 10478. See also note 118 below.
118. MS 4975 at the Royal Library, Rabat, Morocco, is a large volume described on the flyleaf as 'Part of the commentary of al-Shaikh Aḥmad Bāba on *Mukhtaṣar Khalīl*'. However, this seems to fall into the same category of commentaries of anonymous Timbuktu authorship mentioned in note 117 above.
119. Aḥmad Bāba, *Nayl*, pp. 113–4, 343. Cf. al-Sa'di, pp. 36–7.
120. See Aḥmad Bāba, *Nayl*, pp. 217–8. This commentary is no longer extant, but another one on the subject of intention, entitled *Ghāyat al-Amal fi Faḍl al-Niyya 'ala al-'Amal*, is extant in two copies (from Tunis and Tamghrout) and have been discussed in Zoubeir, *Ahmad Baba*, pp. 179–184.
121. Al-Sa'di, pp. 36, 169–70. The genealogy of the Misir-And-'Umar family is unfortunately uncertain.
122. The *Muwaṭṭa'* was often studied in conjunction with a commentary by al-Bajā'i (sometimes al-Bāji) which became the subject of a versification by Muḥammad Bāba b. Muḥammad al-Amīn. See al-Sa'di, p. 218. Aḥmad Bāba studied the *Mukhṭasar* eight times during the course of his training and spent three years on the *Muwaṭṭa'* and its commentators. See *Fatḥ al-Shukūr* in Hunwick, 'A new source', p. 575.
123. Our discussion is based on the Muslim jurists' own definition of the science of *uṣūl*.
124. On al-Suyūṭi's numerous works, see his autobiography, *al-Taḥadduth*, *passim*.
125. Zoubeir, *Ahmad Baba*, has a list of Aḥmad Bāba's works which updates Hunwick, 'A new source' (see especially p. 128).
126. Unfortunately, Zoubeir did not classify the works according to their subject matter.
127. *Jami' al-Mi'yār* is a collection of *fatwas* or rulings on various aspects of Muslim law. Cf. Zoubeir, *Ahmad Baba*, p. 125.
128. These are *Jalb al-Ni'ma* and *Jawāb 'an al-Qawānīn al-'Urfiyya*, both to be discussed in Chapter 5.
129. This classification of Aḥmad Bāba's works is not complete. Not all the extant works were accessible in the course of this study. The subject matter of others, known only by the title, is uncertain.
130. This is according to Sīdi Aḥmad b. 'Ali al-Sūsi as quoted in al-Qādiri, *Nashr al-Mathāni*, p. 152.
131. Paris: Bibliothèque Nationale, Fonds Arabes, MS 5442, fos 249r. Some of the earlier linguists, however, including Sībawayh, are quoted indirectly.
132. Aḥmad Bāba, *Kifāyat al-Muḥtaj*, fo. 292.
133. Askia Daūd kept a royal library at Gao. See *Tārīkh al-Fattāsh*, p. 94.
134. Aḥmad Bāba, *Nayl*, pp. 93–5. See also al-Sa'di, p. 37 (tr. 61). Commenting on books, in the margins, was in most cases a preliminary for writing a full-fledged commentary.

135. Aḥmad Bāba, *Nayl*, pp. 93–5. Al-Sa'di, p. 42.
136. Al-Qādiri, *Nashr al-Mathāni*, p. 152. One book which has been preserved in Morocco from the library of Aḥmad Bāba is volume 22 of Ibn Sīda's *Muḥkam fi'l-Lugha*, see fo. 981.
137. See Leo Africanus (John Leo), *A geographical historie*, p. 287.
138. See Aḥmad Bāba, *Nayl*, pp. 340–2. Al-Sa'di, p. 44. Baghayughu's students did not always return the books, it seems, but the master continued to be liberal despite the great loss.
139. See *Tārīkh al-Fattāsh*, p. 108. Elsewhere (p. 103) this source mentions that 50 to 80 *mithqāls* was the price of the more desirable slaves.
140. Ibn Sīda, *Muḥkam fi'l-Lugha*, vols 17–18, fo. 244; vol. 19, fo. 168; vol. 20, fos 278–9; vol. 22, fo. 981; vol. 23, colophon. The last folios of each volume actually carry the text of the agreement between owner and copyist. The colophon of the last volume indicates that the book came into the possession of Aḥmad Bāba's son Muḥammad.
141. See Anonymous 'Acte du vente'. This includes the text and translation of a purchase contract found at the end of a Timbuktu copy of *Sharḥ al-Aḥkām*. It is not clear where this copy has since been deposited.
142. Henry Barth, *Travels and discoveries*, vol. V, p. 43.
143. For example, Aḥmad Bāba relies rather extensively in his *Jalb al-Ni'ma* on Ibn Khaldūn's *Kitāb al-'Ibar*, a voluminous and unconventional work which nonetheless found its way to Timbuktu in the sixteenth century.
144. See, for example, the biography of al-Maghīli in Aḥmad Bāba, *Nayl*, p. 230.
145. In fact both commentaries were on al-Maghīli's *rajz* in that field. See Aḥmad Bāba, *Nayl*, pp. 93–5, 399.
146. Aḥmad Bāba, for example, studied *Naẓm Abu Muqra'* in astronomy. The author (flourished *c.* 1331 A.D.) composed another *Unẓūma* on the hours. Another work studied in astronomy was al-Tajūri's (d. 1590) commentary on *al-Hāshimiyya*. The *Muqaddima* by al-Tājuri is on the seasons. Cf. Hunwick, 'A new source', especially p. 583 and n. 145.
147. The author of *Tadhkirat al-Nasyān* (pp. 86–7) quotes Muḥammad al-'Irāqi following a composition by Sa'īd b. Muḥammad b. Muḥammad Gurdu. Geneologically (being the seventh-generation ancestor of an early-twentieth-century figure) Muḥammad al-'Irāqi seems to have flourished *c.* 1650, but he is mentioned neither by al-Sa'di nor by *Tārīkh al-Fattāsh*. Cf. Marty, *Etudes sur l'Islam*, vol. II, p. 17.
148. See, for example, al-Sa'di, p. 217 and *Tadhkirat al-Nasyān*, p. 5. It is probable that a yearly record of the Niger flooding towards Timbuktu was kept.
149. See Chapter 2, note 147.
150. See al-Sa'di, p. 218. Cf. Hunwick, 'A new source', p. 583, n. 147.
151. See al-Sa'di, p. 218.
152. Al-Sa'di, pp. 49, 218. Muḥammad Bāba also commemorated his teachers, Muḥammad Baghayughu and 'Abd al-Raḥmān al-Mujtahid, in two separate poems.
153. *Tārīkh al-Fattāsh*, pp. 178–9. Al-Sa'di, p. 21, paraphrases the *Maqāmāt*.
154. See Mawlāy Qāsīm b. Mawlāy Sulaimān, *Dhikr al-Wafayāt*.
155. See Aḥmad Bāba, *Nayl*, pp. 217–8. Al-'Āqib al-Anṣamuni's study under al-Suyūṭi (d. 1505) lends credence to an early *floruit*. Al-'Āqib b. Maḥmūd b. 'Umar may have been named after him, in which case the relations between al-Anṣamuni and Maḥmūd would date as early as 913 A.H. (1507/8 A.D.).
156. *Ibid.*; also al-Sa'di, p. 41.
157. This according to a nineteenth-century tradition peculiar to the defective MS C of *Tārīkh al-Fattāsh*, p. 58. There seems to be some basis for this tradition in the case of Jenne. Cf. al-Sa'di, p. 18.
158. Aḥmad Bāba, *Nayl*, pp. 217–8. Al-Sa'di, p. 41.
159. See, for example, *Tadhkirat al-Nasyān*, p. 21.

160. Aḥmad Maghia's Walāta origin is known only from traditions recorded in the twentieth century. See Marty, *Etudes sur l'Islam*, vol. II, p. 18.
161. Al-Sa'di, p. 30.
162. See al-Sa'di, pp. 55–6, 219, 246–247. Al-Amīn b. Aḥmad died at an old age in 1041 A.H. (1631/2 A.D.) but he and 'Abd al-Raḥmān belonged to the same generation as Aḥmad Bāba.
163. See al-Sa'di, p. 211. See also Chapter 6.
164. Al-Sa'di, pp. 36, 52–6.
165. The last-named had a deputy and close friend in 'Abd al-Salām b. Muḥammad Dikko al-Fulāni who also belonged to the first rank among scholars. See al-Sa'di, p. 241. Dikko is a *nisba* to the warrior clan of chiefs among the Fulānis.
166. Al-Sa'di, p. 215. The Zagharāni *nisba*, though possibly referring to Zāgha, also designates certain Songhai officials (see, for example, al-Sa'di, p. 160).
167. See al-Sa'di's obituaries, pp. 210ff., especially p. 240. On the antiquity of the Kel Antasar (Kel Ansar), see *infra.*, Chapter 5.
168. The two brothers may be grandsons of Aḥmad al-Ṣaqali on their mother's side. In that case, al-Shaikh Muḥammad b. 'Uthmān could be the highly praised scholar Muḥammad b. 'Uthmān b, 'Abdullāh b. Abu Ya'qūb. See al-Sa'di, pp. 36–7, 166–7.
169. *Ibid.*, p. 167. The delegation, sent by al-Qāḍi 'Umar, was headed by his nephew Shams al-Dīn b. Muḥammad b. Maḥmūd.
170. Al-Sa'di, p. 322 (tr. p. 488).
171. See *Tadhkirat al-Nasyān*, p. 148. Compare with al-Sa'di, p. 35.
172. Qāsim b. Sulaimān, *Dhikr al-Wafayāt*, especially fo. 24r.
173. See Marty, *Etudes sur l'Islam*, vol. II, pp. 6–30. More on these notables below.
174. The title of '*Ālim* (scholar) or *Faqih* (jurist) continues to be more prestigious, but both became interchangeable with Alfa.
175. A grandson of Aḥmad Bāba, Muḥammad b. al-Faqīh Sīdi (Muḥammad) b. Aḥmad Bāba, is described as Shaikh al-Maddāḥīn in the Sankore quarter. See *Tadhkirat al-Nasyān*, pp. 72, 64.
176. This discussion is partly based on Dupuis-Yakouba, *Industries*, and Hacquard, *Monographie*, especially pp. 40–4.
177. *Tārīkh al-Fattāsh*, p. 180.
178. In the late nineteenth century to the present, the tailor–Alfas worked primarily in embroidery, but in earlier times they practised more widely in the textile trade.
179. See Dupuis-Yakouba, *Industries*. Hacquard, *Monographie*, p. 44, suggests a larger number of 'ateliers'.
180. See Barth, *Travels and discoveries*, vol. V, pp. 19ff. Cf. Miner, *The primitive city*, p. 62.
181. See *Tadhkirat al-Nasyān*, p. 4. The anonymous author was descended on his mother's side from a scholar named al-Faqīh Muḥammad b. Muḥammad b. Abu Bakr Ṣādiq.
182. Dupuis-Yacouba, *Industries*, p. 179.
183. See Leo Africanus (Jean-Leon l'Africain), *Description de l'Afrique*. As already indicated, Leo confuses Timbuktu with the Songhai capital.
184. See *Tārīkh al-Fattāsh*, pp. 23, 55. Such claims, peculiar to MS C, tended to rationalize the reduction of certain tribes and villages to servile status in the nineteenth century.
185. See al-Sa'di, pp. 87–8 on the austerity of Askia Muḥammad.
186. *Tārīkh al-Fattāsh*, p. 82. Al-Sa'di (pp. 33–4) says: 'No sooner was [Muḥammad] born than he had already a thousand *mithqāls* in his property from the gifts of men who were happy at the arrival of a first-born to Abu'l-Barakāt al-Faqīh Maḥmūd'. The gift came partly (or perhaps largely) from Askia Muḥammad.
187. *Tārīkh al-Fattāsh*, p. 115. It is not clear whether these farms were in the form of a permanent endowment (*hubūs*) nor do we know their number or locality.
188. See al-Sa'di, p. 47.

189. See *Tadhkirat al-Nasyān*, for example, p. 117, p. 146, for the years 1738 and 1740, respectively.
190. *Ibid.*, p. 146.
191. Barth, *Travels and discoveries*, vol. V, p. 89. Al-Bakkā'i's nephew Hammādi, who rivalled him for the leadership of the Kunta, received an additional ten slaves, besides the same quantity of grain.
192. *Tārīkh al-Fattāsh*, pp. 180–1.
193. The Ruma have never produced a full-fledged scholar, though, as we shall see, some of the Pashas sought to adopt that posture.
194. Muḥammad b. Aḥmad Baghayughu died in 1066 A.H. (1655 A.D.). Al-Sa'di, p. 322.
195. At a rate of 5–10 cowries per student, the donations of the students allegedly amounted to 1725. This suggests that Takariyya had as many as two or three hundred students.
196. Cissoko, *Tombouctou et l'Empire Songhay*, p. 160.
197. In the sixteenth century, a *mithqāl* may have purchased as little as 500–1000 cowries. In the eighteenth century, the value of a *mithqāl* ranged between 2000 and 3000 cowries, the exchange rate of 700 in 1711 being exceptional. See *Tadhkirat al-Nasyān*, especially p. 40.
198. See Marty, *Etudes sur l'Islam*, vol. II, p. 84. An average of 20 students per elementary school is suggested there.
199. *Tārīkh al-Fattāsh*, pp. 145–6. Cf. Raymond Mauny, *Tableau*, pp. 495–503.
200. *Tārīkh al-Fattāsh*, pp. 150–1. The source offers the following breakdown of boats available at short notice in and around Gao: 400 large boats belonging to the Askiate; 1000 large boats under provincial officials and some 600–700 boats, some large and some small, belonging to merchants and other inhabitants of Gao. The large boats (*kanta*) are believed similar to the boat in which Caillié travelled to Timbuktu, a large canoe which carried a load of some 80 tons. See M. Tymowski, 'Le Niger', especially p. 87. Also René Caillié, *Journal d'un voyage*, vol. II, pp. 240–5.
201. See Barth, 1890, II, p. 322. Also Oscar Lenz, *Timbouctou*, p. 150. Caillié's estimate of 12 000–13 000 (*Journal d'un voyage*, vol. II, p. 312), was made in the hottest month of April when commerce was at its lowest ebb in the aftermath of the insecurity caused by the Fulāni conquest.
202. See Barth, 1890, II, p. 322. Lenz was given to believe that the city possessed 3500 houses. He, however, attributed this figure to an earlier period. Barth estimated a total of some 1000 houses along with a few hundred huts. A count based on an aerial photograph by Miner (*The primitive city*, p. 15) produced a similar result.
203. Since these remains cover a rather extensive area, it seems doubtful that they all formed part of the compactly built-up city. They may have been merchant houses which were used during, and even before, the Songhai period. Excavation may answer this question with the proviso that even the stone used by the masons in the area is of a soft quality and is believed to withstand the rains no more than a hundred years. Such stone used to be clay-coated, but mud bricks have always been the main construction material.
204. Barth (1890, II, p. 290), for example, mentioned the Sane Gungu quarter as inhabited by rich Ghadāmsi merchants on the southwest edge of the city. This quarter was no longer existent by the end of the century (see Miner, 1953, p. 37, for an alternative explanation).
205. See, for example, General Joffre, *My march to Timbuktu*, p. 95, for an estimate of 5000–8000. Hacquard, *Monographie*, p. 25, estimated 5000 'fixed' inhabitants in addition to a 'floating' population of some 4000. Now the population is generally, but very roughly, estimated at 10 000.
206. Caillié, *Journal d'un voyage*, vol. II, p. 331. The affiliations established by this traveller during his brief sojourn in Timbuktu suggest that his information on this question is quite reliable.

207. This discussion is based primarily on Dupuis-Yakouba, *Industries*, *passim*.

4. The scholars as administrators

1. The classical legislative process in Islam evolved two central principles concerning the governance of society and state in Islam. The first was the concept of the caliphate (*khilāfa*, or successorship to the prophet) and the second was the concept of the infallibility of the community of believers (*'ismat al-Umma*) on matters covered by consensus. Both of these concepts influenced future administrative and ideological developments but along lines which are most difficult to investigate. See, for example, Ibn Khaldūn, *Al-Muqaddima*, section VI, chapters 7, 9 and *passim*.
2. See al-Mawardi, *Al-Aḥkām*, *passim*. In fact, Ḥukm al-Maẓālim was often in the hands of the *Qāḍi* while the *Muḥtasib* was sometimes the latter's delegate as overseer of roadways and markets. See *Al-Muqaddima*, section III, chapter 31.
3. *Al-Muqaddima*, section VI, chapter 7.
4. To take one example, Mālik denied the validity of *bī'a* (or act of allegiance to a ruler) made under compulsion or duress. This stipulation was not strictly retained by his school but elements of the same orientation are perceptible in the Sūdān. *Ibid.*, section III, chapter 29.
5. See for example, Hodgkin, 'Islam and national movements', p. 323. The Almoravids, in Hodgkin's view, 'checked the possibility of the spread southwards from the Maghrib of "deviant" forms of Islam'.
6. We have no evidence on the sectarian identity of the early Islamic presence in Bornu. But by the late fifteenth century, there and in Hausaland, the emerging tradition of learning was Māliki.
7. Several recent studies have suggested a dominant role for the judge in early Muslim cities. See, for example, S. D. Gotein, 'Cairo: an Islamic city in the light of the Geniza documents', in Lapidus, *Middle Eastern Cities*, especially p. 91.
8. In some cases, the coexistence of the Shāfi'i, Ḥanafi and Māliki schools, represented each by its own judge, tended indirectly to reduce the influence of the main judge.
9. See *al-Muqaddima*, book I, section III, chapter 31.
10. See *Tadhkirat al-Nasyān*, p. 83.
11. See note 1, above.
12. Barth, 1890, II, p. 314.
13. Mūlāy (Sīdi) Aḥmad Bābīr, *Al-Sa'āda*, fos 49, 62.
14. See F. H. Ruxton, *Māliki law*, p. 275.
15. Al-Sa'di, pp. 15–6 and *passim*.
16. See above, pp. 38–9.
17. Al-Sa'di, pp. 16–9. Excepting Mur-Magha Kankoy, a Soninke scholar it seems, also migrating from near Bīṭu, al-Qāḍi Muhammad Sānu (Saghanughu) al-Wangari is the earliest known scholar from Jenne.
18. Al-Sa'di, pp. 158–9.
19. For the most part the scholars seem to have reconciled themselves by this time that the Ruma were there to stay. *Ibid.*
20. We have consistently assumed that scholars bearing Mūr (or Mūri) in their nomenclature are Soninke. *Tārīkh al-Fattāsh* (p. 48), says, 'Mūr Hūkār, the ancestor of the Mūri-Kuyra and their scholars, are all . . . originally from the West, Wa'kuri (Soninke) and Wankari'.
21. Al-Sa'di, p. 158.
22. *Ibid.*, *passim*. The genealogy of the al-Ḥājj family in Appendix 4 shows quite a few scholars, but most of these are known only by name.
23. Ruxton, *Māliki law*, pp. 273ff., especially p. 275. The Judge 'should not be too sharp and searching of eye'. See al-Sa'di, p. 40, for the comparison between al-Qāḍi

Muḥammad b. Maḥmūd, a master politician it seems, and his straightforward and fearless brother, al-Qāḍi al-'Āqib.

24. Ruxton, *Māliki law*, p. 275. The Judge should also be 'of a well-known and respected family'.
25. Al-Sa'di, p. 302.
26. When al-Sa'di was dismissed from the imamate of the Sankore Mosque in Jenne, al-Qāḍi Aḥmad b. Mūsa Dābu did not, it seems, intercede to prevent this highly unconventional action by a *ḥākim*. More details on this below. Al-Sa'di (p. 11) qualifies his high praise of the people of Jenne by saying that 'competition over worldly affairs was so much a part of their character that if one of them attained prestige, they all turned against him . . .'.
27. See Ruxton, *Māliki law*, p. 276. 'It is further expedient that the Qāḍi should have attached to the court the least possible number of officers and attendants . . . Within his jurisdiction, a Qāḍi cannot authorize a substitute unless the district is of very considerable area.'
28. Aḥmad Bāba, *Jalb al-Ni'ma.*
29. See above, p. 55. So far as we could tell, al-Sa'di has no reference to the Tusur Mundhu, a factor suggesting that his role was limited.
30. Aḥmad Bāba, *Nayl*, p.343.
31. Verbal communication by Sīdī Aḥmad Bābīr of Timbuktu.
32. We seem to have several cases of succession by favoured students; however, while their succession was not always direct, they were at times in-laws of the deceased judge.
33. The list in Appendix 1 is based on a sequence of sources and, so far as the latest judges are concerned, on information received during field research.
34. See Appendix 2 for a full breakdown of the family affiliations of judges.
35. Aḥmad Bāba, *Mi'raj al-Su'ūd*, Rabat: Bibliothèque Générale, MS D1724. Several other copies are extant. Also Zoubeir, *Ahmad Baba*, pp. 129ff.
36. *Ibid.* Zoubeir's analysis (p. 137) of Maḥmūd b. 'Umar's view emphasizes that the burden of proof lies upon the pretended owner rather than the slave.
37. See *Al-Maghili's replies.*
38. Al-Sa'di, p. 74. The Soninke Mūr Ṣāliḥ Jūr acted as intermediary between the Askia and the Mossi, to satisfy the prescription that 'pagans' be formally invited to Islam before the '*jihād*'.
39. Aḥmad Bāba, *Mi'raj al-Su'ūd*, and Zoubeir, *Ahmad Baba*, especially p. 138.
40. For example, Aḥmad Bāba, *Al-Lam'*.
41. See Aḥmad al-Nāṣiri, *Kitāb al-Istiqṣa*, vol. V, pp. 131–4.
42. Mounted charts of the inheritance shares (which are most complex) today dominate the rooms in which scholars in Timbuktu receive their visitors.
43. Many houses in the Jingerebir and Sarekeina quarters stand deserted and dilapidated today because, whether through disagreement or absence of the lawful heirs, the buildings were at some times unoccupied. Restoring such buildings is made difficult owing to the devastating effect of rains on mud-brick structure.
44. Aḥmad Bāba, *Nayl*, pp. 340–2.
45. See al-Sa'di, pp. 31, 96. And-Agh-Muḥammad al-Muṣalli was 'the greatest among the *shuhūd* of his Majlis'. Maḥmūd Bāghayughu served in a similar capacity *vis-à-vis* al-Qāḍi al-'Abbās Kab of Jenne.
46. The role of the *shuhūd* seems different from that of notaries who served as witnesses to legal deeds. Even the controversial document drawn in favour of the Ahl Mūri-Kuyra by Askia al-Ḥājj Muḥammad was witnessed by lesser literati than the *shuhūd.* See *Tārīkh al-Fattāsh*, p. 74.
47. See *Tadhkirat al-Nasyān*, p. 138.
48. *Ibid.*, p. 78. The attorney for the plaintiffs, the 'Ali al-Mubārak Ruma family, was Bāba b. Muḥammad Baghayughu (b. Gurdu).

49. This is certainly suggested by the events which took place at the time of the Moroccan conquest. See al-Sa'di, especially, pp. 155–6.
50. *Tārīkh al-Fattāsh*, p. 11. Other listed particulars of the Songhai system tended to favour the scholars as a whole.
51. To emphasize the plenipotentiary position of al-'Āqib, *Tārīkh al-Fattāsh* (p. 124) claims that this Judge ordered the pursuit and, presumably, the execution of a fleeing *mu'adhdhin* (mosque functionary) who was ostracised for having deliberately misrepresented a known phrase in praise of the Prophet. However, the wording of the text (and especially the final detail that 'they captured him after a year etc.') suggests caution in accepting this story. It seems to be an extension of an earlier paragraph, peculiar to MS C, which makes al-'Āqib 'beautiful of voice in reciting the Qurān as also Askia Daūd and his son Askia al-Ḥājj' (p. 123).
52. *Ibid.*, pp. 60–1.
53. Al-Sa'di, pp. 155–60 and *Tārīkh al-Fattāsh*, p. 122.
54. Recent studies have suggested wide powers for the Muḥtasib in Muslim cities, but Ibn Khaldūn (*al-Muqaddima*, section III, chapter 31) indicates that the Muḥtasib oversaw 'those laws whose implementation was beneath the *qāḍi*, because they were routine and simple'. The Ashra' Mundhu apparently held a similar position.
55. We are inclined to believe that the imprisonment of offenders in Songhai times was discharged by the Ashra' Mundhu.
56. Al-Sa'di, pp. 304–14.
57. *Tadhkirat al-Nasyān*, pp. 160ff.
58. Indeed, the Saharan approaches to Timbuktu being difficult to control, taxation was centred principally at Kabara.
59. *Tārīkh al-Fattāsh*, pp. 88–9. The jurist apparently invited the monarch to begin by punishing himself.
60. Al-Sa'di (pp. 99–100) tends to confirm *Tārīkh al-Fattāsh*, though very indirectly, on the confrontation between Askia Isḥāq and Maḥmūd Baghayughu.
61. *Ibid.*, p. 100. The two agents did not occupy an official fiscal post. Rather, they seemingly acted as spies for Isḥāq over the fortunes of the Timbuktu merchants.
62. See *Kano Chronicle*, vol. III, p. 110, for state-owned plantations manned by slaves in Hausaland.
63. See Jean Mansuy, *Maçons*, especially, p. 6. The masons also refer to a certain Misir Bīri, a Sanhāja, as founder of the corporation. Since Misir generally prefaces the names of Walātans, the two traditions seem to be the same. Compare with Mansuy pp. 15–6 on masons from Zāgha.
64. *Tadhkirat al-Nasyān*, p. 21.
65. Dupuis-Yakouba, 'Note sur la population', p. 236.
66. See R. Brunschvig, 'Urbanisme'.
67. See Mansuy, *Maçons*, p. 6. There were three circles of membership of the corporation it seems. Entry to the third, and highest, circle was attained at around the age of 50.
68. At times, the procession was accompanied by a body of Ruma soldiers.
69. The location of Timbuktu itself, let alone Kabara on the Niger, has always been considered unhealthy (at least in the rainy and flood season) for camels, and because of this, camels were driven back to the more arid encampment places as soon as they were unloaded.
70. See Anonymous, 'Act du vente'. The Judge, Muḥammad b. Muḥammad b. 'Ali Sili, may perhaps be the scribe's nephew. *Fatḥ al-Shukūr*, Paris: Gironcourt MS, fo. 17r.
71. See *Risālat Ibn Abu Zaid*, fo. 796 (colophon). I am indebted to J. O. Hunwick for directing my attention to this source, which is also listed in el-Kettani, 'les manuscrits'. The copyist is identified as Aḥmad b. Abu Bakr b. 'Ali b. Danbu Sili.
72. See Barth, *Travels and discoveries*, p. 23. The author mentions that the *mithqāl* of Mango, near Yendi, was 1¼ that of Timbuktu.

73. See Dubois, *Tombouctou la mystérieuse* p. 262. Also Miner, *The primitive city* pp. 19ff.
74. The relationships between these clans will be explored further below, especially in Chapter 6.
75. Particularly devastating were the internal struggles of 1148 A.H. (1735/6 A.D.). See *Tadhkirat al-Nasyān*, pp. 98–9.
76. Barābīsh and Arwāni notables who have settled in Timbuktu have always tended to settle in the Sankore quarter.
77. Miner, *The primitive city*, p. 21, is ambiguous on this point. He sees only Ruma and Ghabibi among the Songhai, designating the latter as 'serfs'. Yet clearly Maḥaman Tafa Idye, chief of the Sankore quarter at the beginning of this century, hardly qualifies as a serf. See Marty, *Etudes sur l'Islam* vol. II, pp. 24–5.
78. Hacquard, *Monographie*, p. 40, says: 'The various corporations have their chiefs or amirs but, excepting the amir of the butchers, their rights amount to very little'. Unfortunately, this author does not elaborate on the butchers either, except that the corporations standardized the prices to an extent. The special position enjoyed by butchers is also suggested by the fact that during Songhai times, they took over the Ma'Dughu (the old Malian government house) at the western edge of the city and transformed it into a slaughterhouse. See al-Sa'di, pp. 7–8.
79. In his list of the occupations, Dupuis-Yacouba, *Industries*, mentions also 'measurers of grain' and says that a measure was deposited in the hands of one of the descendants of the 'Kaya'.
80. *Ibid.* This source also mentions metal- and wood-workers (Dyam and Garasa), Tanners (Kuru-Mundyo), shoe-makers (Tamta-Koy), barbers and inn-keepers (Dyumudi, often the Teifa themselves). Hacquard, *Monographie*, p. 40, indicates that the tanners were a class on their own, being composed largely of craftsmen originally from Sasanding.
81. See al-Sa'di, p. 110. Also *Tārīkh al-Fattāsh*, p. 122. Neither source indicates when the Market Mosque was first built.
82. Mūlāy Aḥmad Bābīr quotes Sīdī al-Mukhtār al-Kabīr al-Kunti to the effect that every point of entrance to Timbuktu was guarded by the tomb of a *walī* and that Sīdi Yaḥya, buried in the centre of the city, was the *Quṭb* among all the *walīs*. This in a short composition entitled *Ṣifat Tunbuktu wa-Awliyā'uha Muḥīṭūn Biha*, MS in the possession of J. O. Hunwick. A similar account is to be found in Bābīr's *Al-Sa'āda al-Abadiyya*, *op. cit.*, pp. 92ff.
83. Lenz (*Timbouctou*, p. 151) in fact says that Sankore was completely outside the city at the time of his visit.
84. See Chapter 2, p. 24. See also al-Sa'di, p. 21.
85. Al-Bakri, *Al-Mughrib*, p. 175. Al-Idrīsi, *Ṣifat al-Maghrib*, p. 1ff.
86. The water generally rises enough to receive tolerably large boats at Kabara by early November. Smaller canoes make their way along the canal to Timbuktu in January and February. Hacquard, *Monographie*, *passim*. The canal leading from Kabara to Timbuktu is natural, but it has an artificial look about it on account of the custom whereby it is yearly cleared of sand when the Niger begins to swell towards the city.
87. Barth (1890, II, p. 324) learned that Badyindi (Bagindi) was fully flooded in an inundation which took place in or around 1640. The date is almost certainly in error; al-Sa'di records an exceptional flood reaching Timbuktu as early as November in the year 1616. See al-Sa'di, p. 221.
88. See, for example, Trimingham, *A history*, p. 98n, and Levtzion, *Ancient Ghana and Mali*, pp. 202ff.
89. See al-Sa'di, pp. 48–9, 51.
90. *Ibid.*, p. 63. For some reason, two other scholars declined the post at the time, though the imamate of Sankore was closely linked to the judgeship. Cf. *infra*.

91. *Tārīkh al-Fattāsh*, pp. 91–2, includes a list of the earliest *walīs*. Muḥammad al-Kāburi, 'Uthmān al-Kāburi, Mūri Hūkār, Bukāri Sunna, Muḥammad Tūli, Mūri Mana Bakua, Kusura Bir al-Wangari, Fudiki Muḥammad Sānu and Sanba Tanini all seem to be Malinke and Soninke scholars. Sīdi Yaḥya and a certain al-Faqīh Ibrāhīm (probably of the al-Ḥājj family) are the only *walīs* listed who would have been considered 'white'. Compare with al-Sa'di, *passim*.
92. Al-Sa'di, p. 48.
93. *Ibid.*, pp. 216–7. 'Ali Sili, a friend of al-Sa'di's father, was a grandson through a daughter of the Soninke Bāba Misir Bīru.
94. The kinship and intermarriage patterns suggest that the names Sili, Misir and Muri are Soninke.
95. See, for example al-Sa'di, p. 71. The last Askia before the Moroccan conquest is sometimes identified as Isḥāq al-Zagharāni, probably a *nisba* to his mother's descent. See *Tārīkh al-Fattāsh*, p. 133.
96. *Ibid.*, pp. 51–2. 'Abd al-Raḥmān became *imām* of Sankore.
97. *Ibid.* 'Abd al-Raḥmān Aqīt b. Maḥmūd Aqīt respected the Zagharānis, honouring the memory of his teacher, but others it seems did not.
98. *Ibid.*, p. 215.
99. See *Dhikr al-Wafayāt*, fo. 27v. Bamoy died in 1181 A.H. (1767/8 A.D.). *Tārīkh al-Fattāsh* mentions Mūri Bakr b. Ṣāliḥ Wangarab (p. 36) and we know historically of a certain Alfa 'Abdullāh b. al-Imām Ibrāhīm b. Muḥammād Wangarab. *Tadhkirat al-Nasyān*, p. 71, mentions a certain Alfa 'Abdullāh, son of the erudite Ag Muya Wangarab.
100. Al-Sa'di, pp. 35–6. It seems that a fraction of the Fulānis (the Jaghyati Fulāni) were at one point considered Wangara. According to one composition attributed to Aḥmad Bāba, 'the Fulanis are Muslims even though there are among them those whose conduct is unsatisfactory; evil-doings, treachery and raids predominate among them, but this does not disqualify them as Muslims'. See facsimile, fo. 516, included in the Appendix to Zakari Dramani-Issifou, *Les relations*, pp. 512ff.
101. Racial overtones, though not in a serious context, are present in a poem composed at the time of Barth's visit against Aḥmad b. Aḥmad b. Aḥmad Lobbo.
102. The Fulāni *Imāms* of Jingerebir included principally the Gidadus, the Gurdu and, most recently, the descendants of the seventeenth-century settler Muḥammad al-'Irāqi. This last family, as Marty (*Etudes sur l'Islam*, vol. II, p. 17) observed, became 'naturalized Fulani'. The present *Imām* of Jingerebir, Alfa Humal, belongs to this family.
103. *Tadhkirat al-Nasyān*, p. 75. *Dhikr al-Wafayāt*, *passim*, also records the obituaries of a few prominent *mu'adhdhins*.
104. Caillié, p. 340. 'There are five mosques [besides Jingerebir, Sankore and Sīdi Yaḥya] . . ., but they are small and built like private homes, with the exception that each is surmounted by a minaret; all of them have an inner court'.
105. Barth, 1890, vol. II, p. 324.
106. See al-Sa'di, p. 146. The Qaṣba Mosque, and partly the Qaṣba, survived until 1185 A.H. (1771/2 A.D.). See *Dhikr al-Wafayāt*, fo. 28v.
107. See al-Sa'di, p. 205. In fact, *fanā'* also means courtyard and, in another sense, has mystical Sufi connotations.
108. This tradition, widely adopted in Timbuktu, is also reported by Mūlāy Aḥmad Bābīr in *al-Sa'āda al-Abadiyya*, fo. 93. However, *Dhikr al-Wafayāt* (fo. 28v) does not mention any such calamity in connection with the ruin of the mosque.
109. In fact, the mosque was built under the auspices of the Pasha 'Ali b. 'Abd al-Qādir who, as we shall see, sought to establish a dynasty independent of Morocco. See al-Sa'di, p. 232.
110. Ibn Khaldūn, *al-Muqaddima*, section III, chapter 31.
111. *Tadhkirat al-Nasyān*, p. 83, mentions that Bāba b. Muḥammad b. Muḥammad

Baghayughu b. Gurdu was invested as *imām* of the Market Mosque by al-Qāḍi al-Mukhtār b. al-Qāḍi Muḥammad (Zankanu).

112. See, for example al-Sa'di, p. 113, on the transfer of state property from Sunni 'Ali to Askia Muḥammad.
113. Al-Sa'di himself (*ibid.*, p. 235) acted as witness on some occasions. Sometimes when a Pasha refused to submit to deposition, the *imām* found himself in a difficult position. See *Tadhkirat al-Nasyān*, p. 44.
114. *Tārīkh al-Fattāsh*, p. 131, mentions '*imāms* of the mosques', but does not specify which mosques were involved.
115. *Tadhkirat al-Nasyān*, p. 90. The mosque of the Qaṣba is also mentioned in this connection, but none of the others.
116. Barth, *Travels and discoveries*, vol. V, p. 81. The Lobbo sovereigns allegedly also 'increased the ruin of Sankore'.
117. An anecdote is recorded by al-Sa'di (p. 47) suggesting that Sīdi Yaḥya preferred to teach pupils of his own quarter, in the centre of town, where learning was not as widespread as at Sankore.
118. Al-Sa'di, compare pp. 56–63 with p. 309.
119. 'Abdullāh Bābīr b. al-Qāḍi Sayyid Aḥmad b. Ibrāhīm b. 'Abdullāh b. Aḥmad Maghia became *imām* in 1155 A.H. (1742/3 A.D.) and later retained the post when he became Judge in 1162 A.H. (1748/9 A.D.). See *Tadhkirat al-Nasyān*, pp. 83, 148.
120. Al-Qāḍi Sayyid Aḥmad b. And-Agh-Muḥammad took over the imamate of Sankore after having become Judge. See al-Sa'di, p. 63.
121. *Ibid.*, p. 60. A scribal error may be involved. Possibly the *imām's* name was Aḥmad Nāna Surgu.
122. *Ibid.*, pp. 59–60.
123. *Ibid.* This presumably explains why an individual whose family is not otherwise mentioned could attain such a high post.
124. *Ibid.*, pp. 61–2.
125. The title Commander of the Faithful is applied sparingly in the chronicles and would seem to have extended only theoretically to Askia Muḥammad's successors.
126. Al-Sa'di, p. 60.
127. *Ibid.*, p. 62.
128. *Ibid.*, p. 309. The text has Duku ('Abd al-Salām b. Muḥammad), but current pronunciation renders the name Dikko.
129. Al-Sa'di, p. 142; Barth, 1890, II, p. 324.
130. There exists some ambiguity concerning the Alfasin Kunda; the Fāsiyyīn eventually came to be identified with the Jingerebir quarter. Cf. Hacquard, *Monographie*, pp. 1–2 and *Tadhkirat al-Nasyān*, *passim*.
131. Today there exists a small mosque at Sarekeina, in the east-central part of the quarter, not larger than the houses there, which is presided over by an *imām* believed to be of Ruma descent.
132. In a sense, the Qaṣba Mosque was an extension of Jingerebir, for the exclusive use of the soldiery. See al-Sa'di, p. 146.
133. The two Waddāni families were descended from al-Hādi al-Waddāni, whose son Santā'u was once *imām* of Sankore, and from Muḥammad Tashfīn al-Waddāni. See, for example, *Tadhkirat al-Nasyān*, pp. 75, 85 and 115. (Also p. 152 on Bāba al-Mukhtār b. Muḥammad, a Zankanu.)
134. *Ibid.*, p. 83.
135. *Ibid.*, p. 47. The three markets probably served each of the three main quarters – Sankore, Jingerebir and Sarekeina.
136. The earliest reference to a chief of a quarter (in this case a 'Shaikh') dates to 1211 A.H. (1796/7 A.D.) and implicates Sarekeina. See *Dhikr al-Wafayāt*, fo. 33v. Cf. *Tadhkirat al-Nasyān*, p. 72.

137. In Gao a special status had been allotted to a family of *sharīfs* there in the sixteenth century. The elder is identified as ‘Ali b. Aḥmad, presumably son of Aḥmad al-Ṣaqali. See *Tārīkh al-Fattāsh*, p. 107. The detail is confirmed by the authentic MSS A and B, though MS C makes its own additions on the subject. Cf. *Tadhkirat al-Nasyān*, especially p. 29 on the Sharīfs of Timbuktu.
138. See Hacquard, *Monographie*, p. 60. The presence of the dyers from Sasanding appears strictly to be the result of a nineteenth-century development.
139. More on this below in Chapter 6.
140. See, for example, Marty, *Etudes sur l'Islam*, vol. II, pp. 6–25. Idji originally means ‘son’. The obituaries of a few notables identified by this ‘surname’ are featured from the mid-eighteenth century onwards in *Dhikr al-Wafayāt* (see especially fo. 33r). In the *Tadhkirat al-Nasyān* (especially pp. 180ff), the lines of descent backwards to the Askias are fully specified.
141. Mali, Archives, ‘Notes’. Also, Marty, *Etudes sur l'Islam*, vol. II, p. 24.
142. *Ibid.* (Mali Archives, Dec. 1893, indicates that Alfa Sa‘īd had once been chief of Sarekeina). Also, Marty, *Etudes sur l'Islam*, vol. II, p. 17.
143. See especially Marty, *Etudes sur l'Islam*, vol. II, p. 21.
144. *Ibid.*, pp. 24–5; Mali, Archives, ‘Notes’.
145. Marty, *Etudes sur l'Islam*, vol. II, p. 17, says that Alfa Sa‘īd, while chief of Sarekeina presumably, had been put in charge of imposts on the salt-trade by Hamdia sometime after November 1893, when the latter became chief of Timbuktu.
146. Al-Sa‘di, pp. 60–1.
147. Barth, 1890, vol. II, pp. 340–45. A *mithqāl* could indeed purchase some 300–400 pigeons, birds widely bred for local consumption.
148. We do not know the sequence of *imams* at Sankore prior to Maḥmūd b. ‘Umar. See al-Sa‘di, pp. 62–3.
149. *Ibid.*, p. 47.
150. *Ibid.* The French translation (pp. 77–8) offers an alternate reading. Elsewhere (Arabic, p. 34), al-Sa‘di emphasizes the wealth of ‘Abd al-Raḥmān's brother, ‘Abdullāh, and adds: ‘As for . . . ‘Abd al-Raḥmān, he turned away from the affairs of this world altogether; he would not accept them even for a moment. He had *mukāshafāt* and the people of his school relate many stories about that . . . .’
151. See, for example, *Tadhkirat al-Nasyān*, p. 87, on Sān Alfa Aḥmad b. Aḥmad Tagh (Baghayughu) al-Wangari.
152. Al-Mawardi, p. 101. A *ḥāfiẓ* (pl. *ḥuffāẓ*) is someone widely read in the Qur'ān and the *Tafsīr*.
153. See, for example, *Tadhkirat al-Nasyān*, p. 138.
154. *Dhikr al-Wafayāt*, fos 28v, 31r, 34r.
155. See especially al-Sa‘di, p. 156. At that time, the Sharīfs had apparently a recognized chief (Shaikh al-Muwalladīn) in ‘Umar (b.Zayyān?) b. Aḥmad al-Ṣaqali.
156. See Aḥmad Bāba, *Nayl*, pp. 217–8, 343–4. Al-Balbāli had other *nawazil* with Muḥammad b. Aḥmad b. ‘Abd al-Raḥmān al-Yastani al-Fasi (p. 338).
157. Al-Mawardi, *Al-Aḥkam*, p. 103.
158. One other Anṣamuni scholar, Al-Najīb b. Muḥammad al-Kidawi was a commentator on Khalīl and al-Suyūṭi who flourished up to the early sixteenth century. See Aḥmad Bāba, *Nayl*, p. 348. Cf. Norris, *The Tuaregs*.
159. Aḥmad Bāba, *Ajwiba*, fo. lr.
160. Tobacco apparently first reached Walāta from the Sūdān. See *Receuil de Textes de Touat*, fo. 201r.
161. More on this in Chapter 6 below.
162. Al-Sa‘di, pp. 59, 75. Fayyāḍ was one of the *shuhūd* of Maḥmūd b. ‘Umar.
163. For example, the author of *Tadhkirat al-Nasyān* refers to his own great-grandfather, an elementary school teacher, as Alfa al-Amīn b. Muḥammad Mūdu (mis-spelt Sūdu,

p. 4). Likewise, his grandfather was Alfa al-Amīn. Yet, he refers to his own elementary school teacher as al-Faqīh Aḥmad al-Muryani (p. 96).

164. Compare *Tadhkirat al-Nasyān*, pp. 61, 72.
165. *Ibid.*, *passim.* We have no evidence on learning among the Shurfa prior to 'Abd al-Qādir al-Sanūsi and Sān Sirfi.
166. See, for example Marty, *Etudes sur l'Islam*, vol. II, pp. 10ff. By the nineteenth century, in fact, learning alone sustained the influence of the Shurfa.
167. *Tadhkirat al-Nasyān*, pp. 111ff.
168. 'Timbuktu Notables, *Letter to the French Government*'.
169. 'Timbuktu Jamā'a, *Letter to Aḥmad al-Bakkā'ī*'. The formal reference to whites and blacks is also found in the above-mentioned letter to the French government.
170. Timbuktu Notables, *Letter to Mūlāy al-Ḥasan.*
171. Timbuktu Notables, *Letter to French Governor-General.*

5. *The scholars as regional notables*

1. See Gray C. Boyce, 'Erfurt schools'.
2. Helene Wieruszowski, *The medieval university*, p. 67.
3. S. M. Stern, 'The constitution', p. 33.
4. Richard Bulliet, *The patricians*, *passim*, especially p. IX.
5. Carl Petry, *Autonomy*, to be published by Princeton University Press. I am grateful to Dr Petry for allowing me to consult his MS.
6. Al-Sa'di, p. 141.
7. See 'Umar al-Naqar, 'Takrur'.
8. Al-Shinqīṭi (*al-Wasīt*, pp. 422–3) argued that his Saharan town belonged to the Maghrib rather than the Sudan on the grounds that its scholars in Mecca and Medina, when on the pilgrimage, were qualified to draw upon the resources of the Maghribi *waqf* (endowments).
9. The Songhai traced a line of descent from Za al-Ayman, believed to have migrated in obscure times from Yemen. See, for example, al-Sa'di, p. 4.
10. See al-Sa'di, p. 7.
11. See Norris, *The Tuaregs*, p. 115.
12. Al-Sa'di, p. 22. The author no doubt meant that the Sanhāja in Massina, with the exclusion of the Fulānis, were originally from the area of Tishīt.
13. Al-Bartīli, *Fatḥ al-Shukūr*, Nouakchott MS, fos. 59r–60v.
14. See al-Sa'di, p. 35, p. 108. On genealogical grounds (allowing a thirty-year average between generations) Muḥammad b. Yadghūr was a direct descendant of Muḥammad Gāb.
15. Walāta Jamā'a, *Letter to Aḥmad al-Madani*. In this case, the pressure was exerted against the notables of Walāta so that they would (as seems to have subsequently happened) acknowledge the sovereignty of Aḥmad al-Madani's 'Umarian state in Segu.
16. Al-Bartīli's *Fatḥ al-Shukūr*, of course, exemplifies this sense of belongingness.
17. See especially A. D. H. Bivar and M. Hiskett, 'The Arabic literature'.
18. Though renovated in various periods, the Main Mosque of Jenne owes its origin, at the latest, to the sixteenth century. Al-Sa'di (pp. 18–9) indicates that Muḥammad Sānu al-Wangari, the first known Judge of the city, was buried at the mosque.
19. Al-Sa'di, p. 249.
20. *Wafayāt Jenne: 1164–1180* A.H. In this document, as in the *Tadhkira* and the *Dīwān*, the Ruma are featured far more pronouncedly than is justified by the evidence of earlier and later sources.
21. See Brown, *The Caliphate*, *passim.*
22. Al-Bartīli, *Fatḥ al-Shukūr*, Paris: Gironcourt MS, fo. 17r.

23. *Ibid.*, Nouakchott MS, fos 81r–83v.
24. This is evident from the nomenclature of Walāta notables whereby the pedigrees of al-Bartīlis, Maḥjūbis and Muslimis, for example, show the scholars of each clan to be only distantly related to each other. Cohesiveness, nonetheless, in each group is emphasized by the recourse in most cases to a most elaborate genealogical nomenclature.
25. Max Weber, *Economy and Society*, vol. III, p. 1231. The precommunal 'stage' persisted in Islamic times, according to Weber, 'wherever the autonomy of the city and its patriciate was not, as in large territorial states, completely destroyed by the monarchy'.
26. See, for example, Jack Goody, 'The impact'.
27. See Sanneh, 'The origins'. As early as the eleventh century, al-Bakri (*Al-Mughrib*, p. 177) mentioned that no Muslims lived in the Kingdom of Ghuruntul 'but they are well-received there and people step out of their way to allow them passage'.
28. R. Jobson, *The golden trade* (London, 1623, p. 99), quoted in J. O. Hunwick, 'The influence', p. 34.
29. Al-Sa'di, pp. 266–7, 275.
30. Quoted in Norris, *The Tuaregs*, p. 86.
31. Al-Bartīli, *Fatḥ al-Shukūr*, Nouakchott MS, fo. 13v (biography of al-Ḥājj Aḥmad b. al-Ḥājj al-Amīn al-Ghalāli).
32. *Ibid.*
33. See al-Sa'di, *passim*, and *Tadhkirat al-Nasyān*, especially pp. 173–8.
34. Interviews with Alfadi Muḥammad, son of Muḥammad al-Amīn, son of Imām al-Suyūṭi, resident of Mopti. Also interview with Alfa Humal, *Imām* of Jingerebir, Timbuktu. It seems that Zayyān, father of Abu'l-'Abbas, was especially wealthy. Abu'l-'Abbas combined wealth with some learning, while his son Aḥmad Bāba, was especially noted for his learning and acumen.
35. Capt. L. Marc-Shrader, 'Quand j'étais Maire'.
36. See Ivor Wilks, *Travels of Wargee*.
37. A striking example is the problematical account recorded by Jackson from the information of a North-African merchant. James Grey Jackson, *An account of Timbuctoo*, *passim*.
38. René Caillié, *Journal d'un voyage* (London, 1830) vol. II, p. 53.
39. *Ibid.*
40. Lenz, *Timbouctou*, p. 154. Cf. Mardochée, 'Recit'.
41. Mali, Archives, 'Notes'.
42. *Ibid.* Among the 'foreign' merchants was Muḥammad al-Bashīr wuld 'Abd wuld al-Ḥarṭāni. As our source reads, 'he belongs to a merchant family of the Masā'id fraction of the Tajkant, which has had relations with Timbuktu for around eighty years . . . He has a great influence over the Tajkant and the Barabish, and possesses a fortune amounting to as much as 500,000 francs. He is the richest merchant at Timbuktu. He is married, has three children and five brothers, and all his family resides at Tindouf. He possesses houses at Timbuktu and at Arwān.' It seems almost certain that the family had been well represented at Timbuktu and Arwān before the French conquest. Its members had assisted Major Laing during his journey in 1825–6.
43. Barth (*Travels and discoveries*, vol. V, p. 48) mentions a Ghadāmsi merchant who died leaving an estate worth 2000 *mithqāls*. The merchant in this case was merely an agent of the Tīni family in Ghadāmis and the funds were repatriated to them.
44. *Ibid.*, vol. V, p. 34.
45. Al-Bakkā'i, *Two letters to al-Ḥājj 'Umar*, fos 66v–70r, especially fo. 69v.
46. Al-Sa'di (p. 60) suggests that Abu'l-Qāsim's family was established at Tuāt and Timbuktu at the same time.
47. One of the Waddāni families, descendent from Muḥammad Tashfīn, is known from notices on a few members, including al-Imām Maḥmūd b. al-Amīn b. Aḥmad b. Muḥammad. The Kuri family contributed *imāms* to the Hanā' mosque, including Bāba

Laṭuāj b. Bāba Aḥmad b. al-Muṣṭafa b. ‘Abdullāh al-Kūri. The Kūri *nisba* may have been interchangeable with ‘Kara’. See *Tadhkirat al-Nasyān*, pp. 75, 115.

48. See al-Sa‘di, p. 162.
49. Jackson, *An account of Timbuctoo*, p. 348.
50. *Ibid.*, pp. 464–5. Jackson, or some associate of his, actually used Ḥamed al-Wangari as a pen name in a letter to one of the European magazines.
51. Thus, for example, *Dhikr al-Wafayāt* (fo. 33r) mentions the death of Nāna bint al-Imām Aḥmad (al-Wangari), Imam of Sīdi Yaḥya, in 1214 A.H. (1799/1800 A.D.). Her father, al-Imām Aḥmad, may himself be our Ḥamed al-Wangari. See the genealogy of the Baghayughu family in the appendices. The repetition of the name Aḥmad is dramatized in the case of Alfa Aḥmad b. ‘Abdullāh b. Aḥmad Ṭāgh b. Ibrāhīm b. Aḥmad, a mid-eighteenth-century merchant *alfa* whose son, if named Aḥmad, may also be our Ḥamed al-Wangari. See *Tadhkirat al-Nasyān*, p. 87.
52. Wilks, ‘The transmission’, p. 171. A wealthier family often allowed the eldest son and sometimes even a sequence of sons, to become karamokos. ‘More commonly, however, older brothers are required by their father to trade and farm . . . and it is only a younger brother who can be released for studies.’
53. Al-Sa‘di, p. 33.
54. The fourth generation of Aqīts in Timbuktu produced at least nine full-fledged scholars, all sons of the two brothers Maḥmūd and Ḥājj Aḥmad. The fourth generation of Baghayughus, on the other hand, are represented by eight scholars who belonged to four different nuclear families all descended from Aḥmad b. Maḥmūd Baghayughu. See the genealogies in the appendices.
55. See *Tadhkirat al-Nasyān*, pp. 43, 145. The present-day *Imām* of Jingerebir, Alfa Humal, is descended through one of his female ancestors, a certain Yaya bint ‘Abd al-Raḥmān Suyūṭi, from Isma‘īl Yoro. Interview, July 11, 1978. See genealogy of the Gurdu family, *infra*.
56. Al-Sa‘di, p. 156. Alfa ‘Abdu is specifically identified as brother of al-Faqih ‘Abdullah b. al-Qādi Maḥmūd.
57. *Tadhkirat al-Nasyān*, p. 87.
58. Al-Sa‘di, pp. 50–1.
59. *Ibid.*, pp. 243–4.
60. *Tārīkh al-Fattāsh*, pp. 122–3. The wealth of the Kānu (Gānu) family is confirmed by al-Sa‘di, p. 211.
61. *Tārīkh al-Fattāsh*, p. 122.
62. Al-Sa‘di, p. 170.
63. See Aḥmad Bāba’s biography in Hunwick, ‘A new source’, p. 569.
64. Aḥmad Bāba, *Kifāyat*, fo. 290.
65. Wilks, *Travels of Wargee*, p. 180.
66. In the mid-nineteenth century the repair of the Sankore Mosque from a state of virtual ruin was financed by the Lobbo state at the insistence of al-Bakkā’i, to a total sum equivalent to 600 blocks of salt, or some 600–1000 *mithqāls*. This contrasts sharply with the evidence of earlier times when the expenses of the workers in a single day during the repairs amounted to 77 *mithqāls*. Compare *Tārīkh al-Fattāsh*, p. 122, with Barth, *Travels and discoveries*, vol. V, p. 82. It is quite clear that the mosque, and building in general, was on a much grander scale than in more recent times.
67. Al-Sa‘di, p. 170.
68. *Ibid.*, p. 171.
69. *Ibid.*, pp. 171–4. This complaint reached al-Manṣūr with al-Qā‘id Ḥammu b. Haq al-Dara‘i who himself was found to have ‘stolen’ 20 000 *mithqāls*.
70. Al-Sa‘di, p. 141. Iṣḥāq offered 100 000 *mithqāls* and 1000 slaves on the condition that the Moroccan army would return to Morocco.

71. Aḥmad Bāba, *Nayl*, pp. 243–4. Cf. *Tārīkh al-Fattāsh*, p. 178, especially the addition to the effect that religion and wealth 'are contradictory in meaning', peculiar to MS C.
72. Aḥmad Bāba, *Nayl*, p. 244, '*Wa-kāna mālan dha bāl.*'
73. Massina itself was probably not an importer of cattle, but the areas to the south and west are to this day.
74. Abu Bakr b. al-Qā'id Bāḥaddu al-Drāwi, *Sale of half the Farm Shurunburku.*
75. Juma (Alfa) b. Abṭallāh, sons thereof, *Sale of Farm Ashurfār.*
76. We do not know of any Abu Bakr b. al-Qā'id Baḥaddu either, but al-Qā'id (later al-Pasha) Baḥaddu b. Abu Bakr was foremost among the Ruma up to his death in 1189 A.H. (1775/76 A.D.). As explained in Chapter 6, the sequence of judges after al-Qādi Abkar's tenure is obscure, a factor suggesting that, even before that, the leaders of the Maghia and Zankanu families held the judgeship informally and perhaps conjointly.
77. See, for example, Robin Maugham, *The slaves*. This has no real information on the 'slaves' of Timbuktu.
78. Caillié, *Journal d'un voyage*, (English trans.), vol. II, p. 55.
79. Barth, *Travels and discoveries*, vol. V, pp. 36–7. The traveller mentioned the slave-trade incidentally at the tail-end of his account on the commerce of the city and was able to provide no details.
80. A survey of the various views is available in Aḥmad Bāba's *Mi'raj al-Su'ūd.*
81. Al-Sa'di, pp. 97–8. The official in question was later ostracized and, in flight, was captured and enslaved.
82. *Ibid.*, pp. 157–8.
83. *Ibid.*, p. 165. The Sanḥāja of Massina, who apparently intermarried with Fulānis and Zughrānis, are described as 'the Sanḥāja of the braided hair'.
84. *Ibid.*, pp. 52, 180.
85. This perhaps explains the all-encompassing *fatwa* advanced by al-Balbāli which has been mentioned in Chapter 4.
86. Indeed, even MS C purports to have been written by Maḥmūd Ka'ti who died in 1002 A.H. (1593/94 A.D.).
87. *Tārīkh al-Fattāsh*, p. 12.
88. The writer, presumably Ibn al-Mukhtār Qunbulu, prefaces his account of the sale of Ahl Mūri Kuyra by saying: 'Even this unique ruling [affirming the special rights of Ahl Mūri Kuyra], which al-Qāḍi Isma'īl said was still in force, was revoked after the death of Askia Muḥammad Bankanu b. Balma' al-Ṣādiq . . . by the people of Songhai'. We know from al-Sa'di (p. 299) that Bankanu b. al-Ṣādiq reigned as Askia in Timbuktu, under the auspices of the Ruma, till his death in 1052 A.H. (1642/43 A.D.) and was succeeded by his son Askia al-Ḥājj. The statement above implicitly blames the latter for compromising Ahl Mūri Kuyra, though their sale took place under his successor, Askia Hārūn b. Daūd b. Askia al-Ḥājj (1067–79 A.H. = 1656/56–1668/69 A.D.). It is remarkable that Hārūn is associated with commissioning the composition of a variant upon *Tārīkh al-Fattāsh*, which has been published in French translation as an Appendix (pp. 325–41) by Houdas and Delafosse. It appears almost certain that a seventeenth-century controversy over the status of Ahl Mūri Kuyra gave rise to variant copies of *Tārīkh al-Fattāsh* long before the drastic emendations which were introduced into the text in the early nineteenth century.
89. The legend was related to the present writer by Alfa Yaḥya Ibrāhīm of Timbuktu. Gurdu threated the *Imām* of Sankore that he would cause hair to grow on his palm if he insisted that his *protegé* should marry the maiden. The latter threatened, in turn, that he would cause Gurdu to disappear altogether. The rest of the story is ambiguous, but both threats were allegedly carried out successfully. The legend would make more sense if it pertained to Gidados (also Fulānis, and *imāms* of Jingerebir) rather than the Gurdu. For after the eighteenth century, they seem to have disappeared altogether from the annals and traditions of Timbuktu.

90. See *Tārīkh al-Fattāsh*, p. 107.
91. Barth, *Travels and discoveries*, vol. IV (very end of this volume) and (1890, II, p. 339).
92. Al-Sa'di, p. 170. Reference to an independent *ḥarrāt* (*ḥarṭān*). See note 42, above, for a usage of the Harṭāni *nisba* by a wealthy person.
93. Barth, *Travels and discoveries*, vol. IV, *passim* (1890, II, p. 286). Today Kabara has very few dwellings, though a modern building for storage is in planning.
94. Barth, *Travels and discoveries*, vol. V, p. 22. Wargee also noted that the northern caravans on reaching Arwān 'often separate, some going to Sasanding and Segu, some to Timbuktu'.
95. Jackson, *An account of Timbuctoo*, pp. 345–6. By contrast, the cost of escort through the Sahara, in addition to the taxation exacted by the Tuareg–Hassani clans, did not amount to more than 120 dollars.
96. Bonamy, *Mission de Bonamy*.
97. Barth, *Travels and discoveries*, vol. V, p. 10.
98. *Ibid.*, *passim*. In December, the influx of Saharans, including a 1000-camel caravan, had raised the price of corn from 6000 to 7500 cowries per *suniyya*, while the price of rice nearly doubled from 3750 to 6000 cowries in a few days. See vol IV, *passim* (1890, II, p. 333).
99. See Wilks, *Travels of Wargee* p. 184. Gunpowder cost two dollars per pound at Salaga and three at Timbuktu. It was taken north mainly by the merchants established at Kong.
100. Bonamy, *Mission de Bonamy*.
101. Wilks, *Travels of Wargee*, *passim*.
102. Summary of *Kitāb al-Tarā'if* by Paul Marty, *Etudes sur l'Islam*, vol. I, p. 32. A relative of al-Mukhtār found him in a humble state at Timbuktu, under the patronage of a certain 'Sarf Nacia al-Kouhini', and caused him to return to the Sahara against his wish.
103. Caillié, *Journal d'un voyage*, (English translation), vol. II, p. 70.
104. See Dupuis-Yacouba, *Industries*, shoe-makers (tamtaboy), The shoe-making profession was also featured in *Mission de 'Abd al-Qādir*.
105. This would seem to be an early-eighteenth-century, and perhaps even a seventeenth-century, development, to be discussed again in Chapter 6.
106. Hacquard (*Monographie*, p. 47), indicated that the sending of a slave to market amounted to 'a sort of liberation'. Elsewhere (p. 49), he says that many of the retailers were slaves and ex-slaves who live on what they earn. Rejou says he knew many 'slaves' (captifs) who were richer than their masters. See Commandant Rejou, 'Huit mois', pp. 421–2. A slave born to a family could not be sold and enjoyed rights of inheritance to his father's property.
107. Muḥammad al-Kunti, *Kitāb al-Tarā'if*, fos 137–40.
108. Marty, *Etudes sur l'Islam*, vol. II, p. 21.
109. Al-Sa'di, *passim*. See also genealogy in the appendices.
110. *Ibid.*, p. 258.
111. *Ibid.*, p. 254.
112. *Ibid.*
113. *Ibid.*, p. 293.
114. *Ibid.*, pp. 125, 129.
115. Maḥmūd b. Zarqun to al-Qadi 'Umar b. Maḥmūd Aqīt, Ar. text published in E. Levi-Provencal, 'Un document'.
116. Barth, *Travels and discoveries*, vol. V, pp. 99–100. The traveller describes the Inkundar as a clan of *ṭulba*, 'all able to read'.
117. See especially *Tadhkirat al-Nasyān*, pp. 51, 77.
118. Barth referred to the Wangara as the merchants 'who carry on almost the whole commerce with the countries south of the Niger'. (1890, II, p. 303).

119. See, for example, Muḥammad b. ‘Abdullāh al-Wufrāni, *Nuzhat*, pp. 115ff.
120. *Kano Chronicle*, pp. 104–5.
121. See Sanneh, ‘The origins’, pp. 59ff. Also a variant on Aḥmad Bāba’s *Mi‘rāj al-Su‘ūd*, included in facsimile in Dramani-Issifou, *Les relations*, pp. 512–21.
122. *Tārīkh al-Fattāsh*, pp. 179–80.
123. See, for example, Nehemia Levtzion, *Muslims and chiefs*, *passim*.
124. Lucie Gallistel Colvin, ‘Islam’.
125. John Ralph Willis, ‘The Torodbe clerisy’.
126. In the nineteenth century it was observed that ‘All gold countries, as well as any people coming from the gold country, or bringing Goroo [kola] nuts, are called *Wangara*’. Quoted in Paul E. Lovejoy, ‘The role’, p. 176.
127. See, for example, Hacquard, *Monographie*, p. 25. Everywhere the ‘*alfa*’ are distinguished from Ruma and Songhai, though no doubt the latter had some representatives, albeit of modest stature, among the former.
128. C. C. Stewart, ‘Southern Saharan scholarship’, especially p. 75.
129. *Tadhkirat al-Nasyān*, p. 63.
130. Stewart, ‘Southern Saharan scholarship’, p. 75.
131. Al-Bartīli, *Fatḥ al-Shukūr*, Paris: Gironcourt MS, fo. 17r.
132. Aḥmad Bāba, *Ajwiba*, *passim*.
133. The social differentiation became most formal and stable in the area of Shingīṭ. Yet a local author who described the system conceded that ‘Some of the people of the Zwāya too, in the south, have clients among the [dependent] Laḥma, and impose tribute upon them, and the same is true of some of the people of Tiris’. See Aḥmad b. al-Amīn al-Shingīti, *Al-wasīt*, p. 476.
134. Al-Bartīli, *Fatḥ al-Shukūr*, *passim*, includes the biographies of several Muslim scholars.
135. Norris, *The Tuaregs*, pp. 98–9. Indeed, the mid-nineteenth century chief of the Wulmdān, Quṭub, is known as son of al-Sultan Kāwi b. al-Sultan Amma b. al-Sultan Agashīkh b. al-Sultan Karidenna.
136. Al-Sa‘di, p. 312.
137. See Norris, *The Tuaregs*, p. 110. A further complication arises from the fact that the grandfather of Karidenna (see note 135 above) is known as Alad (Alladda, al-Adda?) al-Tadmekkatti. Both Agadda and Alad flourished around 1600 A.D.
138. *Tārīkh Arwān*. ‘They came to Arwān and lived there with the people of that town who were Maghsharen and Idnan . . . Then Aḥmad b. ‘Ali [here the text is damaged] married a woman from Kel Antassar’. A marginal comment says that the woman was from Idnan; ‘their sons were Muḥammad Ag Anfa, ancestor of Kel Antassar, and Aggina, ancestor of all the Arwān from whom the Keltina al-Ḥājj branch out’.
139. The sons of Muḥammad Aggina inherited the warrior chieftaincy. *Ibid.*
140. *Tārīkh Arwān* indicates that, after some time, the *kalima* (temporal rule) in Arwān went to Sayyid Muḥammad Bu-Umam, while the *kalima* among the Barābīsh went to his maternal uncles, Ahl Yūsuf Awlād Sulaimān.
141. *Za‘āmat Kunāta* (*Kunta*), fo. 3.
142. See, for example, Aḥmad al-Shingiṭī, *Al-wasiṭ*, pp. 506–9, on the wars of the Western Kunta. Later struggles between Kel Antassar and Kunta are the subject of epic poetry related to the present author by Wantaghat Ag esh-Shamasen ag al-Jou ag al-Qadid, the Agou (literally the ‘master-smith’, in practice ‘griot’) of the Kel Antassar.
143. See Marty, *Etudes sur l’Islam*, vol. I, p. 262. Also, *Tārīkh Kel Antassār*.
144. Al-‘Umari, selections of Arabic text in al-Munajjid, *Mamlakat*, p. 46. The evidence suggests that Yantasar designated a confederation of clans of whom some acknowledged Malian sovereignty. The confederations, Shighrasen (Yasighras), Madiunna and Lamtuna, are said to have been fully independent.
145. For example, Nūri Muḥammad al-Amīn, mentioned in note 147 below, is Ag

Muḥammad al-Amīn Ag Muḥammad al-Hādi Ag Interegan Ag Muḥammad al-Tayyib ag Hamma. The latter (Hamma = Khamma) was a chief of the Idnan who crossed over to the Kel Antasar during the dual reigns of Hualen and Dua Dua. Patrilineal succession among the Kel Antasar (but not seemingly the Idnan) dates at least nine generations backwards to *c.* 1600. Information of Abu Bakr al-Ṣādiq Ag Maḥamma-doun Ag Muḥammad Abba Ag Animaghan Ag Muḥammad al-Muṣṭafa Ag Quṭub (Qaitbou) Ag Muḥammad Ag Infa. Muḥammad Ag Infa is believed to be the common ancestor of all the Iguellad, including the Kel Antasar, Kel Haoussa (Kel Tabora) and Kel Cherfug (Esh-Cherifen).

146. In more recent times, up to the present, the Kel al-Sūq have been more or less uniformly literate and exceptionally skilled in calligraphy.
147. Information of Nūri Ag Muḥammad al-Amīn and others of Timbuktu. The place where the 'massacre' took place, due northwest of Timbuktu, is still remembered.
148. Quoted in Norris, *The Tuaregs*, p. 99.
149. Aḥmad al-Bakkā'i, *Two letters to al-Ḥājj 'Umar*, fos 66v–70v, especially fo. 67v.
150. The title roughly translates as follows: *Attaining grace and averting evil by avoiding tyrannical rulers.*
151. Al-Maqqari, *Rawḍat al-Ās*, p. 305.
152. Aḥmad Bāba, *Jalb al-Ni'ma.*
153. See Zoubeir, *Ahmad Baba*, pp. 156ff.
154. Aḥmad Bāba, *Ma Rawāh*. Only the first folio is extant. Cf. Zoubeir, *Ahmad Baba*, pp. 72–3, 109–10.
155. Aḥmad Bāba, *Jalb al-Ni'ma*, opening paragraph.
156. Aḥmad Bāba, *Ajwiba*, fo. 1r.
157. Aḥmad Bāba, *Jalb al-Ni'ma*, cites the authority of Ibn Rushd, Ṣaḥnūn and others on this subject.
158. *Al-Maghili's replies*, Mas'ala IV.
159. See, for example, 'Abd al-'Aziz al-Fishtāli, *Manāhil al-Ṣafa*, especially pp. 265ff.
160. *Al-Maghili's replies*, opening paragraph.
161. *Tārīkh al-Fattāsh*, p. 11. This statement is exclusive to the defective MS C, but its contextual relevance seems confirmed by an isolated folio which forms the beginning of MSA.
162. In old age, Askia Muḥammad was deposed by his son Mūsa and the latter was deposed by his cousin Muḥammad Bankānu b. 'Umar Kumzāghu. The old monarch did not concede till the ascension of his son Isma'īl who was ceremoniously invested. See *Tārīkh al-Fattāsh*, p. 86. The status of Askia Muḥammad in old age bears remarkable resemblance to that of the Malian king Mansa Mūsa II who, after being deposed by his vizier, became the subject of special public reverence (*marjuw li'l-Hidāya*). See Ibn Khaldūn, *Histoires des Berbères*, vol. II, p. 276.
163. *Tārīkh al-Fattāsh*, pp. 109–10. Balma' Jindi may conceivably have given its name to Badyindi.
164. *Ibid.*
165. *Ibid.*, p. 150. Al-Sa'di (p. 139) confirms that 'every reasonable advice that was given to [Askia Iṣḥāq and his generals] they threw behind their backs'.
166. See *Tārīkh al-Fattāsh*, pp. 108–9.
167. Institut Fondamental d'Afrique Noire, Fonds Brevié, cahier no. 7.
168. *Tārīkh al-Fattāsh*, pp. 113–4.
169. The anecdote is related in different sources. See, for example, al-Wufrāni, *Nuzhat*, p. 97.
170. See Dramani-Issifou, *Les relations*, p. 172.
171. Related to the present writer by Alfa Yaḥya Ibrāhīm of Timbuktu. Cf. Marty, *Etudes sur l'Islam*, vol. II, p. 7. Among the Dyula, the institution of the turban as a mark of distinction for the karamoko is attributed to al-Ḥājj Sālim al-Suwāri. See Wilks, 'The transmission', p. 169.

172. For al-Manṣūr's claims, see for example al-Maqqari, *Rawḍaṭ al-Ās*, p. 97.
173. Information of Alfa Yaḥya Ibrāhīm of Timbuktu. It seems doubtful that any Ruma would today identify themselves as 'Ulūj.
174. Testimony of Alfa Sālum, present-day *Imām* of Sankore, Timbuktu.
175. Related to this writer by Alfa Yaḥya Ibrāhīm and others in Timbuktu.
176. Though several traditionists are acquainted with the legend, none are aware of its context nor of which scholar, among the Gurdus, was involved.
177. More on this in Chapter 6.
178. Al-Bartīli, *Fatḥ al-Shukūr*, Nouakchott MS, fo. 69.
179. Al-Imām Sa'd al-Waddāni, *Al-Damlūk*, fos 201r–214v. This is a collection of treatises, mostly in verse, on tobacco and tea. MS 6399 bears the title of *Receuil de Textes de Touat*. A biography of Sa'd, including a reference to the fact that he authored several *fatwas*, is to be found in *Fatḥ al-Shukūr*, Paris: Gironcourt MS, fo. 35v.
180. See, for example, the reference to 'Abd al-Raḥmān (d. 1162 A.H.) b. al-Ḥabīb Bāba (d. 1114 A.H.) b. al-Imām Sa'd b. al-Ḥabīb Bāba b. al-Hādi al-Waddāni in *Dhikr al-Wafayāt*, fo. 1. Cf. *Tadhkirat al-Nasyān*, p. 9.
181. Al-Bartīli, *Fatḥ al-Shukūr*, Nouakchott MS, fos 33v–33r.
182. Al-Bartīli, *Fatḥ al-Shukūr*, *passim*. Aḥmad al-Zaidi's composition was entitled *Rawy al-Fishtātliyya*. This composition is of special interest because Aḥmad, and especially his father Muḥammad b. Mūsa b. Ijil, were products of the Timbuktu school.
183. Al-Bartīli, *Fatḥ al-Shukūr*, Paris: Gironcourt MS, fo. 35r. Elsewhere (fo. 16) al-Bartīli refers to Muḥammad Gurdu as 'the grandfather of Muḥammad Baghayughu (b. Muḥammad Baghayughu) who, in turn, was the *shaikh* of Sīdi Aḥmad Ag al-Shaikh'.
184. *Tadhkirat al-Nasyān*, p. 138.
185. Al-Bakkā'i, *Two letters to al-Ḥājj 'Umar*, fo. 69v.
186. Marty, *Etudes sur l'Islam*, vol. II, p. 14.
187. The Tuareg have always had a predilection for wearing numerous charms, usually verses from the Qur'ān enclosed in decorated leather amulets.
188. Barth says that the *alfa* or *mallam* 'is the confidential factotum of every Tarki chief'. Barth, 1890, II, p. 332.
189. One *alfa* today in Timbuktu is sought for healing the spiritual ills, or perhaps the psychological troubles, of people.
190. Mūlāy Aḥmad Bābīr, *Ṣifat Timbuktu*.
191. For example, Muḥammad b. Aḥmad Baghayughu al-Wangari, the mid-seventeenth-century commentator on al-Sanūsi, was considered *walī* after his death, but the location of his grave is no longer remembered.
192. See al-Maqqari, *Rawḍat al-Ās*, p. 313.
193. Aḥmad Bāba, *Nayl*, pp. 93–5. 'I saw after his death in the world of sleep one of my acquaintances who had died after him . . . He said: "Your father has been given more than has been given to Aḥmad b. Sa'īd, grandson of al-Faqīh Maḥmūd". He saw that I was surprised at that and he told me that he [was surprised] too. After that someone told me that he saw the same vision. He related it to me before I told him of my own, and my belief in it therefore increased.'
194. Al-Sa'di, p. 48.
195. *Ibid.*, p. 55. 'Stories which are of a similar nature about [Mūsa] are numerous.'
196. *Ibid.*, p. 173. *Tārīkh al-Fattāsh* (pp. 174–5) attributes a variant on the same story to the eye-witness testimony of Aḥmad Bāba.
197. See Chung-Li Chang, *The Chinese gentry*, *passim*.
198. Compare *Ibid.*, p. 32, with Ping-Ti Ho, *The ladder*, pp. 38–9.
199. Al-Sa'di, pp. 254, 293.
200. *Tārīkh al-Fattāsh*, p. 160.
201. Sān Sirfi became secretary under the scholar–*amir*, 'Abd al-Qādir al-Sanūsi.
202. Wilks, 'The African travels', pp. 156–163.

203. J. O. Hunwick, 'Ṣalīḥ al-Fulāni', unpublished article, kindly shown to this writer by the author.
204. Franz Michael in the introduction to Chang, *The Chinese gentry.*
205. See above, p. 150. *Za'āmat Kunāta.*
206. Willis, *The Torodbe clerisy*, p. 195.
207. The Centre Aḥmad Bāba has acquired a collection of *nawāzil*, entitled *Nawāzil al-Takrūr* which, however, deal with obscurantist rather than substantive issues in the law. The first collection of *nawāzil*, *Nawāzil Arwān*, was written by one of the Adda scholars.
208. Chang, *The Chinese gentry*, pp. 52ff. Also Robert Marsh, *The Mandarins*, especially p. 15. 'Of all the elites, only two per cent were actually in office.'
209. See especially Ho, *The ladder*, *passim.*
210. Al-Bakkā'i, *Two letters to Ḥājj 'Umar*, fo. 69.
211. Al-Sa'di, pp. 250–1.
212. Al-Bartīli, *Fatḥ al-Shukūr*, Nouakchott MS, fo. 36.
213. See, for example, Ho, *The ladder*, pp. 43ff.
214. Chang, *The Chinese gentry*, p. 13. 'The title of *en-chien-sheng* was sometimes granted also to descendants of early sages who were originally feng-ssu-sheng . . ..'
215. See Ho, *The ladder*, p. 36.
216. The marriage of Muḥammad Zankanu to a daughter of al-Qāḍi al-'Aqib also raised the family's status.
217. See *Tadhkirat al-Nasyān*, pp. 4, 71, 84, 96 and *passim.*
218. *Ibid.*, p. 15.
219. Al-Sa'di, pp. 266–7. Al-Sa'di refers to Mansa Muḥammad b. Mansa 'Ali, the Lord of Fadaku, as 'my friend'.
220. Phyllis Ferguson, *Islamization in Dagbon*, pp. 55–63.
221. Al-Ḥājj Marḥaba, *Tārīkh Islām Būbu*, especially fos 16–7, p. 25.
222. Wilks, 'The African travels', p. 158.

6. Persistence of the patriciate

1. See, for example, Marion Johnson, 'Calico caravans'
2. The *alfas* in the late nineteenth century linked the decline of learning directly to the declining wealth of the city. See Dubois, *Tombouctou la mystérieuse*, pp. 360–1.
3. Miner, *The primitive city*, *passim.*
4. *Ibid.*, pp. 84–5.
5. The *Diwān al-Mulūk* (fos 88r–185v) provides a coherent chronological narrative up to the second reign of Mas'ūd b. Manṣūr (Sanībar) b. Mas'ūd (erroneously referred to as Manṣūr b. Sanībar b. Manṣūr) in 1716–9, a period which witnessed a dramatic conflict between Pasha and scholars. After that, the information of the extant copy is disoriented and disordered. Most references will henceforth be made to the more coherent *Tadhkira.*
6. Michel Abitbol, *Tombouctou.*
7. For example, Willis' contribution in Ajayi and Crowder, *History of West Africa*, pp. 441–83.
8. Abitbol, *Tombouctou*, pp. 185ff.
9. Caillié, *Journal d'un voyage*, vol. II, p. 306.
10. Mas'ūd b. Manṣūr was singled out in the *Tadhkirat al-Nasyān* for the fact that he spoke good Arabic. *Tadhkirat al-Nasyān*, p. 22. Other Ruma notables were modestly learned in the early eighteenth century.
11. There was a tendency for many Songhai along the Niger east of Timbuktu to be identified as Ruma. Barth, *Travels and discoveries* vol. V, *passim.*
12. Al-Sa'di, p. 141.

13. Hama Boubou, *Histoire*, *passim*.
14. Al-Sa'di, pp. 151–2; *Tārīkh al-Fattāsh*, pp. 160ff.
15. Al-Sa'di, p. 152.
16. *Tārīkh al-Fattāsh*, p. 169.
17. The attitude of the Khaṭīb, Maḥmūd Darami, is ambiguous. For, while he readily tendered the submission of Gao to the Moroccans, he was evidently more sympathetic to the Askias. Al-Sa'di, p. 151.
18. The peace began taking shape *c.* 1610, but was not finalized until around 1630. According to al-Sa'di, p. 176, Sulaimān got most of his supporters from forces captured by Pasha Manṣūr after a defeat of Askia Nūḥ in an engagement dating to 1595.
19. *Tadhkirat al-Nasyān*, p. 181.
20. The lineage factor seems pertinent especially in the case of Askia al-Mukhtār (*c.* 1130 A.H. = 1717/18 A.D.) who reigned at Timbuktu. His uncles and great-uncles, like his grandfather, had reigned only at Dendi.
21. *Tadhkirat al-Nasyān*, p. 182.
22. *Ibid.*, pp. 183–4. The struggle was between descendants of Askia Daūd I, and hence descendants of Askia al-Ḥājj Muḥammad I, on the one hand, and between descendants of the latter's brother, 'Umar Kumzāghu. It lasted three years up until 1117 A.H. (1705/6 A.D.).
23. See *infra*.
24. Al-Fishtāli, *Manāhil al-Ṣafa*, pp. 163–4.
25. Al-Sa'di, p. 191.
26. See al-Fishtāli, *Manāhil al-Ṣafa*, p. 203.
27. *Ibid.* Also al-Sa'di, pp. 181–2.
28. By 1150 A.H. (1737/38 A.D.), the Shraqa among the Ruma, at least, resided principally in the desert. See *Tadhkirat al-Nasyān*, p. 111.
29. Al-Fishtāli, *Manāhil al-Ṣafa*, p. 203.
30. *Tadhkirat al-Nasyān* (p. 93) mentions that the presence of 44 Ruma from Ahl Dayir, with their Kahia, was necessary for investing a Pasha. But the Ahl Dayir represented a minor detachment, compared to the Fāsi, Marākushi and even Shrāqa divisions. Al-Sa'di, p. 193, allows for the possibility that the reorganization of the army in the Sudan, dating sometime around 1605/6, was done without authorization from Mūlāy Bu Fāris, who at that time briefly succeeded al-Manṣūr.
31. See al-Sa'di, p. 139, on Ḥammu b. 'Abd al-Ḥaqq al-Dara'i.
32. See al-Bartīli, *Fatḥ al-Shukūr*, *passim* and Nouakchott MS, fo. 28r.
33. See G. S. Colin, 'Chronique'.
34. *Tārīkh al-Fattāsh*, pp. 155–6.
35. Al-Sa'di, p. 142.
36. Al-Manṣūr, al-Sultān Aḥmad, 'Letter to al-Qāḍi 'Umar b. Maḥmūd Aqīt'. The text of this letter is included in al-Fishtāli, *Manāhil al-Ṣafa*, pp. 131–2. 'Since you are in that kingdom [of Songhai] in charge of its *sharī'a* laws . . . we have addressed ourselves to you on the occasion [of sending our army] so that you might be the first to respond [favourably] to its call . . .' Al-Manṣūr had previously sent a letter of a similar sort to Askia Isḥāq, but had received a rebuff. That letter treated the Songhai monarch as a provincial *amīr*, describing him as 'the chief of Gao, and its grandee' and claiming Sa'did right of sovereignty over him. Al-Manṣūr, al-Ṣulṭān Aḥmad, 'Letter to Askia Isḥāq'. Al-Sa'di comments on the letter, p. 137.
37. When Jūdār asked for quarters for himself and his army, al-Qāḍi 'Umar told him' 'I am not a king and I cannot give away anybody else's home [except my own] . . .' *Tārīkh al-Fattāsh*, pp. 155–6.
38. Compare *Tārīkh al-Fattāsh*, pp. 156–8, with Maḥmūd b. Zarqūn, *Letter to al-Qāḍi 'Umar*.
39. *Tārīkh al-Fattāsh*, p. 158.
40. Al-Sa'di, pp. 147, 155–6. Yaḥya's attack on the Ruma fort is dated *c.* October 10, 1591,

while the uprising began *c.* October 19–29, 1591 (See French translation, pp. 229, 240).

41. Al-Sa'di, pp. 155–6.
42. Compare al-Fishtāli, *Manāhil al-Ṣafa*, p. 276, with *Tārīkh al-Fattāsh*, pp. 167–8.
43. Al-Sa'di, pp. 164–5.
44. *Tārīkh al-Fattāsh*, p. 170.
45. *Ibid.*, pp. 171–2.
46. Maḥmūd b. Zarqūn, 'Letter to al-Qāḍi 'Umar b. Maḥmūd Aqīt'.
47. Al-Sa'di, pp. 166–7.
48. See al-Wufrāni, *Nuzhat*, p. 173, apparently quoting al-Fishtāli.
49. Al-Maqqari, *Rawḍat al-Ās*, p. 314.
50. Aḥmad Bāba, *Al-La'āli'*, fo. 1.
51. Al-Maqqari, *Rawḍat al-Ās*, p. 314; al-Wufrāni, *Nuzhat*, p. 98.
52. Aḥmad Bāba, *Nayl*, p. 114.
53. Aḥmad Bāba, *Minan al-Rabb*, colophon.
54. Colin, 'Chronique anonyme'.
55. Zaidan is quoted after Aḥmad Bāba as saying: 'My father lost these forces in vain'. Al-Sa'di, p. 191.
56. Al-Wufrāni, *Nuzhat*, p. 97.
57. See al-Nāṣiri, *Kitāb*, vol. V, *passim.*
58. Al-Maqqari, *Rawḍat al-Ās*, p. 304.
59. A fuller discussion of Aḥmad Bāba's Moroccan students is in Zoubeir, *Ahmad Baba*, pp. 56ff.
60. Al-Wufrāni, *Nuzhat*, p. 98. Compare with Abu'l-Mahd b. Aḥmad al-Fāsi who states that Aḥmad was more highly honoured in Morocco than in his hometown. See the preface to Aḥmad Bāba's *Mi'rāj al-Ṣu'ūd*, Rabat: Bibliothèque Générale, MS J100.
61. Quoted, among others, by al-Wufrāni, *Nuzhat*, p. 206.
62. This is according to Abu'l-Mahd al-Fāsi (see note 60 above). According to this source, Zaidān soon regretted that he allowed Aḥmad Bāba to leave and sent someone after him into the Sahara, but the emissary could not convince the old scholar to return.
63. See al-Wufrāni, *Nuzhat*, p. 203. This source, like al-Nāṣiri, says Abu'l-Maḥalli himself mentioned Aḥmad Bāba among his teachers, but it has not been possible to confirm this in Abu'l-Maḥalli's works.
64. Al-Sa'di, pp. 173, 205–6.
65. Abu'l-Maḥalli (Aḥmad b. 'Abdullāh), *Aṣlīt*, MS 100, fo. 29r (MS 4442 is more legible, but the folios are disordered).
66. *Ibid.*
67. Al-Sa'di, pp. 10–11.
68. *Ibid.*, p. 152. Cf. *Tārīkh al-Fattāsh*, pp. 152ff.
69. Al-Sa'di, pp. 180–1.
70. *Ibid.*, pp. 166–7.
71. Muḥammad Aḥmad al-Gharbi, *Muritānia wa-Mashāghil al-Maghrib al-Ifrīqiyya* (Rabat, 1964), p. 159. Other particulars of this interpretation, much like Kodjo's, are not supported by the evidence (see, for example, p. 161).
72. Al-Sa'di, pp. 144–5.
73. *Ibid.*, pp. 175–6.
74. Idrīs of Bornu, 'Bī'a to al-Sultān Aḥmad al-Manṣūr. The *bī'a* was drafted in Morocco by al-Fishtāli himself and later merely endorsed by Idrīs.
75. See al-Wufrāni, *Nuzhat*, pp. 208–66. Judging from correspondence which is cited here between Zaidān and Sīdi Yaḥya, the relations between the two after the initial alliance were strained.
76. *Ibid.*, *passim.*

77. Al-Sa'di, especially p. 193; al-Wufrāni, *Nuzhat*, p. 196.
78. Al-Sa'di, p. 170. Muḥammad b. al-Amīn Gānu could, of course, have held the title-nickname Bābu Gūr or Bāba Gūru. 'Gūru' is now a title among the Fulānis of the Gundam area. In Songhai its meaning is obscure but it could stand for 'hyena'.
79. Quoted in *Tārīkh al-Fattāsh*, p. 176.
80. *Ibid.*, pp. 176–7. It is possible that Aski Alfa Bakr Lunbāri, the Songhai secretary, had testified against the Aqīts, but there is no reference or allusion to any notables or full-fledged scholars who might have done so.
81. Al-Sa'di, pp. 76–7.
82. *Tārīkh al-Fattāsh* (p. 182) dates the accession of Muḥammad to October–November 1593, though also saying that it took place after the departure of the Aqīts, an event dating to March 1594. Cf. al-Sa'di, p. 173.
83. Al-Sa'di (p. 211) says briefly: 'Al-Faqīh Muḥammad b. Aḥmad b. al-Qāḍi 'Abd al-Raḥmān took charge of the judgeship by the order of the Pasha Maḥmūd at the hands of Ḥabīb b. Muḥammad Bāba . . .'.
84. *Tārīkh al-Fattāsh*, p. 182.
85. Al-Sa'di, p. 198.
86. *Ibid.*, p. 180. Al-Qā'id al-Muṣṭafa, on the other hand, sold all who fell to his portion and that of his companions.
87. *Ibid.*, pp. 199–200. 'Ali saw that 'the seizure of the Jennekoy is not in the [ṣtate's] interest and would result in wounds which would be difficult to heal'.
88. *Ibid.*, p. 193.
89. *Ibid.*, p. 201.
90. Al-Sa'di (p. 312) praises Askia al-Amīn very highly and suggests that the bribery charge against Kara Idji was not unfounded.
91. *Ibid.*, p. 223. 'They dispersed the *rumāt* who came with al-Qā'id Māmi in the countryside whereby each group joined one of the 'Ulūj and Andalusi detachments. As for Māmi, they sent him to Gao and he stayed there till he died.'
92. *Ibid.*, pp. 223–4.
93. *Ibid.*, p. 227; *Tārīkh al-Fattāsh*, p. 178.
94. Al-Sa'di, p. 228.
95. *Ibid.*, p. 232.
96. *Tārīkh al-Fattāsh*, p. 34. Al-Qāḍi Sayyid Aḥmad allegedly proclaimed that Mansa Mūsa had marched with 8000 men at the time of his own pilgrimage. The Judge must have made the statement immediately after Pasha 'Ali's departure for he also reportedly added: 'Ali b. 'Abd al-Qādir's purpose may not be accomplished'.
97. Al-Sa'di, p. 232.
98. *Ibid.*, p. 237. Cf. p. 172 on Shams al-Dīn b. al-Qāḍi Muḥammad Aqīt.
99. Al-Wufrāni and other Moroccan chroniclers barely mention the reign of al-'Abbās b. Muḥammad al-Shaikh. Cf. al-Sa'di, p. 322.
100. Abitbol, *Tombouctou*, *passim.*
101. *Tadhkirat al-Nasyān*, p. 90.
102. *Ibid.*
103. *Dhikr al-Wafayāt*, *passim*, especially fo. 29r.
104. Abitbol, *Tombouctou*, *passim.*
105. Ismā'il, Mūlāy al-Sulṭān, *Letter to Timbuktu.* Cf. *Tadhkirat al-Nasyān*, *passim*, on the Mujtahid scholars.
106. Ismā'īl, *Letter to Timbuktu*, fo. 215v.
107. *Ibid.*, fo. 214r.
108. *Tadhkirat al-Nasyān*, p. 95.
109. *Ibid.*, pp. 116–8.
110. In 1736, when a grandson of Mūlāy Ismā'īl, 'Abdullāh b. Nāṣir, appeared in Jenne, he was told: 'We know no one but the Pashas. As for you, we do not know your status,

nor who you are, nor do we care.' Later, the same 'Abdullāh was honoured and given presents by all the notables, excepting, it seems, the local Shurfa. See *Tadhkirat al-Nasyān*, p. 65.

111. *Tārīkh Wulmdān.* The sequence of the Askias is likewise confused in this source. The first investiture of an Amenokal by a Pasha at Timbuktu took place in 1690. At that time, Karidenna, who had long been reigning, came for formal recognition to Timbuktu. This might suggest weakness of the Wulmdān at this juncture, or alternatively, that they now established a formal basis for influence in the region of Timbuktu. See also Norris, *The Tuaregs*, pp. 100–1.
112. See Timbuktu Notables, *Letter to Mūlāy al-Ḥasan*, (dated Dhu'l Qi'da, 1310 A.H. = 1892/3 A.D.). Extracts from Mūlāy al-Ḥasan's answer are quoted in Marty, *Etudes sur l'Islam*, vol. II, p. 69.
113. Al-Sa'di, p. 278.
114. *Ibid.*, p. 291. Besides honouring the chronicler's brother (p. 293), Pasha Ḥamad b. Ḥaddu witnessed the accession of the first Maghia scholar to the judgeship.
115. *Tadhkirat al-Nasyān*, *passim.*
116. *Ibid.*, p. 172.
117. *Ibid.*, pp. 92–3.
118. *Ibid.*, pp. 91–2.
119. Al-Sa'di, p. 264.
120. *Tadhkirat al-Nasyān*, pp. 16, 172.
121. *Ibid.*, pp. 5–6. The information of the *Tadhkirat* on the period from 1655 to 1700 is brief and rather sketchy.
122. *Ibid.*, pp. 187ff (list of Kabara Farmas).
123. *Ibid.*, p. 185. Also al-Sa'di, p. 284 on Manṣūr.
124. See *Tadhkirat al-Nasyān*, for example, p. 17. The French translation (p. 27) has 'We no longer want him' for *'ma hana' fīh'*.
125. *Ibid.*, p. 60.
126. *Dhikr al-Wafayāt*, fo. 24r. 'Abd al-Ghaffār reigned five months.
127. *Ibid.*, p. 51. Leghbu is possibly gum arabic.
128. *Ibid.*, pp. 16ff. More on this *infra.*
129. *Ibid.*, p. 77.
130. See James Grey Jackson, *An account of the Empire of Marocco*, pp. 282ff.
131. *Tadhkirat al-Nasyān*, p. 45.
132. *Ibid.*, pp. 41–9.
133. *Ibid.*, p. 22. Mas'ūd was befriended by a Tuareg scholar identified as Muḥammad b. Tāhir al-Targi. This man was killed in the wake of Mas'ūd's fall (p. 143).
134. *Ibid.*, p. 17.
135. *Ibid.*, p. 37.
136. Information of Alfa Yaḥya Ibrāhīm of Timbuktu.
137. *Tadhkirat al-Nasyān*, pp. 140–1.
138. See *Ibid.*, pp. 50–3, on Mas'ūd's (Manṣūr's) re-entry to Timbuktu. He aligned himself with the Tazarkīnis for a short time, then switched over to the side of the Dara'is. At that time, the Tibshāsha remained vacant for almost four years (1723–6).
139. *Ibid.*, especially pp. 124, 129.
140. *Ibid.*, pp. 6–7.
141. The practice survived at least for one century from 1690 to *c.* 1795.
142. *Tadhkirat al-Nasyān*, p. 33.
143. *Ibid.*, pp. 107–8.
144. More on this below.
145. *Ibid.*, p. 114.
146. *Ibid.*, p. 116.
147. See genealogy of the Askia dynasty and its successors in the Appendices.

148. *Tadhkirat al-Nasyān*, p. 155.
149. See, for example, *ibid.*, p. 69.
150. We do not know the sequence of Askias at Dendi after the mid-seventeenth century. A century later, Askia al-Ḥājj resided mostly away from Timbuktu and the *Tadhkirat al-Nasyān* (p. 185) says of his successor, Maḥmūd b. Kunfāri 'Ammār, 'He is now in the provinces, but we heard that they have deposed him'.
151. As known from several sources, 'Uthmān b. Bābakr (Abu Bakr) was son of Bābakr b. Bāḥaddu who, in turn, was Bāḥaddu b. Bābakr b. Alfa Manṣūr b. Muhammad b. 'Ali al-Mubārak al-Dara'i. See *Dhikr al-Wafayāt*, fos. 26r and *passim*; *Tadhkirat al-Nasyān*, p. 164.
152. The copy in question is at Dakar: Institut Fondamental d'Afrique Noire, Fonds Brevié, Cahier no. 23. The same copy came into the ownership of 'Abdullāh b. al-Imām b. 'Abdullāh b. al-Imām Zungu Iji, a Songhai or Ruma it seems, judging by the Idji surname, whose father served as *imām* at an unspecified mosque. Aḥmad himself (the copyist) was Pasha in 1709 and was known as Ḥammādi Zungu. See *Tadhkirat al-Nasyān*, p. 94.
153. *Tadhkirat al-Nasyān*, p. 179.
154. It seems that the Ruma notables feigned obedience to Mas'ūd for some time, but neglected his orders after having secretly deposed him. The old *Qāḍi* was unaware of this. *Ibid.*, p. 17.
155. *Ibid.*, p. 138.
156. *Ibid.*
157. *Tadhkirat al-Nasyān*, pp. 79–80.
158. *Ibid.*, pp. 112–3.
159. *Tārīkh Arwān.*
160. *Tadhkirat al-Nasyān*, pp. 106–7. The author apparently received his information on these events from a certain 'Abdullāh al-Kunti, a brother or nephew of 'Abd al-Mu'min.
161. *Ibid.*, p. 78. The occasion was the murder of one of the Dara'is, Kāhia 'Ali b. al-Jasīm, followed by a retaliation against merchants affiliated to the Tazarkīnis.
162. *Ibid.*, p. 148.
163. *Dhikr al-Wafayāt*, fo. 33r. By this time, the briefly reigning Bābakr b. Baḥaddu had been deposed, but continued to be looked upon as 'Pasha'.
164. *Ibid.*, fos 28vff. The Tingeregif eventually broke away, under the leadership of Ḥamati, from the rest of the Tadmekkat in 1227 A.H. (1812/13 A.D.).
165. See Barth, *Travels and discoveries*, vol. V. *passim.* Cf. Awwāb, 'Amān Document in favour of 'Abd al-Karīm al-Inglīsi [Barth]', quoted in 'Abdelqader Zebadia, pp. 67–8.
166. Wilks, 'African travels of Wargee', p. 185.
167. *Dhikr al-Wafayāt*, fo. 32v.
168. Wilks, 'African travels of Wargee', p. 184.
169. Marty, *Etudes sur l'Islam*, vol. I, p. 26.
170. *Dhikr Waqāi'*, fo. 4.
171. See Zebadia, *The career*; al-Baṭrān, 'An introductory note'.
172. *Kitāb Tārīkh al-Fūtāwi.*
173. *Ibid.*, fo. 5.
174. *Dhikr Waqāi'*, fo. 5.
175. Al-Bakkā'i, *Letter to al-Ḥājj 'Umar*, fo. 67.
176. *Kitāb Tārīkh al-Futāwi*, fos 6ff.
177. 'Abd al-Qādir b. Muḥammad b. Aḥmad, *Letter to Aḥmadu Lobbo.* The writer may be possibly al-Qāḍi 'Abd al-Qādir al-Sanūsi.
178. *Wafayāt Timbuktu.*
179. See, for example, Lenz, *Timbouctou*, vol. II, p. 150.
180. *Dhikr al-Wafayāt*, fos 28ff.

181. See, for example, al-Mukhtar, *Ajwiba*, fos 219r ff. Cf. Aḥmadu [Lobbo] b. Muḥammad, '*Proclamation*'; this prohibits contact between men and women not married or closely related.
182. Aḥmad b. Aḥmad [b. Aḥmadu Lobbo], *Letter to Gūru b. Sa'īd*, fo. 3.
183. The success of Ḥājj 'Umar remains problematical though Robinson has emphasized that he relied on recruits from his native Futa Toro. See David Robinson, 'Abdul Qādir', p. 286.
184. According to a fragment (Fonds Gironcourt, MS 2406, pièce 70), Bakkā'i's army included 'Urbān (presumably Kunta and Barābīsh clansmen), Tuareg and students of the Shaikh.
185. Sa'īd b. Abu Bakr al-Fūti, '*A letter to Amīr al-Mu'minīn Sīdi Aḥmad al-Bakkā'i*', Recueil 2, MS 30. Similarly al-Bakkā'i is addressed as a monarch in Recueil 2, MS 28.
186. A version of *Dhikr Waqāi'* which is favourable to the Tijānis is found at Paris: Institut de France, Fonds Gironcourt, MS 2406, pièce 75.
187. *Dhikr Waqāi'* (Timbuktu MS), fo. 16.
188. *Ibid.*
189. Lenz, 1887, II, p. 132.
190. Ibrāhīm, al-Kāhia, *Letter to the French.*
191. Mali National Archives, 'Notes et fiches'.
192. *Dhikr Waqāi'*, fo. 14.
193. Information of the Timbuktu Ruma elder Aḥmadu Badiji.
194. Aḥmad Bāba b. Abu'l-'Abbās, *Letter on behalf of Timbuktu to the Lieutenant Boiteux.*
195. Timbuktu Notables, 'Letter to the French Government'.
196. See Marty, *Etudes sur l'Islam*, vol. II, pp. 15–8.
197. See *ibid.*, p. 18.
198. *Ibid.*, pp. 19–20.
199. *Wafayāt Timbuktu*, fo. 1.
200. Interview with Alfa Humal, *Imām* of Jingerebir, Timbuktu.
201. Aḥmad Bāba's descent is recorded by Marty, *Etudes sur l'Islam*, vol. I, Annexe III, and was related to this writer by Aḥmad Bāba's son, Alfa Ẓubair.
202. Information of Alfa Humal, Timbuktu.

Glossary

Unless otherwise indicated, the following terms are either Arabic or locally derived from Arabic.

Alfa Songhai term for a literatus and, later, for a scholar. Tamashagh equivalent is Alfagha

Amenokal Chief of the Tuareg Wulmdān (Ouillimiden)

Arukoy Songhai: Chief of the Corporation of Muleteers

Ashra' Mundhu Songhai: Chief of Police. Under authority of the Qāḍi. (Cf. Khadim al-Shar')

Baraka 'Divine Grace'. Complex concept relating to *Wilāya* and *Karamāt*

Bashut Officer in the Ruma military hierarchy, subordinate to the *Kāhia*

Fatwa Formal legal opinion

Ḥadith Sayings of the Prophet. Corpus of traditions on precedents set by the Prophet

Ḥarrāṭīn Farmers, client farmers. Singular sometimes *Harṭān*

Ijāza Certificate authorizing the teaching of a specific book or a branch of learning

Ijmā' Consensus of Muslims in the classical legislative process

Ijtihād Independent reasoning in Muslim legislation

Kabara Farma Songhai: Governor of Kabara, in charge of collecting duties on passage of goods

Kāhia Lieutenant-Commander in charge of one of the main Ruma divisions

Karāmāt Special 'gifts', supernatural abilities

Kātib Secretary or scribe

Khadim al-Shar' Arabic equivalent of *Ashra' Mundhu*

Khaṭīb Literally a scholar who delivered the Friday *Khuṭba*. A post combining parochial, administrative and judicial functions at Gao

Maktab Elementary literacy school where the *Qur'ān* is taught.

Mithqāl Measure of gold; in Timbuktu roughly equal to four grams

Mu'adhdhin Caller to prayers; mosque functionary

Mu'allim Elementary school teacher. (Cf. *maktab*)

Mu'āmalāt Legal and commercial transactions

Muddāh Praise singers. Literati who specialize in recitation of poetry in praise of the Prophet (also *Maddāhin*, singular *Maddāh*)

Mujaddid Renovator of the Faith; usually in reference to a scholar
Mujtahid A person who exercises *ijtihād*
Musabbibīn Body of merchants and other propertied individuals in Ruma times
Nisba Reference to place or clan of origin, or to descent
Qiyās Analogy. Relating novel legal problems to precedents
Rumāt Soldiers carrying firearms
Ruma A derivation from *Rumāt* from which Arma (Al-Ruma = Ar-Ruma) is derived
Sanad Chain of attribution of information to its original source. Also chain of teachers of a particular book traced backwards to the author
Shar' Also *Shari'a*. Corpus of Muslim law
Sharīf Person tracing his descent to the Prophet (or sometimes to the Prophet's clan, the Quraish)
Shurfa Plural of *Sharīf*. Locally, often called *Shurfa*, *Shirfi* or *Sirfi*
Silsila Chain of transmission of learning
Tafsīr Exegesis. Qur'ānic exegesis
Taqlīd Emulation. Emulation of early jurists (contrasts with *ijtihād*)
Tarīqa Literally 'way' or 'path'. Sufi ('mystic') order or confraternity
Tawḥīd Doctrinal theology, emphasizing unity or oneness of God
Teifa Songhai: Commercial brokers
Tibshāsha Local name for the post of Pasha (Pashalik).
Timbuktu-Mundhu 'Governor of Timbuktu during Songhai times. Earlier *Timbuktu-Koy*
Tindi Songhai: Tailors, tailoring houses, tailor–alfas
Uṣūl Field of study relating Muslim legislation to the original sources (*usul*) of the law
Walī 'Saint'. Person (usually a scholar) believed graced with special *baraka* and *karāmāt*
Wilāya State of being a *walī*; 'sainthood'
Wird Litany of a Sufi order

Bibliography

Unless otherwise specified, all references to the *Institut de France*, Paris, pertain to the *Fonds Gironcourt* there, while all references to the Bibliothèque Nationale in Paris pertain to its *Fonds Arabes*.

Correspondence and related documents

'Abd al-Qādir b. Muḥammad al-Sanūsi, *Ijāza in Kitāb al-Shifa to Sān Sirfi b. Muḥammad al-Kāburi*, MS in possession of Alfa Humal, *Imām* of Jingerebir, Timbuktu

'Abd al-Qādir b. Muḥammad b. Aḥmad (al-Sanūsi?), *Letter to Aḥmadu Lobbo b. Muḥammad b. Abu Bakr al-Māsini*, MS in possession of Alfa Humal, Timbuktu

Abu Bakr b. 'Ali b. Danbu Sili, *Contract between Aḥmad b. And-Agh-Muḥammad b. Maḥmūd b. And-Agh-Muḥammad and Mālik b. Muḥammad al-Fulāni*, published as 'Acte du vente passé à Tombouctou – Manuscrit Arabe venue de Tombouctou', in *Journal Asiatique*, 1840, vol. 9, pp. 375–89

Abu Bakr b. al-Qā'id Baḥaddu al-Drāwi, *Sale of half the Farm Shurunburku, 1175 A.H., to Hungudu b. al-Murdu*, Paris: Institut de France, MS 2406, pièce 80

Aḥmad b. Aḥmad (b. Aḥmad Lobbo), *Letter to Gūru b. Sa'īd*, Paris: Institut de France, MS 2405, pièce 36

Aḥmad Bāba (Aqīt), *Ijāzas to Aḥmad al-Maqqari*, included in al-Maqqari, *Rawḍat al-Ās*, pp. 304–5. (see below)

Aḥmad Bāba b. Abu'l-'Abbās al-Qāḍi, *Letter on behalf of Timbuktu to the Lieutenant Boiteux, Dec. 1893*, Arabic text published in Pefontan, *Histoire*, 1922, p. 112. (see below)

Aḥmad b. Muḥammad Bīru, *Ijāzas in al-Bukhari and al-Muwatta' to 'Umar b. Aḥmad*, MS in possession of 'Issa wuld Muḥammad Mawlūd, Timbuktu

Aḥmad b. Muḥammad b. Muḥammad Bīru, *Ijāza to Bāba 'Uthmān b. Muḥammad b. 'Uthmān al-Kāburi*, MS in possession of 'Issa wuld Muḥammad Mawlūd, Timbuktu

Aḥmad Lobbo, *Letter to Bāba b. 'Uthmān (father of Sān Sirfi?)*, Paris: Institut de France, MS 2406, pièce 69

Aḥmadu (Lobbo) b. Muḥammad, *Proclamation to the Amīrs and Qāḍis*, Paris: Institute de France, MS 2406, pièce 66

Awwāb al-Tārgi, *Letter to Aḥmad b. Aḥmad b. Muḥammad (Lobbo)*, Paris: Institut de France, MS 2406, pièce 64

Al-Bakkā'i, Aḥmad, *Letter to Aḥmad b. Aḥmad b. Ag-Gīg al-Sūqi*, Paris: Bibliothèque Nationale, MS 5259, fos 70–72r. Also included in Zebadia, *The career*, 1974, pp. 533–57. (see below)

Letter to Aḥmad b. Aḥmadu (Lobbo), Timbuktu: Centre Aḥmad Bāba, Recueil 1
Letter to al-Ḥājj 'Umar, Dakar: Institut Fondamental d'Afrique Noire, Fonds Brevié, Cahier 12
Three letters to 'Umar al-Hausi and the latter's answers, Paris: Bibliothèque Nationale, MS 5716, fos 32–6, 182–5. Also included in Zebadia, *The career*, 1974, pp. 477–503. (see below)
Two letters to al-Ḥājj 'Umar Tal (c. 1862), Paris: Bibliothèque Nationale, MS 5259, fos 66v–70
al-Hasan, Mūlāy al-Sulṭān, *Letter to Timbuktu Notables*, French translation published in Marty, *Etudes*, 1920, II, p. 69 (see below)
Ibrāhīm, al-Kāhia, *Letter to the French at St. Louis*, Dakar: Senegal National Archives, 1G70 (1884)
Idrīs of Bornu, Bī'a to al-Sultān Aḥmad al-Mansūr, Arabic text in al-Fishtāli, *Manāhil al-Ṣafa*, pp. 69–73 (see below)
Ismā'īl, Mūlāy al-Sulṭān, *Letter to Timbuktu*, Paris: Bibliothèque Nationale, MS 6399, fos 214v–218r
Juma (Alfa) b. 'Abṭallāh, sons thereof, *Sale of Farm Ashurfār, 1174* A.H., *to al-Qāḍi Bāba b. al-Qāḍi al-Bakr (Abkar)*, Paris: Institut de France, MS 2406, pièce 77
Al-Maghīli, Muḥammad b. 'Abd al-Karīm, *Ajwiba 'āla Askia Muḥammad*, Dakar: Institut Fondamental d'Afrique Noire, Fonds Brevié, Cahier no. 23. Cf. Hunwick, 1974
Maḥmūd b. Zarqūn, *Letter to al-Qāḍi 'Umar b. Maḥmūd Aqīt*, published in Levi-Provençal, 'Un Document Inédit sur l'Expedition Sa'dide au Soudan', *Arabica: Revue d'Etudes Arabes*, 1955, vol. II, 1, pp. 89–96
Al-Manṣūr, al-Sulṭān Aḥmad, 'Letter to Askia Ishāq b. Daud,' text in al-Fishtāli, *Manāhil al-Ṣafa*, pp. 123–4 (see below)
Muḥammad al-'Ābid b. Muḥammad b. 'Ali al-Anṣāri, *Letter to Aḥmadu Lobbo al-Fulāni*, Timbuktu: Centre Aḥmad Bāba, Recueil 1, MS 6
Muḥammad (Sīdi) b. Sīdi al-Mukhtār al-Kunti, *Ajwiba 'ala Nūh b. Tāhir al-Fulāni*, Timbuktu: Centre Aḥmad Bāba, Recueil 2, MS 25
Letter to Aḥmadu Lobbo, King of Massina, Timbuktu: Centre Aḥmad Bāba, Recueil 1, MS 12
Al-Mukhtār b. Yarki Talfi, *Letter to Aḥmad al-Bakkā'i*, Paris: Bibliothèque Nationale, MS 5697, fos 30r–42r. Also included in Zebadia, *The career*, 1974, pp. 504–30. (see below)
Al-Mukhtār, Sīdi (al-Kabīr al-Kunti), *Ajwiba (On questions of law and custom)*, Paris: Bibliothèque Nationale, MS 6399, fos 219r–265v
Sa'īd b. Abu Bakr al-Fūti, *A letter to Amīr al-Mu'minīn Sīdi Aḥmad al-Bakkā'i*, Timbuktu: Centre Aḥmad Bāba, Recueil 2, MS 30
Timbuktu Jamā'a, *Letter to Aḥmad al-Bakkā'i*, Arabic text published in Pefontan, *Histoire*, 1922, p. 112. (see below)
Timbuktu Notables, *Letter to French Governor-General of the Soudan, 28 March 1895*, Senegal: National Archives at Dakar, File 15G212
Timbuktu Notables, *Letter to Mūlāy al-Ḥasan b. Mūlāy Muḥammad (1892)*, MS in possession of Alfa Aḥmad Bānio, *Imām* of Sīdi Yaḥya, Timbuktu
Timbuktu Notables, 'Letter to the French Government,' Translation in *Bulletin du Comité de l'Afrique Française*, 25e Année, 1915, Jan.–Fev., pp. 90–4
Walāta Jamā'a, *Letter to Aḥmad al-Madani*, Paris: Bibliothèque Nationale, MS 5713, fo. 43

Other primary sources

Abu'l-Maḥalli (Aḥmad b. 'Abdullāh), *Aṣlīt al-Khibrīt fi Qat' Bal'ūm al-'Ifrīt*, Rabat: Bibliothèque du Palais Royal, MS 100. (MS 4442 is another copy)

Aḥmad b. And-Agh-Muḥammad, *Al-Futūh al-Qayūmiyya fi Sharh al-Ajerrūmiyya*, Paris: Bibliothèque Nationale, MS 5442, fos 195r–250v. (The latter is the most complete among several extant copies)

Aḥmad Bāba (Aqīt), *Ajwiba fi'l-Qawānīn al-'Urfiyya*, Rabat: Bibliothèque du Palais Royal, MS 5813

Al-Nukat al-Mustajāda fi Musāwāt al-Fa'il li'l-Mubtada' fi Sharṭ al-Ifāda, Rabat: Bibliothèque du Palais Royal, MS z3720

Jalb al-Ni'ma wa-Daf' al-Naqma bi-Mujānabat al-Wulāt al-Zalama, Rabat: Bibliothèque du Palais Royal, MS 5534

Kifāyat al-Muḥtāj li-Ma'rifat man Laysa fi'l-Dībāj, Cairo: Egyptian National Library (Dar al-Kutub), History, MS 1068

Al-La'āli' al-Sundusiyya fi'l-Fadā'il al-Sanūsiyya, Rabat: Bibliothèque Générale, MS D984

Al-Lam' wa'l-Ishāra ila Ḥukm Tibgh, Rabat: Bibliothèque du Palais Royal, MS 3627

Ma Rawāh al-Ruwāt, Rabat: Bibliothèque Générale, MS 3299k

Minan al-Rabb al-Jalīl fi Bayān Muhimmāt Khalīl, Rabat: Bibliothèque du Palais Royal, MS 4975

Mi'raj al-Ṣu'ūd fi Ḥukm Bay' al-Sūd, Rabat: Bibliothèque Générale, MS D1724

Nayl al-Ibtihāj bi Taṭrīz al-Dībāj, on the margins of *al-Dībāj al-Mudhahhab fi Ma'rifat A'yān 'Ulamā' al-Madhhab*, by al-Ya'muri, Cairo: n.p., 1351 A.H.

Tuḥfat al-Fudalā' bi-Ba'd Fadā'il al-'Ulamā', Rabat: Bibliothèque Générale, MS D1641, fos 302–411

Aḥmad Bāba b. Muḥammad b. Yūsif b. Ibrāhīm Fadika al-Zaghawi, *Anwa' al-Kufr fi'l-Sūdān*, Paris: Bibliothèque Nationale, Fonds Arabes, MS 6106

Ansāb Ahl Gurdu wa'l-'Iraqi, MS in possession of Alfa Humal, Timbuktu

Aṣl al-Wangāriyyin . . . bi Kano, edited and translated by Muḥammad al-Ḥājj, in *Kano Studies*, 1968, No. 4, pp. 17–42

Bābīr, Mūlāy Aḥmad, *Al-Sa'āda al-Abadiyya fi'l-Ta'rīf bi-'Ulamā' Timbuktu al-Bahiyya*. This work, by a living scholar in Timbuktu, was drawn in several copies of which one was presented by the author to the present writer

Ṣifat Timbuktu wa-Awlayā'uha Muḥītūn Biha, MS copy in possession of J. O. Hunwick

Al-Bakri, *Al-Mughrib fi Dhikr Ifrīqiya wa'l-Maghrib, Juz' min al-Masālik wa'l-Mamālik* (*Description de l'Afrique Septentrionale*), Alger: Imprimeur du Gouvernement, 1857. (reprinted by Maktabat al-Muthna, Baghdad)

Barrows, David Prescott, *Berbers and Blacks: Impressions of Morocco, Timbuktu and the Western Sudan*, Westport, Connecticut: Negro Universities Press, 1970

Barth, Henry, *Travels and discoveries in North and Central Africa*, 5 vols. London: Longman, 1858. References are also made to the two-volume edition, New York, 1890

Al-Bartili, *Fatḥ al-Shukūr fi Ma'rifat A'yān 'Ulamā' al-Takrūr*, Paris: Institut de France, MS 2406, pièce 118. References are also made in this study to the more complete Nouakchott MS. I am grateful to Dr John Hunwick for allowing me to consult his own copy of this MS

Bonamy, *Mission de Bonamy, Administrateur des Colonies en 1917, Commission Interministerielle des Affaires Musulmans, Mission Transsaharienne,* unpublished report, with confidential annex, No. 2, Paris: Institut de France, Fonds Terrier, MS 5949 (I), fos 49–137

Caillié, Rene, *Journal d'un Voyage á Tombouctou et à Jenne dans l'Afrique Centrale Pendant les Années 1824–1828*, 2 vols., Paris, 1830. References are also made to the 1830 London edition

Colin, G. S. (ed.), 'Chronique anonyme de la dynastie Saadienne', *Collection de Textes Arabes publiées par l'Institut des Hautes-Etudes Marocaines*, 1934, II, Rabat

Curtin, Phillip D., *Africa remembered: narratives of West Africans from the era of the slave trade*, Madison: University of Wisconsin Press, 1967

Dar al-Kutub al-Misriyya, *Fihrist al-Makhtūtāt al-Lati Iqtanatha al-Dār*, 3 vols, Cairo, 1961–63

Dhikr Fuqahā' Tunbuktu, Timbuktu: Centre Aḥmad Bāba, MS 42

Dhikr al-Wafayāt, see Qāsim b. Sulaimān below

Dhikr Waqāi' al-Qarn al-Thālith 'Ashar, Timbuktu: Centre Aḥmad Bāba, Recueil 1, MS 1

Dubois, Felix, *Tombouctou la mystérieuse*, Paris: Flammarion, 1897

Dupuis-Yacouba, 'Note sur la population de Tombouctou, castes et associations', *Revue Ethnographique*, 1910, Nos. 8–9, pp. 233–236

Industries et principales professions des habitants de la région de Tombouctou, Paris: E. Larose, 1921

Al-Fishtāli, 'Abd al-'Azīz, *Manāhil al-Ṣafa fi Akhbār Mawālīna al-Shurafa*, ed. by 'Abd al-Karīm Krayyim, Rabat: Ministry of Awqaf, n.d.

Hacquard, Mgr. A., *Monographie de Tombouctou*, Paris: Societé des Etudes Coloniales et Maritimes, 1900

Hall, Leland, *Timbuctoo*, New York: Harper Brothers, 1927

Hourst, Lieut., *Sur le Niger et au pays des Touaregs*, Paris: Plou, 1898

Ibn Baṭūṭa, *Tuḥfat al-Nuzzār fi Gharā'ib al-Amṣār wa-'Ājā'ib al-Asfār* (*Voyages*), Arabic text and translation by C. Defremery and B. R. Sanguinetti, 4 vols., Paris, 1854

Ibn Ḥauqal, *Configuration de la terre*, 2 vols., translated by H. Kramers and G. Wiet, Paris: Maisonneuve et Larose, 1964

Ibn Idhāri, *Histoire de l'Afrique du Nord et de l'Espagne musulmane: Kitāb al-Bayān al-Mughrib*, edited by G. S. Collin and E. Levi-Provencal, 2 vols., Leiden: J. Brill, 1951

Ibn Khaldūn, *Histoire des Berbères* (*Kitāb Tārīkh al-Duwal al-Islāmiyya bi'l-Maghrib, al-Jiz' al-Awwal*), Arabic text, 2 vols. Alger: Imprimeur de Gouvernement, 1847

The Muqaddima: An introduction to history, 3 vols., translated by Franz Rosenthal, New York: Pantheon Books, 1958

Ibn Sīda, *Muḥkam fi'l-Lugha*, Rabat: Bibliothèque Générale, MS Q75

Al-Idrīsi, *Ṣifat al-Maghrib wa-Ard al-Sūdān wa-Misr wa'l-Andalus* (from *Kitāb Nuzhat al-Mushtāq*, *Description de l'Afrique et de l'Espagne*), edited and translated by Reinhart P. A. Dozy and Michael J. de Goeje, Amsterdam: Oriental Press, 1969

Jackson, James Grey, *An account of the Empire of Marocco*, London: Wm. Bulmer and Co., 1814

An account of Timbuctoo and Housa . . . by El Hage Abd Salam Shabeeny . . ., London: Longman, 1820

Jaime, Lieut., *De Koulikoro a Tombouctou, a Bord du 'Mage', 1889–1890*, Paris: E. Dentu, n.d.

Al-Jazūli, 'Abd al-Raḥmān b. Muḥammad al-Tamanarti, *Al-Fawā'id al-Jamma bi-Asnād 'Ulamā' al-Umma*, Rabat: Bibliothèque Générale, MS D1420, fo. 45

Joffre, General, *My march to Timbuctoo*, London: Chatto & Windus, 1915

Kano Chronicle, translated by H. R. Palmer, *Sudanese Memoirs*, 3 vols., Lagos: 1928, reprinted in London: Frank Cass, 1967, III, pp. 92–132

Ka'ti, Maḥmūd, *Tārīkh al-Fattāsh*, edited and translated by M. Delafosse and O. Houdas, Paris: Adrien–Maisonneuve, 1964

Kitāb al-Tarā'if, Rabat: Bibliothèque Générale, MS K2294, fos 134–154

Kitāb Tārīkh al-Fūtāwi, apparently by 'Abd al-Raḥmān b. Sān Sirfi, Paris: Institut de France, MS 2406, pièce 72

Al-Kunti, Muḥammad b. Sīdi al-Mukhtār, *Kitāb al-Ṭarā'if wa'l-Talā'id*, Rabat: Bibliothèque Générale, MS K2294

Lenz, Oscar, *Timbouctou: voyage au Maroc, au Sahara et au Soudan*, translated Pierre Lehautcourt, Paris: Hachette, 1887

Leo Africanus (John Leo), *A geographical historie of Africa written in Arabic and Italian by John Leo . . .*, translated by John Pory, London: Imperis Georg, 1600

Leo Africanus (Jean-Leon l'Africain), *Description de l'Afrique*, translated and edited by A. Epaulard, Paris: Librairie d'Amérique et d'Orient, 1956

Al-Maghīli's replies to the questions of Askia al-Ḥājj Muḥammad, edited and translated with an introduction by J. O. Hunwick, unpublished PhD Dissertation, University of London, June 1974

Mali, Archives, 'Notes et fiches de renseignements sur les chefs et notables, Cercle de Tombouctou, 1897–1917', Bamako-Koulouba: Archives Nationales, Politiques Indigènes, file 2E, 71, 1900

Al-Maqqari, Aḥmad, *Rawḍat al-Ās al-Ātirat al-Anfās fi Dhikr man Laqiytuhum min A'lām al-Ḥadratayn Marākish wa-Fās*, edited by 'Abd al-Wahhab Ben Manṣūr, Rabat: Al-Maṭba'a al-Malakiyya, 1964

Marc-Shrader, Capt. L., 'Quand j'étais Maire de Tombouctou', *Le Tour de Monde, Nouvelle Ser.*, 1913, vol. 19, pp. 397–432

Mardochée, 'Recit du Rabbin Abi-Seror Mardochée, sur Tombouctou', *Bulletin de la Société de Geographie de la Province d'Oran*, 1878–1881, vol. I, pp. 169–72

Marḥaba, al-Ḥājj, *Tārīkh Islām Būbu* (MS copy in possession of Ivor Wilks, Northwestern University)

Marty, Paul, *Etudes sur l'Islam et les tribus du Soudan: I, Les Kounta de l'Est . . ., II, La Région de Tombouctou . . .*, Paris: Leroux, 1920

Al-Mawardi, *Al-Aḥkām al-Sulṭāniyya*, Cairo: Al-Babi & Co., 1973

Mission de 'Abd al-Qādir, Embassadeur de Tombouctou à St.-Louis, 1885–1886, Dakar: Senegal National Archives, 1G70

Muḥammad b. Aḥmad b. Maḥmūd Baghayughu, *'Aqīdat Ahl al-Tawhīd al-Ṣughra*, Paris: Bibliothèque Nationale, MS 5602, fos 102r–110v

Muḥammad Bāba b. Muḥammad al-Amīn, *Al-Minah al-Ḥamīda fi Sharh al-Farīda*, Rabat: Bibliothèque Générale, MS K1746, fos 3–4

Muḥammad b. al-Ḥājj Ḥasan b. al-Ḥājj b. Sulaimān, *Shifā' al-Nās min Dā' al-Ghafala wa'l-Wiswās*, (1241 A.H.), Paris: Bibliothèque Nationale, Fonds Arabes, MS 6108

Al-Munajjid, Ṣalāh al-Dīn (ed.), *Mamlakat Māli 'Ind al-Jughrāfiyyin al-Muslimīn*. Beirut: Dar al-Kitab al-Jadid, 1963

Al-Nāṣiri, Aḥmad (Abu'l-'Abbās) b. Khālid, *Kitāb al-Istiqṣā li-Akhbār Duwal al-Maghrib al-Aqsa*, edited by the author's sons Ja'far and Muḥammad, 5 vols., Casablanca: 1955

Park, Mungo, *Travels in the interior districts of Africa*, New York: Arno Press, 1971. (Reprint in facs. of London edition, 1799)

Peyrissac, Léon, *Aux ruines des grandes cités Soudanaises: notes et souvenirs de voyage*, Paris: 1910

Al-Qādiri, Muḥammad b. al-Ṭayyib, *Al-Iklīl wa'l-Tāj fi Tadhyīl Kifāyat al-Muḥtāj*, Rabat: Bibliothèque du Palais Royal, MS 1897, fo. 10r.

Nashr al-Mathāni de Mohammad al-Qadiri, I: 1594–1640, translated by A. Graules and P. Paillard, Paris: Ernest Leroux. This is volume XXI of *Archives Marocains*. (Also Moroccan facsimile publication, n.p., n.d.)

Qāsim b. Sulaimān, Mawlāy, *Dhikr al-Wafayāt wa-mā Ḥadath min al-Umūr al-'Izām*, Paris: Bibliothèque Nationale, MS 5259, fos 24v–34r

Rattray, R. Sutherland, *Hausa folklore, customs, proverbs . . .*, New York: 1969

Recueil de Textes de Touat, Arabic MS, Paris: Bibliothèque Nationale, MS 6399

Rejou, Commandant, 'Huit mois a Tombouctou et dans la région Nord', *Le Tour du Monde, Nouvelle Ser.*, 1898, vol. 4, pp. 409–32

Risālat Ibn Abi Zaid, Rabat: Bibliothèque Générale, MS K5

Ruxton, F. H., *Māliki law: a summary from French translations of Mukhtasar Sīdi Khalil*, London: Luzac & Co., 1916

Sa'd, al-Imām, b. al-Ḥabīb Bāba . . . al-Waddāni, *Al-Damlūk 'ala Hadhayān al-Hashtūq*, Paris: Bibliothèque Nationale, MS 6399 (Recueil de Textes de Touat), fos 201r–214v

Al-Sa'di, 'Abd al-Raḥmān, *Tārīkh al-Sūdān* (*Tarikh es-Soudan*), edited and translated by O. Houdas, Paris: 1898–1900, reprinted in Paris: Adrien–Maisonneuve, 1966

Sakhāwi, Muḥammad b. 'Abd al-Raḥmān, *Al-Daw' al-Lāmi' li-Ahl al-Qarn al-Tāsi'*, 12 vols., Beirut: Dar Maktabat al-Hayat, n.d.

Al-Shinqīṭi, Aḥmad b. Al-Amīn, *Al-Wasīṭ fi Tarājim Udabā' Shinqīt*, Cairo: Maktabat al-Khanji, 1961

Al-Suyūṭi, 'Abd al-Raḥmān, *Risāla ila Mulūk al-Takrūr*, Cairo: Egyptian National Library, MS Majami', No. 416, fos. 139a–140b

Al-Tanbi'a bi-man Yab'athuhu Allah 'ala Ra's Kull Mi'a, Rabat: Bibliothèque Générale, MS K486, fos 345–79

Al-Suyūṭi, Jalāl al-Dīn ('Abd al-Raḥmān), *Al-Taḥadduth bi-Ni'mat Allah*, (*Autobiography*), edited by E. M. Sartain, 2 vols., Cambridge: Cambridge University Press, 1975

Tadhkirat al-Nasyān fi Akhbār Mulūk al-Sūdān, edited and translated by O. Houdas, Paris: Adrien–Maisonneuve, 1899–1901

Tārīkh Arwān, MS in possession of Mawlay Aḥmād Bābīr of Timbuktu

Tārīkh Kel Antasār, (Original composition attributed to 'Ali b. Muḥammad al-Najīb, c. 1122 A.H. = 1710/11 A.D., additions by later scholars), MS edited by Nūri Muḥammad al-Amīn, Centre Aḥmad Bāba, Timbuktu

Tārīkh Wulmdān, Paris: Institut de France, MS 2405

Tāriq Ahl al-Maghrib ila Bayt Allāh al-Ḥarām, Paris: Bibliothèque Nationale, Fonds Arabes, MS 5713

Wafayāt Jenne: 1164–1180 A.H. (Obituaries of Jenne: 1751–1767 A.D.), Paris: Institut de France, MS 2405, pièce 5

Wafayāt Timbuktu, apparently by Sān Sirfi, Paris: Institut de France, MS 2405, pièce 3

Wilks, Ivor, (ed.) 'The African travels of Wargee', in Curtin, *Africa remembered*, 1967 (see above)

Al-Wufrāni, Muḥammad b. 'Abdullāh, *Nuzhat al-Hādi bi-Akhbār Mulūk al-Qarn al-Ḥādi*, edited by Houdas, Paris: Librairie de la Société Asiatique, 1888

Za'āmat Kunāta (Kunta), Paris: Institut de France, MS 2406, pièce 90, 7 fos

Al-Zuhri, Muḥammad, *Kitāb al-Jughrāfiya*, edited by Muḥammad Hadj-Sadok, in *Bulletin d'Etudes Orientales*, 1968, vol. XIX, pp. 122–7

Secondary sources

Abitbol, Michel, *Tombouctou et les Armas (1591–1833)*, University of Paris: Unpublished PhD dissertation, 1974–5

Abun-Nasr, Jamil M., *The Tijaniyya: a Sufi order in the modern world*, London: Oxford University Press, 1965

Ajayi, J. F. A. and Crowder, Michael, (eds), *History of West Africa*, New York: Columbia University Press, 1972

Al-Baṭrān, 'Abd al-'Āzīz, 'A contribution to the biography of Shaikh Muḥammad Ibn 'Abd-al-Karīm Ibn Muḥammad ('Umar-A'mār) al-Maghilị, al-Tilimsāni', *Journal of African History*, 1973, vol. XIV, 3, pp. 381–94

'An introductory note on the impact of Sīdi al-Mukhtār al-Kunti (1729–1811) on West African Islam in the 18th and 19th centuries', *Journal of the Historical Society of Nigeria*, 1973, vol. VI, 4, pp. 347–52

Anonymous, 'Acte du vente passé à Tombouctou', *Journal Asiatique*, 1840, vol. 9, pp. 375–89

Bell, Nawal Morcos, 'The age of Mansa Mūsa of Mali: problems in succession and chronology.' *International Journal of African Historical Studies*, 1972, vol. V, part 2, pp. 221–34

Bivar, A. D. H. and Hiskett, M., 'The Arabic literature of Nigeria to 1804: a provisional account', *Bulletin of the School of Oriental and African Studies*, 1962, vol. XXV, 1, pp. 105–48

Boahen, A. Adu, *Britain, the Sahara and the Western Sudan, 1788–1861*, Oxford: Clarendon Press, 1964

Boubou, Hama, *Histoire des Songhay*, Paris: Presence Africaine, 1968

Boyce, Gray C., 'Erfurt schools and scholars in the thirteenth century', *Speculum*, 1949, No. 24, pp. 1–18

Brocklemann, Carl, *Geschichte der Arabischen literatur*, 5 vols, 1898, 1938, Leiden

Brown, William A., *The Caliphate of Hamdullahi, ca. 1818 1864*, University of Wisconsin, Unpublished PhD Dissertation, 1969

Brunschvig, R. 'Urbanisme medievale et droit Musulman', *Revue des Etudes Islamique*, 1947, vol. XV, pp. 127–55

Bulliet, Richard, *The patricians of Nishapur: a study in medieval Islamic social history*, Cambridge, Mass.: Harvard University Press, 1972

Cahen, Claude, 'Mouvements populaires et autonomisme urbain dans l'Asie Musulmane du Moyen Age', in two parts in *Arabica*, 1958, vol. V, 3, pp. 225–50 and 1959, vol VI, 1, pp. 25–6

Campbell, Dugald, *On the trail of the veiled Tuareg*, Philadelphia: Lippincott, n.d.

Cat, E., *A travers le désert*, Paris: Librairie Gedalge, n.d.

Chang, Chung-Li, *The Chinese gentry: studies on their role in nineteenth-century China*, Seattle: University of Washington Press, 1955

Charbonneau, Col. Brevete Jean, *Sur les traces du Pasha de Tombouctou: la pacification du Sud-Marocain et du Sahara Occidental*, Paris: Charles-Lavanzelle & Cje., 1936

Cissoko, Sekene Modi, 'L'Intelligentsia de Tombouctou aux XVe et XVIe Siècles', *Bulletin de l'Institut Fondamental d'Afrique Noire*, 1969, *Sér. B*, vol. XXXI, no. 4, pp. 927–52

Tombouctou et l'Empire Songhay, Dakar: Nouvelles Editions Africaines, 1975

Colvin, Lucie Gallistel, 'Islam and the state of Kajoor: a case of successful resistance to Jihad', *Journal of African History*, 1974, vol. XV, no. 4, pp. 587–606

Dramani-Issifou, Zakari, *Les relations entre le Maroc et l'Empire Songhai seconde moitié du XVIe siecle*, University of Paris: Unpublished PhD Dissertation, 1974–5

Ferguson, Phyllis, *Islamization in Dagbon: a study of the Alfanema of Yendi*, Newnham College: Unpublished PhD Dissertation, 1972

Fisher, Humphrey, 'Leo Africanus and the Songhai conquest of Hausaland', *The International Journal of African Historical Studies*, 1978, vol. XI, 1

Gardet, Louis, *La cité Musulmane: vie sociale et politique*. Paris: Librairie Philosophique, 1954

Gardner, Brian, *The quest for Timbuctoo*, London: Cassel, 1968

Goitein, S. D., 'Cairo: an Islamic city in the light of the Geniza Documents', in *Middle Eastern cities: a symposium*, edited by I. M. Lapidus, Berkeley: University of California Press, 1969, pp. 80–96

Goody, Jack, 'The impact of Islamic writing on the oral cultures of West Africa', *Cahiers d'Etudes Africaines*, 1971, vol. XI, 3, pp. 455–66

Grabar, Oleg, 'The architecture of the Middle Eastern city from past to present' in *Middle Eastern cities: a symposium*, edited by I. M. Lapidus. Berkeley: University of California Press, 1969

Ho, Ping-Ti, *The ladder of success in Imperial China: aspects of social mobility, 1368–1911*, New York: Columbia University Press, 1962

Hodgkin, T., 'Islam and national movements in West Africa', *Journal of African History*, 1962, vol. III, part 2, p. 323

Hunwick, J. O., 'Aḥmad Bāba and the Moroccan invasion of the Sudan (1591)', *Journal of the Historical Society of Nigeria*, 1962, vol. II, 3, pp. 311–28

Al-Maghili's replies to the questions of Askia al-Ḥājj Muḥammad, edited and translated with an introduction. Unpublished PhD dissertation: University of London, June 1974

'The dynastic chronologies of the Central Sudan states in the sixteenth century: some reinterpretations', *Kano Studies, New Series*, vol. i, I, 1973

'The influence of Arabic in West Africa: a preliminary historical survey', *Transactions of the Historical Society of Nigeria*, 1964, vol. VII, pp. 24–41

'The mid-fourteenth century capital of Mali', *Journal of African History*, 1973, vol. XVI, 2, pp. 195–208

'A new source for the biography of Aḥmad Bāba al-Tunbukti (1556–1627)', *Bulletin of the School of Oriental and African Studies*, 1964, vol. XXVII, 3, pp. 568–93

'Notes on a late fifteenth-century document concerning al-Takrur', in *African Perspectives*, edited by C. Allen and R. W. Johnson, Cambridge: Cambridge University Press, 1970, pp. 7–33

'Religion and state in Songhai', in *Islam in Tropical Africa*, edited by I. M. Lewis, London: Oxford University Press, 1966, pp. 296–317

'Ṣāliḥ al-Fulāni of Futa Jallon: An eighteenth century scholar and *Mujaddid*', unpublished article

Johnson, Marion, 'Calico caravans: the Tripoli–Kano trade after 1800', *Journal of African History*, 1976, vol. XVII, 1, pp. 95–117

Kanya-Forstner, A. S., *The conquests of the Western Sudan: a study in French military imperialism*, Cambridge: Cambridge University Press, 1969

El-Kettani, Mohammed Ibrahim, 'Les manuscrits de l'Occident Africain dans les Bibliothèques du Maroc', *Hesperis-Tamuda*, 1969, vol. IX, 1, pp. 57–63

Kodjo, Niamkey Georges, 'La Chutte des Aqits (1585–1594)'. *Annals of the University of Abidjan, Series I, (History)*, 1975, vol. 3

Lapidus, Ira M. (ed.), *Middle Eastern cities: a symposium*, Berkeley: University of California Press, 1969

Muslim cities in the late middle ages, Cambridge: Harvard University Press, 1967

Le Tourneau, Roger, *Fez in the age of the Marinids*, translated by Besse Alberta Clement, Norman: University of Oklahoma Press, 1961

Levi-Provencal, E., 'Un document inédit sur l'expedition sa'dide au Soudan', *Arabica: Revue d'Etudes Arabes*, 1955, vol. 2, part 1, pp. 89–96

Levtzion, N., *Ancient Ghana and Mali*, London: Methuen, 1973

Muslims and chiefs in West Africa: a study of Islam in the Middle Volta Basin in the pre-colonial period, Oxford: Clarendon Press, 1968

'A seventeenth century chronicle by Ibn al-Mukhtar: a critical study of *Ta'rikh al-Fattash*', *Bulletin of the School of Oriental and African Studies*, 1971, vol. XXXIV, no. 34, pt. 3, pp. 571–93
'The early states of the Western Sudan', in *History of West Africa*, edited by J. Ajayi and M. Crowder, 2 vols. New York: Columbia University Press, 1972, I, pp. 114–51
Lewicki, Tadeusz, 'Un etat Soudanais mediéval inconnu: le royaume de Zafun(u)', *Cahiers d'Etudes Africaines*, 1971, vol. XI, 4, pp. 501–25
'A propos du nom de l'Oasis de Koufra chez les géographes Arabes du XIe et du XIIe siècle', *Journal of African History*, 1965, vol. VI, 3, pp. 295–306
Lewis, Bernard (ed.), *Islam: from the Prophet Muhammad to the capture of Constantinople*, 2 vols., New York: Harper & Row, 1976
Lloyd, Christopher, *The search for the Niger*, London: Collins, 1973
Lovejoy, Paul E., 'The role of the Wangara in the economic transformation of the Central Sudan in the fifteenth and sixteenth centuries', *Journal of African History*, 1878, vol. XIX, 2, pp. 173–93
Marsh, Robert, *The mandarins: the circulation of elites in China, 1600–1900*, Glencoe: Free Press, 1961
Maugham, Robin, *The slaves of Timbuktu*, London: Longman, 1961
Mansuy, Jean, *Maçons et maisons de Tombouctou*, unpublished memoir, Paris: Institut International d'Administration Publique, Bibliothèque, no. 8, 1948–49
Mauny, Raymond, *Tableau géographique de l'Ouest Africain au moyen age*, Dakar: Institut Française d'Afrique Noire, Memoires, 61, 1961
Mills, Lady Dorothy, *The road to Timbuktu*, London: Duckworth and Co., 1924
Miner, Horace, *The primitive city of Timbuktu*, Princeton University Press, 1953
Monteil, Charles, *Djenné: une cité Soudanaise*, Paris: Société d'Editions Géographiques . . ., 1932
Monteil, Vincent, *L'Islam Noir*, Paris: Editions du Seuil, 1971
Morias Farias, P. F. 'Du nouveau sur les steles de Gao', *Bulletin de l'IFAN*, 1974, *Ser. B*, vol. XXXVI, 3, pp. 511–24
Al-Naqar, 'Umar, 'Takrur: the history of a name', *Journal of African History*, 1969, vol. X, 3, pp. 365–74
Norris, H. T., *Saharan myth and saga*, Oxford: Clarendon Press, 1972
'Sanhaja scholars of Timbuctoo', *Bulletin of the School of Oriental and African Studies*, 1967, vol. XXX, pp. 634–40
The Tuaregs: their Islamic legacy and its diffusion in the Sahel, Warminster: Aris and Phillips Ltd., 1975
Pefontan, Capt., 'Histoire de Tombouctou, de sa fondation a l'occupation Francais', *Bulletin de la Comité d'Etude Historique et Scientifique de l'AOF*, 1922, pp. 81–113
Petry, Carl, *Autonomy in adversity: The civilian elite in Cairo in the later middle ages*, MS to be published by Princeton University Press
Robinson, David, 'Abdul Qādir and Shaykh 'Umar: a continuing tradition of Islamic leadership in Futa Toro', *The International Journal of African Historical Studies*, 1973, vol. VI, 2, pp. 286–303
Saad, E. N., 'Islamization in Kano: sequence and chronology', *Kano Studies*, (in press)
Sanneh, Lamin, 'The origins of clericalism in West Africa', *Journal of African History*, 1976, vol. XVII, 1, pp. 49–72
Sartain, E. M., 'Jalāl Ad-Dīn As-Suyūṭi's relations with the people of Takrur', *Journal of Semitic Studies*, 1971, vol. 16, pp. 193–8
Sauvaget, J., 'Les epitaphes royales de Gao', *Bulletin de l'Institut Française d'Afrique Noire*, *Sér. B*, 1950, vol. XII, pp. 418–40

Skolle, John, *The road to Timbuctoo*, London: Victor Gollancz, 1956

Stern, S. M., 'The constitution of the Islamic city', in *The Islamic city: a colloquium*, edited by A. H. Hourani, Oxford: Bruno Cassirer, 1970, pp. 25–50

Stewart, C. C., 'Southern Saharan scholarship and the *Bilād al-Sūdān*, *Journal of African History*, 1976, vol. XVII, 1, pp. 73–93

Triaud, J. L., *Islam et sociétés Soudanaises au moyen age*, Paris: Recherches Voltaiques, 16, 1973

Trimingham, J. S., *A history of Islam in West Africa*, London: Oxford University Press, 1962

The influence of Islam upon Africa, New York: Praeger, 1968

Tymowsky, Michal, 'Le Niger, voie de communication de Grands Etats Soudan occidental jusqu'à la fin du XVIe siècle', *Africana Bulletin*, 1967, vol. 6, pp. 73–95

Weber, Max, *Economy and society*, edited by Guenther Roth and Claus Wittich, 3 vols., New York: Bedminister Press, 1968

Wieruszowski, Helene, *The medieval university*, Princeton: Van Nostrand Co., 1966

Wilks, Ivor, 'A medieval trade-route from the Niger to the Gulf of Guinea', *Journal of African History*, 1962, vol. III, 2, pp. 337–41

'The transmission of Islamic learning in the Western Sudan', in *Literacy in traditional societies*, edited by J. Goody, London: Cambridge University Press, 1968, pp. 162–95

Willis, John Ralph, 'The Torodbe clerisy: a social view', *Journal of African History*, 1968, vol. XIX, 2, pp. 195–212

Zebadia, 'Abdelquader, *The career and correspondence of Aḥmad al-Bakkā'i of Timbuktu*, London: School of Oriental and African Studies, Unpublished PhD Dissertation, 1974

Zoubeir, Mahmoud, *Ahmad Baba de Tombouctou (1556–1627): sa vie et son oeuvre*, Paris: Maisonneuve et Larose, 1977

Index

The entries for most scholars, notables, kings, etc., are under their personal names with cross-references under family names and entries for posts.

Women's Agency in
Muslim Marriage
Fatwas from
Timbuctu
Mathee

Journal for Islamic Studies

Presence vs. Absence
of voices

CPSIA information can be obtained
at www.ICGtesting.com
Printed in the USA
LVHW010439061222
734664LV00001B/88

9 780521 136303